Early Christianity

Early Christianity

A Brief History

✝

Joseph H. Lynch

Joe R. Engle Designated Professor of
the History of Christianity
Department of History
The Ohio State University

New York   Oxford
OXFORD UNIVERSITY PRESS
2010

Oxford University Press, Inc., publishes works that further Oxford University's
objective of excellence in research, scholarship, and education.

Oxford   New York
Auckland   Cape Town   Dar es Salaam   Hong Kong   Karachi
Kuala Lumpur   Madrid   Melbourne   Mexico City   Nairobi
New Delhi   Shanghai   Taipei   Toronto

With offices in
Argentina   Austria   Brazil   Chile   Czech Republic   France   Greece
Guatemala   Hungary   Italy   Japan   Poland   Portugal   Singapore
South Korea   Switzerland   Thailand   Turkey   Ukraine   Vietnam

Published by Oxford University Press, Inc.
198 Madison Avenue, New York, New York 10016
http://www.oup.com

Oxford is a registered trademark of Oxford University Press

Library of Congress Cataloging-in-Publication Data

Lynch, Joseph H., 1943–
  Early christianity : a brief history / Joseph H. Lynch.
    p.   cm.
Includes bibliographical references and index.
ISBN 978-0-19-513803-0 (pbk.)—978-0-19-513855-9 (hardcover)
1. Church history—Primitive and early church, ca. 30–600.   I. Title.
  BR165.L98 2010
  270.1—dc22   2008049590

Printed in the United States of America
on acid-free paper

To my beloved grandchildren
Matthew, Daniel, Charles, Katherine,
Samuel, Erin, and Nicholas

Contents

PART II Christianity in the Second and Third Centuries   51

5 ✝ Christian Diversity in the Second and Third Centuries   54

6 ✝ The Emergence of a Proto-Orthodox Christian Consensus: Bishop, Creed, and Canon of Scripture   62

PART III The Creation of a Christian Empire   121

10 ✤ Diocletian, the Great Persecution, and the Conversion of Constantine   123

11 ✤ The Christian Empire and the Imperial Church   131

17 ✛ Fourth- and Fifth-Century Christian Thinkers 212

18 ✛ Conversion and Christianization 223

Preface

When Benedict of Nursia (about 480-about 545) described his *RULE* for monks, he called it "a little rule that we have written for beginners" (ch. 73). I have tried to write a book for beginners and their teachers. I have taught the history of early Christianity for more than twenty years, during which I have used a half-dozen different textbooks to provide the narrative framework. From the start, I was troubled that the textbooks sometimes presupposed a great deal of knowledge on the part of the reader. For instance, Hebrew, Greek, and Latin words might be used with little or no explanation. Some authors took for granted that their readers were familiar with the technical terms of Christian theology such as "christology," "soteriology," "sacrament," and the like. I assumed, perhaps incorrectly, that the authors often had in mind a readership of seminary students or at least students whose main interest (and earlier training) was in church history or ancient history. Yet, my classes consisted of undergraduate students of chemistry or history or English or fine arts or business who were curious about the historical origins and development of Christianity. Many were intelligent and eager but were often ill-equipped to tackle the sort of book that is written for those in training to be clergy. Gradually, I adapted my lectures to my audience, but I continued to feel the need for a book that would be accessible to a student audience. In the present book I have made a conscious effort to reach a readership of beginners, whether they are students enrolled in courses or informal learners who want to read about early Christianity while they sit in their favorite chair.

Not only is this a book for beginners but also it is a mere beginning. Some, perhaps many, read-ers will want to read more on specific topics. For that reason, I have ended each chapter with a brief list of ancient sources and modern books. The sheer number of books (not to mention articles) on early Christianity is astounding. I tried to make my recommendations about further reading with an audience of beginners in mind. Some authors of histories of ancient Christianity have taken different approaches to suggested reading. After every chapter they offer tightly printed pages of dozens of suggested readings. In my experience beginners can be discouraged by the sheer number of suggested readings among which they have little way to choose. I have recommended a relatively few books that I think are both scholarly and accessible to beginners, perhaps even potentially interesting to them. I became a historian in part because I love to read original sources, which can enlighten, instruct, even surprise. I wanted beginners to have that experience. After each chapter I also suggested some sources written in the ancient world (translated, of course) that I think are accessible to beginners.

One approach to the study of ancient Christianity can be called "encyclopedic": Every important person and idea gets a paragraph or two. There is nothing wrong with that, but I chose a different approach. In this book I emphasized large themes that I think will lay a foundation for further reading and thought. I chose not to provide a thumbnail sketch of the life and theology of every important early Christian. Of course, I mention such people as Tertullian, Cyprian, Origen, Eusebius, Athanasius, Basil of Caesarea, Martin of Tours, Augustine of Hippo, and Gregory I. But if readers want to know more about them, I strongly recommend that they read a rounded, relatively brief treatment in a scholarly encyclopedia or hand-book. Teachers can also adapt their syllabi to complement my approach, for instance, by using a book of source readings or a biography of an important thinker.

Students often want to know where to go if their interest in a topic surpasses what I provide. I regularly recommend three reference works:

1) The *Encyclopedia of Early Christianity*, two volumes, second edition by Everett Ferguson (New York, 1997).
2) *Encyclopedia of the Early Church,* two volumes, translated from Italian by Adrian Walford, with a foreword and bibliographic amendments by W. H. C. Frend (New York, 1992).
3) *The Oxford Dictionary of the Christian Church*, third edition, by F. L. Cross and E. A. Livingstone (Oxford, 1997), which treats Christianity to modern times but includes excellent entries on early Christian topics.

Not only do these reference books provide reliable treatments of more topics than you can imagine, but also they provide some bibliography on the topics.

Translations. "The Scripture quotations contained herein are from the New Revised Standard Version Bible copyright 1989 by the Division of Christian Education of the National Council of the Churches of Christ in the U. S. A., and are used by permission. All rights reserved." Many translations of the Bible will be adequate, but if students ask me to suggest one, I recommend THE NEW OXFORD ANNOTATED BIBLE WITH THE APOCRYPHAL/ DEUTEROCANONICAL BOOKS, augmented third edition by Michael D. Coogan et al. (New York, 2007).

An important and intellectually demanding way to approach the study of ancient Christianity is to read the original sources in modern scholarly translations. There are two major series of translations that provide introductions and explanatory notes that make early Christian texts more accessible to modern readers:

1) *The Fathers of the Church* (Washington, DC, 1947–), 110 volumes so far.
2) *Ancient Christian Writers* (New York, 1946–), sixty volumes so far.

They do not duplicate one another. Look in them first if you want to read such things as the two Apologies of Justin Martyr, the letters of Augustine of Hippo, the letters of Saint Jerome or Athanasius' LIFE OF ANTHONY There is another collection of translations, but I recommend it to students only if no modern translation exists. The ANTE-NICENE, NICENE AND POST-NICENE FATHERS was a vast undertaking (thirty-eight stout volumes with each page packed with small print), published between 1885 and 1900 in Edinburgh and reprinted by Eerdmans in 1989. You can find this series at the website www.ccel.org/. The nineteenth-century translations are often written in such formal and old-fashioned English that they can be difficult for beginners to understand. For most of the sources cited in this book I use existing translations, but I "alter" some of them so that students can more easily understand them. I keep the meaning of the text while making it clearer for readers, usually by changing no more than a few words.

Dates. In the modern West, historical dates are expressed in two ways. The traditional system, which goes back to the Anglo-Saxon historian Bede (died 735), made the birth of Christ the pivotal point in history. Everything after Christ's birth was AD, which means "in the year of the Lord" (ANNO DOMINI). Everything before Christ's birth was logically BC ("before Christ"). Some scholars have replaced this overtly Christian way of expressing dates with a more neutral system: CE meaning "the common era" and BCE meaning "before the common era." Whichever system is used, no date actually changes. For instance, 325 AD becomes 325 CE, and 1000 BC becomes 1000 BCE. I shall use the BCE/CE system of dating. But if you see a date such as 451 without any modifier, it is a CE/AD date. I add BCE or CE only when I think that its omission will confuse readers.

I owe a great deal to many people. Before all others, I want to thank my teachers in church history, especially the late Professor William M. Daly of Boston College, the late Professor George Williams of Harvard Divinity School, and Professor Emeritus Giles Constable of the Institute for Advanced Study and of Harvard University. Each of them influenced me as a scholar and a person far more than they know. I also want to thank a generation of undergraduate and graduate students whose members have taken my courses in ancient church history and have challenged me to meet their intellectual needs. I want to thank colleagues with whom I have discussed chapters, especially Professor Emeritus Martin Arbagi of Wright State University. I want to thank the National Endowment for the Humanities, the American Council of Learned Societies, the Institute for Advanced Study, and the John Simon Guggenheim Foundation for support over the many years that this book was taking shape. I am grateful to my department, to my college, and to the Ohio State University for support and encouragement. I want to thank Robert Miller, my editor at Oxford University Press, for his patience and his advice. Finally, I want to thank my wife Ann, who has supported me in this project for more than a decade.

Abbreviations and Signs

ACW	*ANCIENT CHRISTIAN WRITERS* translation series
altered	A translation has been modified for clarity
ANF	*THE ANTE-NICENE FATHERS*. Translations of the writings of the Fathers down to AD 325, ten volumes (Buffalo, 1885–1896)
c.	chapter
EH	Eusebius, *BISHOP OF CAESAREA, THE ECCLESIASTICAL HISTORY AND THE MARTYRS OF PALESTINE,* translated with introduction and notes by Hugh Jackson Lawlor and John Ernest Leonard Oulton, two volumes (London, 1927)
FOC	*FATHERS OF THE CHURCH* translation series
LCL	Loeb Classical Library
NPNF	*A SELECT LIBRARY OF NICENE AND POST-NICENE FATHERS OF THE CHURCH,* first series, fourteen volumes (New York, 1905–1917)
NPNF second series	*A SELECT LIBRARY OF NICENE AND POST-NICENE FATHERS OF THE CHRISTIAN CHURCH,* second series, fourteen volumes (Oxford and New York, 1890–1899)

CHAPTER 1

Jesus

Many readers might think that a book on the history of early Christianity should begin with a detailed treatment of Jesus. But, in fact, that is not usually the way scholars organize their material. In a well-developed, sophisticated field called "New Testament Studies," scholars study Jesus historically and theologically. The history of the movement that emerged out of his life and teaching is usually studied separately in the field of Church History, which is also well-developed and sophisticated. This book is an introduction not to New Testament studies but rather to the history of early Christianity.

But we need to say something about Jesus. Before we do, we need to get a grasp on *how* we know about Jesus. He wrote nothing that has survived, although in the third century some believed that they had a letter he had written to King Abgar of Edessa. What was written about him and when? In the first hundred years (about 29 to about 130) after his death, a few believers and a few non-believers wrote about him. It might surprise some readers that Paul wrote his authentic letters decades before the evangelists wrote the gospels. Paul provides the oldest accounts of Jesus. But if we put aside for the moment documents that first- and second-century Christians wrote, the sources about Jesus are sparse. In the light of Jesus' immense impact on subsequent history, it might seem surprising that no non-believers living in his lifetime or for decades afterward mentioned him. If those non-Christian sources were all that survived, what would we know? Let's try an intellectual experiment. What would the "Gospel According to the Outsiders" look like? Of course, there was *no such gospel*, but if we imagined one, we might learn something about Jesus.

NON-CHRISTIAN SOURCES ABOUT JESUS

Between sixty and one hundred years after Jesus' death one Jewish writer and three pagan Roman writers mentioned him briefly. The Jewish historian Josephus (about 38–about 100) wrote about Jesus twice. In his brief account of the execution in 62 of James, the leader of the Jewish Christians at Jerusalem, he identified James as "the brother of Jesus, the so-called Christ" (Josephus, *The Antiquities of the Jews*, XX.200). Elsewhere in the *Antiquities*, there is a remarkable but suspicious paragraph about Jesus:

> About this time there lived Jesus, a wise man, if indeed one ought to call him a man. For he was one who did surprising feats and was a teacher of such people as accept the truth gladly. He won over many Jews and many of the Greeks. He was the Messiah. When Pilate, upon hearing him accused by men of the highest standing amongst us, had condemned him to be crucified, those who in the first place had come to love him did not give up their affection for him. On the third day he appeared to them restored to life, for the prophets of God had prophesied these and countless other marvelous things about him. And the tribe of the Christians, so called after him, has still to this day not disappeared. (Josephus, *Jewish Antiquities* XVIII.63–64, in *Josephus*, with an English translation by Louis H. Feldman, LCL [Cambridge, MA, and London, 1965], vol. 9, pp. 48–51, altered)

The pro-Christian tone of this passage is puzzling because Josephus lived and died a Jew: He was not a follower of Jesus. Its openly Christian content is usually explained as follows. In the *Antiquities* Josephus probably did devote a few sentences to Jesus, as he did to other religious and political figures of first-century Palestine, for instance, John the Baptist (*Antiquities* XVIII.5). Perhaps a Christian scribe, copying the *Antiquities*, thought Josephus's account of Jesus was inadequate or hostile or wrong. The scribe "corrected" it by writing what we read today. Unless an uncorrected manuscript is found, we shall never know what Josephus actually wrote about Jesus. The paragraph is, however, a nice summary of what a third-century Christian thought about Jesus.

Pliny the Younger (about 61–about 112) wrote the second non-Christian source that mentions Christ. When Pliny became governor of Bithynia-Pontus in what is now northern Turkey he learned that numerous Christians lived in the area. In about 110 he wrote a letter to the Roman Emperor Trajan (98–117) asking for advice on how to deal with them. His letter and Trajan's reply (Pliny's *Letters*, book 10, letters 96 and 97) will be analyzed more fully in chapter 8, which treats persecution. Apparently Pliny knew nothing about Christ except what his on-the-spot investigation revealed. He knew that the Christians took their name from a person named *Christus*. He noted in passing that the Christians told him that they met on a certain day before dawn and sang in alternate verses a hymn to Christ as to a god. That was all that he mentioned about Christ himself. He tortured two Christian women but dismissed what they said as a depraved and excessive superstition. (Wouldn't we be grateful if he had thought it worthwhile to inform the emperor in a paragraph or two about what he found out during his interrogations? But he did not.)

The Roman senator and historian Tacitus (about 56–about 118) wrote the third non-Christian source. In his *Annals*, he recorded events that occurred about fifty years earlier during the reign of the Emperor Nero (54–68). In 64, a major fire devastated much of the city of Rome. Rumors spread that Nero had set it to make way for his ambitious building projects. Nero shifted the blame to Christians, whom he ordered to be arrested, tortured, and executed in horrible ways. In telling about the fire and Nero's reaction, Tacitus informed his readers briefly about the founder of the Christians who had died about eighty years before Tacitus wrote: "Christus, the founder of the name [Christian], had undergone the death penalty in the reign of Tiberius, by sentence of the procurator Pontius Pilate, and the pernicious superstition was checked for a moment, only to break out once more, not merely in Judaea, the home of the disease, but in the capital itself [Rome]...." (Tacitus, *Annals* XV.44 in *Tacitus in Five Volumes*, with an English translation by John Jackson, LCL no. 322 [London and Cambridge, MA, 1937], vol. 5, p. 283).

Finally, in the 120s, the gossipy historian Suetonius (about 70–about 130) summarized events in the reign of the Emperor Claudius (41–54). At one point, he might have referred to Christ: "Since the Jews constantly made disturbances at the instigation of Chrestus, he [Claudius] expelled them [Jews] from Rome" (Suetonius, *Claudius*, ch 25, in *Suetonius*, with an English translation by J. C. Rolfe, LCL no. 38 [London and Cambridge, MA, 1914], p. 53). The name *Chrestus*, which was a Greek word meaning "useful," was sometimes given to slaves to encourage them to be what they were called. Is Suetonius referring to Christ or to an otherwise unknown Chrestus who had caused a disturbance among the Jews at Rome? Even if Chrestus was Christ, we learn little beyond the fact that his followers might have provoked disturbances among the Jews of Rome. You have now been alerted to every scrap of information about Jesus that survives from non-Christian writers during the hundred years after Jesus' death. The harvest of information is meager. If there was a "Gospel According to the Outsiders" (*which there is not!*) it would say that Jesus lived in Judea; he had a brother named James; he claimed to be, or his followers said he was, the Christ, that is, the Jewish Messiah ("the Anointed One"); he was executed in the reign of Emperor Tiberius (14–37) when Pontius Pilate was procurator of Judea; and he continued to have followers in the late first and early second century, called "Christians," who lived in such diverse places as Judea, Rome, and northern Turkey. But if such a "Gospel According to the Outsiders" was the only source about Jesus, we would have no idea what Jesus taught, what he did, and most of what his followers believed about him. The conclusion is inescapable. Virtually everything known about Jesus comes from documents that Christians wrote during the sixty or seventy years after his death. That fits the pattern of other founders of religions, including Zoroaster and the Buddha: They are known primarily from the writings of their admirers and followers.

CHRISTIAN SOURCES ABOUT JESUS

Early Christians wrote a lot. In the later first, second, and third centuries Christians with different views composed many gospels, letters, apocalypses, meditations, and stories about individual apostles and other early followers of Jesus. Only twenty-seven of those documents were eventually regarded as scripture and included in the "canon" of the New Testament, a matter to be treated in chapter 7. By the fourth century, the canon of scripture included four gospels (Matthew, Mark, Luke, and John); twenty-one letters (thirteen of them attributed to Paul, one anonymous letter to the Hebrews, one attributed to James, two attributed to Peter, three attributed to John, and one attributed to Jude); one historical text called the *Acts of the Apostles;* and one apocalypse, called the *Revelation to John.* Scholars generally agree that only the four canonical gospels (and perhaps the non-canonical *Gospel of Thomas*) contain much information about the man Jesus who lived in Palestine, taught, died, and, as his followers believed, rose from the dead, ascended into heaven, and was expected to return.

Word-of-Mouth Good News

The four canonical gospels are not simple documents. Generations of scholars have tried to understand their origins, their purposes, and their messages. Most New Testament scholars believe that the gospels were not written immediately after Jesus died. Perhaps because Jesus' earliest followers expected him to return quickly, they did not feel the need to write about him until several decades after his death. With their certainty that time was short, Jesus' earliest followers spread in oral ways the gospel, an English word that means "good news" (*euangelion* in Greek). They preached in public and private, taught converts, retold stories of Jesus when they worshipped, sang about him in hymns, and referred to the oral gospel when they debated among themselves and with their Jewish and pagan opponents. Memories of what Jesus did and said were preserved in talk and perhaps in a few written documents that do not survive.

As long as apostles and disciples (or people who had been instructed directly by them) were still alive, oral transmission of Jesus' words and deeds was possible. Can we make a reasonable estimate of how long the period of oral transmission was? If Jesus died around 29 and had disciples in their twenties and thirties, some of them might have lived to the seventh and eighth decades of the first century. The sparse information we have supports that view: Paul, Peter, and James, the brother of Jesus, were killed in the 60s, and the evangelist John is said to have lived into the 90s. Irenaeus of Lyons claimed that Polycarp of Smyrna, who was at least eighty-six years old when he was burned to death in 156, had heard the Apostle John teach and had been appointed bishop by the apostles. Polycarp might have been one of the last survivors of those who had known an early follower of Jesus. But that date, almost 130 years after Jesus' death, must be the outer limit of the possibility of oral transmission. By then, oral transmission was fading out, and reliance on written documents was dominant.

What were the consequences of a generation or more of oral transmission of the sayings and doings of Jesus? What was likely to be remembered? What was likely to be forgotten? Oral tradition tends to preserve material that is useful to those who repeat it. Accounts of the death and resurrection of Jesus must have been a central feature of the oral good news. For instance, each of the four canonical gospels included an account of Jesus' trial, death, and resurrection, which represented a high percentage of all the words in each of them. Early preachers apparently gave detailed accounts of Jesus' suffering and death, called "Passion narratives," which they repeated often when they tried to make converts and to instruct believers. Oral accounts of Jesus were repeated in other settings as well. When Christians worshipped they repeated Jesus' sayings and deeds. For instance, Pliny wrote that the Bithynian Christians sang "a hymn to Christ as to a god." We do not know the content of the hymn, but it is reasonable to think that it taught something about Jesus that the congregation (or its leaders) thought was useful. From very early, the central religious ritual of the Christians was the meal of bread and wine. When Christians ate the meal, someone told the story of Jesus' Last Supper with his apostles. In his first letter to the Corinthians, which was written before any gospel was composed, Paul already knew the story about Jesus' final meal, presumably in an oral form (1 Cor 11:23–26). When Christians taught, they also repeated stories about what Jesus had said and done. If a Christian community convinced someone to join it, that was just a first step. The convert had to be instructed in what to believe and how to behave. Accounts of Jesus that were useful for instruction must have been repeated often. For instance, the Beatitudes (Mt 5:3–11; Lk 6:20–23) were useful for moral teaching, and the Lord's Prayer (Mt 6:9–13; Lk 11:1–4) was a model of how the believers should pray.

A Jesus movement took shape within a whirl of controversies, some with Jews and some among Christians. The repetition of Jesus' words and deeds was useful in those debates. The early Jewish-Christian claims about Jesus received a positive reception from some Jews but were rejected by others. For generations, Christian Jews and non-Christian Jews disagreed over how the Hebrew scriptures, later called the "Old Testament" by Christians, should be interpreted. For instance, was the Mosaic Law still binding in such matters as circumcision, the clean and the unclean, and the observance of the Sabbath; and had Jesus been the Messiah foretold by the Hebrew prophets? In those debates, Jewish Christians repeated Jesus' words and deeds, especially to show that he had fulfilled the prophecies of the Hebrew scriptures. Christians also debated among themselves about who Jesus was and how they should react to him. The Christian combatants repeated sayings and doings of Jesus to support their views and to refute the views of their Christian opponents.

The oral tradition also included accounts about Jesus that were useful to strengthen and console the believers in the frequent hard times they experienced. Christians faced not just debate but also occasional violence from their Jewish and pagan opponents. For instance, in defending himself against Christian critics, Paul offered an insight into the difficulties and dangers of his life as a missionary. He reported that he had been imprisoned, had received countless floggings, had been given thirty-nine lashes on five occasions by Jewish opponents, had been beaten with rods three times, and had been stoned once (2 Cor 11:23–25). He was not alone. Some first-century Christian communities were under pressure and wracked by fear. The telling of a story that Jesus had already predicted such troubles offered useful comfort. For instance, the Gospel of Mark, which might have been written at Rome within a decade of Nero's attack on Christians in 64, reported a comforting message to a beleaguered community. It told them that Jesus had predicted these terrible things, so they did not need to be afraid:

> …for they will hand you over to councils; and you will be beaten in synagogues; and you will stand before governors and kings because of me, as a testimony to them. And the good news must first be proclaimed to all nations. When they bring you to trial and hand you over, do not worry beforehand about what you are to say; but say whatever is given to you at that time, for it is not you who speak, but the Holy Spirit. Brother will betray brother to death, and a father his child, and children will rise against parents and have them put to death; and you will be hated by all because of my name. But the one who endures to the end will be saved. (Mk 13:9–13)

If "usefulness" increased the chances that information from and about Jesus would survive, what was likely to be forgotten during the decades of oral transmission? Information that was not useful and that found no regular occasions for repetition among struggling Christian communities was often not transmitted orally. For instance, it is striking that no physical description of Jesus survives. Apparently in the decades when oral transmission was normal, there were few or no occasions that called for repeating a physical description of Jesus. When later generations of Christians wanted to visualize Jesus, it was too late to get oral or written descriptions. The uncountable images of Jesus as a bearded, long-haired, dignified, well-proportioned man that have appeared for about eighteen hundred years in mosaics, stained glass, statues, paintings, prints, books, movies, and in people's heads are not based in the oral tradition or in early documents. Similarly, when oral transmission was the normal way that Jesus was remembered, there was apparently no strong need to remember events that occurred between Jesus' birth and his brief public life as a preacher and healer. The thirty or so years between birth and ministry are a blank, except for Luke's account of the twelve-year-old Jesus teaching in the Temple (Lk 2:41–51). Some second- and third-century Christians wanted to know about Jesus' childhood and family, but by their time the information was irretrievably lost. To fill the gap, unknown authors wrote the "infancy gospels," such as the *Protoevangelium of James*, which promoted the idea of Mary's perpetual virginity, and the *Infancy Gospel of Thomas*, which depicted little Jesus as both human and divine.

For decades it must have seemed sufficient to transmit by word of mouth stories about Jesus that were useful for worship, instruction, controversy, and encouragement. For example, between twenty and thirty years after Jesus' death, Paul had no access to a written gospel but instead relied on oral traditions. He wrote letters that are earlier than the canonical gospels, but in those letters he gave no connected account of what Jesus said and did during his lifetime in Palestine. In fact, to judge from what survives in Paul's writings, he was more interested in the Risen Jesus who was to come back soon than in the Jesus who taught, acted, lived, and died in Palestine. Even when some Christians wrote documents, they did not immediately replace the oral forms, which continued to be used for a while alongside the written gospels.

Written Good News

As years passed and circumstances changed, a tiny number of Jesus' followers began to write about him, although oral accounts were still respected and relied upon. By the 60s or 70s, Jesus had not returned. Those who knew him were dead or aging. The Roman destruction of Jerusalem in 70 fell hard on the Jewish Christians living in that city, who were the most likely to have known both Jesus

and his earliest followers. It is probably not coincidental that about 70 the writing of accounts of Jesus, called "gospels," began. The four canonical gospels are more complex than they might appear. The writers of the canonical gospels are shadowy figures because they did not tell us who they were, when they wrote, or where they wrote. No gospel writer clearly identified himself or declared that he was an eyewitness to anything he recorded. The author of the Gospel of Luke made clear that he was *not* an eyewitness when he wrote: "Since many have undertaken to set down an orderly account of the events that have been fulfilled among us, just as they were handed on to us by those who from the beginning were eyewitnesses and servants of the word, I too decided, after investigating everything carefully from the very first, to write an orderly account for you, most excellent Theophilus, so that you may know the truth concerning the things about which you have been instructed" (Lk 1:1–4). So why are the canonical gospels attributed to men called "Matthew," "Mark," "Luke," and "John"? As those gospels gained circulation and authority during the second century, the Christians who used them wanted to know who wrote them. In each case, the traditional linking of a particular named author to a particular gospel is based on evidence from the second century. Of course, the second-century writers could have been correct in some or all of their attributions, but it is difficult to be sure. The scholarly consensus is that the Gospel of Mark is the oldest, written about 70, perhaps at Rome. The author, whom I shall call "Mark" for convenience, was a pioneer who invented a literary form—the gospel—which had not existed before. The gospels attributed to Matthew and Luke are based in part on Mark and are generally thought to have been written between 80 and 90, but there is no way to tell which came first. The gospel attributed to John, which is different in important ways from the other three, was perhaps written in the 90s. The production of gospels continued in the second and maybe even the later first century, but only those attributed to Mark, Matthew, Luke, and John were later included in the collection of documents called the "New Testament."

The four canonical gospels are not biographies of Jesus. They are probably best described as theology presented in a narrative form. They try to answer a complicated set of questions, such as "Who was/is Jesus?" and "What is his significance for Israel and for humanity?" Theologians classify the answers to such questions as christology, which is the investigation of the meaning and significance of Jesus Christ. Christological questions have remained issues of debate throughout the history of Christianity. The gospel writers, who were not copyists or stenographers, participated in the christological investigations and disagreements. They worked independently of one another. There was nothing neutral about them. They had distinct viewpoints, according to which they actively shaped the oral and written materials that they had at their disposal. They recounted Jesus' teachings and actions not just to tell a story but also to convert readers and hearers to faith in Jesus, to instruct and strengthen those who already believed, and to refute those, including Jews and other Christians, with whom they disagreed. The Gospel of John is clear about its purpose: "But these are written so that you may come to believe that Jesus is the Messiah, the Son of God, and that through believing you may have life in his name" (John 20:31). Each gospel contains what its author, and perhaps the community for which he wrote, believed about Jesus anywhere from forty to sixty years after his death. There is no substitute for a careful, thoughtful reading of the four canonical gospels. But it is possible to describe briefly some of the distinctive features of each gospel as a guide to that reading.

The Gospel of Mark. According to a second-century Christian writer, Mark's gospel was associated with the teaching of Peter. The church historian Eusebius quoted Papias of Hierapolis, who had reported what a man called "John the Elder" used to say: "Mark having been the interpreter of Peter, wrote accurately, although not in order, all that he recalled of what was either said or done by the Lord. For he [Mark] neither heard the Lord, nor was he a follower of His, but at a later date (as I said) of Peter" (EH 3.39). Mark's is the shortest gospel and contains the fewest words from the mouth of Jesus. Mark portrayed a situation in which Jesus performed mighty deeds (primarily healings and exorcisms), but in spite of them his disciples did not recognize who he was. Mark was critical

of the disciples because they repeatedly failed to comprehend what Jesus told them and failed to understand what they saw him do. A feature of Mark's Gospel that has puzzled many readers is its insistence that Jesus tried to keep his deeds and his identity a secret during his lifetime. For instance, he forbade exorcised demons (1:25; 3:12) and the recipients of his cures (5:43; 7:36) to tell anyone what he had done. He told his disciples not to make known that he was the Messiah (8:30). Mark implied that only after Jesus died and rose was his true nature revealed. In a surprising paradox, Mark seemed to think that he and his readers understood more about Jesus than Jesus' disciples did during his lifetime. Mark wrote for a community that was under pressure, perhaps the community at Rome that was recovering from Nero's attack in 64.

The Gospel of Matthew. Eusebius of Caesarea (EH 3.39) also reported that Papias of Hierapolis attributed a gospel to Matthew: "So then, Matthew compiled the oracles in the Hebrew language; but everyone interpreted them as he was able." Papias' statement is puzzling because there is no evidence that the existing Greek Gospel of Matthew was translated from Hebrew or Aramaic. Matthew presented Jesus as a royal person, descended from King David. He was the long-awaited fulfillment of the hopes of Israel, the expected outcome of Jewish history, the Messiah who would correct the wrongs of the world. Matthew emphasized continuity with Judaism. He often concluded his account of a deed of Jesus with an observation such as "This was done to fulfill what the Lord had spoken through the prophet" (4:14; 12:17; 13:35). Matthew was respectful of Jesus' disciples but highly critical of the Jewish leaders, especially the scribes and Pharisees. He also is the most Jewish of the gospel-writers, emphasizing that Jesus introduced a perfected and purified Judaism (Mt 5:17–20). Matthew portrayed Jesus as a teacher like Moses. In five well-organized scenes of teaching, Jesus instructed his followers on moral attitudes and behavior ("the Sermon on the Mount," chs 5–7), on the life that apostles and missionaries should lead (ch 10), on the nature of the kingdom of the heavens (ch 13), on church discipline (ch 18), and on the last judgment (chs 23–25). Only the Gospel of Matthew used the word "church" (ekklesia), and early church leaders valued it for its usefulness in teaching. Perhaps that is why it was placed first when the separate gospels were collected together at an unknown, but early time.

The Gospel of Luke. The arrangement of the New Testament obscures the fact that the Gospel of Luke is actually volume one of a two-volume work. It was meant to be read with the Acts of the Apostles, which is now separated from it in New Testaments by the Gospel of John. During the second century, Luke was identified as Paul's companion, a physician, and a gentile, which is a term that includes anyone who is not a Jew. Luke's is the least Jewish of the gospels. He emphasized the universality of Jesus' message: It was always intended for all of humanity. He openly welcomed the eventual inclusion of gentiles, a controversial issue in the first-century Jesus Movement. Luke made his point about universality by tracing Jesus' descent from Adam (Lk 3:23–38), the Father of all human beings, whereas Matthew had traced Jesus' descent from Abraham, the Father of the Jews (Mt 1:1–17). Luke's gospel emphasized that Jesus was compassionate and sympathetic to outsiders, including the poor (2:7; 6:20; 9:58; 14:21), women (7:11; 9:38; 18:15), Gentiles (4:24f; 23:28f), and even the hated Samaritans (10:25–37; 17:16).

The Synoptic Problem

Careful readers have long recognized that the Gospels of Mark, Matthew, and Luke are quite similar, although not identical, in their treatment of the geography, chronology, and episodes of Jesus' career. Mark, Matthew, and Luke have been called "synoptic gospels," from the practice of studying those gospels in parallel columns in which they are "seen together." They are so similar that most modern scholars think they are interrelated, although there is debate about how that interrelationship should be explained. The scholarly consensus (although details differ, and not every scholar agrees) is that both Matthew and Luke used the Gospel of Mark when they composed their gospels. The Gospel of Luke, 1:1, explicitly referred to "many others [who] have undertaken to draw up accounts of the events that have taken place among us." Mark was probably one of those "many others."

The authors of the Gospels of Matthew and Luke adopted not only Mark's words but also much of Mark's outlook, geography, and chronology of Jesus' life. But they adapted them to their own viewpoints. Each expanded and recast Mark's account by adding material from the oral tradition or perhaps from written sources that they had but that are now lost to us. For instance, Matthew and Luke record similar sayings of Jesus that are not in Mark. Scholars have theorized that both of them had a now-lost source (or perhaps sources), which has been called "Q" from the German word *Quelle*, which means "source." Matthew and Luke also had material that appeared only in their respective gospels. For example, only Matthew (ch 2), included the story of the wise men from the East, and only Luke (1:26–38) included the Angel Gabriel's annunciation to Mary and the story of the Good Samaritan (ch 10).

Why might Matthew or Luke rewrite Mark? The simplest answer is that they thought his gospel was incomplete and inadequate. It is the shortest, "plainest" gospel. If only it survived, Christians would be without some of the most influential, colorful, and appealing texts of their tradition. Mark has no stories of Jesus' birth. Matthew wrote down an elaborate story about the circumstances surrounding Jesus' miraculous birth, with which he opened his gospel. Only after adding his particular birth and infancy stories did Matthew begin to follow Mark's account again. In addition—and these are just a few instances—Mark has no Sermon on the Mount, no story of the Good Samaritan, no Lord's Prayer, and very little ethical teaching. But it is not just that Matthew and Luke had more material than Mark did. It appears that they differed, at least somewhat, from Mark's christology, that is, from his view of who Jesus was/is. Mark attributed to Jesus weakness, human emotions, and even ignorance. His christology may be described as "low" in the sense that in some circumstances he depicted Jesus as very human.

Mark and Matthew on Christology

As a mental experiment, let's assume that the author of Matthew had a copy of Mark in front of him. We shall focus on just two issues. What did the author of

Matthew do to make Mark fit his own view of Jesus, that is, his christology? What did he do to make Mark fit his own view of Jesus' apostles? In each case, Matthew introduced significant, if sometimes subtle, changes to Mark's account. On the basis of those changes, Matthew had a somewhat "higher" christology than what he found in Mark. Matthew quietly fixed statements where Mark implied or said that Jesus was weak or ignorant.

1) In Mark 6:1–6, Jesus went to his hometown in Galilee, was not accepted, and "he *could* work no miracle there." Matthew 13:53–58 told the same story but changed the verb in a way that avoided declaring that Jesus was not able to work a miracle: "and he *did not work* any miracle there."

2) In Mark 10:17–18, a rich young man addressed Jesus as "Good master." Jesus denied that he was good, rebuking the young man, saying "why do you call me good? No one is good but God alone." Matthew 19:16–17 has the rich young man call Jesus "Master" and ask a different question, "what good deed must I do to possess eternal life?" Jesus answers "Why do you ask me about what is good. There is one alone who is good." In Matthew's revision, Jesus no longer says that he is not good.

3) In Mark 1:41, Jesus felt sorrow for a leper and healed him. In Matthew 8:3, Jesus cured him with no expression of emotion.

4) In Mark 5:30, a woman with a flow of blood that had persisted for twelve years touched Jesus' clothes and was cured. Mark portrays Jesus as not knowing who touched him: "Immediately aware that power had gone out from him, Jesus turned to the crowd and said, 'Who has touched my clothes?'" In Matthew 9:21–22, Jesus knew immediately who touched him, picked her out of the crowd, and said to her, "Courage my daughter your faith has restored you to health."

Mark and Matthew on the Disciples

Matthew apparently felt the need to correct his source, Mark, about the disciples of Jesus. The Gospel of Mark was hard on Jesus' disciples, criticizing them for their thick-headedness and

timidity. Matthew apparently had a more positive view and edited Mark to express that.

1) In Mark 6:51–52, just after Jesus multiplied the loaves and fishes, he walked on the Sea of Galilee, to which the disciples reacted: "They [the disciples] were utterly and completely dumbfounded because they had not seen what the miracle of the loaves meant; their minds were closed." In Matthew 14:27–33, the same episode provoked a different reaction among the disciples: "The men in the boat bowed down before him and said, 'Truly you are the son of God.'"

2) In Mark 9:30–32, Jesus predicted his own death: "But they [the disciples] did not understand what he said and were afraid to ask him." In Matthew 17:22–23, they apparently did understand what was coming "and a great sadness came over them."

3) In Mark 4:13–14, Jesus told the parable of the sower and the seed. When he was alone with his disciples, he explained the parable but criticized them at the same time: "Do you not understand this parable? Then how will you understand any of the parables?" Matthew 13:18–23 repeated the same parable but with no hint that the disciples did not understand.

The three synoptic gospels share a great deal but also differ in some content and in some attitudes. The authors, whoever they were, had their own viewpoints, their own experience in Christian communities, and their own sources of information, which they skillfully wove into their accounts.

The Gospel of John. An alert reader who studies the three synoptic gospels might be surprised at reading the Gospel of John. That gospel has almost no overlap with the synoptics. The author of the Gospel of John either did not know any of the synoptic gospels or chose to ignore them. For instance, the only miracle they share is Jesus' multiplication of the loaves and fishes (Mt 14:13–21; Mk 6:30–44; Lk 9:10–17; John 6:1–13). During the second century, the author of the Gospel of John was identified with John, the son of Zebedee, one of the apostles. From an assessment of what the Gospel of John emphasized, many modern scholars believe that it was composed in a community where the

Jewish synagogue had expelled those members who accepted Jesus as Messiah (John 16:2). The author was negative about what he called simply "the Jews," who may have been the leaders of the community rather than the rank-and-file. The author wrote from a tradition that emphasized a particular view of Jesus, another christology. Clement of Alexandria (about 160–215) described the Gospel of John as the "spiritual" gospel, which emphasized what can be called a "high christology." John wrote that Jesus was the eternally preexisting Divine Word that became flesh (John 1:1–18). Whereas Mark thought that Jesus had kept his identity secret, John thought that Jesus proclaimed openly and often who he was. In John's Gospel, Jesus' deeds are different from those reported in the synoptic gospels. John recorded only seven miracles, which he called in Greek "signs." John reported no exorcisms, which were common in the synoptic gospels. In John's Gospel, Jesus' preaching, often called "discourses," is long and "philosophical," not pithy and down-to-earth as in the synoptics.

This chapter began with the questions, "What do we know about Jesus and how do we know it?" The answers are not simple. Once in a while someone will declare that Jesus never existed. Such a view is just wrong. The four non-Christians who wrote before 130 demonstrate that Jesus came briefly to the attention of contemporary non-believers. Josephus, Pliny, Tacitus, and Suetonius recorded a few things about Jesus and certainly his existence. But Christians wrote the sources, called "gospels," that report their beliefs about Jesus' life, activities, teaching, death, resurrection, ascension into heaven, and expected return. A superficial reading of the gospels may lead one to believe that they all tell the same story. But a more careful reading indicates that each gospel writer was an author with a point of view that shaped what he chose to report and how he interpreted his story. Right from the moment that Christians began to talk about Jesus, there was a diversity of views, and that diversity was evident from the moment they began to write about him.

JESUS

Since the time when Christians began to talk and write about Jesus, he has been an object of contro-

versy. It seems safe to say that he was a Jew from Galilee who, as an adult about thirty years old, began to preach that the Kingdom of God was near and that Jews should repent to prepare for the kingdom's arrival. His preaching career was short, perhaps about one year or perhaps about three years. He was arrested at Jerusalem, tried before a Jewish court and a Roman official, and executed in about 29. His crime seems to have been political. The placard placed above his head on the cross described him as "Jesus of Nazareth, King of the Jews." His followers believed that on the third day after his death on the cross, he was raised from the dead and was alive again. They said that they talked and ate with him for forty days, after which he ascended into the heavens. They were sure that he was coming back soon to judge the world. They told stories about him as a healer, an exorcist, and a worker of wonders. They also talked about him as Messiah and Son of God. His earliest followers, all of them Jews, spread orally what they called the good news about Jesus. Some other Jews and some gentiles believed them. A disorderly, uncoordinated movement—the Jesus Movement—began in the first century. This book traces the complicated developments of the Jesus Movement during the six centuries after Jesus was executed.

FURTHER READING

Ancient Sources

There is no substitute for reading the gospels themselves. At a minimum, a student might read the Gospel of Matthew and the Gospel of John for an introduction to the variety of early Christian thought contained even in the canonical gospels. If you use a reliable, scholarly biblical commentary, such as *The Oxford Companion to the Bible*, edited by Bruce M. Metzger and Michael D. Coogan (New York and Oxford, 1993) to illuminate your reading, you will learn an immense amount. If you are feeling ambitious, each of the gospels has been translated with an introduction and commentary in the Anchor Bible series. Well-known experts wrote each volume, which are long and detailed. *Matthew: Introduction, Translation and Notes* by W. F. Albright and C. S. Mann, Anchor Bible, vol. 26 (Garden City, NJ, 1971); *Mark, Chapters 1–8: A New Translation with Introduction and Commentary* by Joel Marcus,

Anchor Bible, vol. 27 (New York, 2000); *The Gospel According to Luke (I–IX): Introduction, Translation and Notes* by Joseph A. Fitzmyer, S.J., Anchor Bible, vol. 28 (New York, 1981); *The Gospel According to Luke (X–XXIV): Introduction, Translation and Notes* by Joseph A. Fitzmyer, S. J., Anchor Bible, vol. 28A (New York, 1985); and *The Gospel According to John, Introduction, Translation and Notes* by Raymond E. Brown, Anchor Bible, vols. 29–29A (Garden City, NJ, 1966–1970). *The Infancy Gospel of Thomas* and *The Protoevangelium of James* are translated in J. K. Elliott, *The Apocryphal New Testament* (Oxford, 1993), pp. 48–83.

Modern Works

The bibliography on the New Testament in general and on the gospels in particular is immense. I can suggest only a few useful and readable books. Bart D. Ehrman, *The New Testament: A Historical Introduction to the Early Christian Writings* (New York and Oxford, 1997), especially chapters 1–10 on the oral traditions and the writing of the canonical gospels.

Jesus remains a subject of fascination. Some modern studies from differing viewpoints include Geza Vermes, *Jesus in His Jewish Context* (Minneapolis, MN, 2003) and C. H. Dodd, *The Founder of Christianity* (New York, 1970); John Dominic Crossan, *The Historical Jesus: The Life of a Mediterranean Jewish Peasant* (San Francisco, 1992); Paula Fredriksen, *Jesus of Nazareth, King of the Jews: A Jewish Life and the Emergence of Christianity* (New York, 1999); or E, P. Sanders, *The Historical Figure of Jesus* (London, 1993).

John Gabel, Charles Wheeler, and Anthony D. York, *The Bible as Literature*, fourth edition (New York, 2000), especially pp. 213–232 on the gospels.

Robert M. Grant, *A Historical Introduction to the New Testament*, second edition (New York, 1972) is still a readable, sensible introduction to the topic.

Bruce Metzger, *The New Testament: Its Background, Growth and Content*, third edition (Nashville, TN, 2003).

PART I

✢

The Contexts of
Early Christianity

Timeline for First-Century Christianity

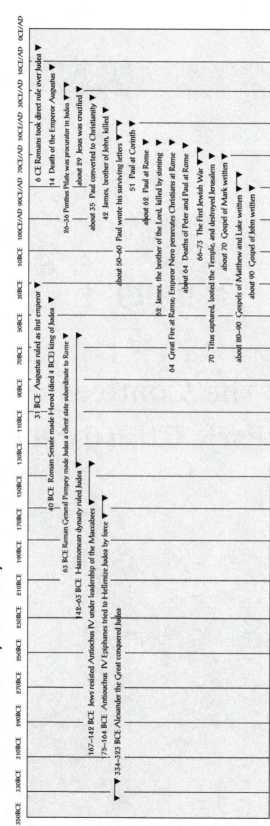

350BCE 330BCE 310BCE 290BCE 270BCE 250BCE 230BCE 210BCE 190BCE 170BCE 150BCE 130BCE 110BCE 90BCE 70BCE 50BCE 30BCE 10BCE 0CE/AD 10CE/AD 30CE/AD 50CE/AD 70CE/AD 90CE/AD 100CE/AD 110BCE

334–323 BCE Alexander the Great conquered Judea

175–164 BCE Antiochus IV Epiphanes tried to Hellenize Judea by force

167–142 BCE Jews resisted Antiochus IV under leadership of the Maccabees

142–63 BCE Hasmonean dynasty ruled Judea

63 BCE Roman General Pompey made Judea a client state subordinate to Rome

40 BCE Roman Senate made Herod (died 4 BCE) king of Judea

31 BCE Augustus ruled as first emperor

6 CE Romans took direct rule over Judea

14 Death of the Emperor Augustus

26–36 Pontius Pilate was procurator in Judea

about 29 Jesus was crucified

about 35 Paul converted to Christianity

42 James, brother of John, killed

about 50–60 Paul wrote his surviving letters

51 Paul at Corinth

about 62 Paul at Rome

62 James, the brother of the Lord, killed by stoning

64 Great Fire at Rome; Emperor Nero persecutes Christians at Rome

about 64 Deaths of Peter and Paul at Rome

66–73 The First Jewish War

70 Titus captured, looted the Temple, and destroyed Jerusalem

about 70 Gospel of Mark written

about 80–90 Gospels of Matthew and Luke written

about 90 Gospel of John written

CHAPTER 2

The Jewish Context of the Jesus Movement

Historians try to make people and developments understandable by looking into their background, sometimes called their "context." First-century Judaism was the main context for the rise of the Jesus Movement. In this chapter I shall lay out features of that period in the long history of Judaism, with my eye on providing a context for the development of what is often called "Jewish Christianity," that is, groups of Jews who both accepted Jesus as the Messiah and remained Jews. Jesus' relatively brief life was lived on a small stage. Galilee, where he spent much of his public ministry, and Judea, the heartland of the Jews and the site of their Temple at Jerusalem, were like small islands in a sea of other peoples, most prominent of whom were Greeks and Romans. Jesus and his early followers lived in the midst of political and cultural tensions that had deep historical roots. After his death, Roman political domination, coupled with Greek cultural threats to the Jewish way of life, provoked unrest among Palestinian Jews that exploded in unsuccessful revolts in 66 and again in 132. Jesus' earliest followers were influenced by the complex world in which they lived.

Between about 700 and 400 BCE, in the region around the Aegean Sea, Greek-speaking peoples created a remarkable civilization that still influences the modern world. Because Greece and western Turkey were relatively poor lands, for centuries Greek-speaking people had emigrated out of their homeland to settle in colonies, especially around the Black Sea, in southern Italy, and in southern France. When Alexander the Great (356–323 BCE), a successful Macedonian Greek general, conquered Egypt and the Near East, including Judea, he set in motion a massive expansion of Greek culture.

His conquests opened rich opportunities for Greeks, who poured out of their traditional homeland around the Aegean Sea. Some found jobs as mercenary soldiers and bureaucrats who controlled the millions of people conquered by Alexander; others enriched themselves as merchants, manufacturers, and tax collectors; and still others earned a living as teachers, artists, sculptors, and architects. Wherever the Greek emigrants settled, they recreated as well as they could their traditional way of life, whose focus was the city-state, called in Greek a *polis*. They brought their gods, and they built temples, gymnasia, public baths, and marketplaces. The Greek settlers also tried to preserve their language and their values, which were embodied in their literature. Teachers in Greek cities instructed the young in the Greek language, literature, and way of life, especially the poems of Homer and other central documents of Greek civilization. A simplified form of Greek, called "Koiné" ("common Greek"), developed for everyday use and for written documents as well. The Christian New Testament was written in Koiné Greek. The simplified form of Greek was spoken, written, and understood, especially in cities, from what is now Pakistan to the Atlantic Ocean. Like English today, Koiné Greek became the language for business and for documents of all sorts across a broad area around the Mediterranean Sea.

In political, economic, and military matters, the Greeks dominated the conquered peoples, including Egyptians, Babylonians, Persians, Syrians, and Jews. To a large degree the local ethnic groups continued to use their own languages and to live in their own ways, especially in the countryside. But the opportunities for worldly success that the Greek way of life offered were attractive to ambitious non-Greeks, some of whom aspired to live that way, too. In general, Greek prejudices were cultural rather than racial. Greeks called people who lived in non-Greek ways "barbarians." But if non-Greeks learned Greek and absorbed Greek values, they might be able to join the dominant group. Because the Greeks called themselves "Hellenes," the process of learning to live like a Greek has been called "Hellenization." The Greek expansion into Egypt and the Near East—and the Hellenization after that expansion—had a lasting impact. For at least a thousand years, urban peoples all over the Near East lived more or less in a Greek way. Hellenization influenced many conservative rural subjects as well.

THE JEWS AND HELLENIZATION

Judea, the Jewish homeland, was just one of the areas swept up in the Greek conquests. When Alexander died unexpectedly at Babylon in 323 BCE, at the age of thirty-three, his vast empire was divided among his leading generals. Although most Jews cherished memories of the independent kingdom of David and Solomon (about 1000–about 920 BCE), they were ruled from the fourth century BCE to the sixth century CE first by Greek kings, then by Jewish rulers who were to one degree or another Hellenized, and finally by Romans. The pressure to adopt a Greek way of life provoked profound divisions within Judaism. Some Jews were attracted to the Greek way of life; other Jews hated it; and some held positions in between.

Judea was disputed territory, claimed by the descendants of Alexander's General Antiochus, who ruled to the north in Syria, and by the descendants of Alexander's General Ptolemy, who ruled to the south in Egypt. King Antiochus IV Epiphanes (175–164 BCE) was troubled by his Jewish subjects' aloofness and strong desire for independence. He decided that a thorough Hellenization, by force if necessary, would increase his control of this border territory. His strong measures provoked a crisis within Palestinian Judaism. In 171 BCE, Antiochus ousted the high priestly family and sold the chief priesthood to the highest bidder, a Jew who had accepted much of the Greek way of life. In 168 BCE, Antiochus forbade Jews to observe their ancestral

law and customs. He tried to impose Greek law and religious practices on the Jews. There were to be no more burnt offerings to the God of Israel, no circumcision of male children, and no observance of the dietary laws. Because Jews believed that their God should not be represented in art, there were no statues in his Temple. Antiochus placed statues of Greek gods in the Jewish Temple and worshipped them with Greek religious rituals. This was probably the "Abomination of Desolation" condemned in Daniel 11:31 and 12:11. The Jews fervently believed that their God was the only god, but Antiochus IV demoted him to a local god among many others. Some Jews, favorable to Hellenism, accepted Antiochus' measures. But other Jews, particularly conservative and rural Jews, rose up in a long, bitter war (167–142 BCE) under the leadership of Judas Maccabeus ("the Hammer") and his brothers. By 142 BCE, the Syrian rulers were forced to concede defeat. For about eighty years (142–63 BCE), relatives of Judas Maccabeus, called the "Hasmonean dynasty," ruled a small independent Jewish kingdom centered on Jerusalem.

The crisis over forced Hellenization and the long war that followed had profound consequences that still shaped the Judaism of Jesus' lifetime and of generations thereafter. First, the Jewish sense of separation from (and superiority to) non-Jews intensified. Second, in reaction against Antiochus' direct attack on the Law of Moses, the pious parties within Judaism promoted strict observance of the Law, which was to them not just a set of beliefs but a detailed way of life given directly by their God. Third, the Jewish avoidance of outsiders, who were called "goyim" or "gentiles," was met with a corresponding dislike of Jews in much of the Greco-Roman world. Fourth, the Jewish martyrs (literally "witnesses") who died for their religion set a precedent for future struggles. The ancient Mediterranean religions generally did not encourage dying for one's religious beliefs. But in reaction to twenty-five years of bitter warfare, Judaism (and later Christianity) exalted those who chose death rather than compromise in religion. Fifth, during the long war, there were times when defeat led to discouragement for the Jews. To assure their fellow Jews that things would turn out well in the end, some Jews wrote books or pamphlets that predicted that God was about to intervene on their side, to smash the gentiles, and to usher in an age of Jewish independence. Such views are called "apocalyptic" (from a Greek word meaning "uncovering"). Apocalyptic hopes persisted and perhaps even intensified within Judaism in the time of Jesus and in the first generations of the Jesus Movement.

From 142 to 63 BCE, the Hasmonean rulers of Judea presented themselves to their Jewish subjects as the high priests of the God of Israel and to outsiders as Hellenized kings. For instance, some coins had Hebrew inscriptions on one side and Greek inscriptions on the other. The years of Hasmonean rule were strife-ridden, both because the Hasmoneans fought among themselves and because some of their Jewish subjects disapproved of their religious policies and personal behavior. In 63 BCE the Roman general Pompey conquered much of the eastern shore of the Mediterranean Sea for Rome. He made the Kingdom of the Jews a "client" state, that is, he left the Hasmonean dynasty in charge but under Roman supervision. The Romans were gentiles and Hellenized: Their rule was no more welcome to pious Jews than that of any non-Jewish ruler would have been. The strife and unrest continued. In about 40 BCE, the Romans tried a new strategy to control Judea without ruling it directly. The Roman Senate appointed as king a man named Herod, later called "the Great" (37–4 BCE), who was hated by many of his Jewish subjects. Herod undertook important building projects, including fortresses, palaces, roads, new cities, and the port at Caesarea. Above all, he began the renovation of the Temple in Jerusalem. But he was also ruthless and kept order in brutal ways. After Herod's death in 4 BCE his sons succeeded to his subdivided kingdom, although Roman officials still maintained general control through a Roman legate in Syria who had a significant army. After a revolt in Judea in 6 CE, the Romans took direct rule of Judea and its chief city, Jerusalem, but left outlying areas under the control of Herod's descendants. Most Jews hated the rule of the gentile Romans over their sacred city but disagreed among themselves about what to do. Jesus' ministry and the lives of his earliest followers took place against the background of bitter struggles about Roman political control and Greek cultural threats to Judaism.

THE TEMPLE

Long before Jesus' lifetime, Jews had concluded that the Temple at Jerusalem was the only place where Jews could properly worship their God with the animal sacrifices and rituals that the Law demanded. In 586 BCE, the Babylonians destroyed the first Temple, which had been built by King Solomon in about 964 BCE. When the Persian King Cyrus allowed Jews to return from exile in Babylon to Jerusalem in 538 BCE, they built a second Temple on the same site. To win favor with his hostile Jewish subjects, King Herod began a massive renovation of that second Temple in 20 BCE. In Jesus' lifetime, the Temple was an impressive complex of walls, courtyards, and buildings. It was also a busy place where Jewish priests and other Temple attendants carried out the elaborate worship of the God of Israel. Perhaps as many as twenty thousand priests and Levites served in the Temple in shifts. Twice daily there were sacrifices of animals and food, which were burned to the accompaniment of music. Twice daily incense was burned as an offering to God. There were special offerings on each Sabbath. Individual Jews could arrange private offerings in the Temple to atone for their sins and to express thanks for a divine favor. During the important annual festivals, great numbers of Jews came to the Temple, sometimes from long distances, to pray, make offerings, and witness the impressive spectacle. The Temple was also a major employer and economic engine for Jerusalem. Every male Jew over the age of twenty, wherever he lived, was expected to pay an annual tax to support the Temple. In addition, the priests and other personnel of the Temple received a share in the offerings, fees, and sacrificial animals, which could be considerable, especially during feast days when great crowds came to the Temple. A gentile, that is, anyone who was not a Jew, could enter an outer courtyard of the Temple but was forbidden under pain of death from entering the Temple's inner courtyards.

SYNAGOGUES

There was only one Jewish Temple, and its primary role was to worship God as the Mosaic Law prescribed. Synagogues (a Greek word meaning "a coming together" or a "congregation") or "houses of prayer" developed to meet the religious needs of the vast majority of Jews who lived away from the Temple, whether they were seventy-five miles away in Galilee or hundreds of miles away in Greece. The early history of the synagogues is murky, but by the first century CE, the weekly gathering in a house of prayer had an important place in Judaism. A synagogue was often a building, but it did not have to be. Jews who met to worship anywhere, perhaps in a private home, could constitute a synagogue. The synagogue was a flexible institution that kept Judaism alive in places distant from the Temple. The organization of first-century synagogues is not well documented. There was variation in first-century synagogue services, which probably consisted of different combinations of reading from the scriptures in Hebrew, with a paraphrase in Aramaic or Greek for those who needed it. The reading was followed by an explanation of what had been read. The attendees sang, offered a series of blessings and curses, and prayed. In a synagogue there were no sacrifices because they could be offered only in the Jerusalem Temple. The synagogue became essential to Jewish communal and religious life, including the knowledge of the Law. The Mosaic Law directed not just religious ritual and worship but also moral conduct and social behavior. Taken as a whole, the Law laid out a way of life. The complexity of the Law and the seriousness with which many wanted to observe it gave rise to a body of experts and teachers called "scribes" in the Christian gospels. Synagogues were not just places of worship and instruction in the Law. The Jews had a reputation in antiquity for their generosity to their needy fellow Jews. The synagogue was often the place where charity was organized for Jewish widows, orphans, the ill, and the aged. Synagogues were places of worship, community organization, teaching, and charity. They were common in the eastern Mediterranean, where many first-century Jews lived.

ORDINARY JUDAISM IN PALESTINE

There were hundreds of thousands of Jews in Judea and Galilee. Many were fervent about their reli-

gion, but they disagreed about many topics. As a result, a precise, uniform description of Jewish belief and practice is not possible. But it is possible to describe briefly "ordinary" first-century Judaism and then describe the activist sects or parties within Judaism. Almost all Jews agreed on the central features of their religion. They believed that their God was the only God, the creator and controller of the universe. They believed that he had made a pact, a covenant, with their ancestors and with them that made them God's special people, whom he would protect. They believed that through Moses God had given them a Law that they must obey if they wanted to maintain their side of the covenant. The English word "Law" can be misleading here. The Law of Moses prescribed a full way of life, including such matters as how to worship God, how to treat one's neighbor, and how to carry out some agricultural tasks. The Jews believed that the holiest place on Earth was the Temple at Jerusalem. God was thought to dwell in the innermost chamber of the Temple, called the "Holy of Holies," although he was also thought to be everywhere in his creation. Following detailed instructions in the Law, the hereditary priests offered sacrifices of incense, food, and above all birds, lambs, rams, and cattle to God in his Temple. Jews who were not priests willingly supported the Temple and the priesthood. Ordinary Jews also came to the Temple in great numbers for annual festivals, especially Passover (in the spring), Weeks (fifty days after Passover), and Booths or Tabernacles (in the autumn). In their homes Jews recited the Shema (Deut 6:4 "Hear, O Israel, the Lord is our God, the Lord is one....") and offered personal prayers, often twice a day. In day-to-day life, many Jews sought to observe the Law correctly, although they might be puzzled or disagree about exactly how to do that. The priests claimed the authority to interpret the Law. But because the Law was written down, they had rivals. Non-priests could and did study it and expressed a broad spectrum of opinions about it.

I cannot describe everything most Jews did, but a few things stand out. One way to look at first-century Judaism is to study what contemporary pagans found noteworthy in it. Some non-Jewish writers commented on the Jews' observance of the Sabbath, on the seventh day of the week, which was a visible characteristic of Judaism. On the Sabbath, Jews went to the synagogue for scripture study, refrained from all work, and ate a festive meal. Gentiles were also aware that Jews circumcised their sons. The Jews were not the only ancient peoples to do so, but their practice drew comment from outsiders, much of it negative. Gentiles were also aware that Jews ate certain foods and avoided other kinds of food. Some observers judged that to be fussy and superstitious. Outsiders sometimes made fun of their avoidance of pork, a meat common in the diets of non-Jews. Gentiles were also aware that Jews were willing to die for the sacredness of the Temple and their right to observe their ancestral Law. The frequent riots and uprisings in Jewish Palestine when Jews thought the Temple or the Law was in danger demonstrated the point. The major rebellions in 66 and 132 were motivated in large part by zeal for the Law.

Sects and Parties

The ordinary Judaism of the first century CE was not the whole story. Jews generally agreed on the importance of the five books of Moses (Genesis, Exodus, Leviticus, Numbers, and Deuteronomy), called the "Torah" or "the Law." Pious Jews were concerned to observe the Law properly, which is often called "orthopraxy" ("correct behavior"), but they were less concerned with uniformity of belief, which is often called "orthodoxy" ("correct belief"). Judaism had no official creed beyond a strict monotheism. No person or group was universally recognized as having a binding teaching authority. Thus, Jews who *believed* rather different things could accept other people as Jews, provided that they were orthopractic, that is, that they carried out the commands and obeyed the prohibitions of the Law of Moses. A life of orthopraxy was demanding. Many, perhaps most, Jews in Palestine were uneducated, poor, downtrodden, and hard-pressed by taxes. Such people were often not willing or able to observe every provision of the Law, but they certainly considered themselves Jews.

In Jesus' lifetime, Judaism in Palestine was split by serious internal divisions. The pressures of Greek culture and Roman political domination had created within Judaism groups of activists, sometimes called "sects" or "parties," the best known of which are Sadducees, Pharisees, Essenes, and the followers of Jesus whom I shall call "Jewish Christians." The sects, which were often rather small, observed the Law strictly, although they disagreed with one another vigorously about what was proper and improper. They also competed with one another for influence among the ordinary Jewish people.

Because no sources survive that were written by Sadducees, general statements about them need to be cautious. The Sadducees were not numerous but were important because they were often aristocrats and major landholders. They included the higher members of the hereditary priesthood, who controlled the Temple. Wherever they could, the Romans tried to rule through cooperation with local elites. In Judea, they gave significant political power to the Sadducees and their aristocratic allies, who already had wealth, high social status, and religious authority. The Sadducees often represented the interests of the Jews to the Roman authorities and the interests of the Roman authorities to their own people. Some rival sects perceived them as collaborators with the Romans. This was not an entirely fair accusation. Although they could not avoid all contact with the Roman rulers, like all orthopractic Jews the Sadducees kept their distance when possible from the gentiles. The Sadducees were conservative in their religious views, accepting as authoritative only the written Torah, embodied in the books of Genesis, Exodus, Leviticus, Numbers, and Deuteronomy. In particular they rejected the rich body of oral traditions that the rival sect of the Pharisees accepted. Because the Sadducees believed that they could not find in the five books of Moses a clear teaching about the resurrection of the dead, the existence of angels, and the expectation of a coming Messiah, they rejected those beliefs. The Sadducees did not favor armed resistance to Roman rule, perhaps because they had so much to lose.

The first-century Jewish historian Josephus, a priest who joined the sect of the Pharisees, wrote that there were six thousand Pharisees, probably the largest group of Jewish activists. They were strict observers of the Law, but what set them apart was their desire to adapt it to changing circumstances and to make it relevant to their own times. They were skilled interpreters of the Law and, unlike the Sadducees, also revered an oral law, sometimes called the "traditions of the fathers," that they believed had been handed down from Moses through a succession of teachers. They thought that the oral traditions were as binding as the written Law itself. They were generally not aristocrats or religious "professionals." Instead, they were often non-priestly Jews who earned their living in some occupation, perhaps as farmers or merchants. They devoted themselves to intense study and meditation on the Law, which they tried to observe in every detail. Many Jews respected them for their religious zeal and their detailed knowledge of the Law. People consulted them about difficult religious matters. They urged other Jews to follow their interpretations of the Law, they gave religious advice, but ordinarily they could not force anyone to do anything. The Pharisees may have been influential in at least some synagogues, where the teachers, called "scribes," were often their allies. Because they accepted a wide selection of books as authoritative and added to them the traditions of the fathers, they believed in the resurrection of the dead, rewards and punishments in the next world, and the existence of angels and demons. They were anti-Hellenic and anti-Roman but did not call for revolt. They expected God to set things right without violence on their part. They hoped for the expulsion of foreign rulers, the return of Jewish exiles and emigrants, and the restoration of Jewish independence. They were the main rivals to the Sadducees for leadership within Palestinian Judaism. The gospels gave the Pharisees a negative reputation as "hypocrites" that still survives in some places. The writers of the Christian gospels, who criticized the Pharisees severely, probably saw them as important rivals precisely because the Pharisees shared many ideas with the Jesus Movement.

The Alexandrian Jewish writer Philo (20 BCE–50 CE) wrote that there were four thousand Essenes, who had separated completely from other Jews whom they regarded as impure and impious. The Essenes were a closed, secretive society that can be described as monastic. Some Essene men lived in a community with strict rules that regulated diet, property, prayers, discipline, celibacy, and ritual baths to restore purity. They had mar-ried followers as well, although we know almost nothing about them. The Essenes rejected the Sadducee high priests as illegitimate and avoided the Temple. They saw the Pharisees as not strict enough. The Essenes eagerly expected a battle between the children of light, who were themselves, and the children of darkness, who were the gentiles and unworthy Jews. They may have thought the final battle had begun in 66 when Palestinian Jews rebelled against Roman rule. But they were destroyed in the Roman victory. The famous Dead Sea Scrolls, which were found in 1947 in clay jars near the Essene settlement at Qumran, were probably their library. Although the Essenes were contemporaries of Jesus, they were never mentioned in the four canonical gospels.

The most militantly anti-Roman sect was that of the Zealots, who saw the Sadducees as collaborators and the Pharisees as too pacifistic. Depending on your viewpoint, the Zealots were terrorists, rebels, freedom fighters, or uncompromising nationalists who would accept only God as their king. They took the lead in the violence that led up to the uprising of 66. There were other activists in Jesus' lifetime who are more difficult to identify with specific sects. Some Palestinian Jews had a strong apocalyptic conviction that the end of this world was near. Apocalyptic preachers, often working on their own or with a few disciples, criss-crossed the land. John the Baptist is the best known, but there were others. Finally, the Jewish Christians, who were Jews who accepted Jesus as Messiah, were also a sect within Judaism in the years between Jesus' death in about 29 and the rebellion of 66. The Jewish Christians will be treated more fully in chapter 4.

DIASPORA ("DISPERSION")

One prominent feature of Judaism had an important influence on the Jesus Movement. The majority of first-century Jews lived outside Palestine, concentrated in the cities of the eastern Mediterranean and farther east in Babylonia, which is in modern Iraq. Palestine was a relatively poor place, and for centuries Jews migrated out of their homeland. As a result of Alexander the Great's conquests in the fourth century BCE, Greeks gained the most opportunities, but members of other ethnic groups also migrated, primarily for economic or political reasons. The Jews who migrated and their descendants are said to have lived in the Diaspora, a Greek word meaning "dispersion" or "scattering." The Diaspora was not a particular place; it was a state of being. It was where Jews lived who did not dwell in Judea but who still regarded it as their homeland and themselves as Jews. Although there are no reliable numbers, Jews were numerous in the Roman Empire. They were a minority large enough to be politically and socially important. In the Diaspora there was a wide spectrum of Jewish life. Some Jews adopted a Hellenized way of life, but others continued to observe the Law, which they sometimes adapted to the circumstances in which they lived. Because Jews in the Diaspora were far from the Temple, they found their religious and social center in synagogues, the scriptures, and customs. Many Diaspora Jews made, or wished to make, at least one pilgrimage to the Temple in Jerusalem. Even Jews who never saw Jerusalem—and there must have been many—kept ties to the holy city and its Temple. They had with them the sacred books of their ancestors, although they often read them in a Greek translation called the *Septuagint* because many no longer knew Hebrew after living for generations in the Diaspora. Male Jews over the age of twenty, including those in the Diaspora, paid a tax to support the Temple.

To the degree that the Law governed their behavior, the Jews of the Diaspora were quite distinct from their gentile neighbors. They socialized among themselves—a good Jew should not eat with gentiles. Jews refused to participate in pagan worship because they were strict monotheists who regarded Greek and Roman gods with contempt. Where the Jews were very numerous, as they were in the city of Alexandria in Egypt, they obtained a privileged status, which often meant some degree of self-government. In reaction, many gentiles, although attracted to Jewish monotheism, were puzzled or repelled by the requirements of the Jewish religious practices. Life for Jews in the Diaspora was a combination of fitting in and feeling tension with their gentile neighbors. Violence between gentiles and Jews was a recurring reality in the cities of the eastern Mediterranean. In some

places Jewish communities looked to the central Roman state to protect them from local governments. In return, they were often supporters of the empire against local interests.

Proselytes and God-Fearers

On the one hand, Judaism was the religion of a particular people; on the other hand, it had an appeal to some Greeks and Romans. Some gentiles were attracted by Judaism's elevated moral code, its prestigious antiquity, and its clear assertion that there was just one god. Some gentile admirers, called "proselytes," converted to Judaism. But Judaism had features that made other sympathetic gentiles hesitant to go so far as to convert. The Law of Moses required that converts give up their gentile families and friends. Circumcision for adult men in an era before anesthetics or antibiotics was also a serious step. The gentiles who admired Judaism but would not convert had a special status. They could attend Sabbath services, where they heard the reading of scripture and sermons, often in Greek, a language they could understand. Jews called these people "God-fearers." They were at the margins of the synagogue, never members. It was from the ranks of the god-fearers that some of the earliest gentile converts came to the Jesus Movement.

ROMAN RULE AND THE JEWS

In a vast empire that stretched from northern Gaul to southern Egypt, the Romans wanted peace, quiet, and taxes. The Jews were numerous, and, as they showed in their struggle against Antiochus Epiphanes and in urban strife in places such as Alexandria, they were willing to fight and die as martyrs for their God, their Law, and their traditional rights. The Roman authorities were forced to take into account Jewish numbers and willingness to resist. The Roman authorities often protected Jews from their fellow citizens, who sometimes resented Jewish aloofness and political privileges. The Romans granted Judaism a special status on the grounds that it was an ancient national religion to which its members owed allegiance, even when they lived in the Diaspora. For instance, Jews were exempt from the worship of the emperor, to which other conquered peoples were subject. In the Temple, the Jewish priests offered daily sacrifices to their God *for* the emperor. Roman tolerance for Judaism, occasionally leaning toward favor or toward repression, was usually successful in keeping peace in the Diaspora.

The situation in Palestine was different from that in the Diaspora. After 6 CE, direct Roman rule of Judea (and Jerusalem) created ongoing tension. Some Roman magistrates tried to respect Jewish sensitivities that could easily be inflamed by a gentile presence in the holy city. As a concession, the Roman procurator, who governed Judea, lived not in Jerusalem but in Caesarea, a mostly gentile city on the sea coast. Much of the day-to-day governance of Jerusalem and Judea was left in the hands of the high priest, the chief priests, and a council called the "Sanhedrin," dominated by Sadducees and Pharisees. But the Roman rulers still occasionally offended their Jewish subjects. For instance, Pontius Pilate, the procurator of Judea from 26 to 36, once brought into Jerusalem Roman military standards, called *signa*, which had pagan symbols on them. Rioting followed. He also took money from the Temple treasury to pay for an aqueduct. What he probably regarded as a reasonable way to pay for a public works project also led to rioting. The Emperor Gaius Caligula (37–41), who did not like Jews and had an exalted view of himself, ordered his statue to be put up in Temple. The Roman authorities in Judea delayed carrying out the emperor's order because they foresaw the explosion that would occur in Judea and perhaps in the Diaspora. Caligula was assassinated at Rome in 41, and the crisis passed.

The Roman policy of limited concessions to the Jews did not work in Palestine. Almost all Jews in Palestine yearned for their God to rule them directly or at least through legitimate Jewish rulers. The Jewish sects differed in their reaction to Roman rule, but none welcomed it. The Essenes expected a great war that would lead to the destruction of the sons of darkness; the Zealots agitated for warfare; and the Pharisees kept a hostile distance from the gentile rulers. To end the profound resentment of their rule, the Romans could do nothing short of giving Judea independence, which they were not going to do. Apocalyptic preachers and apocalyptic documents stirred up the political and religious atmosphere by proclaiming that the time was near when gentile rule would be overthrown. The agitated times were favorable to prophets, messiahs, and rebels.

The hatred of Roman rule was not just talk. In the decades before war broke out in 66, there were assassinations, riots, and unsuccessful uprisings. Roman repression of political threats in Palestine was swift and bloody, as it was wherever conquered people resisted Roman rule. Luke made a passing reference to two such episodes: "There was Theudas who became notorious not so long ago. He claimed to be someone important and he even collected about 400 followers; but when he was killed all his followers scattered and that was the end of them. And then there was Judas the Galilean at the time of the census who attracted crowds of supporters but he was killed too and all his followers dispersed" (Acts 5:36). In Jesus' lifetime and in the three decades thereafter, the Jewish homeland was a powder keg.

The Jewish War of 66–73

Political and economic causes strengthened Jewish religious grievances. Direct Roman rule was relatively recent, only about sixty years old. The Jewish desire for independence was much older, fueled by memories of the kingdom of David and Solomon one thousand years earlier. Roman officials, local Jewish rulers, and landlords imposed heavy taxes and rents in a poor land. Roman repression of small outbreaks of dissent was heavy-handed and fueled more unrest. In 66, a full-scale rebellion broke out in Palestine but not in the Diaspora. In a declaration of revolt, the priests ceased to offer the daily Temple sacrifice for the emperor. The Roman general Vespasian responded with two legions, supported by troops from neighboring client kingdoms. He systematically captured cities and fortified places. While the military campaign was still under way, Vespasian returned in 68 to Rome to become emperor after Nero committed suicide. Vespasian's son Titus besieged Jerusalem with sixty-five thousand troops. The city held out for five months, but famine and factional fighting among Jews raged inside its walls, even as the Roman surrounded it. When the Roman troops captured Jerusalem in August of 70, the Temple was ransacked and burned, the city's walls were destroyed, and the survivors were slaughtered or sold into slavery. The Jews of the entire empire were ordered to pay the traditional Temple tax to the Temple of Jupiter Optimus Maximus ("Jupiter the Best and Greatest") in Rome. Titus built a triumphal arch at Rome to celebrate his victory. On the arch, which is still standing, he depicted his soldiers carrying off the magnificent objects that had been used in the Temple worship, including the altars and the massive seven-branched candelabra.

The Roman victory had tremendous consequences for the future of Palestinian Judaism and for the Jesus Movement. The Temple, the only legitimate site of Jewish worship, was destroyed and with it the base of power of the Sadducees, who controlled the Temple. The Essenes and Zealots, who had probably welcomed the war, were destroyed militarily. Not every sect disappeared immediately after the military defeat, but within a generation

Figure 2.1 The Triumphal Arch of Titus. After the capture of Jerusalem in 70, Roman soldiers looted the Jewish Temple. The victory was significant enough to the Romans that a triumphal arch was built in the Roman Forum, where it still stands. This sculpture from Titus' arch shows sacred objects from the temple, including the large seven-branched candelabra, being carried in a triumphal procession. *(Alinari / Art Resource, NY)*

only two Jewish sects with a future ahead of them survived the catastrophe: the Pharisees from whom rabbinic Judaism gradually developed over the following centuries and the Jewish Christians from whom the Christian Movement developed. Defeat did not end Jewish unrest. In 115–117 there was a Jewish rebellion in Egypt, Libya, and Cyprus over Jewish political rights in the cities. The Emperor Trajan (98–117) put down the uprising, but the legacy of intense hatred persisted.

The Jewish War of 132–135

The Romans had decisively defeated the Jews by 73, but Palestine continued to bubble with anger. A second significant Jewish rebellion began in 132. Akiba, a leading rabbi, declared that the leader of the second rebellion, Simon bar Kochba ("Son of the Star"), was the Messiah. After initial successes, including the recapture of Jerusalem and perhaps the reinstitution of sacrifices on the site of the ruined Temple, the Roman army prevailed. Simon bar Kochba was killed in battle. A bitter, desperate war ended in massive defeat. The victorious Emperor Hadrian (117–138) took severe measures to prevent a future uprising. Because Hadrian forbade Jews to live in Jerusalem or close to it, the city was inhabited primarily by gentiles for at least two centuries. He renamed Jerusalem "Aelia" (based on his name) "Capitolina" (in honor of Jupiter, whose temple was on the Capitoline hill in Rome). Jupiter was worshipped on the site of the Jewish Temple. The Christian Emperor Constantine (306–337) allowed the name "Jerusalem" to be used again, although Jews could not legally live in the city until the Emperor Julian the Apostate (361–363) gave them permission.

The two unsuccessful rebellions changed Judaism in significant ways. The end of the Temple meant that the synagogue gradually emerged between the second and fourth centuries as Judaism's main religious and social institution. Many Jews intensified their devotion to those aspects of the Law that could be observed without the Temple. In earlier times, Judaism had been to some degree open to converts, but after the Second War it generally turned in on itself in order to survive. Some Jewish teachers went so far as to forbid or discourage conversion, although some conversions did occur. The "new" Judaism rejected—or at least tried to reject—the Hellenic way of life and its dominant language, Greek, at least for religious purposes. Jews stopped using the Greek translation of the Hebrew scriptures, the Septuagint, which had by then become the scriptures of the Christians. Judaism gradually gave religious authority only to books written in Hebrew or Aramaic, that is, they created a "canon," an official list, of the Hebrew scriptures.

The Romans allowed surviving teachers, who were mostly Pharisees in their orientation, to reconstitute Judaism as a religion. Although the Pharisees could not live in Jerusalem, they were allowed to set up a school at Jamnia, where the prince or patriarch of the Jews, called the *Nasi*, lived. After two disastrous defeats, most Jews were suspicious of the violent forms of apocalyptic views, which never disappeared. Jews still prayed for their deliverance from gentile rule and for a return to Jerusalem. In return for acceptance of their rule, the Roman state again tolerated and protected Jews.

Thus, Jesus and his earliest followers lived in and were shaped by a tumultuous period in the history of the Jews in which they, as Jews, shared.

FURTHER READING

Ancient Sources

C. K. Barrett, *The New Testament Background: Selected Documents* (New York, 1956), pp. 105–266. A good selection of translated documents that illustrates the complicated history of first- and second-century Judaism.

Josephus, *On the Jewish War* (many translations). A gripping account of the First Jewish War (66–73).

Geza Vermes, trans., ed., *The Complete Dead Sea Scrolls in English*, translated and edited with an introduction by the editor (London, 2004). If you want to read one document from the Dead Sea scrolls, choose "The War Scroll."

Modern Works

W. H. C. Frend, *Martyrdom and Persecution in the Early Church: A Study in Conflict from the Maccabees to Donatus*

(Oxford, 1965), especially chapter 2, on "Judaism and Martyrdom."

E. P. Sanders, *Judaism: Practice and Belief, 63 BCE–66 CE* (London and Philadelphia, 1992). A long, challenging book. But a careful reading will help you understand the beliefs, practices, and complexities of Judaism in the century before the First Rebellion.

Peter Schäfer, *Judeophobia: Attitudes toward the Jews in the Ancient World* (Cambridge, MA, 1997). An interesting account of how outsiders regarded Jews.

Emil Schürer, *The History of the Jewish People in the Age of Jesus Christ*, three volumes in four parts, a new English version revised and enlarged by Geza Vermes and Fergus Millar (Edinburgh, 1973). A detailed history of the period.

Marcel Simon, *Jewish Sects at the Time of Jesus*, translated by James H. Farley (Philadelphia, 1967). A brief, insightful treatment of the internal divisions of Palestinian Judaism just before, during, and after Jesus' lifetime.

CHAPTER 3

The Greek and Roman Context of Early Christianity

Within a few decades of Jesus' death, his followers began to spread their messages beyond their Jewish audience to gentiles, that is, to non-Jews, especially Greeks and Romans. The missionaries had to cope with a religious world larger and more diverse than the Judaism within which the Jesus Movement had been born. It is to that wide religious context that we turn now. By Jesus' lifetime, the Roman Empire had united under its control the shores of the Mediterranean Sea and much of the inland territory. Until about 175, the empire continued to expand. The migrations in the Mediterranean area that had been going on at least since the fourth century BCE intensified in the empire. The ancient migrants brought their gods with them, just as modern migrants do. In American history each new wave of immigrants has meant new religions—mostly Protestants in the seventeenth and eighteenth centuries (with small numbers of Jewish and Catholic immigrants), large numbers of Catholics and Jews in the nineteenth and early twentieth centuries, and, more recently, Muslims, Buddhists, Hindus, and others. For several centuries peoples and religions mixed on a large scale in the Roman Empire. When Christian missionaries approached gentiles with their messages, they encountered a complex situation where their hearers already had many religious choices. The modern opinion that the Roman Empire was somehow religiously deprived and yearned for Christianity is inaccurate. Christianity became one more choice in a religiously crowded society.

Modern popular culture, especially in films, tends to portray the ancient Greeks and Romans in a lurid light: orgies, gross banquets, and gladiatorial fights. Roman life was coarser and cruder than would fit most modern American or European sensibilities. The gap between rich and poor was huge, slavery was prominent, sports that shed the blood of animals and human beings were wildly popular, and a sex industry that catered to every taste flourished. But there was another side to the picture. Christianity appeared when the Greco-Roman world was in the midst of a long-term religious revival, marked by a growing interest in otherworldly matters. It simplifies, but not too much, to divide the religious development of the Greco-Roman world into three long phases. Before the fifth century BCE, the myths ("stories") about the gods and the rituals to worship them developed. In the second phase from the fifth to first centuries BCE, many intellectuals in the Greek world embraced an intense skepticism about the traditional myths and rituals. Philosophers in particular kept up a withering attack on traditional beliefs and practices. In fact, it is hard to think of any modern criticism of religion that was not expressed by someone in those centuries. Without the means of mass communication, the waves of doubt and criticism probably influenced only educated elites and some urban people. Agricultural societies are generally conservative. In the countryside there was no mass revolt against traditional religion, but in some places there was growing neglect of temples and rituals. Because Romans were generally more conservative than their Greek contemporaries, the criticism of their traditional religious ways was slower to emerge. But as Greek education permeated the Roman upper classes from the second century BCE onward, some Hellenized Romans expressed religious doubts. For instance, before Roman magistrates undertook any official action, they consulted the gods in a process called "augury." Experts, called "augurs," looked at the flight of birds or the entrails of animals to discern if the gods were favorable to a proposed undertaking. Augury was firmly rooted in Roman public religion and preceded many official actions even though some Romans expressed cynicism about it. Cato the Censor, a prominent Roman senator who died about 150 BCE, is said to have remarked that he could not understand why the examiners of entrails did not laugh when they encountered one another (Cicero, *De divinatione*, II.52). The age of religious skepticism did not last forever. The third phase of religious development began late in the first century BCE, when a wave of seriousness about religion began to build. The first Roman emperor, Augustus (31 BCE–14 CE), consciously presented himself as pious in the old ways. In a famous inscription in which he summed up his achievements, he boasted that he had restored eighty-two neglected temples in the city of Rome itself and that he had reinvigorated dying rituals. His actions were symptoms of a deepening concern with religion that continued for centuries, in fact, even beyond the end of the Roman Empire. Christianity emerged during this third phase of ancient religious development. On the one hand, the intense and growing interest in religion gave the Christians an audience. On the other hand, that same interest gave them many rivals.

The religious choices in the first-, second-, and third-century Roman Empire ranged across a broad spectrum, from state-supported temples and rituals to voluntary groups and on to freelance astrologers, magicians, healers, fortune-tellers, and philosophers. There was no limit on how many gods an inhabitant of the empire could embrace or abandon. This openness to adopting new religious practices without necessarily giving up the old ones can be called "adhesion": It was possible for a person who worshipped several gods to adhere to more gods without abandoning the earlier ones. Only the Jews and the Christians, because they were strict monotheists, refused to allow adhesion

and demanded "conversion," that is, that their believers abandon all other gods besides their God. Because the demand of the religious authorities was not always effective, we should not draw too sharp a line between second- and third-century Christianity and its rivals. The attractions of the traditional religions must have been strong even for Christians. That is a reasonable conclusion from Christian literature, which is filled with denunciations of the gods and of those who worshiped their images. In order to make sense of the complex Greco-Roman religious life that the Christian missionaries encountered and in which Christians lived, I shall treat some important categories of religious expression—but in real life, Greeks and Romans sampled all sorts of religious activity in a range of choices that was potentially unlimited.

First we need a definition of "cult," a word often used with reference to ancient religions. In modern speech, "cult" is often a negative way to refer to a smallish religious group of which one disapproves. That is not what is meant here. In the study of religion, "cult" is the word for the external, visible features that accompany the worship of any god. Every religion has its "cult," that is, its own places for worship, objects, and practices of worship. Worshippers know, usually from past practice, what their god wants in his or her cult, whether it is simplicity or magnificence, words or actions, sacrifices of animals or not, images or no images, and so on. Cult is, then, a way of carrying out worship.

OFFICIAL CULTS

Every Greco-Roman community, from the humblest rural village to the mighty empire, held a deep conviction that the gods—its particular gods—were important to its well-being. Consequently governments at every level supported the worship of their gods, often at public expense. The public officials supported such things as altars, temples, sacrifices, processions, and festivals to honor the gods and keep their favor. Wealthy people were encouraged, even pressured, to subsidize public worship and were rewarded by public esteem, expressed in such things as statues and inscriptions that praised the donors. The leaders of the Roman state visualized their relation to the Roman gods as a treaty, called the *pax deorum* ("the peace of the gods"). At the core of the treaty, magistrates promised on behalf of the Roman state to offer correct worship to the gods in return for divine favor. The magistrates were very careful to keep their promises. They believed that the gods generally wanted the sacrifice of animals. For instance, Jupiter was worshipped in his great temple in Rome with the carefully orchestrated killing of bulls, rams, and boars. Rural communities often sacrificed to their gods and goddesses on simple open-air altars. Heads of individual households offered wheat cakes and other humble food to their family gods, whose images were in their homes.

These official cults had no creed in the Christian sense, no tight set of required beliefs. Because most people thought that what the gods wanted was reverence expressed in proper cult, the worshiper's beliefs were a secondary matter. The state-supported temples and rituals generally did not have professional priests. The magistrates performed the ceremonies, with experts in religious lore at their elbows, telling them what must and must not be said and done. State-sponsored worship was careful, carried out by public officials acting in front of an altar or behind the closed doors of a temple. The temples were built as the god's house, not as a place where congregations gathered. In the important public rituals, private individuals had only a secondary role, perhaps just to stand in the crowd watching the magistrates do their religious duty. At every level of society, these official cults went on at state expense until the fourth century, when Christian emperors gradually withdrew their support, which they transferred to the Christian church's clergy, buildings, and rituals. Christianity then became the official way, the official cult, to worship God.

Because the official cults were primarily the religions of groups, carried out for the safety and prosperity of society as a whole, they had only a small role for the individual citizen, who swelled the crowd while the magistrates carried out the rites or who joined in the festivals of eating, drinking, singing, and dancing that honored the gods. The official cults were serious matters because society's welfare was thought to depend on them. This is why modern notions of separation of church and state do not fit the ancient world. Most ancient people believed that preserving a correct relationship with the gods was as important to the state as maintaining a sufficient army. The official cults usually promised nothing specifically to individuals, except insofar as they benefited from the safety and prosperity of society. Because some official cults could draw on the great wealth of the state and of rich donors, particularly the emperor, they possessed the fine temples and statues that still amaze visitors to Italy, Greece, or Turkey or to a museum well-stocked in ancient art.

Jews were not entirely exempt from the views of their pagan contemporaries. Like the pagan gods, the Jewish God demanded the sacrifice of animals and other things in his Temple at Jerusalem. In other ways, however, the God of the Jews was unusual when compared with the gods of the Greeks and Romans. He was a "jealous" god, that is, he demanded exclusive worship from his followers: "I am the Lord your God . . . you shall have no other gods before me. You shall not make for yourself an idol. . . . You shall not bow down to them or worship them; for I the Lord your God am a jealous God. . . ." (Exodus 20:2–5). In contrast, the Greco-Roman gods were not "jealous." Most Greeks and Romans did not believe that their gods were the only gods. On the contrary, they were sure that all peoples had their own gods who should be worshipped in whatever way was traditional. The Roman authorities were generally tolerant in religious matters and ordinarily did not upset local religious arrangements, probably because disrupting other people's religions is a sure way to produce a rebellion. In addition, Romans hoped to win the support of the gods of the people whom they conquered. Every community subject to the Roman Empire was allowed, even encouraged, to carry on its traditional official cults. However, Roman religious tolerance was not unlimited. The Roman authorities sometimes had hesitations about how far Roman citizens could go in adding other religions to their practices. Initially, they were slow to allow foreign cults inside the sacred boundary—the *pomerium*—of the city of Rome itself or to allow Roman citizens to join in the worship of foreign gods. But over time those barriers broke down. During the imperial period, Roman citizens enjoyed the same wide religious choices as everyone else. The Roman authorities would not tolerate religions that promoted anti-Roman feeling. For example, the druids, priests of the Celtic religion, resisted Roman rule in Britain and were ruthlessly suppressed. Sometimes the Romans frowned on rituals that they thought too barbaric to tolerate, such as human sacrifice, which the Druids practiced in addition to their resistance to Roman rule. Groups, including religious groups, that met in secret or at night might be repressed because the Roman magistrates feared plots against their rule. For instance, the Roman magistrate Pliny (about 61–about 112) suppressed fire brigades in northern Asia Minor because he was uneasy about their meetings and unsure of their loyalty.

The official cults were conservative but not completely static. The last century of the Roman Republic (133–31 BCE) had been disrupted by bloody civil wars, political murders, brutal exploitation of subject peoples, and frightening insecurity. As a result, Roman citizens and conquered subjects were grateful when Octavian, later called "Augustus," defeated his rivals Anthony and Cleopatra in 31 BCE and brought peace and stability. Their gratitude to the emperors was expressed in religious terms. In the eastern Mediterranean, people had for centuries treated their rulers as gods. When the empire spread into the east, the new subjects began to worship both living and deceased Roman emperors. At first the Romans, who had no tradition of worshipping their rulers, were reluctant to participate in the worship of living emperors but acknowledged that the Senate could deify—make into gods—deceased emperors who were judged worthy of the honor. After his assassination in 44 BCE, the Senate granted Julius Caesar divine status, with a publicly funded temple and priests within the city of Rome. When the emperor Augustus died in 14 CE, he was accorded divine honors. An important person swore that he saw the Augustus' spirit ascending to heaven out of the flames of his funeral pyre. The Senate deified most deceased emperors but refused the honor to those of whom it disapproved. Living emperors were in a hazy intermediate zone: not yet gods but potentially gods. In the later first, second, and third centuries, the goddess Roma, who personified Rome, and the reigning emperor (or his *genius*, a sort of life spirit) were joined as the focus of an important official cult. They were honored with priesthoods, altars, statues, temples, animal sacrifices, laudatory inscriptions, and annual festivals. The cult of Roma and the emperor was patriotic, a sign of loyalty, and a force for unity in a diverse empire. The worship of living emperors grew in importance as their position grew in power. Many cults around the empire added emperor worship to their existing practices. In fact, the religious life of the empire was restructured to integrate the emperor into it. For instance, Jews would not worship the emperor, but until the beginning of the Jewish Revolt in 66, the Jewish priests at Jerusalem prayed for the emperor every day in the Temple. Christians never had a formal ritual of prayer for the pagan emperor, although some second-century defenders of Christianity wrote that Christians prayed for emperors. Over time, the Roman emperors became the most powerful figures in every aspect of Roman society, including religion. When the Christians refused to participate in the cult of Roma and Augustus because their god was "jealous," they brought down on themselves the wrath of the Roman state and suffered persecution.

VOLUNTARY CULTS

Greco-Roman civilization achieved remarkable things, even though modern people are sometimes repelled by the fact that ancient urban life was built on the exploitation of the rural majority and on slavery. By 150, it had attained a level of literacy that was not seen again in the West until the sixteenth century and a level of urban comfort not achieved until the eighteenth century. For about 250 years (31 BCE–235 CE), called the "Pax Romana" ("the Roman Peace"), the empire unified the Mediterranean shores and their hinterlands into a large zone of peace, stability, and trade—something never achieved again. The official cults were important directly to the state and indirectly to individuals, but they did not try to satisfy the *personal* religious desires of individuals. To put it another way, the official cults sought to guarantee immortality for the group—Roman coins proclaimed "Roma Aeterna" ("Eternal Rome")—but not for individuals. Greco-Roman culture had no single, firm belief in a personal afterlife. For pagans who did believe in an afterlife, it was often imagined not as a paradise but rather as a sad, cold, dark place. Greco-Roman society also had no firm belief in progress. Common ancient views of history were either cyclical, that is, things repeated themselves over vast stretches of time, or degenerative, that is, the world had declined from a golden age to ever worse conditions. In addition, the Roman Empire was not invigorated by powerful movements that swept up individuals in a cause bigger than themselves. There was, for instance, nothing comparable with an anti-slavery movement, a feminist movement, an ecological movement, or a democratic movement that gives meaning to many modern peoples' lives. As memories of the Roman Republic faded and the emperors became more dictatorial, ordinary citizens found it safer to be politically passive. The mobility characteristic of the empire, both from country to city and from one region to another, fed the anxiety of many ordinary people, who must have felt rootless, cut off from their ancestral homes, relatives, and religions. Life was biologically fragile in ways we find hard to imagine. Medicine was primitive and mostly ineffective. Life expectancies were low. There was no insurance, only a rudimentary welfare system, and no workmen's compensation. If a worker broke a leg or died, his widow and orphans could live in terrible poverty or could starve to death. The legal system was harsh to the lower classes, which included slaves, freedmen, and foreigners, who had few of what we call "civil rights." Many people, who had nothing against which to contrast their lives, took all this as normal, but they had significant reasons for anxiety and fear.

Some ancient concepts of the universe also fed fear. The gods of Mount Olympus, such as Zeus, Hera, and Athena, and their Roman counterparts, Jupiter, Juno, and Minerva, were not alone in the universe. Few people doubted that there were uncountable, unnamable, invisible powers that could help or hurt humans. The angels and devils of the Bible are well-known examples, but they jostled for space with lots of others. Paul, for instance, spoke of dominions, powers, and principalities that were apparently cosmic beings (Col 1:16). In Greek, such beings were called *daimones*,

which is the origin of the English word "demon," but originally not every *daimon* was thought to be evil. Some would or at least could help their human followers. Many Greeks and Romans had the fatalistic feeling that they were playthings of *daimones* who controlled, helped, hurt, and even tormented them. The widespread worship of the goddess Fortuna ("Luck") grew out of the sense that the unseen powers in the universe were arbitrary and that such a goddess might help. The state religions offered little or no help for an individual to deal with the *daimones*.

The ruling elites and intellectuals ate and dressed better than the lower classes, but they were not untouched by fear and anxiety. Bacteria and viruses killed them, too. In addition, the upper classes, including the senatorial aristocracy, had special reasons for fear that emerged from their high status and wealth. Emperors feared attempts to assassinate them (they had good reason to fear them). Such attempts almost always originated with the powerful people around them. Some emperors struck out after detecting a plot or on mere suspicion. A considerable number of senators were killed and their property was confiscated. Many in the upper classes had an acquaintance or relative who had perished in a suspected or unsuccessful plot.

The literature of the Greeks and Romans was generally produced by and for the upper classes. It contains remarkable, beautiful achievements, such as the Greek *Iliad* and *Odyssey* attributed to Homer and the Latin *Aeneid* of Virgil, which have influenced Western civilization to the present time. But by and large classical literature offered little hope for a better future. By the second century CE, literature was increasingly marked by feelings of alienation from the world and by a contemptuous resignation to fate. Divisions of body from soul and matter from spirit grew sharper, with body and matter regarded as inferior, if not evil. The Roman writer Seneca (about 4 BCE–65 CE), who committed suicide at the command of his former pupil, the Emperor Nero (54–68), expressed the view that the body and the world are pointless and empty and that life is short. To avoid slavery to one's desires, he recommended that his readers put aside striving for wealth and fame. They should be constantly ready to die (Seneca, *Natural Questions*, bk. III, preface, c. 16). This effort to maintain a stiff upper lip in the face of fear and hopelessness was the creed of only an educated few, but it might have nourished in them a sense of anxiety or at least resignation.

One can emphasize too much the notion of anxiety—there were no doubt many ancient people content with their lives, including perhaps the overwhelming majority who lived in the countryside and observed the seasonal rhythms of agricultural life and traditional worship. But in an age of rising religious interest, the traditional state cults, which had never been personal religions, were supplemented by cults that offered something to individuals, who often sought from the gods security and material well-being in this world and a happy situation after death. Perhaps in response to growing individual desires, the first-, second-, and third-century empire bubbled with religious ferment and individual religious choices. Alongside the state-supported cults, individuals supported voluntary cults that had their own officials, rituals, meeting places, and beliefs. The religious history of the empire can be visualized as a flow of these unofficial cults from the religiously creative eastern Mediterranean into the rest of the empire. Judaism and Christianity followed that pattern, but so did many other cults. Generally, the voluntary cults did not demand absolute allegiance: A person could join as many as his or her time and wealth allowed (initiation into some cults could be quite expensive) while also honoring the state religion, worshipping the emperor and the goddess Roma, and consulting astrologers or magicians. Judaism and Christianity were exceptions in demanding the complete allegiance of their members, not always successfully. Between the first and third centuries, the voluntary cults expressed a bewildering variety of beliefs and practices. But we can make sense of much (not all) of the complexity if we remember that the voluntary cults generally responded to personal, practical needs—to help individual people escape from fear, from the power of the *daimones*, and from the power of fate.

Some of the most important voluntary cults are called "mystery religions" because their central beliefs and rituals were revealed only to members who had been initiated into them step by step. The adherents to mystery religions took the secrecy seriously, so that we often do not know the "mystery," although we can reconstruct some of it from literary references, inscriptions, and archaeological remains. The mystery religions differed widely in details, but generally they promised adherents three things: a rebirth of some sort, purification from guilt and sin, and immortality. A mystery religion usually had three interrelated components: a story or myth about the god(s) of the mystery cult, a ritual that in some way acted out that story, and a secret interpretation that explained to the initiated person what the myth and the ritual meant personally for him or her. Initiation into a mystery religion was designed to be an emotionally moving, life-changing experience, sometimes called an "enlightenment." Dio Chrysostom (between 40 and 50–after 110) described initiation into the mysteries: "...if anyone were to place a man, a Greek or a barbarian, in some mystic shrine of extraordinary beauty and size to be initiated, where he would see many mystic sights and hear many mystic voices, where light and darkness would appear to him alternately, and a thousand other things would occur; and further, if it should be just as in the rite called enthronement, where the inducting priests make the novices sit down and then dance round and round them—is it likely that the man in this situation would not be moved in his mind and would not suspect that all which was taking place was the result of a more than wise intention and preparation, even if he belonged to the most remote and nameless barbarians...?" (Dio Chrysostom, *The Twelfth, or Olympic, Discourse*, c. 33 in *Dio Chrysostom* with an English translation by J. H. Cohoon, LCL no. 339 [Cambridge, MA, and London, 1939], vol. 2, pp. 34–37, altered).

Hungry from fasting, exhausted from lack of sleep, excited, fearful, full of expectations, the initiates into some mystery cults thought they gained profound insights that saved them from fear and oppression by the *daimones* and other cosmic forces. The initiates, who were a tiny minority of the empire's population, sought salvation, which was often interpreted in practical ways: long life, healing from illness, safe completion of a sea voyage, success in business or in war or in love, and the like. Four examples of voluntary cults, chosen out of many, will make the range of personal religious choices clearer. Christianity and Judaism had to compete in this marketplace of religious choices.

Rebirth at Eleusis

The Eleusinian mysteries, which were unusual because they could be performed at only one place, Eleusis, about twelve miles from Athens, originated in ancient rituals based on the visible cycle of seasonal death and rebirth of vegetation. At the core of the Eleusinian mysteries was the myth of Demeter and Persephone. Hades, the god of the underworld, kidnapped Demeter's daughter Persephone and brought her to the underworld. In her grief, Demeter ceased to protect vegetation, which died. Zeus, Persephone's father, persuaded Hades to let the girl come back into the upper world, but by a trick Hades made sure she had to return periodically to him in the underworld. Hence, when Persephone was in the upper world with her mother Demeter, vegetation flourished, and when she was in the underworld with her husband Hades, vegetation died. At Eleusis, the observation that vegetation "died" in the autumn and was "reborn" in the spring was applied to individuals: They could die and be reborn through rituals.

The celebrations and initiations at Eleusis took place in late September or early October. There was a public aspect to the Eleusinian mysteries. A procession from Athens to Eleusis culminated at night in a building capable of holding thousands—it was perhaps the largest building in Greece. There was also a secret aspect. The people to be initiated were washed to purify them. They were shown visual representations of the myth of Demeter and Persephone to reveal the myth's real meaning, which was probably interpreted as referring to their own rebirth. The Eleusinian mysteries were immensely prestigious. Emperors, generals, and wealthy people were initiated. In our time, billionaires, rock stars, and trendy actors would flock there. The Christian Emperor Theodosius (378–395) prohibited them in 393, and in 396 invaders looted and destroyed the thousand-year-old sanctuary where the mysteries had been celebrated.

The Cult of Mithras

The Eleusinian mysteries were sober, Greek, high-toned, and ancient. Some mystery religions attracted followers in part because they had a colorful and exotic origin, which was adapted to the tastes of Greeks and Romans. Unlike the agrarian mysteries at Eleusis, which were tied to one shrine, many of the exotic mysteries had missionaries or at least devotees who spread them to many places. The myth of the warrior god Mithras was a version of the widespread contrast between light and darkness or between good and evil. Mithras, a Persian god, led the forces of light against those of darkness. The main symbol of Mithraism was a statue of Mithras cutting the throat of a bull, which was the embodiment of evil. The rites of Mithras took place in a cave, called a "Mithraeum" because Mithras had been born in a cave. If there was no natural cave, believers built an artificial one in a dark room or even underground. The Mithraea were generally small. Archaeologists have found many Mithraea, including about sixty in the city of Rome alone. The cult of Mithras was open only to men and was especially popular with soldiers. A man initiated into the mystery of Mithras passed through seven stages until he knew the complete myth and its real meaning. At each stage of initiation, there was a visual display or play that conveyed new information. The culmination was a meal of bread and wine at which the initiate communed with his fellow initiates and with Mithras himself.

The Cult of Isis

Egyptian "wisdom" had great prestige because it was thought to be unimaginably old. Egyptian religion fascinated many because it was so different from Greek and Roman religions. Egypt had mummies of people and animals, gods with the heads of animals, mysterious hieroglyphics, and pharaohs who married their sisters. The Egyptian goddess Isis gained many adherents outside of Egypt, although her cult was Hellenized to make it more attractive to Greek worshippers. The myth underlying the cult of Isis fit the pattern of death and rebirth. In the story, the god Seth killed and dismembered his brother Osiris, also known as

"Serapis." Isis, the sister and wife of Osiris/Serapis, gathered his scattered remains. He was restored to life as Lord of the Underworld. The annual reenactment of Osiris/Serapis' death, Isis' search for his remains, and his rebirth was the public ritual that presented the myth for all to see. The cult of Isis had an Egyptian air about it—Egyptian music in the temples, hieroglyphics, and actual Egyptians as priests with shaved heads and special clothing who carried on daily worship of Isis in temples called "Isaea." Accompanied by hymns and prayers, the goddess was awakened each morning, clothed, given food, worshipped, and solemnly put to bed in the evening.

Individuals were initiated privately into the mysteries of Isis during an elaborate light and sound show. In his *Metamorphoses* (sometimes called *The Golden Ass*), Apuleius of Madaura (about 125–about 170) wrote a description of initiation into the cult of Isis. His book's hero, Lucius, had been turned into an ass by magic. After many adventures, Isis restored him to human form. In gratitude, Lucius began to worship her and was eventually initiated into her cult. Lucius warned, perhaps teased, the readers of the *Metamorphoses* that he could not tell them everything. But some of the atmosphere and emotion surrounding an individual's initiation into the cult of Isis are accessible to us. Lucius described in guarded language his night of visions and extraordinary experiences that accompanied his initiation.

> Therefore listen, but believe: these things are true. I came to the boundary of death and, having trodden the threshold of Proserpina, I traveled through all the elements and returned. In the middle of the night I saw the sun flashing with bright light. I came face to face with the gods below and the gods above and paid reverence to them from close hand.

After Lucius had been initiated, he was dressed as a god and probably worshipped (temporarily) in the very temple of Isis:

> When morning came and the ceremonies were completed, I came forth wearing twelve robes as a sign of consecration. This is very holy attire, but no obligation prevents me from talking about it since at that time a great many people were present and saw it. Following instructions I stood on a wooden platform set up in the very centre of the holy shrine in front of the goddess's statue, the focus of attention because of my garment, which was only linen, but elaborately embroidered....In my right hand I carried a torch alight with flames, and my head was beautifully bound with a crown made of leaves of shining palm, jutting out like rays of the sun. After I had been thus been decorated in the likeness of the Sun and set up in the guise of a statue, the curtains were suddenly opened and the people wandered round to view me. (Apuleius of Madaura, *Metamorphoses*, XI, 23–24 in *Apuleius*, *Metamorphoses*, edited and translated by J. Arthur Hanson, LCL no. 453 [Cambridge, MA, and London, 1989], vol. 2, pp. 340–343)

Lucius regarded his initiation into Isis' cult as the turning point of his life. He loved the goddess and believed that she personally protected him.

The Cult of the Great Mother

The cult of Isis was dignified and moral, but some of the mystery religions were rooted in fertility rites that depended for their power on sexual acts and the shedding of blood. The worship of the Great Mother, sometimes called "Cybele," was deep rooted in Anatolia, which is a region in modern Turkey. Contact between Romans and the Great Mother began in the Roman Republic. The Romans feared defeat by the Carthaginian general Hannibal. At the command of an oracle, they brought the Great Mother to Rome in 204 BCE. She was entitled to be worshipped in her usual way, but the Romans were shocked when they saw what that involved. The priests of the Great Mother were eunuchs who had cut off their genitals and offered them to her. Their behavior imitated the myth of Attis, the lover of the Great Mother, who was unfaithful to her and was castrated for his sin. One feature of the Great Mother's cult was the spectacular public ceremony of the *taurobolium*: The person to be initiated crouched in a pit covered with wooden planks; a bull was slaughtered above him to drench him in blood. When the initiate emerged from the pit, he was adored by other worshippers as one who had escaped from ordinary life. As an inscription from 376 put it, he was "reborn unto eternity." The ever-practical Romans hit on a solution to keep the Great Mother's favor and at the same time to shield the Roman citizenry from her bloody, unseemly rites. They allowed devotees and priests from Asia Minor to worship her behind closed doors in their temple at Rome. But gradually the barriers broke down, and by the first century BCE, Roman citizens could participate in the cult of the Great Mother.

Thus, there were voluntary forms of worship to suit almost every temperament, from the exclusive, high-toned mysteries celebrated at Eleusis to the bloody sexual mutilations practiced by the devotees of the Great Mother. As Christianity spread in the gentile world, many people probably classified it as a voluntary religious association with its own rituals and beliefs that were made known in detail only to the initiated, which in the case of Christianity meant the baptized members.

Astrology, Oracles, Magicians

Alongside the state cults and the voluntary cults, a vast number of religious entrepreneurs also provided services in return for a fee. The variety of these entrepreneurs is bewildering, but we can make sense of many of them if we recall that they were offering practical services for which their clients were willing to pay. Because the world was thought to be in the power of good and evil spiritual beings, people who could find ways to please or control them hoped to get along or even to escape an unhappy fate. The religious entrepreneurs promised to help people cope with such negative forces as the evil *daimones,* and the power of fate, fear, and ignorance.

Astrology flourished in response to the desire to know the future. Astrology was rooted in the belief that the stars were *daimones* or at least the homes of *daimones,* which controlled people born under their influence. There was an abundant literature describing the nature of the cosmic powers and explaining how to control or escape them. Astrology was a serious matter for individuals and for the government. For instance, to ask an astrolo-

ger about the death of an emperor was an offense that could bring on a death sentence. Every now and then, Roman officials took measures against astrologers, especially those who gave their advice without witnesses or inquired into the time that anyone would die. But generally, astrologers flourished in the empire.

Oracles also flourished in the empire. At certain favored places, a god was believed to speak, usually through a priest or priestess. An Egyptian papyrus preserves ninety-two common questions posed to an oracle. As you might expect, they are the problems that in our society might appear in a personal advice column. Oracle-seekers wanted to know about their finances, the situation of distant loved ones, whether they were going to get a job or a spouse, and how long they were going to live.

Wonder-workers and magicians were also common figures who found welcome even in the highest social circles. They also gave advice about personal problems, made amulets to ward off evil, interpreted dreams, and even worked cures. But they were also suspected of being able to cause deaths and to force people to fall in love. When Jesus' followers claimed that he cured the sick and expelled demons, that claim had less impact than we might expect because Greeks and Romans could quite easily categorize him as one of the magicians and wonder-workers with whom they were quite familiar.

There were some intellectuals who criticized the religious entrepreneurs. The second-century pagan satirist Lucian of Samosata delighted in debunking what he saw as their frauds. In one of his satires he denounced Alexander of Abunoteichos, who had ingeniously created an oracle at which the healing god Asclepius appeared in the form of a snake. Lucian was disgusted that so many people rushed to pray to the snake/god, from whom they sought wealth, health, and other gifts (Lucian, *Alexander the False Prophet,* c. 12–16). But as the wave of intense religiosity grew stronger, skeptics grew quieter, even disappeared. Virtually everyone—pagan, Jew, and Christian—took astrology, oracles, and magic seriously. Christians disapproved of magic, oracles, and the like but did not deny their reality. They interpreted them as tricks of evil *daimones.* Some Christians consulted astrologers, wonder-workers, and amulet makers, much to the annoyance of their leaders.

Some educated pagans had doubts about the thick cloud of gods, goddesses, and *daimones* who were so prominent in popular religion. Such people might participate in all sorts of religious cults, but they could be monotheists of a vague sort who believed that there might be just one god behind the names of the many gods. The Romans had a long tradition of merging gods who had different names but shared similar characteristics. For instance, the Greek god Zeus, who was a sky god and the father of the other gods, was identified with the Roman god Jupiter, who was also a sky god and divine father. The process of merging gods suggested to some that all gods could be merged into one god. Apuleius of Madaura recounted that when the goddess Isis spoke in a dream to her devotee Lucius, she identified herself as the chief god who was discernible behind the other gods:

> I am she that is the mother of the nature of things, mistress of all the elements, the initial progeny of the ages, highest of the divine powers, queen of the departed spirits, the first of the heavenly deities, the uniform manifestation of the gods and goddesses. The luminous summits of the sky, the wholesome breezes of the sea, and the lamented silences of the dead below I control at my will. My sole divine power is adored throughout all the world in manifold guise, with varied rites, and by varied names....and the Egyptians who are preeminent in ancient lore and worship me with special ceremonies, call me by my true name, Queen Isis. (Apuleius, *Metamorphoses*, XX.5 as cited in Naphtali Lewis and Meyer Reinhold, *Roman Civilization: Sourcebook II: The Empire* [New York, 1955], p. 578)

PHILOSOPHIES

In the intensifying religious atmosphere of the Roman Empire, many educated people turned to philosophers for guidance on how to cope with the problems of life. The study of philosophy in the Roman Empire was a prestigious pursuit; in fact,

it was the very top of the intellectual hierarchy, rivaled only by the study of rhetoric. Philosophical training was long, expensive, and often involved seeking out prominent teachers in the philosophical tradition that the student found most convincing. Athens remained an important center for the teaching of philosophy, although there were other places as well. In many cities, there were philosophers who opened a school and taught disciples. Some philosophers had personal fortunes or lived on students' fees, but others were employed by rich people as tutors for children and as advisers (almost chaplains) for the master and mistress of the house. There were about a half-dozen competing philosophical traditions, sometimes called "schools," that claimed to teach what prominent Greek philosophers of the fifth and fourth centuries BCE, including Plato, Aristotle, and Zeno, the founder of Stoicism, had taught. By Roman times, these philosophical traditions had hardened into relatively fixed systems of belief that were passed from masters to disciples. They were comparable in some ways with modern religious denominations or with the circles of disciples who gather around a modern charismatic preacher, television psychologist or guru.

The detailed teachings of the philosophical schools differed widely, but what they had in common was that they gave ethical and moral advice about how to live or at least how to cope. Many upper-class Romans favored the Stoic philosophy, founded by Zeno in the fourth century BCE. Stoicism taught that the universe was permeated with reason, called "logos" in Greek, which was benevolent, positive, and just, but it was not a person. Some Stoics were troubled by "unreasonable" things such as slavery, war, and poverty. But they thought that in the long run, the reason shaping the universe would correct these examples of unreason. Because all humans are part of a grand design that is rational, Stoics thought that reason had put everyone—rich, poor, slave, free, well, ill—in a place for a purpose. Wise men or women—that is, the Stoics—chose to live in accord with reason, to accept their lot, and to control their desires. The Stoics taught their adherents how to achieve *apatheia*, which did not mean "apathy" but rather "tranquility," that is, freedom from tension within yourself or between yourself and others. They also taught that people could gain "self-sufficiency" by restricting their desires: If you do not desire a thing you cannot have, then you are not tortured by the lack of it. Stoicism had a limited appeal because it demanded a great deal from its followers, although Stoics came from many walks of life. One important Stoic teacher, Epictetus, was a former slave; another prominent Stoic, Marcus Aurelius, was an emperor. But in general, Stoicism tended to attract well-educated and probably prosperous people.

Romans in particular were attracted to Stoicism because it emphasized devotion to duty, which was an important cultural value for them. Stoicism could encourage a passive attitude toward life, but Romans reshaped it to fit their more vigorous view of how to live. They saw in it a call to do the best one could wherever one was. If a Stoic was a general, a magistrate, or an emperor, the reason of the universe had put him in that position and he must behave in an honorable way. Stoicism encouraged a high-minded view that all in authority should treat justly those under their control. Stoicism probably influenced early Christianity. Both a Stoic and a Christian would agree to the statements: "I have been put here for a reason," "I must do what is right," and "I must control my desires." Paul used Stoic terminology to explain Christian ideas. For instance, in his First Letter to the Corinthians, he tried to counter the Corinthian Christians' disorders and religious one-upmanship by emphasizing the stoic image of a body in which each part has its function and all parts are needed to make a perfect body. Luke wrote that Paul used Stoic ideas in his speech to educated pagans at Athens (see Acts 17:22–31). In 1 Corinthians 12, Paul used a common, perhaps Stoic discussion of the parts of a body united to create a harmonious whole when he defended the underlying unity in the Corinthians' diversity of spiritual gifts. But there were significant differences between Stoicism and Christianity. Unlike Christians, Stoics did not believe in a personal God who cared about humans and to whom humans could pray. But Stoics' views on the harmony of the universe as well as their calls for strict moral conduct appealed to Christian thinkers.

Another philosophical tradition, Epicureanism, founded by Epicurus (341–270 BCE), taught that humans needlessly feared the gods and death. Epicureans explained how those disturbing fears could be eliminated. Epicurus taught that the gods existed but did not trouble themselves about human beings: They hurt no one, and they helped no one. He also assured followers that death was not to be feared. He expounded what might be called "Epicurean physics." Tiny particles, called "atoms" ("indivisible things") because they could not be divided into smaller units, fell in a vast emptiness. At times, the atoms swerved and linked up to make things, including people. When the atoms separated again, the things, including people, just evaporated, reabsorbed into the cascade of falling atoms. Death should induce no fear because there was no afterlife of pain (or pleasure). The Epicurean school advised its followers to reject religiously inspired fear, to withdraw from active life, and to seek quiet pleasures.

In the fourth century BCE, several philosophers contributed to a stream of philosophical thought called "Cynicism." Do not be misled by the modern meaning of that word. In Greek, it means "like a dog." It refers to philosophers who saw in the dog a kind of freedom from conventional behavior that humans should adopt. The Cynics loved to violate ordinary practices and to live free from moral and social restraints. They wanted a "natural" life, free from the need to conform to society's artificial ways. Some adopted a wandering life wearing a short cloak, not cutting their hair or beards, and rejecting wealth. They spoke in public places, denouncing or ridiculing every form of ordinary social and religious behavior. Their vigorous oral attacks on the existence of the gods and on what ordinary people thought of as right were called "diatribes." Christians sometimes adopted for their use Cynic attacks on the pagan gods. Christian preachers might have imitated the diatribe in their own denunciations of the world around them. Christian ascetics may have imitated some aspects of the poverty and simplicity of the Cynic philosopher's life.

Platonism was the most widely admired philosophical school between the second and sixth centuries CE. Plato (about 429–347 BCE) taught in the grove of Academos at Athens, so his school has been called the "Academy." Plato had written twenty-five philosophical dialogues in which his teacher Socrates (about 470–399 BCE) was the central figure. Plato's Socrates prodded, criticized, and challenged his fellow discussers on profound questions that concerned ethics, politics, and education. In addition to being great literature, Plato's dialogues inspired a long succession of teachers in the Platonic Academy at Athens and elsewhere. Over more than nine hundred years, the Platonic school changed. When Christian thinkers encountered Platonism, it was what is called "Middle Platonism" (about 68 BCE–about 250 CE) and then Neo-Platonism (about 250–about 500). Christian thinkers pointed to some Platonic teachings as precursors or dim reflections of their beliefs. Plato and his followers taught that the soul was immaterial, that there would be rewards and punishments after death, that reality grew greater the further one got from matter. Neo-Platonists encouraged their followers to transcend their burdensome bodies and rise toward that which was most real, which they called "the Good, the Beautiful, the One and the First." If I had to pick one Platonic belief that influenced Christianity, it would be the teaching about the nature of God. For the Platonists, the origin of everything is the being called "the One" (also called "the First"), who/which was beyond description and beyond human understanding. The One was perfect in itself, serene and unimaginably distant from the created world. The One had no direct contact with the world in which humans lived. Instead the One brought the world of matter into existence through intermediaries. By a process called "emanation," literally "an outflowing," a cascade of beings flowed out from the One, but each emanated being was less like the being from which it emanated because it was further away from the ultimate source, the One. The One emanated from itself the Logos or Word, which could also be called "Intelligence." The Logos emanated the World Soul. Thus, the Platonists taught that at the heart of the universe there is a three, a triad. The visible world, which the Platonists regard as not quite real, was far down in the long chain of emanations. But in humans there was an immaterial soul that yearned to climb up so as to be united with the One.

The influence of philosophy was greater than the number of philosophers or their disciples might suggest. First, the man or woman in the street, angry at Christians for their rejection of society's gods and their political disloyalty, occasionally attacked Christians physically. But people with philosophical training were equipped to attack Christianity intellectually. Second, some of the intellectual leaders of Christianity, including Justin Martyr (died in 165), had received philosophical training, which they used to defend Christianity from their pagan counterparts. In their efforts to refute philosophers' arguments against Christianity, philosophically educated Christians adopted or adapted philosophical arguments for their own use. Christian theology was often formulated in terms that Christian thinkers borrowed from philosophy, especially Platonic philosophy, which Christian thinkers thought was most compatible with their religion. Third, the Christian criticism of the gods and popular religion owed a great deal to the criticism that philosophers had expressed for centuries.

Thus, Christianity did not spread out of Judaism into a context of irreligion or unbelief. Quite the opposite, the Greco-Roman world of the first, second, and third centuries was deeply concerned with religion and the other world. Many people sought to find out how to live well and happily. Christianity had many rivals.

FURTHER READING

Ancient Sources

Apuleius, *The Golden Ass* (many translations, including a Penguin Classic translated by J. Kennedy, 1999). A lively, readable trip through the religious stew of the second century.

Frederick C. Grant, *Hellenistic Religions* (New York, 1953). A rich collection of sources.

Frederick C. Grant, *Ancient Roman Religion* (New York, 1957). See especially pp. 169–252 on religion in the Roman Empire.

Modern Works

Mary Beard, John North, and Simon Price, *Religions of Rome*, vol. 1: *A History* and vol. 2: *A Sourcebook* (Cambridge, 1998). The best introduction to Roman religion; read especially volume 1, pp. 167–388, on religious developments in the imperial period.

Walter Burkert, *Ancient Mystery Cults* (Cambridge, MA, and London, 1987). A demanding book but up-to-date and generally readable on the important mystery cults.

Ramsey MacMullen, *Paganism in the Roman Empire* (New Haven, 1981). Significant insights into the nature of Greco-Roman paganism.

Arthur Darby Nock, *Conversion: The Old and the New in Religion from Alexander the Great to Augustine of Hippo* (London, 1931; reprinted 1961). A classic treatment of the religious journeys of some educated Greeks and Romans who were not interested in the religious conversion of the many ordinary people.

CHAPTER 4

The Jesus Movement in the First Century

The conviction that Jesus rose from the dead set in motion an explosion of energy that was expressed in visions, dreams, preaching, writing, and the creation of communities of believers. The movement that began in Judea and Galilee and spread into the rest of the Roman Empire was not under anyone's direction. It was marked from as early as can be seen by strongly held disagreements about such fundamental matters as who Jesus was, what belief in him meant, which aspects of a convert's preconversion life could continue, and which had to change. The beginnings of Christianity are broad and diverse enough to justify referring to a "movement," the Jesus Movement.

We know less than we would like about the means by which Christianity spread in the first and early second centuries. In a world that had no mass media—no radio, no television, no newspapers, no magazines, and nothing remotely resembling the Internet—much depended on person-to-person contact. Some evidence, supported by common sense, suggests that there were many missionaries at work in the decades after Jesus' death. Paul, who was such a missionary, opened a small window on other missionaries when he referred in his letters to his supporters and fellow missionaries, including Barnabas, Titus, Timothy, Aquila, Epaphras ("our beloved fellow servant"), Epaphroditus, Luke, Mark, Onesimus, Onesiphorus, Silas, Silvanus, Stephanas, and Tychicus and some women, including Prisca, Junia, Chloe, and Phoebe. These men and women probably did many things to spread their views of Jesus, but we have no clear evidence about them. If we had a collection of *their* letters, our perspective on the spread of Christianity beyond the boundaries of Judaism might be different—but we do not have such letters. In his second letter to the

Corinthians, 8:18, Paul mentioned in passing that he was sending to the Corinthians "the brother who is famous among all the churches for his proclaiming the good news"—but he never gave the brother's name. The letter's recipients knew who the famous proclaimer of the good news was, but we shall never know. Except for a single sentence, we would never know that "the brothers of the Lord" (and perhaps their wives) were missionaries (1 Cor 9:5). When Paul arrived as a Roman prisoner at Puteoli in southern Italy, Luke wrote that there were believers to greet him, but there is no historical record to tell us how they got there (Acts 28:14–15).

One missionary, named "Apollos," emerges briefly from the shadows because Paul and Luke happened to write a few lines about him. "Now there came to Ephesus a Jew named Apollos, a native of Alexandria. He was an eloquent man, well-versed in the scriptures. He had been instructed in the Way of the Lord; and he spoke with burning enthusiasm and taught accurately the things concerning Jesus, though he knew only the baptism of John. He began to speak boldly in the synagogue; but when Priscilla and Aquila heard him, they took him aside and explained the Way of God to him more accurately. And when he wished to cross over to Achaia [Greece], the believers encouraged him and wrote to the disciples to welcome him. On his arrival he greatly helped those who through grace had become believers, for he powerfully refuted the Jews in public, showing by the scriptures that the Messiah is Jesus" (Acts 18:24–28).

Apollos had some success as a missionary in Corinth, where Paul had worked before him. Paul complained that some Corinthian Christians identified themselves as members of Apollos' faction

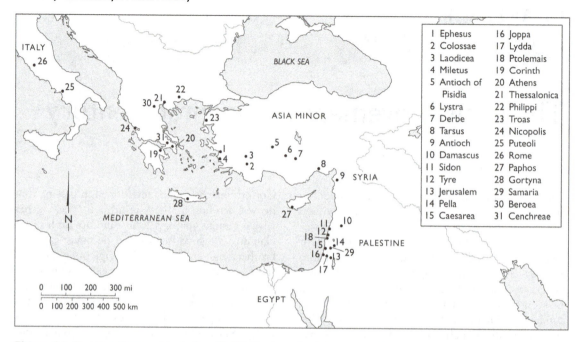

1 Ephesus	16 Joppa
2 Colossae	17 Lydda
3 Laodicea	18 Ptolemais
4 Miletus	19 Corinth
5 Antioch of	20 Athens
Pisidia	21 Thessalonica
6 Lystra	22 Philippi
7 Derbe	23 Troas
8 Tarsus	24 Nicopolis
9 Antioch	25 Puteoli
10 Damascus	26 Rome
11 Sidon	27 Paphos
12 Tyre	28 Gortyna
13 Jerusalem	29 Samaria
14 Pella	30 Beroea
15 Caesarea	31 Cenchreae

Figure 4.1 Christian Communities before 70 CE. Thanks to Paul's letters and Luke's Acts of the Apostles, a tentative and incomplete map of places where Christians are mentioned before 70 CE can be made. There probably was a handful of Christians in each place, but the trend is clear. Christians first found a toehold in Palestine, Asia Minor, and eastern Greece. *(After Frend, The Rise of Christianity)*

(1 Cor 1:12), but Paul apparently got along with Apollos. They were together at Ephesus when Paul wrote to the Corinthians (1 Cor 16:12). Paul also commented on the missionaries who disagreed with him. He did not approve of the unnamed "superapostles" who came to Corinth after he left (2 Cor 11) and the unnamed Jewish-Christian missionaries from Jerusalem, whom he criticized in his letter to the Galatians. Paul rejected those missionaries, and presumably they rejected him. Whatever Paul thought of them, they thought they were right and he was wrong. They spread their understandings of Christianity as they preached and organized congregations, just as Paul did. There must have been many other missionaries who left little or no trace in the scanty sources. Without the unknown missionaries, it is hard to understand how in three or four decades differing kinds of Christianity gained small footholds in many places scattered around the eastern and central Mediterranean. During the second century, the Jesus Movement divided

into recognizable communities, including those usually called "churches." But in the first century and the early second century, I shall refer to the "Jesus Movement" in order to remind readers of the broad, diverse, and somewhat unshaped nature of the earliest expansion.

JEWISH CHRISTIANITY

It is often repeated that Jesus and his earliest followers were Jews. The historical implications of that statement are more complicated than might at first appear. In its earliest form, Christianity was a movement *within* Judaism. As noted in chapter 2, first-century Judaism was not a unified religion. In Palestine it was divided into what modern scholars call "sects," that is, relatively small groups of religious activists. In the four decades between Jesus' death in about 29 and the Roman destruction of Jerusalem in 70, his followers at Jerusalem would have appeared to their fellow Jews as a sect of Judaism. I shall call Jesus' earliest Jewish followers "Jewish Christians" because they combined a continuing attachment to Judaism with their belief that Jesus was the Messiah ("the Anointed One"), who was going to return soon. By the middle of the first century, Jesus' followers had different names, depending on who was talking. The Jewish Christians may have named themselves "The Way" (Acts 19:9 and 23; 24:22). When Paul was brought before the Roman governor Felix, the spokesman for his accusers declared that Paul was "a ringleader of the sect of the Nazarenes" (Acts 24:5). Acts asserted that it was at Antioch that the group first began to be called "Christians" (Acts 11:26). The historical sources for the first forty years of the Jewish-Christian sect are few, the most important of which are Paul's letters, written between about 50 and 60, and Luke's Acts, chapters 1–12, written in the 80s. Paul was contemporary with the Jewish Christians at Jerusalem and knew many of them, but he was not one of them. He championed the growing gentile forms of Christianity. Luke's Acts must be read with the awareness that he was not a Jewish Christian, that he thought conversion of gentiles was right, and that he wrote after the destruction of the Jewish-Christian community at Jerusalem.

Both Paul and Luke described Jesus' early followers as orthopractic Jews who faithfully observed the Mosaic Law. For instance, they went to the Temple to worship (Acts 2:46–7; 3:1) and to teach (Acts 5:26; 5:12–14); they practiced circumcision (Acts 15:1–2); and they observed the dietary laws. Even their practice of washing (baptizing) converts would have been familiar to their fellow Jews, who purified converts to Judaism in a ritual bath. The Jewish-Christian practice of eating a meal together ("the breaking of bread") did not set them apart either. Meals in common were central to the social and religious life of some other Jewish sects. Luke wrote that the Jewish Christians had a good reputation in Jerusalem and even attracted as members some Pharisees and priests (Acts 5:12–13; 15:5; 6:7). They also had opponents among their fellow Jews, but even that was not unusual. The Jewish sects constantly criticized one another as they struggled for religious influence within Palestinian Judaism. Although the Jewish Christians shared a great deal with the other sects within Judaism, they had at least one distinctive belief that set them apart: They proclaimed publicly that Jesus of Nazareth was the Messiah. They told their fellow Jews that Jesus had been unjustly killed but that God had raised him from the dead. They believed fervently that he was going to return soon to judge everyone. They told their fellow Jews that there was only a brief time to correct the mistake they had made when they rejected Jesus.

Luke emphasized that the Jewish Christians experienced visions, dreams, prophesies, and healings, which were interpreted as the signs predicted by the prophet Joel (2:28–32) that the "Day of the Lord" was near. The Jewish Christians' belief in the approaching end had real-life consequences. For instance, Luke wrote that at Jerusalem the Jewish Christians pooled their property (Acts 2:44–45; 4:34–35), a practice that apparently did not take root elsewhere. In Acts 2:14–38, Luke attributed a revealing sermon to Peter. The sermon's context is that by-standers were amazed when Jewish Christians began to speak in foreign languages, a phenomenon called "glossolalia" ("speaking in tongues"). Peter's sermon, which Luke thought contained the early Jewish Christian message, can be summarized thusly: The final age has begun, ushered in by Jesus' ministry, death, and resurrection, of which the Jewish-Christian preacher Peter gave a brief account, accompanied by references to the Jewish scriptures to show that all happened through the "foreknowledge of God." Peter presented Jesus as God's instrument. God worked wonders through him; God raised him from the dead; and God made him both Lord and Messiah. Peter said that Jesus would return soon to end the present age in a judgment. In the period of waiting, the Jewish Christians interpreted their prophecies, visions, and speaking in tongues as signs that Jesus' Holy Spirit was active among them. Peter called on his fellow Jews to repent while there was still time and be baptized in the name of Jesus so that they also would receive the Spirit's gifts.

The forty years between Jesus' death and the Roman destruction of Jerusalem are a relatively long time, during which Jewish Christianity evolved in ways that we can only barely see. It spread geographically. Jewish Christians lived in

Galilee, Antioch, and Damascus (and probably other places), but in the few written sources the community at Jerusalem stands out. The leadership at Jerusalem changed over time. According to Acts, Peter was the leading figure for a time. Then Peter was joined by John and James, who was identified as Jesus' brother. Paul called the three the "acknowledged pillars" (Gal 2:9). Eventually James, the brother of the Lord, emerged as the leader of Jewish Christianity at Jerusalem. He had not been a follower during Jesus' lifetime, but at some point he became a believer, perhaps when, as Paul wrote, he believed that the risen Christ appeared to him (1 Cor 15:7). Even after James' death by stoning in 62, he continued to be revered as the leading figure in Jewish Christianity, just as Peter was in the communities that read the four canonical gospels, and as Paul was in Luke's Acts and in the Pauline churches. Jewish Christians remembered James as an extraordinarily pious Jew, nicknamed the "Just" or the "Righteous." Hegesippus, a second-century Christian writer who may have been of Jewish origin, wrote that James' "knees became hard like a camel's, for he was continually bending the knee in worship to God, and asking forgiveness for the people" (EH II.23). In the early *Gospel of Thomas*, "The disciples said to Jesus, 'We know that you will go away from us; who will be our leader?' Jesus said, 'Wherever you are, you are to go to James the just; heaven and earth came into being for him'" (*Gospel of Thomas*, c. 12, in *The Apocryphal New Testament*, edited by J. K. Elliott [Oxford, 1993], p. 137). Under James' leadership, the Jewish-Christian community at Jerusalem had two or three decades of relative peace in a thoroughly Jewish context.

Jewish Christians and Gentile Converts

The early Christian community at Jerusalem was Jewish in its membership and in its orthopractic way of life. Like all orthopractic Jews, Jewish Christians regarded gentiles, that is, non-Jews, as outsiders who should be avoided to the degree that was possible. A pious Jew—and that included Jewish Christians—could not ordinarily have a close relationship with a gentile. Eating with gentiles was especially sensitive because of the Mosaic Law's commands about food and purity. But it was a crucial development that the Christian message began to cross the boundaries between Judaism and the Greco-Roman world. The Jesus Movement attracted some gentiles, especially the gentile "god-fearers" who already knew and admired some aspects of Judaism but had not formally converted to it. Luke wrote about a Roman centurion, Cornelius, whom he said was a "devout man who feared God" and "gave alms generously to the [Jewish] people and prayed constantly" (Acts 10 and 11). Cornelius was one of those gentiles sympathetic to Judaism, but he remained a gentile, a fact that presented problems for Jewish Christians. In response to a vision, Cornelius sent for Peter. Before Cornelius' messengers arrived, Peter also had a vision in which a sheet was lowered from heaven full of the unclean things that no orthopractic Jew could eat. When a voice told Peter to eat them, he responded as he should, "By no means, Lord; for I have never eaten anything that is profane or unclean." The voice then told him "What God has made clean, you must not call profane." The vision puzzled Peter, but when Cornelius' messengers arrived, he went with them. Luke then attributed to Peter a revolutionary view for any Jew or Jewish Christian: "You yourselves know that it is unlawful for a Jew to associate with or to visit a Gentile; but God has shown me that I should not call anyone profane or unclean." Peter preached about Jesus to Cornelius and his household. "While Peter was still speaking, the Holy Spirit fell upon all who heard the word. The circumcised believers [that is, Jewish Christians] who had come with Peter were astounded that the gift of the Holy Spirit had been poured out even on Gentiles." When Peter reported these events to the Jewish Christians at Jerusalem, they at first criticized him for associating with and especially eating with uncircumcised men. After Peter told them about his vision of the sheet from heaven, Cornelius' vision, the meeting with Cornelius, and the descent of the Holy Spirit on the gentiles, his critics relented, saying, "Then God has given even to the Gentiles the repentance that leads to life." Luke, who wrote these words in the 80s, favored the inclusion of gentiles in Christianity and knew that in his day gentiles had become an important source of new believers.

Luke's account of Cornelius' conversion and of Peter's change of heart about gentiles makes no sense unless we understand that Jewish Christians were seriously divided about what to do when gentiles sought to join the group. Some Jewish Christians argued that gentiles must first become Jews and that only then could they enter the community that accepted Jesus as Messiah. Luke recorded their view, with which he disagreed: "Then certain individuals came down from Judea and were teaching the brothers [Christian believers of gentile origin], 'Unless you are circumcised according to the custom of Moses, you cannot be saved'" (Acts 15:1–2). Other Jewish Christians, whose spokesman was Paul, defended the revolutionary view that gentiles could become followers of Jesus without the need to observe the Mosaic Law, including circumcision. On one occasion at Antioch, Paul criticized Peter for first eating with and then refusing to eat with gentiles. He said that Peter's willingness to eat with gentile Christians was undermined by emissaries from James, the leader in Jerusalem. In the face of the criticism from the circumcision faction, as Paul called it, Peter refused to eat any longer with gentile Christians. Other Jewish Christians joined Peter, including Paul's fellow missionary Barnabas (Gal 2:11–13). The split was serious.

Paul's opinion was controversial; indeed, his life was in danger because his views on gentile converts offended some Jews and Jewish Christians. Luke wrote that Paul went to Jerusalem and met with James and the elders. "Then they said to him, 'You see, brother, how many thousands of believers there are among the Jews, and they are all zealous for the law [these are Jewish Christians]. They have been told about you that you teach all the Jews living among the Gentiles to forsake Moses, and that you tell them not to circumcize their children or observe the customs. What is to be done?'" (Acts 21:17–40). James and the Jewish-Christian elders encouraged Paul to show that he "observed and guarded the law" by paying the expenses for four men who were taking a Nazirite vow (Num 6:1–12). Paul did so and took the vow himself, but it was not enough for his critics. Jews from Asia

Minor, who presumably knew his missionary work there, stirred up a riot when they said, "Fellow Israelites, help! This is the man who is teaching everyone everywhere against our people, our law, and this place [the Temple]...." (Acts 21:28). They tried to kill Paul, who was rescued by the intervention of Roman troops.

Because hindsight is usually perfect, it may seem obvious that Christianity would spread among gentiles. But the first-century debate within Jewish Christianity was serious. If the stricter (and probably larger) group of Jewish Christians had won the argument that a gentile had to convert to Judaism in order to be a follower of Jesus, the history of the Jesus Movement would have been quite different. But they did not win. Luke reported that at a meeting in Jerusalem in about 49, Paul, spokesman for the "liberal" Jewish-Christian view of gentile conversion, and James, spokesman for the strict Jewish-Christian point of view, reached a compromise: "Therefore I [James] have reached the decision that we should not trouble those Gentiles who are turning to God, but we should write to them to abstain only from things polluted by idols and from fornication and from whatever has been strangled and from blood" (Acts 15:19–20). Thus, the gentile Christians were to observe some dietary restrictions so that Jewish Christians could eat with them. The omission of a requirement that gentile converts be circumcised was a major victory for Paul and his party.

In spite of Luke's optimistic view that the matter of gentile conversion had been settled during the meeting at Jerusalem, some Jewish Christians never accepted the direct conversion of gentiles. For centuries Jewish Christian communities, many of them in Galilee and east of the Jordan River, continued to honor Jesus as Messiah, to observe the Mosaic Law, and to hate Paul, whom they blamed for leading astray both the gentiles and the Jesus Movement itself.

Jewish Christians and the Jewish Rebellions

In the 60s, tension and violence escalated in Judea as resistance to Roman rule moved toward open revolt. Jews not only opposed Roman rule but also struggled among themselves. In 62, Festus, the Roman procurator in Judea, died. Because his replacement, Albinus, had not yet arrived, there was a brief power vacuum. In the interval, some Jewish opponents took the opportunity to kill James, the brother of Jesus. James' disappearance from the scene revealed that Jewish Christians preferred leadership by relatives of Jesus. Hegesippus reported that when the Jewish-Christian community reorganized after the Romans captured Jerusalem in 70, "those apostles and disciples of the Lord who were still surviving met together from all quarters and, *together with our Lord's relatives after the flesh (for the more part of them were still alive)* . . . ." They chose Symeon, the son of Clopas, probably Jesus' cousin, to succeed James as leader at Jerusalem (EH III.2). Symeon was executed as a very old man in the reign of the Emperor Trajan (98–117). Hegesippus also reported that the descendants of Jude, "one of the Savior's reputed brothers," "ruled every church, as being martyrs and of the Lord's family" (EH III.32). The leadership of Jesus' relatives did not continue when gentiles became the ordinary members of the religion.

When the Jewish rebellion against Roman rule broke out in 66, the Jewish Christians were unavoidably swept up in the events that engulfed all of the Jews in Palestine. The Jewish Christians faced a crucial choice: How should they react to the rebellion? Many Jewish rebels hoped that the outbreak of violence would cause the Messiah to come and save his people. Jewish Christians believed that Jesus, the Messiah, had *already* come and would soon return. As a consequence, at least some Jewish Christians probably did not support their fellow Jews in the desperate revolt against the Romans. The historian Eusebius (EH III.5) reported that a Christian prophet told the Jewish Christians to flee across the Jordan River to the city of Pella to await the outcome of the revolt (Mk 13:14–16 may refer to this event). The utter failure of the rebellion had important consequences for all Jews, including Jewish Christians. After the war, Palestinian Judaism, which did survive the massive defeat, became different than it had been before the war. Only some Jewish sects survived. The Essenes and Zealots were militarily annihilated. The Sadducees vanished because

their power center, the Temple, no longer existed. In contrast, the Pharisees grew in importance after the war because they were prominent in the synagogues, which adapted to the new situation. The leadership of the Pharisees kept Judaism alive in the many houses of prayers and synagogues that survived or were founded after the war. The Jewish Christians also survived the war, but their position *within* Judaism deteriorated. Perhaps because they had not embraced the national uprising against Rome, the attractiveness of their message to their fellow Jews declined. Judaism increasingly rejected the Jewish-Christian sect. For instance, the Gospel of John, composed twenty or thirty years after the capture of Jerusalem, said that the Christian community for which it was written had been expelled from the synagogues (John 12:42 and 16:2). Late in the first century (the date is uncertain), a curse on the renegades, heretics, and *minim* (perhaps Jewish Christians) may have been added to the synagogue service.

During the second century, the rift between Jewish Christians and other Jews widened. During the second revolt in Palestine between 132 and 135, the Jewish rebels not only fought the Romans but also persecuted Jewish Christians. In his *First Apology*, the Christian Justin Martyr wrote that "in the Jewish war which lately raged, Barcochebas, the leader of the revolt of the Jews, gave orders that Christians alone should be led to cruel punishments, unless they would deny Jesus Christ and utter blasphemy" (Justin, *First Apology*, c. 31 in ANF, vol. 1, p. 173).

The Jewish defeat in 135 affected all Palestinian Jews. The Roman Emperor Hadrian (117–138) ordered the expulsion of all Jews from Jerusalem, which became a city of gentiles, renamed "Aelia Capitolina." Although Hadrian probably did not know that Jewish Christians existed, his stern measures ended whatever remained of the Jewish-Christian community in Jerusalem, which had its origins with Jesus and the first believers. It had survived about one hundred years. After 135, Christians in Jerusalem were of gentile background. By the middle of the second century, it was clear that the Jewish Christians had failed in their efforts to convince the majority of their fellow Jews that Jesus was the Messiah.

In addition to being cut off from the mainstream of Jewish development, the Jewish Christians were isolated within the Jesus Movement by the increasing number of gentile converts. Gentile Christians owed a great debt to Jewish Christianity but diverged from their Jewish-Christian parent in precisely those matters that made it "Jewish." For instance, gentile Christians abandoned circumcision, the Hebrew language in their scriptures, the dietary laws, and in general the authority of the Mosaic Law. Some gentile Christians, including groups of gnostic Christians, rejected the Jewish background entirely.

Later Jewish Christianities

Jewish-Christian communities continued to exist even after the Jewish defeat in 135. Some ancient sources refer to the later forms of Jewish Christianity under a variety of names, including "Ebionites," "Nazoreans," and "Elkesaites." The diversity of names points to the multiplication of kinds of Jewish Christianity. For instance, the Jewish-Christian Elkesaites, who arose in Mesopotamia in the second century, relied on a prophet named "Elkesai," who left a book of prophecies to guide his followers. Some Jewish Christians had their own written gospels, including a Hebrew or Aramaic version of the Gospel of Matthew, which was the canonical gospel most favorable to Judaism. If the Gospel of Matthew is read from a Jewish-Christian perspective, it can support the idea that Christianity is not a radical break with Judaism but rather is a perfected form of Judaism (Mt 5:17–18). Eusebius of Caesarea (260–337), a gentile Christian who lived in Palestine, was puzzled about Jewish Christians who still existed in his day. He recognized that they held theological views and observed practices different from those of orthodox fourth-century Christians. He knew at least two kinds of Jewish Christians, both of which he called "Ebionites" (in Aramaic, "the poor"). Eusebius thought that one group of Ebionites erred because of its christology, its view of Jesus. Eusebius wrote that in spite of the group's adherence to Christ, the devil had misled members of the group: "...that evil demon was unable to detach them from their devotion to the Christ of God, yet found access from another

direction, and so made them his own. Ebionites was the suitable name given them from the first, since they held poor and low opinions about Christ. For indeed, they regarded him as a simple, ordinary person; a man whom progress in character, and this alone, had justified; the fruit of a man's intercourse with Mary. And in their opinion, the worship [of God] enjoined by the [Mosaic] Law was absolutely necessary for them, since faith in Christ by itself and a corresponding life would not secure their salvation." Eusebius regarded the other kind of Ebionites as closer to what fourth-century orthodox Christians believed but still unacceptable: "But there were others besides these, who went by the same name, yet escaped the outlandish absurdity of the persons mentioned. They did not deny that the Lord was born of a Virgin and the Holy Spirit; nevertheless, like the others, they refused to acknowledge that, being God the Word and Wisdom, He preexisted;...they set great store by the observance of carnal worship prescribed by the [Mosaic] Law, as did the other kind of Ebionites. These were of the opinion that the epistles of the apostle [Paul] ought altogether to be rejected, calling him a renegade from the Law; but they used only the Gospel of the Hebrews, as it is called, and gave little importance to the rest [of the gospels]. And they observed the Sabbath and the other Jewish customs...; yet, on the other hand, each Lord's day they celebrated rites similar to ours, in memory of the Savior's resurrection" (EH III.27 altered).

There is much we do not know about Jewish Christians between the second and sixth centuries. But some generalizations are possible. Many Jewish Christians revered the Hebrew scriptures and observed the Law of Moses, in so far as that was possible without the Temple. All had a more or less "low christology," that is, some denied Jesus' divinity, and others denied his pre-existence. Some revered Jesus as a prophet like Moses, purely human, born from ordinary sexual intercourse between Joseph and Mary. Some said Jesus became the Messiah at his baptism when the dove appeared, a theological position called "adoptionism," from the view that God adopted the man Jesus. Others said he was made Messiah when God raised him from the dead.

Jewish-Christian communities survived in the Near East until Islam conquered much of the region after 632. Jewish Christians may have existed for generations more, but they generally recede from the historical record. They did not shape the direction of the Jesus Movement after the first century. About 100, the expanding edge of the movement was already in the gentile world.

GENTILE CHRISTIANITIES

Although Jewish Christians preached primarily to Jews in the earliest days, within two or three decades of Jesus' death, a major cultural barrier was crossed when Jewish-Christian missionaries found a positive reception from some Greek-speaking pagans. Jewish Christians outnumbered gentile Christians for many decades. But the conversion of non-Jews opened the way to new forms of Christianity that may be grouped together as "gentile Christianities," that is, the forms of Christianity practiced by people who did not have the experience of being Jews. Jewish-Christian missionaries gained some of their gentile converts from the ranks of the god-fearers, who saw in the new sect a way to embrace features of Jewish theology and ethics without submitting to the Law of Moses. The Jewish-Christian missionaries' success must have angered some Jewish communities that regarded such conversions from among their god-fearers as a sort of poaching.

Paul and Gentile Christians

Paul (about 10–about 64) is the early Jewish-Christian missionary best known to later generations. He was a contemporary of Jesus, whom he never met during his lifetime. He is the only first-century follower of Jesus for whom a biography, however inadequate, can even be attempted. Two things set him apart from the anonymous or poorly known missionaries. First, late in the first century, some unknown disciple(s) gathered some of Paul's letters into a small collection, which provides a remarkable window, but often only a glimpse, into his thoughts, career, and personality. The thirteen letters attributed to Paul in the New Testament contain about twenty-nine thousand Greek words, perhaps 110 printed pages. Second, Luke made Paul the central figure in Acts of the Apostles, which

treated the spread of Christianity among the gentiles during the thirty years after Jesus' death. Paul's own letters are the firmest basis for knowledge about him, supplemented carefully by reference to Luke's Acts, which did not always agree with what Paul wrote about himself and his work.

New Testament scholars debate the authenticity of some of the thirteen letters attributed to Paul. Most agree that Paul's authentic writings are one letter to the Romans, two letters to the Corinthians, one letter to the Galatians, one letter to the Philippians, the first letter to the Thessalonians, and the letter to Philemon. Most think that the three "pastoral letters" (I and II Timothy and Titus) are not by Paul but rather by later followers who wrote in his name. There is debate about whether or not Paul wrote the letters to the Ephesians and to the Colossians and the second letter to the Thessalonians. The seven generally accepted letters are the earliest surviving writings of the Jesus Movement, composed between about 50 and 60. Aside from his letter to the Romans, which is very much like a theological treatise, Paul's letters are real letters, that is, they were written to specific people about specific problems. They often contain his reactions to oral reports and letters that he had received from distant churches to which he had ties. When we read Paul's correspondence, we have only half the conversation, as if we were listening to one side of a telephone conversation. His letters take a lot for granted and give the reader tantalizing hints about all sorts of things but often not enough information to answer the questions they provoke.

As indicated earlier in this chapter, Paul's views, especially those on the conversion of gentiles, made him a controversial figure among his fellow Jewish Christians. When he identified his opponents and critics, they were ordinarily other Jewish Christians. He was in frequent controversy with strict factions of Jewish Christians, some of whom doubted his credentials to be an apostle; others disapproved of his rejection of the Law of Moses, others criticized his willingness to accept gentile converts on an equal footing with Jewish converts; and others just did not like him. For those reasons he often had to defend himself and in so doing included in his letters details about his life.

In his letter to the believers at Philippi in Greece, he defended himself with a terse "autobiography," which emphasized his Jewish origins and status: "If anyone else has reason to be confident in the flesh, I have more: circumcised on the eighth day, a member of the people of Israel, of the tribe of Benjamin, a Hebrew born of Hebrews; as to the law, a Pharisee; as to zeal, a persecutor of the church; as to righteousness under the law, blameless" (Phil 3:4–6). In his letter to the believers in Galatia, he gave a precious but surely incomplete account of his life. Paul was responding to the accusation that he had no right to call himself an apostle. "You have heard, no doubt, of my earlier life in Judaism. I was violently persecuting the church of God and was trying to destroy it. I advanced in Judaism beyond many among my people of the same age, for I was far more zealous for the traditions of my ancestors. But when God, who had set me apart before I was born and called me through his grace, was pleased to reveal his Son to me, so that I might proclaim him among the Gentiles, I did not confer with any human being, nor did I go up to Jerusalem to those who were already apostles before me, but I went away at once into Arabia, and afterwards I returned to Damascus. Then after three years I did go up to Jerusalem to visit Cephas [Peter] and stayed with him fifteen days; but I did not see any other apostle except James the Lord's brother. In what I am writing to you, before God, I do not lie! Then I went into the regions of Syria and Cilicia, and I was still unknown by sight to the churches of Judea that are in Christ; they only heard it said, 'The one who formerly was persecuting us is now proclaiming the faith he once tried to destroy.' And they glorified God because of me. Then after fourteen years I went up again to Jerusalem with Barnabas, taking Titus along with me. I went up in response to a revelation. Then I laid before them (though only in a private meeting with the acknowledged leaders) the gospel that I proclaim among the Gentiles, in order to make sure that I was not running, or had not run, in vain. But even Titus, who was with me, was not compelled to be circumcised, though he was a Greek. But because of false believers secretly brought in, who slipped in to spy on the freedom we have in Christ Jesus, so that they might enslave us—but we did not submit to them even for a moment, so that the truth of the gospel might always remain with you....when they [the leaders at Jerusalem] saw that I had been entrusted with the gospel for the uncircumcised, just as Peter had been entrusted with the gospel for the circumcised (for he who worked through Peter making him an apostle to the circumcised also worked through me in sending me to the Gentiles), and when James and Cephas and John, who were acknowledged pillars, recognized the grace that had been given me, they gave to Barnabas and me the right hand of fellowship, agreeing that we should go to the Gentiles and they to the circumcised. They asked only one thing, that we remember the poor, which was actually what I was eager to do" (Gal 1:13–2:10).

In Acts, Luke reported some things that Paul never wrote about himself, such as that Paul was born in Tarsus in modern Turkey, that he knew Hebrew and Aramaic, and that he was a Roman citizen (Acts 16:35–40; 22:24–29; 25:12). We might assume that after his conversion Paul preached and organized churches as a full-time occupation. But he tells us that he worked at a trade, tent-making or leather-working, to pay his bills (1 Cor 9:3–18; 2 Thes 3:7–10). He did not want to support himself from the offerings of his converts, although he occasionally accepted gifts and aid. He probably had a long-standing but unidentified illness, which he called a "thorn in his flesh" (2 Cor 12:7). He seems to allude to a serious illness, perhaps involving his eyes (Gal 4:13–15). He was unmarried (1 Cor. 7:7), although it is not clear if he was widowed, divorced, or single. He was a charismatic ("one who has gifts of the spirit"), who wrote that he spoke in tongues (1 Cor 4:18), uttered prophesies, saw visions (2 Cor 12:2–5), and received revelations. Paul conceded to his critics that he was not impressive in person (2 Cor 10:10), but he thought that he wrote strong letters. There are no physical descriptions of any early figures of Christianity—Jesus, Peter, Mary, and others. Later representations of people in the Bible are based on the artistic practices of the third and fourth centuries. Eventually artists and their audiences came to expect that New Testament people would be depicted in ways that had become traditional. For instance, Peter was usually depicted with a full beard and curly hair. But it is just possible that someone remembered what Paul looked like. The *Acts of Paul*, perhaps written in the late second century, described him as "a man small in size, bald-headed, bandy-legged, of noble mien, with eyebrows meeting, rather hook-nosed, full of grace" (*The Acts of Paul and Thecla*, c. 3, in J. K. Elliott, *The Apocryphal New Testament* [Oxford, 1993], p. 364).

Luke wrote that on the road to Damascus Paul had the most influential vision in the history of Christianity. Luke described it three times (Acts 9:1–19; Acts 22:4–16; Acts 26:12–18). Luke reported a version of that vision that he couched in Paul's words. "While I was on my way and approaching Damascus, about noon a great light from heaven suddenly shone about me. I fell to the ground and heard a voice saying to me, 'Saul, Saul, why are you persecuting me?' I answered, 'Who are you, Lord?' Then he said to me, 'I am Jesus of Nazareth whom you are persecuting.' Now those who were with me saw the light but did not hear the voice of the one who was speaking to me. I asked, 'What am I to do, Lord?' The Lord said to me, 'Get up and go to Damascus; there you will be told everything that has been assigned to you to do'" (Acts 22:6–11).

In his own letters, Paul never described the experience on the road to Damascus. But he insisted (perhaps because others were doubtful) that the Risen Jesus had appeared to him, personally singled him out, and called him to be an apostle whose special task was the conversion of the gentiles (Rom 11:13). Paul was convinced that Jesus had given him the mission to carry a message to the ends of the Earth, which apparently meant Spain (Rom 15:23).

Paul devoted about thirty years of his life to vigorous missionary work. He was aided by a network of settled helpers and traveling missionaries. For a long time, his base was at Antioch. Luke wrote that Paul made extended missionary journeys from Antioch to Cyprus, Asia Minor, Greece, Rome, and maybe Spain. Paul felt driven by the task he believed Jesus had given him, and he wrote that he suffered physically and mentally for it. In a letter to the believers at Corinth, he defended himself from critics who challenged his right to be a "minister of Christ" by describing his hard life: "Are they ministers of Christ?...I am a better one:

with far greater labors, far more imprisonments, with countless floggings, and often near death. Five times I have received from the Jews the forty lashes minus one. Three times I was beaten with rods. Once I received a stoning. Three times I was shipwrecked; for a night and a day I was adrift at sea; on frequent journeys, in danger from rivers, danger from bandits, danger from my own people, danger from Gentiles, danger in the city, danger in the wilderness, danger from false brothers and sisters; in toil and hardship, through many a sleepless night, hungry and thirsty, often without food, cold and naked" (2 Cor 11:23–27).

Although Luke wrote about Paul's imprisonment at Rome in the 60s, Luke did not tell his readers what happened to Paul afterward. Paul's death is not recorded in the New Testament. About thirty or forty years later, Clement of Rome wrote to the Corinthian church: "We should set before our eyes the good apostles....Because of jealousy and strife Paul pointed the way to the prize for endurance. Seven times he bore chains; he was sent into exile and stoned; he served as a herald in both the East and the West; and he received the noble reputation for his faith. He taught righteousness to the whole world, and came to the limits of the West, bearing his witness before the rulers. And so he was set free from this world and transported up to the holy place...." (*First Letter of Clement*, c. 5 in *The Apostolic Fathers*, edited and translated by Bart D. Ehrman, LCL 24 [Cambridge, MA, and London 2003], vol. 1, pp. 43–45). Paul was probably executed at Rome under the Emperor Nero (54–68).

Paul the Missionary

As I stressed earlier, Paul was not the only Jewish-Christian missionary, although he is the best documented. In his earliest surviving letter, that to the believers at Thessalonica in northern Greece, Paul sounded a theme that pervaded his writing and shaped his life: The Lord was returning soon. He also expressed his conviction to the Corinthians that end was near: "I mean...the appointed time has grown short; from now on, let even those who have wives be as though they had none, and those who mourn as though they were not mourning, and those who rejoice as though they were not rejoicing, and those who buy as though they had no possessions, and those who deal with the world as though they had no dealings with it. For the present form of this world is passing away" (1 Cor 7:29–31). At some points he seems to have expected to be alive when Jesus returned. As years passed and Jesus did not return, Paul came to think that he might not live to see the return, but he always believed it was close. Because the time of this world was short, Paul was eager to get on with the work of preaching to the gentiles. He and contemporary missionaries moved the Jesus Movement out of a largely Jewish context into the context of Greco-Roman cities.

Paul's career as a missionary took place in the favorable context of the Roman Empire. The empire provided about two centuries of peace and order that helped the work of Paul, other Christian missionaries, and also the missionaries of other gods. For instance, the far-flung Roman Empire was linked together by roads that were built for the movement of troops but that anyone could use. Roman soldiers reduced the danger that travelers faced from highway robbers and pirates. Paul (or anyone) could travel those roads or sail from one end of the Mediterranean Sea to the other without a passport (try that today!). In the first and second centuries, the Roman roads and seaways were the avenues for the movement of many religious entrepreneurs. Paul, who fit into that pattern, would not have attracted much attention from the Roman authorities, except when his activities disrupted public order—which sometimes happened. Paul also benefited from Roman tolerance in religious matters. In his letters, Paul advised believers to obey and honor civil rulers, who held power from God. In Acts, Luke stressed that the Roman authorities had been fair to Paul, who, he said, was a Roman citizen. Luke wrote that it was Jews, Jewish Christians, and some local pagans who actively opposed him, sometimes to the point of imprisonments, beatings, and mob attacks. The geography of languages within the empire also made Paul's work possible. If Paul had preached in Aramaic, his audience would have been small—even many Diaspora Jews could not have understood him. But many inhabitants of the empire knew Koiné Greek, especially those living in the cities of the eastern Mediterranean and in some parts of the

west, including the city of Rome. It is no accident that Paul wrote his letters in Greek.

Paul does not say in his own letters how he went about converting people. But Luke described Paul's missionary work as he thought it had been carried out. In many cities in Asia Minor and Greece, Paul had a ready-made audience in the synagogues of the Jewish Diaspora. As a Pharisee educated in the Law of Moses, he was sometimes invited to give the sermon in a synagogue at the Sabbath service. Luke's description of Paul's experience at Antioch in Pisidia, which is in modern Turkey, is illuminating. "And on the Sabbath day they [Paul and his fellow missionary Barnabas] went into the synagogue and sat down. After the reading of the law and the prophets, the officials of the synagogue sent them a message, saying, 'Brothers, if you have any word of exhortation for the people, give it.' So Paul stood up and with a gesture began to speak" (Acts 13:14–16). Paul addressed his sermon to the Jews and god-fearers. He placed Jesus within the great sweep of the history of the Jews: "And we bring you the good news that what God promised to our ancestors he has fulfilled for us, their children, by raising Jesus [from the dead]" (Acts 13:32–33). The climax of Paul's address was a call to repent and believe: "Let it be known to you therefore, my brothers, that through this man [Jesus] forgiveness of sins is proclaimed to you; by this Jesus everyone who believes is set free from all those sins from which you could not be freed by the law of Moses" (Acts 13:38–39). Luke said that Paul and Barnabas were invited to speak again on the next Sabbath. But some members of the synagogue thought about Paul's message and rejected it. Paul and Barnabas reacted by asserting a powerful break with the past, which may express Luke's view of the inevitable development of Christianity: "It was necessary that the word of God should be spoken first to you [the Jews]. Since you reject it . . ., we are now turning to the Gentiles" (Acts 13:46). A central fact in Paul's letters and in Luke's account of him was that missionary activity among the Jews had only modest success, although individual Jews remained important in the Jesus Movement for several generations.

Some missionaries may have settled down in the churches they founded but not Paul. After he had organized a congregation, ordinarily in a city,

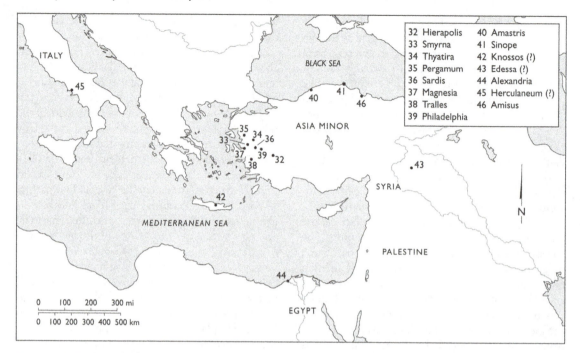

32	Hierapolis	40	Amastris
33	Smyrna	41	Sinope
34	Thyatira	42	Knossos (?)
35	Pergamum	43	Edessa (?)
36	Sardis	44	Alexandria
37	Magnesia	45	Herculaneum (?)
38	Tralles	46	Amisus
39	Philadelphia		

Figure 4.2 Christian Communities between 70 and 100. In the generation after the destruction of Jerusalem, Christian communities emerged primarily in western Asia Minor. When this map is viewed along with Figure 4.1, the geographical extent of Christianity before 100 is clear. Keep in mind that these communities were small. *(After Frend, The Rise of Christianity)*

he moved on to new territory, although he kept in touch with his converts through occasional visits, messengers, and the letters that have made him so significant in the history of Christianity. Paul's success in his own lifetime is difficult to assess. We cannot count the number of Paul's converts, but I think that it was small. Nevertheless, the scattered communities that he and other missionaries founded provided a basis for growth in subsequent years.

Paul the Theologian

Missionaries must have had messages for potential converts, although the messages may have varied significantly. Individual missionaries must have told their converts about their understanding of Jesus. Paul comes closest to telling us what he said to his converts. Anyone interested in understanding the origins of Christianity should read the letters of Paul. But do not expect the intellectual

equivalent of a leisurely walk on a sunny day. Paul's letters are difficult to understand. For instance, the author of the second letter of Peter wrote: "So our beloved brother Paul wrote to you according to the wisdom given him.... There are some things in them [Paul's letters] hard to understand, which the ignorant and unstable twist to their own destruction...." (2 Peter 3:15–16). Paul never laid out in a systematic way a full account of his beliefs—the closest he came was in his letter to the Roman believers, which was his longest and most theologically influential letter. As a consequence, for centuries believers, theologians, and historians have had to pick out of his letters bits and pieces to create a Pauline theology. To this day, there is controversy over what he wrote and what it meant.

We can, however, see some important contours of his teaching. Paul was not a revolutionary in secular matters. The Roman world was full of injustice and oppression, but he was content to leave social and economic arrangements alone. Perhaps he thought that all human structures would pass away when Jesus returned. There were also practical reasons why he did not criticize the Roman Empire. Jesus had been executed for the political claims that swirled around him ("the King of the Jews" in Mk 15). Paul was in similar danger. Luke reported that Paul's success at Thessalonica led to a near riot led by Jews who accused him of a dangerous political crime: "They are all acting contrary to the decrees of the emperor, saying that there is another king named Jesus" (Acts 17:1–9). That sort of talk about another king could lead to execution. But in Paul's own letters there is no hint of political rebellion. Quite the contrary, he urged loyal obedience to the rulers of the Roman Empire. For instance, he advised, that "…every person be subject to the governing authorities; for there is no authority except from God, and those authorities that exist have been instituted by God. Therefore whoever resists authority resists what God has appointed, and those who resist will incur judgment.…There-fore one must be subject, not only because of wrath but also because of conscience. For the same reason you also pay taxes, for the authorities are God's servants, busy with this very thing. Pay to all what is due—taxes to whom taxes are due, revenue to whom revenue is due, respect to whom respect is due, honor to whom honor is due" (Rom 13:1–7).

Paul also expressed no challenge to fundamental features of the Greco-Roman social order that modern people might find wrong. He advised believers to stay in the situation in which they found themselves when they converted. He counseled slaves to accept their situation and be good slaves (1 Cor 7:17–30). He did not advise slave owners to free their slaves but rather to treat them fairly. He never criticized wealth, although he encouraged generosity. Paul welcomed women as co-workers and fellow believers. He wrote that the distinctions of Jew from Greek, slave from free, and male from female no longer mattered because all believers were one in Christ (Gal 3:28). Alongside such spiritual equality, Paul did not oppose the contemporary social inequality of women.

Paul was, however, a revolutionary in religion. As a Pharisee educated in the Law of Moses, he had a deep knowledge of Judaism. Because the gospels were not yet written, the "scriptures" for him were the Hebrew scriptures, which later Christians called the "Old Testament." Like any pious Jew, he believed that there was only one God, who did not want his followers to have anything to do with other gods. Paul's ethical views on such topics as marriage, alms-giving, and brotherly love were within the range of views held in the Judaism of his time. If Paul had just repeated the basic theological and ethical ideas of Judaism, his impact on the development of the Jesus Movement would have been much less profound. But he was a creative thinker who worked out a revolutionary interpretation of the relationship between Judaism and Christianity. Paul broke decisively with Judaism over the significance of the Law of Moses, those positive and negative commands that shaped the life of a pious Jew. He experienced decades of strife because of his forceful declaration that the Mosaic Law, which was central to Judaism and was observed by many Jewish Christians, was no longer binding and could not save anyone. When Jewish-Christian missionaries told Paul's converts in Galatia that they must observe the Law, symbolized by circumcision, Paul wrote indignantly, "For freedom Christ has set us free. Stand firm, therefore, and do not submit again to the yoke of slavery. Listen! I, Paul, am telling you that if you let yourselves be circumcised, Christ will be of no benefit to you. Once again I testify to every man who lets himself be circumcised that he is obliged to obey the entire law. You who want to be justified by the law have cut yourselves off from Christ; you have fallen away from grace. For through the Spirit, by faith, we eagerly wait for the hope of righteousness. For in Christ Jesus neither circumcision nor uncircumcision counts for anything; the only thing that counts is faith working through love" (Gal 5:2–6). Although Paul believed that God had given the Law to Moses, he argued that it was binding in its time, which he thought had passed when Jesus came. In place of the Mosaic Law, Paul argued that faith in Jesus was sufficient for salvation. Such faith was a free gift from God that could not be earned but rather could be accepted by anyone, Jew or gentile. Paul never outlived the resistance to his view that the Law of Moses no longer bound and that Christianity was open to all who accepted Jesus in faith. His role in the process that eventually separated Christianity from Judaism was so important that he is sometimes described as a founder of the religion.

Paul also emphasized the universalism of Jesus' message, which he insisted was not just for Jews but rather for all mankind. In some Jewish circles, there was an expectation that when Israel was restored in the last days, gentiles would come to Mount Zion with gifts to worship the God of Israel (Isaiah 60:10–14; Micah 4). Paul might have interpreted his success among gentiles as a fulfillment of that expectation about the last days. He argued that the Jews had been invited first to believe in Jesus, but he faced the reality that the majority did not respond favorably. He kept hope that his fellow Jews would accept Jesus before the end came.

When Paul died in the 60s, he could not have known that within a decade both Judaism and Jewish Christianity would be engulfed by a disastrous defeat at the hands of the Romans. His work, and that of many unknown or hazily known missionaries, was crucial for the future of Christianity. When Jewish Christianity in Palestine was severely weakened by the Roman victory in 70, there were already mostly gentile Christian communities in Asia Minor, Greece, and Italy that took the lead in the Jesus Movement. The missionaries of the Jesus Movement were under no central control and sometimes taught different and even incompatible things, in part because they depended on oral teaching. By the late first century, there were Christian groups, probably mostly small, scattered from the Near East to Asia Minor, Greece, and Italy. The proliferation of views, documents, and institutions within the Jesus Movement continued into the second century. The next chapters will trace those developments within the broad Jesus Movement.

FURTHER READING ON JEWISH CHRISTIANITY

Ancient Sources

Luke, *Acts of the Apostles*, especially but not only chapters 1–12. The surviving fragments of the Jewish Christian gospels are translated in *The Apocryphal New Testament*, edited by J. K. Elliott (Oxford, 1993), pp. 3–16. For those who

want to read the sources written by Christian writers about Jewish Christianity, see A. F. J. Klijn and G. J. Reinink, *Patristic Evidence for Jewish-Christian Sects* (Leiden, 1973), where the Greek and Latin documents are published with an English translation on the facing page.

Modern Works

In recent years, there has been significant interest in Jesus' family, which was prominent for a time within Jewish Christianity. You might want to read John Painter, *Just James: The Brother of Jesus in History and Tradition* (Columbia, SC, 1997); or Richard Bauckman, *Jude and the Relatives of Jesus in the Early Church* (Edinburgh, 1990).

H. J. Schoeps, *Jewish Christianity* (Philadelphia, 1969).

Marcel Simon, *Jewish Sects at the Time of Jesus*, translated by James H. Farley (Philadelphia, 1967).

Gerd Theissen, *Sociology of Early Palestinian Christianity*, translated by John Bowden (Philadelphia, 1978).

FURTHER READING ON GENTILE CHRISTIANITY

Ancient Sources

Luke's *Acts of the Apostles* is translated with a good commentary in Johannes Muck, *The Acts of the Apostles*, revised by W. F. Albright and C. S. Mann, Anchor Bible, vol. 31 (Garden City, NY, 1967).

Read Paul's letters in a translation with good notes and explanatory passages, such as *The Writings of St. Paul*, edited by Wayne A. Meeks (New York, 1972). If you have to choose, read Paul's First Letter to the Corinthians and his Letter to the Romans.

Modern Works

There are many treatments of Paul the man and his message. You might read E. P. Sanders, *Paul: A Very Short Introduction* (Oxford, 1991, and reprinted 2001), which packs a great deal of insightful analysis in a small book. See also Jerome Murphy-O'Connor, *Paul: His Story* (Oxford, 2004); John Ashton, *The Religion of Paul the Apostle* (New Haven and London, 2000); or F. F. Bruce, *Paul, Apostle of the Free Spirit* (Exeter, 1977).

Wayne Meeks, *The First Urban Christians: The Social World of the Apostle Paul*, second edition (New Haven and London, 2003). A readable and enlightening introduction to Paul's life, work, and world.

PART II

✣

Christianity in the Second and Third Centuries

Timeline for the Second and Third Centuries (All Dates Are CE/AD)

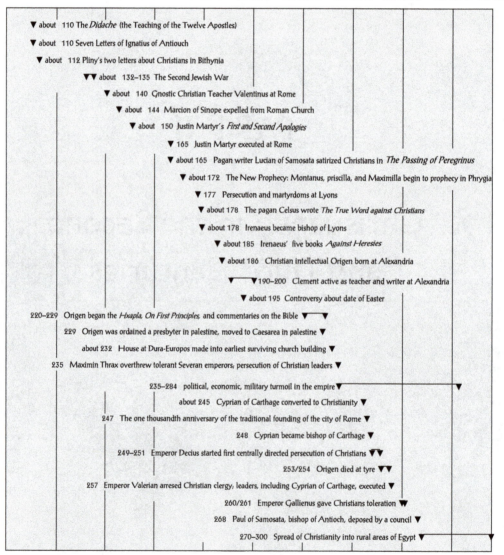

100 CE/AD   120 CE/AD   140 CE/AD   160 CE/AD   180 CE/AD   200 CE/AD   220 CE/AD   240 CE/AD   260 CE/AD   280 CE/AD   300 CE/AD

▼ about 110 The *Didache* (the Teaching of the Twelve Apostles)

▼ about 110 Seven Letters of Ignatius of Antiouch

▼ about 112 Pliny's two letters about Christians in Bithynia

▼▼ about 132–135 The Second Jewish War

▼ about 140 Gnostic Christian Teacher Valentinus at Rome

▼ about 144 Marcion of Sinope expelled from Roman Church

▼ about 150 Justin Martyr's *First and Second Apologies*

▼ 165 Justin Martyr executed at Rome

▼ about 165 Pagan writer Lucian of Samosata satirized Christians in *The Passing of Peregrinus*

▼ about 172 The New Prophecy: Montanus, priscilla, and Maximilla begin to prophecy in Phrygia

▼ 177 Persecution and martyrdoms at Lyons

▼ about 178 The pagan Celsus wrote *The True Word against Christians*

▼ about 178 Irenaeus became bishop of Lyons

▼ about 185 Irenaeus' five books *Against Heresies*

▼ about 186 Christian intellectual Origen born at Alexandria

▼ 190–200 Clement active as teacher and writer at Alexandria

▼ about 195 Controversy about date of Easter

220–229 Origen began the *Hxapla, On First Principles*, and commentaries on the Bible ▼ ▼

229 Origen was ordained a presbyter in palestine, moved to Caesarea in palestine ▼

about 232 House at Dura-Europos made into earliest surviving church building ▼

235 Maximin Thrax overthrew tolerant Severan emperors; persecution of Christian leaders ▼

235–284 political, economic, military turmoil in the empire ▼ ▼

about 245 Cyprian of Carthage converted to Christianity ▼

247 The one thousandth anniversary of the traditional founding of the city of Rome ▼

248 Cyprian became bishop of Carthage ▼

249–251 Emperor Decius started first centrally directed persecution of Christians ▼▼

253/254 Origen died at tyre ▼▼

257 Emperor Valerian arresed Christian clergy, leaders, including Cyprian of Carthage, executed ▼

260/261 Emperor Gallienus gave Christians toleration ▼

268 Paul of Samosata, bishop of Antioch, deposed by a council ▼

270–300 Spread of Christianity into rural areas of Egypt ▼ ▼

A NOTE ON NAMING CHRISTIAN GROUPS

Before I describe the Jesus Movement in the second century and beyond, I need to tell you how I shall name Christian groups. For the first three centuries, the unadorned word "Christian" is rarely adequate. Modern scholars emphasize the diversity within the Jesus Movement during those centuries. Probably every group thought that it contained the true Christians. To treat these matters historically, I accept as Christian every person or group that claimed to be Christian—that involves a wide spectrum. But as I write about them, I need to distinguish them by their names. I usually add an adjective before the word "Christian," such as "Jewish Christian," "gnostic Christian," or "Montanist Christian," although I know that such simple labels can hide complex realities. One kind of Christianity emerged in the later third and fourth centuries as the dominant form of Christianity. How should it and its predecessors be named? They sometimes called themselves "orthodox" ("right thinkers") or "catholic" ("universal") or just plain "Christians." Those three words have the disadvantage that they have later meanings that might not apply in the year 150 or 250. Professor Bart Ehrman (*The New Testament: A Historical Introduction to the Early Christian Writings* [New York, 1997], pp. 7–8) coined the term "proto-orthodox" to designate these second- and third-century groups that were the forerunners of and developed into the catholic/orthodox Christianity that emerged clearly in the fourth century. In the second and third centuries, the proto-orthodox Christians were one group among many, but they are visible in the surviving sources, written by such people as Justin of Rome, Tertullian of Carthage, Hippolytus of Rome, and Irenaeus of Lyons. I shall follow Professor Ehrman in naming such groups "proto-orthodox Christians" in order to single them out within the diversity of Christian groups before the fourth century. After Constantine's conversion in the early fourth century, I use the terms "orthodox" and "catholic" interchangeably, although I generally do not capitalize the words in order to alert readers that the words are not exactly the same as the modern, capitalized forms such as "Orthodox" or "Catholic." When I treat other groups during and after the fourth century I give them their appropriate labels, such as "Donatist Christians."

CHAPTER 5

Christian Diversity in the Second and Third Centuries

GNOSTIC CHRISTIANITIES

Information about many early Christian groups is sparse or distorted. Because the proto-orthodox Christians and their successors, the orthodox or catholic Christians, won the struggles over belief and organization, they shaped to a large degree how the history of early Christianity has usually been understood. Their writers ignored or attacked rival forms of Christianity, pushing them to the margins and making them seem outlandish or demonic. During and after the fourth century, most rivals to orthodox Christianity withered under religious, social, and legal pressure. Some disappeared entirely, although others survived for centuries. Their documents, which were handwritten in small numbers of copies on papyrus or parchment, ceased to be copied, perished in fire, flood, or neglect, or were actively destroyed. As a consequence, many forms of early Christianity are known mostly from the attacks of their proto-orthodox opponents or are just names to us. A remarkable modern discovery made available documents that belonged to an unidentified group of Christians. In 1945, near Nag Hammadi in Egypt, a peasant digging in a hillside found a jar containing thirteen books that preserved a total of fifty-one mostly Christian texts, about one thousand pages in the Coptic language, not one of which is included in the New Testament. (Do not confuse these documents with the Dead Sea scrolls, which were found in Israel in 1947 and contained Jewish documents.) The Nag Hammadi documents reveal the views of some, but certainly not all, relatively unknown second-, third-, and fourth-century Christian individuals and groups.

No single term can capture the rich variety within the second- and third-century Christian movement. In the third century, Hippolytus of Rome wrote a *Refutation of All Heresies* that attacked thirty-three groups that seem to be gnostic. There are other groups, often poorly documented, that cannot be put into a category. Modern scholars sometimes classify *one* broad band within the Christian movement as "gnostic," from the Greek word *gnosis,* which means "knowledge." Recently some scholars have argued that the term "gnosticism" should be abandoned because it is too vague and broad to be useful (and no ancient writer used it). I shall avoid the word "gnosticism" but shall write about gnostics ("knowers") because they certainly existed. There was no single organized movement of gnostics. There was no united gnostic church. The gnostic Christian groups were rivals to one another. They taught a remarkable variety of beliefs and practiced their Christianity in many different ways. But many shared some or all of a set of beliefs and attitudes. They were often pessimistic about the material universe and about human beings. They taught that a completely unknown and unknowable God produced—emanated—an outflow of other beings that probably represented features of that supreme God, such as Mind, Peace, Glory, and Wisdom. Something terrible happened in the higher world of the Supreme God, as a result of which something divine escaped. A lesser being who was ignorant or evil carried out material creation to hold the divine element. In some but not all human beings the divine element slept unaware of itself until a redeemer descended from above to bring knowledge of the real situation and then ascended back to the divine realm. Some human beings became aware of the divine element in themselves and were in that sense saved by knowledge (gnosis).

Gnostic Christians generally claimed to have a *secret* religious knowledge. It was not the kind of knowledge gained from studying books but rather a special kind of knowledge that arose out of a personal insight or out of a revelation that radically changed the recipient. Those who had received the secret knowledge thought that they had learned who Jesus really was, who they really were (trapped divine spirit), and how to escape from the oppressive powers that ruled the universe (by knowledge of themselves). The boundaries among the many Christian groups were not firm in the second century. Some gnostic Christians participated in the emerging proto-orthodox Christian congregations, where they attended services, shared in the Eucharistic meal, and listened to the readings of scripture and to the sermons of the bishop. But they thought that they were superior to the ordinary church members, including the leaders, because they were sure that they knew what the rituals and scriptures *really* meant. Many gnostic Christians thought that the bishops and elders taught a simple-minded version of the gospel, suitable only for the unenlightened members of the congregation. When challenged about their secret knowledge, they could point, for instance, to Paul, who wrote to the Corinthians that he spoke about God's hidden and secret wisdom only among the mature (1 Cor 2:6–7). He also wrote, "I could not speak to you as spiritual people, but rather as people of the flesh, as infants in Christ. I fed you with milk, not solid food, for you were not ready for solid food. Even now you are still not ready, for you are still of the flesh" (1 Cor 3:2–4). Some gnostic Christians identified themselves with the mature people to whom God revealed hidden wisdom and with the spiritual people who were fed solid food, which they interpreted as the secret knowledge that Jesus imparted to his inner circle of followers and to them. Their fellow Christians were the immature and unspiritual people who were fed milk, that is, simple doctrine, because that is all they could digest. Some gnostic Christians thought Jesus endorsed their view when the gospels

reported that he had taught some things openly to the unenlightened and other things secretly to a select few (see, for instance, Mk 4:10–12): "When he was alone, those who were around him along with the twelve asked him about the parables. And he said to them, 'To you has been given the secret [or mystery] of the kingdom of Heaven, but for those outside, everything comes in parables; in order that they may indeed look, but not perceive, and may indeed listen, but not understand; so that they may not turn again and be forgiven.'"

The source of the secret knowledge varied from group to group. Some claimed that their saving gnosis came directly from Jesus in visions and dreams; others claimed that Jesus had taught the secret knowledge to his early followers, who handed it down *orally* and *secretly* by a succession of teachers. On the face of it, this was not impossible. In the second century, the chain of teachers did not have to be very long because many important New Testament people had been dead for only a generation or two. For instance, the influential gnostic Christian teacher Valentinus (active about 120–160) claimed that he had been taught by Theudas, who, he said, had been a disciple of Paul. Gnostic Christians also wrote a great deal, including gospels, about twenty-five of which are known to us at least by name. Sometimes it is difficult for modern people to read the gnostic Christian documents, which were often intentionally mysterious. The early readers and hearers needed the secret knowledge before they could interpret the documents properly. When gnostic Christians read the letters of Paul and the four gospels that were eventually included in the New Testament, they interpreted them in the light of their secret knowledge.

Most religions attempt to answer profound questions about the universe and the human individual. So did early forms of Christianity. Early Christians of all kinds were pessimistic about the universe and generally agreed that there was something deeply wrong with human beings and the world in which they lived. But the rival Christian groups offered different explanations of human misery and ignorance. Proto-orthodox Christians, who relied primarily on Paul and the writers of the Synoptic Gospels, taught that the human problem was sin and that the solution was repentance and acceptance of Jesus as Lord. Mark, 1:14–15, said it briefly: "...Jesus came to Galilee, proclaiming the good news of God, and saying, 'the time is fulfilled, and the kingdom of God has come near; repent, and believe in the good news.'" For many gnostic Christians, the human problem was ignorance of one's true self. The second-century teacher Theodotus wrote that if we have gnosis, we understand "who we were, and what we have become; where we were...whither we are hastening; from what we are being released; what birth is, and what rebirth is" (Theodotus, in Clement of Alexandria, *Excerpta ex Theodoto*, 78.2, and quoted in Elaine Pagels, *The Gnostic Gospels* [New York, 1979], p. xix). In *The Book of Thomas the Contender,* found at Nag Hammadi, Jesus addressed Thomas, who was identified as Jesus' twin brother and true companion, about the liberating power of "knowing," especially knowing himself. He encouraged Thomas to learn who he was, how he existed, and what he would become. Jesus promised that Thomas would be called "the one who knows himself." If Thomas knew himself, he would have knowledge of the all. Jesus declared that those who do not know themselves stumble (*The Book of Thomas the Contender*, II.138, pp. 1–21). Some gnostic Christians compared the majority of humans with sleepers or drunks: They are in such a state that they do not know who they really are. Another revealing image drew on the common human experience of a nightmare. In *The Gospel of Truth*, a person without knowledge was described as trapped in a nightmare filled with terror, fear, confusion, and illusions of all sorts. If gnosis awakened the sleeper, the evil dream would turn out to be nothing (*The Gospel of Truth*, 28.30–30.15).

What do we know about the specific content of the secret knowledge? There was no single piece of secret, saving knowledge on which all gnostic Christians agreed. Some proto-orthodox Christians mocked the diversity of gnostic beliefs as proof that they were making it all up. In the 180s, Irenaeus, bishop of Lyons, wrote a long book against all kinds of gnostics. He asserted that the followers of the gnostic teacher Valentinus "put forth their own compositions, and boast that they possess more gospels than there really are [Irenaeus accepted only the gospels of Matthew, Mark, Luke, and John].... they really have no Gospel which is not full of blasphemy. For if what they have published is the Gospel of truth, yet it is totally unlike those which have been handed down to us from the apostles" (Irenaeus, *Against Heresies*, 3.11.9, in ANF, vol. 1, p. 429, altered). Gnostic Christians often did not feel bound by tradition or restricted by the developing canon of scripture, as the proto-orthodox Christians did. Gnostic Christian teachers—and there may have been hundreds of them in the second and third centuries—felt free to exercise their creativity. The gnostic secret knowledge was often expressed in elaborate accounts of the origin of the universe, in which the gnostic teachers explained how human beings got into their sad predicament and how they could escape from it. The gnostic search for self-knowledge and for an escape from the fear and confusion that often mark human life attracted many second-century people, including members of proto-orthodox Christian congregations who might not feel compelled to choose one or the other.

From proto-orthodox Christian efforts to refute him, we know the details of the teaching of an important gnostic Christian teacher, Valentinus. He was born in Egypt, educated in Alexandria, and came to Rome about 140. Even his opponents acknowledged that he was well-educated and eloquent. He wrote sermons, letters, and other works, which have not survived, although some scholars think he might be the author of the *Gospel of Truth*, which was found at Nag Hammadi. For a while, he was a member of a proto-orthodox Christian congregation in Rome. Apparently, he expected to be chosen bishop, but a confessor (that is, a person who had been persecuted but survived) was elected instead.

Valentinus taught that a being absolutely unknown to humans (certainly not the God of the Old Testament), its companion, "Thought," and fourteen pairs of male-female beings called "Aeons" ("eternities"), which had emanated out of that unknown god made up a perfect, harmonious spirit world called the "Pleroma," which means "the Fullness." The Pleroma existed outside of and before time. A disruption in it led to the escape of some spiritual substance (*pneuma*), which was stabilized by being encased in physical bodies (hyle) and souls (psyche). The Jewish God, who is not the true God but was called the "demiurge" ("the craftsman"), created the material universe in order to trap the escaped spirit in human bodies. The spirits-trapped-in-bodies were absolutely ignorant of their real spiritual selves. The Aeons in the Pleroma took pity on the trapped spirits. The heavenly Christ-Aeon sent another being, Jesus, to save the trapped spirits. Jesus brought to humans the knowledge that some people were really spirits. When the spirits-in-bodies learned who they were, they were able to return to the Pleroma. They were thus "saved." Such a summary of Valentinus' views does not convey the flavor of the gnostic wisdom, which was often couched in purposefully mysterious language. In his book against "the knowledge (gnosis) falsely so called," Bishop Irenaeus described Valentinus' teaching about God, Jesus, and the creation of human beings, using some of Valentinus' own terminology. "They claim that in the invisible and unnamable heights there is a certain perfect Aeon that was before all, the First-Being, whom they also call First-Beginning, First-Father, and Profundity.... And, since he is incomprehensible and invisible, eternal and ingenerate, he existed in deep quiet and stillness through countless ages. And along with him there existed Thought, whom they also name Grace and Silence. At one time this Profundity decided to emit from himself the Beginning of all things. This emission would be as a 'seed' which he decided to emit and deposit as it were in the womb of Silence, who coexisted with him. After she had received this 'seed' and had become pregnant, she gave birth to Mind who was both similar and equal to his Father who emitted him; and he alone comprehended his (Father's) greatness. This Mind they also call Only-begotten, Father and Beginning of all things. Truth was emitted at the same time he [Mind] was. Thus these four constitute the first and principal Pythagorean Tetrad [group of four], for there are Profundity and Silence, then Mind and Truth. This [Tetrad] they also call the root of all things. But when this Only-begotten perceived for what things he was emitted, he in turn emitted Word and Life, since he was Father of all who were to come after him and the beginning and formation of the entire Fullness. Thereupon by the conjugal union of

Word and Life, Man and Church were emitted. That is the principal Ogdoad [group of eight], the root and substance of all things...." Eventually the Valentinian Fullness (Pleroma) included thirty Aeons (Irenaeus, Against Heresies, 1.1.1, in ANF, vol. 1, pp. 316–317, altered).

The last Aeon to be emanated, Wisdom, yearned to know the unknown god but could not because she was so distant from him/it. In her unsuccessful effort to know the Father, she produced a misshapen offspring. Wisdom returned to her place in the Fullness (Pleroma), but her miscarriage, which contained spirit, was separated from her and expelled from the Fullness. Because of Wisdom's disruption of the Fullness, the Aeons blended their most brilliant and beautiful aspects into Jesus, who was sent into the material world to retrieve the scattered spirit (Irenaeus, Against Heresies, 1.2.6 in ANF, vol. 1, p. 323). Valentinus' explanation of the origins of creation and human beings found a receptive hearing in some Christian circles.

During the second century, Christian groups began the long process of sharpening the boundaries that separated them. Gnostic Christians were often excluded from proto-orthodox congregations. The gnostics, who considered themselves the real Christians, protested against such persecution, as they saw it. For instance, in The Second Treatise of the Great Seth, Jesus comforted his gnostic followers who were being rejected by other Christians. Jesus compared the rejecters with dumb animals because they think they are Christians but are in fact "empty" (The Second Treatise of the Great Seth, 9:19–31). The Apocalypse of Peter, found at Nag Hammadi, also interpreted the history of Christianity as the persecution of good gnostic Christians by proto-orthodox bishops and deacons. As Jesus explained to Peter, "And there shall be others of those who are outside our number who name themselves bishop and also deacons, as if they have received their authority from God. They bend themselves under the judgment of the leaders. Those people are dry canals" (Apocalypse of Peter, 79:24–30, translated by James Brashler and Roger A. Bullard in The Nag Hammadi Library in English, edited by James M. Robinson [San Francisco, 1988], p. 376).

Particular religious views often appeal to particular kinds of people. But it is not clear what sorts of people in the second and third centuries became gnostic Christians. It is also not clear what sorts of people became proto-orthodox Christians. To judge from written works, many gnostic believers saw themselves as members of an elite, whose special knowledge made them superior to ordinary, simple-minded believers. For instance, Valentinus taught that there were three categories of human beings, separated from one another by the share of spirit encased in their bodies. Some people had no spirit at all. Such purely material people, who were probably identified as Greco-Roman pagans, completely perished when they died. Those with a generous dose of spirit, called "pneumatics" from the Greek word *pneuma* ("spirit"), were the gnostic Christians themselves, who were sure to be saved if only they were awakened by Jesus' secret message. Other people, called "psychics" from the Greek word *psyche* ("soul"), were very short on spirit but might be saved after death as a reward for self-discipline and good works. These were probably the simple-minded clergy and other members of proto-orthodox Christian congregations.

I must repeat that the variety among gnostics is so great that almost no generalization is true of every teacher. But there are some cautious generalizations that hold for many of them. Gnostics often opposed the tendency, visible among proto-orthodox Christians, to organize churches with clergy, rituals, and specific documents as scripture. Some gnostics organized themselves in churches, but others organized in schools or study groups around charismatic teachers who were generally from Egypt or Syria, some of whose names and teachings are known: Simon Magus, Carpocrates, Basileides, and Valentinus. Many gnostic Christians seem to have valued personal experience, personal exploration of the self, and the creativity that encouraged diverse, even contradictory expressions of Christian belief.

There were large issues at stake. Many Christian groups in the second century wrestled with their evaluation of the Jews and their book, the Old Testament. Jewish Christians maintained a large degree of continuity with the Jewish past and venerated the Law of Moses. The proto-orthodox

Christians insisted that the Hebrew scriptures were God's books but had to be interpreted in their way. They insisted that if the Hebrew scriptures were rightly understood, they belonged to them, not to the Jews. Many gnostic Christians gave little or no respect to the God of Israel and his book. Some gnostic Christians thought that the God of Israel was the evil creator of matter; and others thought that he was the ignorant, spiteful, and petty creator of the material world. In any case, he was not the *real* god of the universe, who had remained hidden from humans until Jesus brought knowledge of him. Many gnostics concluded that the Hebrew scriptures had little or no relevance for them. In varying degrees, gnostics cut off Christianity from its Jewish roots.

All Christian groups also had to work out a view of Jesus, which is called a "christology." For many gnostic Christians, the idea that God became flesh was a repulsive thought. They reasoned that because created matter was a bad thing that existed only because of a disruption in the Pleroma, the purely spiritual Jesus could not have had real contact with it. If he had a real body, he would have been imprisoned in flesh like everyone else. Thus, some gnostic christologies tended to separate Jesus from matter and to regard him as a pure spirit rather than a real human being. Because many gnostics thought Jesus was a spirit, they could see no reason to believe that he actually suffered, died, or had any need to rise from the dead. Such a view of Jesus, which was held by some other Christians, is called "docetism," from the Greek verb *dokein* ("to appear"): Jesus only appeared to be human in order to interact with ignorant humans, including most of his disciples, who could not apprehend his real, spiritual nature. For instance, in *The Acts of John*, the narrator, John, the son of Zebedee, recounted episodes in which Jesus had no fixed appearance but rather adapted himself to the viewer. At one time Jesus appeared to John as a child and at the same time to John's brother James as a handsome man. On another occasion, John saw Jesus as a balding man with a large beard, whereas his brother saw a boy whose beard was just beginning to show. The point of the author of *The Acts of John* was that John and James could not see Jesus as he was because he was continually shifting his appearance

(*The Acts of John*, 88–89, in *The Apocryphal New Testament*, edited by J. K. Elliott [Oxford, 1993], pp. 316–317). The gnostics claimed that their knowledge of Jesus' real nature set them apart from the more simple-minded Christians, who believed that he had been a human being as well as God.

Christians of every sort also had to decide how to interpret whatever sacred texts—scriptures— they accepted. The gnostic Christians composed their own sacred texts in abundance, but some also read the letters of Paul and the gospels of Matthew, Mark, Luke, and John with what I shall call "gnostic eyes." They were sure that they understood the *real* meaning of the documents, which was obscured when too much attention was given the literal words. They were often sure that the true meaning of the scriptural words was hidden and needed to be drawn out in accordance with their special knowledge. Because gnostics often believed that the scriptures meant more than they said when read literally, they were among the earliest Christians to try to interpret scripture rather than just read and repeat it. For instance, about 140 a gnostic named "Heracleon" commented on the Gospel of John in twenty-two volumes. In order to refute the gnostics, the proto-orthodox Christians also began to interpret scripture, but with their own perspectives, with their own eyes, so to speak.

Just as we do not know the social origins of the gnostic Christians, so we do not know much about how their beliefs influenced their behavior. Gnostic beliefs may have had implications for the ways that gnostics behaved, that is, for their ethics. The gnostic Christian ideal was fundamentally individualistic. Gnostics might seek fellowship with other gnostics by belonging to a church or to a circle of disciples gathered around a master, but they had no need for that. After attaining the knowledge that saved, each gnostic pursued a personal journey to escape the flesh in which his or her real self was trapped. To those who knew who they were, differences, including sexual differences, became irrelevant. Some gnostics taught that the male and female would become one, whereas others taught that women would become like men. The *Gospel of Thomas*, over which there is disagreement about whether it is really "gnostic," reported: "Simon Peter said to them, 'Let Mary

leave us, because women are not worthy of life.' Jesus said, 'Look, I shall lead her so that I will make her male in order that she also may become a living spirit, resembling you males. For every woman who makes herself male will enter the kingdom of heaven'" (*The Gospel of Thomas*, 114, in *The Apocryphal New Testament*, edited by J. K. Elliott [Oxford, 1993], p. 147).

The gnostic Christians' effort to escape the misery of the human condition could take many forms, depending on the nature of the gnostic teaching and personal preferences. Some, perhaps most, gnostic Christian teachers advised their followers to defy the inferior creator God whose first command to humans had been to "be fruitful and multiply" (Gen 1:28). They refused to have children because that would continue the enslavement of spirit in flesh. Such gnostics adopted a self-denying way of life. Other Gnostics drew a different conclusion: "If the body I drag around is not the real me, then it can do what it wants." Such gnostics might conclude that there can be no physical acts that are wrong. In either case, the gnostics who were determined to escape the created world and the prison of the flesh may have felt little moral responsibility in this world. At least that is what their proto-orthodox opponents charged in saying gnostics did not practice charity to the needy and did not accept an obligation to die rather than deny Jesus and worship idols.

In the second and third centuries, gnostic Christianity was attractive to many in the broad Jesus Movement, although we shall never have accurate numbers. The proto-orthodox opponents of other forms of Christianity were disturbed by their rivals' successes. In reaction against gnostic views, they created important ways to draw a sharper boundary between themselves and the many kinds of gnostic Christians. Chapter 6 will treat more fully the proto-orthodox responses to competition with other Christian groups, including gnostic Christians.

MARCIONITE CHRISTIANITY

As noted earlier, the God of the Old Testament posed problems for some readers or hearers of the good news of Jesus. He could seem cruel, violent, petty, ignorant, and lax about the morally dubious behavior of his followers. Some gnostic Christians solved the problems by rejecting the God of the Jews. In their view, he was the enemy of the true gnostic, because he had encased spirit in matter and tried to prevent humans from learning who they really were. For many gnostic Christians, the secret knowledge enabled them to escape from the creator God's power.

Marcion of Sinope (about 85–about 164) proposed a view of the Jewish God that was milder than that of the more radical gnostic Christians but still negative and attractive to many. Marcion was the son of a bishop from Pontus, a region on the Black Sea coast of modern Turkey. He emigrated to Rome and joined the proto-orthodox congregation, to which he made a large gift of money. He was not a clergyman, but he was a skilful theologian who developed remarkable views. Marcion put forward no elaborate account of how humans came to be what they are. He taught nothing about Aeons, a Pleroma, or spirits trapped in flesh. He did not base his theology on secret gospels. He read the same scriptures as the proto-orthodox Christians but found in them something radically different from what they found. He was troubled by what he saw as conflicts between the portrayal of God in the Hebrew scriptures and that in the gospels and the letters of Paul. He described those conflicting views in a book called *Antitheses* ("Contradictions"), which does not survive, but we know something about it from what his many opponents wrote. After laying out what he saw as the contradictions between the description of God in the Old Testament and the description of God in the gospels, he concluded that there were actually two gods: a "Just" God in the Old Testament and a "Good" God in the gospels. Marcion did not argue that the God of the Old Testament was evil, as some believed, but rather that he was legalistic, interested in demanding an eye-for-an-eye and in imposing strict justice. Most importantly, Marcion concluded that the God of the Old Testament was not the "good" Father of Jesus, full of mercy, forgiveness, and unlimited kindness. Marcion believed that Jesus' Father—the true God—had been absolutely unknown to humans until Jesus revealed him.

Marcion's hero and theological inspiration was the Apostle Paul, who had contrasted the Law of Moses with the grace of God. Marcion hardened that contrast into an absolute division. He concluded that the God who gave the Mosaic Law could not be Jesus' Father, who was the God who gave grace. He argued that the stern, petty creator was not the perfect, loving Father. After Marcion had his basic insight about two gods, certain conclusions flowed logically. The proto-orthodox Christians regarded as scripture the Old Testament in its Greek translation, called the "Septuagint." In light of his view of the Old Testament God, Marcion could not accept that book. He granted that the Jewish scriptures contained the history and literature of the Jews. For instance, he agreed that the Jewish scriptures foretold the coming of a Messiah, but he argued that the Messiah would be a Jewish military leader and was not Jesus. In Marcion's view, even if the Jewish scriptures were historically true, they told of the doings of the Just God and his people, the Jews. They had nothing to do with Jesus and the Good God. He rejected the *religious* authority of the Old Testament for Christians. By denying any religious authority to the Old Testament, Marcion simply cut the bond between Christianity and Judaism. Because of his teaching about the God of the Old Testament, the Roman proto-orthodox Church excommunicated him in 144, that is, expelled him from the congregation, and returned his monetary gift.

By the middle decades of the second century, many proto-orthodox Christians knew, read, and revered the gospels of Matthew, Mark, Luke, and John and the letters of Paul, but they did not have a fixed list, a canon, of scripture. Marcion was probably the first person to create something that resembled a scriptural canon, that is, an official list of the New Testament books. Marcion thought that the four gospels and the Pauline letters had been contaminated and falsified by Jesus' Jewish followers, including the apostles. To correct those errors, Marcion created a "small" canon, which consisted only of the Gospel of Luke and ten letters of Paul. He chose Luke because he was believed to have been a companion of Marcion's hero Paul. Even then Marcion removed from Luke's gospel many favorable references to the Jewish scriptures, such as the Jewish genealogy of Jesus and the infancy stories about Jesus, which stressed his and his parents' adherence to the Mosaic Law. He also edited the ten Pauline letters to eliminate or correct favorable references to the Jewish scriptures and their Just God.

Like Paul, Marcion was a tireless missionary who created a church that endured until at least the seventh century. The Marcionite church was similar to the proto-orthodox churches in structure and rituals but was intensely ascetic, frowning on marriage, the drinking of wine, encouraging vegetarianism, and producing many martyrs. Married people were not full members. Only virgins, widows, and eunuchs could be baptized. Marcion's christology was docetic: Jesus was not born of a woman and did not have a real body. But Marcion thought that Jesus' death on the cross saved believers.

Marcion's challenge to proto-orthodox Christianity was serious because he faced head-on the problems posed by the God of the Old Testament. Every major proto-orthodox Christian writer between Tertullian (active 180–215) and Origen (died about 251) took up the pen to defend the God of the Old Testament and to insist that he was identical with Jesus' Father. Furthermore, the proto-orthodox Christians were pushed toward the creation of their own canon of scripture, although that was not completed until the fourth century.

In the second century, the Jesus Movement was remarkably wide and internally divided. The situation in the city of Rome is illuminating. As the capital of the empire and a very large city, Rome attracted many immigrants. Ambitious people from all over the empire, including all sorts of Christians, moved to Rome, just as ambitious people today move to New York, Los Angeles, London, Paris, or Tokyo. If you visited Rome between 100 and 200, you would have found a bewildering variety of religions. There was the vast complexity of "pagan" religion, including the official state religion, mystery religions, private cults, astrologers, magicians, and fortune-tellers. You would also have found that Christians, who made up a tiny percentage of the population, were divided among themselves into many groups. There was a proto-orthodox Christian group or perhaps loosely knit groups headed by a bishop, with elders and deacons. There was at least one Christian philosopher, Justin the Martyr, who ran a private school in which Christianity was taught as the "true philosophy." There were many gnostic Christian teachers, including Basileides and Valentinus. Marcion was there. The second-century ferment within the Christian movement had many consequences, which will be explored in the next chapter.

FURTHER READING

Ancient Sources

Documents written by gnostic Christians were almost entirely unknown until the second half of the twentieth century. Frankly, they are difficult to read but well worth browsing. You can learn a great deal from *The Gnostic Scriptures: A New Translation with Annotations and Introductions by Bentley Layton* (New York, 1987), in which many gnostic documents are translated and, more importantly, analyzed.

J. K. Elliot, ed., (Oxford, 1993) *The Apocryphal New Testament: A Collection of Apocryphal Christian Literature in English Translation Based on M. R. James*, contains a collection of the gospels, letters, acts, and other Christian documents that were not accepted into the canon of scripture (it does not contain the fifty-two Nag Hammadi documents). Try the "Infancy Gospel of Thomas" (pp. 68–83) or the "Protoevangeliun of James" (pp. 48–67), which I think are readable and interesting.

Robert M. Grant, *Second-Century Christianity: A Collection of Fragments*, second edition (Louisville and London, 2003), has a readable sample of the sources and issues in second-century Christianity.

Modern Works

E. C. Blackman, *Marcion and His Influence* (London, 1948). Old but still useful.

Bart D. Ehrmann, *Lost Christianities: The Battles for Scripture and the Faiths We Never Knew* (New York, 2003), ranges widely across the spectrum of struggles over scriptures and the beliefs they represented.

Christoph Markschies, *Gnosis: An Introduction*, third edition (London and New York, 2003). A brief introduction to a complex topic.

Elaine Pagels, *The Gnostic Gospels* (New York, 1979).

Elaine Pagels, *Beyond Belief: The Secret Gospel of Thomas* (New York, 2003).

CHAPTER 6

The Emergence of a Proto-Orthodox Christian Consensus: Bishop, Creed, and Canon of Scripture

During the second century, divisions within the Jesus Movement became more severe as competing forms of Christianity jostled with one another. The turmoil within the Jesus Movement had many causes, including the passage of time. By the second century, those who knew Jesus had died, and even those who knew his early followers were passing from the scene. The hope of Jesus' second coming, so prominent in the first century, faded but never disappeared. The vague organizational patterns of the early days were inadequate to cope with the problems that arose when Christians had to live in the world—and a hostile world, at that. Theological differences also contributed significantly to the turmoil. Christian groups interpreted Jesus in different ways, appealed for authority to different people and documents, and organized themselves in different ways, such as synagogues, churches, and circles of devotees. The groups competed with one another for converts from paganism, Judaism, and other kinds of Christianity. There was no violence among them, but heated arguments, mutual verbal abuse, and the expulsion of dissenters were common. In the noise of competing claims, many Christians and curious outsiders must have wondered where they could find reliable authority. How was a person to decide what to believe and how to behave?

Between about 50 and 200, a relatively large group of loosely affiliated congregations took shape within the broad Jesus Movement. Those Christians called themselves "orthodox" ("right-believing") or "catholic" ("universal") and sometimes just "the Church" or "the Christians, but I shall call them "proto-orthodox." In the second and third centuries, the proto-orthodox Christians gradually came to a consensus about how they would organize their churches, defend their theological views, and put barriers between them and their Christian rivals, especially the groups whom we lump together as "gnostic Christians." "Consensus" can be a slippery idea, but it happens frequently. Modern people join a political party because they agree generally with that party. They might not accept every detail, but they are comfortable with the party's aims, structures, and beliefs. In the same way, like-minded second-century Christian congregations joined voluntarily in a loose federation. The proto-orthodox consensus became the seed bed of almost all forms of modern Christianity, whether the modern groups acknowledge the fact or not.

ONE BISHOP, ELDERS, AND DEACONS/DEACONESSES

Jesus left no clear organizational blueprint that could have guided the Jesus Movement. Only Matthew's gospel (16:18 and 18:17) attribute to Jesus the use of the word *ekklesia* (church), but there was no organizational blueprint visible in those few words. His early followers had to improvise organization or borrow it from the synagogues with which they were familiar. We can glimpse some forms of organization in the later first century. The sources reveal two sorts of leaders: Some traveled (itinerant leaders), and some lived permanently in a particular community (local leaders). Paul, the best-known itinerant leader, stayed in a place long enough to establish a church, then moved on, driven by his desire to preach to the ends of the earth before Jesus returned. He kept contact with his converts by the exchange of messengers, letters, and occasional visits. He expected his churches to accept his supervision, although his letters make clear that they did not always do so. The letter to Titus, perhaps written by a disciple of Paul, referred to a time when an itinerant leader and local leaders—in this letter called "elders"—co-existed: "I [Paul] left you [Titus] behind in Crete for this reason, so that you should put in order what remained to be done, and should appoint elders in every town" (Titus 1:5).

Paul was not the only itinerant missionary, although he is the best-known to us. Many unknown people carried differing versions of the Christian message to existing or new churches. They were crucial in the spread of the new religion. Some documents called the itinerant missionaries "teachers," others called them "prophets," and still others called them "apostles," which might indicate that they had different functions. More people were called "apostles" than the twelve whom Jesus had gathered around him. For instance, Paul called himself an "apostle." Luke called both Paul and his fellow missionary Barnabas "apostles" (Acts 14:14). Paul mocked the "superapostles" who challenged his authority at Corinth (2 Cor 11:5), but implicit in his mockery is that they were calling themselves "apostles" and that some Corinthian Christians were accepting them. The itinerant apostles, prophets, and teachers continued their work during the first half of the second century, even after the last people who actually knew Jesus or his immediate followers had died. Some itinerant missionaries may have been active even into the third century. The Alexandrian scholar Origen (about 185–about 251) wrote that "[s]ome [Christians], in fact, have made it their business to visit not only cities but even villages and country houses to make converts to God. And no one would argue that they did this for the sake of gain, since sometimes they would not even accept necessary support...." (Origen, Contra Celsum, III.9, in ANF, vol. 4,

p. 468, altered). Sometimes an itinerant missionary settled down as leader in a community, perhaps one that he had created. As Origen noted, "Let us take an example. In a city where there are not yet any Christians, someone comes along who begins to teach, to labor, to instruct and if he leads men to the faith, he becomes subsequently the prince and bishop of those whom he has instructed" (Origen, Homily 11.4.5 on the Book of Numbers).

Generally, the itinerant missionaries stayed in one place only temporarily. When they left the churches they had founded or in which they had worked, some form of local organization had to keep the communities in existence. We know the titles of some local leaders but not always what the title-holders did or how they were chosen. Some churches had both bishops (episcopoi, literally "overseers") and deacons (diaconoi, literally "servants") (Phil 1:1; 1 Peter 2:25; 1 Tim 3:1–2; Titus 1:7; Didache 15). Other churches had local leaders called elders (presbuteroi) (1 Tim 4:14; James 5:14; Acts 11:30). Local communities might also have influential charismatic members (literally "those with a spiritual gift"). Especially in the later first and early second centuries, the local ministry was often subordinated to the authority and prestige of the itinerant ministry. For about a century after Jesus' death, the itinerant ministry was dynamic and dominant, whereas the local ministry was necessary but secondary.

The balance of authority and prestige between the itinerant and the local forms of leadership was unstable. As years gave way to decades, local forms of ministry became more deeply rooted in their communities, while serious problems emerged in the itinerant ministry. The second-century itinerant apostles, prophets, and teachers were less and less able to claim authority on the basis of direct contact with Jesus' early followers. In addition, as the beliefs prevalent in local churches became more fixed, some itinerant missionaries were rejected for teaching what the local leaders thought was incorrect. Some itinerant ministers also enriched themselves financially at the expense of the local churches they visited.

The pagan satirist Lucian of Samosata (second century) hated the numerous contemporary charlatans, whom he mocked in what we might call "short stories." In one story, he threw vivid light on a man who for a time took advantage of the goodwill of Christian communities. Lucian satirized an actual person named "Peregrinus," whom some ancient writers described as a wise man. Lucian depicted him as exploiting other people. Peregrinus finally dramatically burned himself to death at the Olympic Games in 165. At one point in his career, Peregrinus linked up with Christians, whom Lucian regarded as pathetic simpletons who could provide a good laugh to his sophisticated readers. According to Lucian, Peregrinus encountered Christians in Palestine and soon mastered their lore. He became, as Lucian put it, their prophet, cult-leader, and the head of the synagogue. He rose to such a position, said Lucian, that he was revered as a god, right after the man who was crucified because he introduced the new cult of the Christians into the world. When Peregrinus was imprisoned, Lucian reported that fellow Christians tried to get him released. When that failed they visited him in prison and brought him fine meals. Elderly widows and orphans waited from daybreak to see him. Church officials bribed guards so that they could join Peregrinus in his cell, where they passed the time reading aloud from their sacred books. Christians from distant places brought him encouragement and money. After he was released from prison, he traveled among Christians, receiving attention, respect, and money. Lucian wrote that Peregrinus fell out of favor with the Christians when he committed a serious fault—Lucian speculated that he might have eaten a forbidden food. Lucian thought it was partly the fault of the Christians that Peregrinus exploited them. He wrote that Christians held all things as common property and that they believed in things without any acceptable evidence. He thought they were too simple to ward off charlatans (Lucian, "The Passing of Peregrinus," c. 11–16). Some details in Lucian's satire cannot be taken literally because he hated Peregrinus and was not well-informed about Christians. But even though Lucian was an outsider, he knew that Christians were occasionally persecuted, that their leadership positions were open to strangers whom they accepted as their apostles, prophets, and teachers (Peregrinus was an educated man),

and that Christians rallied to the support of their imprisoned fellow believers.

A second-century Christian document, *The Teaching of the Twelve Apostles*, better known as the *Didache*, confirms Lucian's description of how itinerant missionaries could exploit Christians. The *Didache* was written when the itinerant ministry still functioned but local congregations were becoming wary about unorthodox teachers and freeloaders who claimed the venerable titles of apostle, prophet, and teacher. After the anonymous author of the *Didache* had concluded brief instructions on baptism, fasting, prayer, and the Eucharist, he continued: "And so, welcome anyone who comes and teaches you everything mentioned above. But if the teacher should himself turn away and teach something different, undermining these things, do not listen to him. But if his teaching brings righteousness and the knowledge of the Lord, then welcome him as the Lord. But act towards the apostles and prophets as the gospel decrees. Let every apostle who comes to you be welcomed as the Lord. But he should not remain more than a day. If he must, he may stay one more. But if he stays three days, he is a false prophet. When an Apostle leaves he should take nothing except bread, until he arrives at his night's lodging. If he asks for money, he is a false prophet....No prophet who orders a meal in the spirit shall eat of it; if he does, he is a false prophet...Do not listen to anyone who says in the spirit, 'Give me money' (or something else). But if he tells you to give to others who are in need, let no one judge him" (*The Didache*, c. 11 in *The Apostolic Fathers*, vol. 1, edited and translated by Bart D. Ehrman, LCL 24 [Cambridge, MA, and London, 2003], pp. 435–437).

Imagine telling Paul or Peter, who had been itinerant apostles but who had been dead for many decades when the *Didache* was written, that they could stay only one day! But circumstances had changed by the second century. The itinerant ministry was fading, in part under the weight of Christians' unhappy experience with apostles, prophets, and teachers who were money-grubbers and taught things that the local leaders thought were wrong. But the *Didache* did not say *never* to receive an itinerant missionary. There must have been a period in the second century when acceptable itinerant apostles, prophets, and teach-ers mingled with the unacceptable.

As the itinerant ministry slowly faded in pres-tige, the local ministry grew in self-confidence and importance. One of the shortest documents in the New Testament may give a glimpse of a local community's leader resisting the authority of a non-resident missionary. The author of the Third Letter of John identifies himself not as "John" but as "the Elder" or "Presbyter." Except for what the letter says, we know nothing about the people men-tioned in it. The Elder complained to a man named "Gaius" that he had written a letter to an unidenti-fied church, but a man named "Diotrephes" "did not acknowledge our authority" and was spread-ing within the church what the Elder called "false charges" against him. Diotrephes refused to wel-come brothers, perhaps itinerant missionaries, sent by the Elder, and he prevented other church members from giving hospitality to them. In fact, Diotrephes expelled from the congregation those who welcomed the Elder's messengers. Diotrephes was clearly a powerful leader in an unidentified local church—many members were following his orders. Otherwise the Elder would not have needed to write a letter of complaint. The Elder had some local supporters, including the otherwise unknown Gaius, to whom he wrote his letter. What might be going on? Diotrephes, who is given no title in the letter but whom the Elder described as one "who likes to put himself first," was one of the local lead-ers who no longer wanted this outsider, the Elder, to direct his congregation. In this brief letter, we may see a local church leader and some of his con-gregation refusing to obey an itinerant missionary and his representatives. The author of the early second-century Didache also encouraged the local leaders, whom he called in the plural "bishops" and "deacons," to reject the view that they were infe-rior to the itinerant prophets and teachers: "And so, elect for yourselves bishops and deacons who are worthy of the Lord, gentle men who are not fond of money, who are true and approved. And so, do not disregard them. For these are the ones who have found honor among you, along with the prophets and teachers" (Didache, c. 15, in The Apostolic Fathers, vol. 1, edited and translated by Bart D. Ehrman, LCL 24 [Cambridge, MA, and

London, 2003], p. 441). The Third Letter of John and the Didache point to a period in the first half of the second century when the local ministry was rising in influence even as the itinerant ministry was declining.

The Didache and other sources referred to bish-ops, elders, and deacons in the plural. In circum-stances not clear to us, a different way of organizing proto-orthodox Christian communities developed during the second century. One man, with the title episcopos, meaning "overseer," usually called "bishop" in English, became the leader of each local church. He was assisted and advised by two groups, one called "elders" or "presbyters" and the other called "deacons." The pace at which this three-leveled ministry emerged varied from region to region, although before the end of the second century it was the consensus on church organiza-tion among the proto-orthodox.

Ignatius, bishop of Antioch, provides the earliest clear evidence for the three-level ministry. In about 110 Roman soldiers transported Ignatius to Rome for execution. Ignatius wrote six letters to churches along the way in western Asia Minor, in which he indicated that the three-level ministry was normal in those places, although the local bishops had rivals and were not firmly in control. He addressed by name the bishop of each church to which he wrote in Asia Minor. He also wrote a letter to the Roman Church, but he did not name its leaders. In view of the confusion and strife within the early second-century Jesus Movement, it is no surprise that Ignatius commented on the internal divisions of the churches in Asia Minor. Some Christians, whom he called "judaizers," retained strong ties to Judaism; other Christians, perhaps gnostic in outlook, denied the reality of Christ's humanity. Ignatius belonged to a third group, whom he called "catholic" or "universal," who agreed neither with the judaizing Christians nor with the gnosticizing Christians. As a defense against internal divisions, Ignatius vigorously endorsed the three-level min-istry to the Christians at Smyrna. In that letter, he used the term "catholic" or "universal" for the first time in any surviving document to describe a church organized in the way he thought proper, that is, with a three-level ministry: "All of you should follow the bishop as Jesus Christ follows the Father; and follow the presbytery as you would the apostles. Respect the deacons as the commandment of God. Let no one do anything involving the church without the bishop. Let that eucharist be considered valid that occurs under the bishop or the one to whom he entrusts it. Let the congregation be wherever the bishop is; just as wherever Jesus Christ is, there also is the universal (or "catholic") church. It is not permitted to baptize or to hold a love feast without the bishop. But whatever he approves is acceptable to God...." (Ignatius, *Letter to the Smyrnaeans*, c. 8, in *The Apostolic Fathers*, vol. 1, edited and translated by Bart D. Ehrman, LCL 24 [Cambridge, MA, and London, 2003], pp. 303–305). Ignatius' emphasis on unity around one bishop, who was assisted by elders and deacons, was the earliest statement of what became a decisive feature of proto-orthodox churches. During the second century, the three-level ministry spread to all proto-orthodox churches, which set them apart from the many groups of Christians who were organized in other ways.

Why did the three-level ministry succeed? The historical sources are not adequate to provide a complete answer. As a consequence there has been controversy. I suggest that several factors converged to strengthen that form of organization. First, *liturgy* was crucial in the internal development of proto-orthodox churches. The meaning of the term "liturgy" evolved over time. In Greco-Roman society, citizens were sometimes obliged to perform unpaid labor, called in Greek "liturgies," for the city or state. They did such things as repair roads and city walls. The worship of the state's gods was also obligatory and sometimes called "liturgy." As Christian rituals took form, they were called "liturgy" because believers owed or offered them freely to God.

The main liturgical activities in proto-orthodox churches were baptism and the Eucharist. From early days, they were regarded as holy things, not to be given too easily to those who sought them. Already in the 50s, Paul emphasized to his converts at Corinth the holiness of the Eucharistic meal of bread and wine. He issued a dire warning: "Whoever, therefore, eats the bread or drinks the cup of the Lord in an unworthy manner will be answerable for the body and blood of the Lord.

Examine yourselves, and only then eat of the bread and drink of the cup. For all who eat and drink without discerning the body, eat and drink judgment against themselves. For this reason many of you are weak and ill, and some have died" (1 Cor 11:27–30). The early second-century *Didache* declared "let no one eat or drink from your thanksgiving meal unless they have been baptized in the name of the Lord. For also the Lord has said about this, 'Do not give what is holy to the dogs.'" (*Didache*, c. 9 in *The Apostolic Fathers*, vol. 1, edited and translated by Bart D. Ehrman, LCL 24 [Cambridge, MA, and London, 2003], p. 431). The decision as to who was worthy to be baptized or to eat the bread and drink the wine was—and, in some churches, still is—a serious issue. The reluctance to offer the Eucharist without assurances of the recipient's worthiness strengthened the position of the bishop, who presided at that liturgical ritual. Ignatius indicated that the bishop had (or should have) a monopoly on important liturgical activity. He alone should preside at baptism, the Eucharist, and love feasts, or he could authorize others to act in his place. Because the bishop presided, he probably took a leading role in deciding who was fit for baptism or the Eucharist. He could decide who was and was not a member of the group.

The bishop's importance as chief liturgical figure in his community was strengthened by his claim to special authority to teach. In the second century, there was much disagreement about where to find the true teaching of and about Jesus. Some gnostic Christians based their teaching on visions and dreams in which Jesus spoke directly to them. But most competing Christian groups agreed that reliable teaching must be "apostolic," that is, connected somehow to Jesus' first followers and through them to him. But there was fierce disagreement about how to find that apostolic connection. Some gnostic Christians asserted that they had access to Jesus' teaching because it was passed down to them secretly in an oral form. The uncertainty about where apostolic teaching could be found was made more intense because a bewildering variety of written documents—gospels, acts, letters, and apocalypses—circulated under the names of apostles and other companions of Jesus, such as Mary Magdalene and Jesus' brother James. Finally, the oral teaching of itinerant apostles, prophets, and teachers muddied the waters even further. They claimed to speak in the name of Jesus, but who could be sure?

The proto-orthodox Christians developed their own views on how apostolic teaching was transmitted from Jesus' apostles to them. They emphasized the bishop as the key link in that chain of transmission. In contradiction to gnostic Christians, they argued that their beliefs were not based on *secret* traditions but rather on *public* teaching by bishops, whom they identified as the living successors to the apostles. In the history of theology, the view that bishops teach as the apostles did and hold offices originated by apostles is called the "doctrine of apostolic succession"—bishops are successors to the apostles. To support that view, some proto-orthodox Christians tried to establish specific historical chains of succession from the apostles to their living second-century bishops. They argued that reliable apostolic teaching could be found in the oldest apostolic churches, which generally meant those mentioned in the New Testament. They claimed for those churches a line of named bishops that stretched back to the era of the apostles or even to a particular apostle. They also argued that when living bishops were consistent with one another in the main lines of teaching, that was proof of the continuity of apostolic teaching in their churches. For instance, Hegesippus, who died about 180, talked with bishops while he was traveling to Rome from somewhere in the east. Eusebius of Caesarea quoted in his *Ecclesiastical History* from Hegesippus' lost five books of "Memoirs":

> Now Hegesippus, in his five Memoirs which have come down to us, has left behind a very complete record of his personal views. And in his Memoirs he tells us that on a journey as far as Rome he associated with very many bishops, and that he received the same teaching from all...In fact...., he adds as follows [Eusebius now quoted Hegesippus]:
>
> And the church of the Corinthians continued in the true doctrine until Primus was bishop at Corinth....With them I associated on my voyage to Rome, and I abode with the Corinthians many days; during which we were refreshed together in true doctrine. But when I came to Rome, I made for myself a succession [list] as far as Anicetus [about 155–about 166]....And Soter [about 166–175] received the succession from Anicetus; after whom came Eleutherus [about 175–189]. And in every succession [of bishops] and in every city that which the Law and the Prophets and the Lord preach is faithfully followed [by the bishops]. (EH 4.22)

Thus, Hegesippus not only compared teachings among the bishops he met but also made a list of bishops at Rome that he believed went back to the apostolic era, which by then was more than a century in the past.

In the later second century, Irenaeus of Lyons wrote a long work against gnostic Christians in which he stated at some length the argument that the living bishops succeeded both to the offices and to the teaching of the apostles:

> ...and we are in a position to enumerate those who were by the apostles instituted bishops in the Churches, and [to demonstrate] the successors of these men to our own times; those who neither taught nor knew of anything like what these [heretics] rave about. For if the apostles had known hidden mysteries, which they were in the habit of imparting to the "perfect" apart and privately from the rest, they would have delivered them especially to those to whom they were also committing the Churches themselves. For they [the apostles] were desirous that these men [their successors] should be very perfect and blameless in all things, whom also they were leaving behind as their successors, delivering up their own place of government to these men; which men, if they discharged their functions honestly, would be a great boon [to the Church], but if they should fall away, the direst calamity. (Irenaeus, *Against Heresies*, 3.1, in ANF, vol. 1, p. 415)

To support his claim about unbroken continuity from the apostles to his own day, Irenaeus then named Peter and Paul as the founders of the Roman Church and traced twelve Roman bishops from Linus, reputed to be Peter's appointee, to Eleutherus (171–189), who was bishop at the time Irenaeus wrote. Irenaeus also traced the succession of bishops at Smyrna, his home town in Asia Minor, where he claimed that the long-lived bishop Polycarp, martyred about 156, had been appointed a bishop by the "apostles." Thus, Hegesippus, Irenaeus, and other second-century proto-orthodox Christians argued that the orderly, public succession of bishops in the "oldest churches," such as Rome and Smyrna, guaranteed the authenticity and apostolic origins of their teaching against rival forms of teaching. The position of bishops was strengthened by the belief that in each local church they were the living bearers of the apostles' teaching, which they proclaimed in their public teaching.

The doctrine of apostolic succession had important implications for the church of the city of Rome. The Roman Church was among the most ancient churches and had, so to speak, a double helping of apostolic teaching from Peter and Paul, who were believed to have taught, died martyrs' deaths, and been buried in Rome. Irenaeus argued that if churches encountered an uncertainty or disagreement, they could settle the matter by examining "[t]hat tradition derived from the apostles, of the very great, the very ancient, and universally known church founded and organized at Rome by the two most glorious apostles, Peter and Paul...." (Irenaeus, *Against Heresies*, 3.1 in ANF, vol. 1, p. 415). What was taught or done in the Roman church counted heavily, although in the second century the Roman bishop could not order other independent bishops to do anything.

A third source of authority for bishops was the need for leadership in a hostile society. In the second century, scattered but fierce persecution of Christian communities broke out every now and then. Bishops provided leadership in such times of trouble and often regathered churches when the persecution ended. During the second century, proto-orthodox Christians came to a consensus that each bishop was the leader in the local church. The pace of change varied from place to place, but the move toward enhancing the bishop's authority was clear. His supporters saw him as the successor of the apostles and the living teacher of apostolic truth. He was also the chief liturgical and disciplinary figure, who with advice from the elders determined those who were worthy for baptism and the Eucharist. In some large churches, such as Alexandria, the bishop supervised a school for the numerous converts, called "catechumens," who were being prepared for baptism. Each bishop monopolized the right to ordain an elder or a deacon by laying on his hands, accompanied by appropriate prayers. He supervised and sometimes paid the clergy in his church out of the offerings of the congregation. Other clergy might preside at liturgical services and teach but only in agreement with him. He might be a charismatic himself, able to utter prophecies or speak in tongues, but even if he was not a charismatic he claimed the right to test and supervise the charismatics in his church. In company with other bishops, he could lay hands on a man and make him a bishop. Local bishops and congregations were united to other sharers in the proto-orthodox consensus by the frequent exchange of messengers and letters. Many of the surviving sources are letters from one bishop to another. During the second century, proto-orthodox Christians adopted the three-level ministry of bishop, elders, and deacons. But other patterns of organization survived as long as rival Christian groups did. The proto-orthodox consensus was just that—an agreement among some Christians about important issues.

Developments in the second century also shaped significantly the situation of women within proto-orthodox Christianity. Paul took the activity of women for granted. He called some women "fellow workers," who supported male missionaries. Some of these women were important in their local churches, including Phoebe (Rom 16:1–3) and Pricilla/Prisca (1 Cor 16:19). Paul described his relative Junia as prominent among the apostles (Rom 16:7). Women also received the spiritual "gifts," perhaps especially the gift of prophecy. For instance, the four virgin daughters of Philip the Evangelist were said to be prophetesses (Acts 21:8–9). But even in Paul's day there were also tensions about the roles open to women. At Corinth, women were active in the church assembly, where they prayed and prophesied. Paul did not approve. At one point, he ordered that they cover their heads in worship (1 Cor 11:2–16). After his relatively long argument about the need to regulate the "gifts" of speaking in tongues and prophecy, Paul added, "As in all the churches of the saints, women should be silent in the churches. For they are not permitted to speak, but should be subordinate....If there is anything they desire to know, let them ask their husbands at home. For it is shameful for a woman to speak in church" (1 Cor 14:33–35). If Paul wrote the first letter to Timothy or if, as many scholars believe, a disciple wrote the letter in Paul's name, the growing reluctance to let women take prominent roles in church was reinforced. "Let a woman [perhaps "wife"] learn in silence with full submission. I permit no woman to teach or to have authority over a man; she is to keep silent. For Adam was formed first, then Eve; and Adam was not deceived, but the woman was deceived and became a transgressor" (1 Tim 2:11–14). Such prohibitions would not have been needed if women were not actually praying, prophesying, and otherwise speaking in the assemblies. The gospels, some written decades after Paul's letters, said that women had accompanied and supported Jesus and his earliest followers, although no canonical gospel records that Jesus "called" any woman to be an apostle. Luke wrote that Jesus had seventy disciples, but there is no evidence one way or the other about women being among them (Lk 10). From the second century onward, the roles open to women became a prominent dividing line between proto-orthodox and some other Christians. Even as women were restricted among the proto-orthodox Christians, their prominence among some, but not all, rival groups grew. For instance, the Montanist Christians, who will be treated later in this chapter, believed that their prophetesses Priscilla and Maximilla were inspired directly by the Holy Spirit. Epiphanius of Salamis (310/320–403) reported that the Montanists of his times had female bishops and elders, which appears to be confirmed by an inscription from Asia Minor (Epiphanius, *Panarion*, 48:5–6). In certain gnostic groups, women held prominent religious roles. Tertullian (active about 200) was horrified at what some North African gnostic women did: "The very women of these heretics, how wanton they are! For they are bold enough to teach, to dispute, to enact exorcisms, to undertake cures—it may be even to baptize" (Tertullian, *On Prescription against*

Heretics, c. 41 in ANF, vol. 3, p. 263). But notice that he did not say they performed such clerical functions as presiding at the Eucharist; he was even unsure about whether they baptized. Tertullian also criticized the anti-baptismal teaching of a woman, whom he called a "viper," who led a group in North Africa that was winning converts from his group (Tertullian, *De baptismo*, c. 1).

As proto-orthodox Christians rejected what they regarded as the disorder and error that Montanism and gnostic Christianities seemed to encourage, their exclusion of women from public religious roles and especially from membership in the ordained clergy hardened. There was one exception or perhaps an ambiguous case: the deaconesses. In the churches of the eastern Mediterranean, except for Egypt, some women served as deaconesses, whose main duties were to care for ill women, to help women at baptism, and perhaps to instruct women before or after baptism. When baptismal candidates, including adult women, were baptized, they were naked. It must have seemed inappropriate that male bishops, elders, and deacons see or anoint the naked bodies of adult women. The deaconesses assisted the male clergy in that circumstance and probably in others where modesty was expected.

The Greek word *diakonia* means "service," and the deaconesses surely provided services to women. But the modern debate asks the question whether the ancient deaconesses were clergy, which as a practical matter means whether they were put into office with a laying-on of hands. The ancient sources are divided and vary by region. In canon 19, the Council of Nicaea (325) declared that because deaconesses did not receive a laying-on of hands they were laywomen, not clergy. In the later fourth century, some documents from Syria stated that deaconesses were ordained and hence clergy. But as infant baptism replaced adult baptism, the need for female helpers diminished. Deaconesses were never accepted as clergy in the western church and gradually ceased to be appointed in the eastern churches. The ordained clergy in proto-orthodox churches remained male.

There is some evidence that there were more women than men who were Christians. Women who had wealth or power wielded practical influence as donors of gifts and protectors of churches.

Prestigious religious roles were open to women. Martyrdom did not distinguish between the sexes. Female martyrs were admired and remembered in written accounts, buried in places of honor, and commemorated in the church's prayers. As the ascetic movement gained strength within Christianity, the virgin and the chaste widow also emerged as admired, praised, and influential figures.

In a process that took place across several generations in the second century, the consensus about the need for a three-level ministry set proto-orthodox Christian congregations apart from many rivals. That separation contributed stability and continuity and set up boundaries against rival forms of Christianity.

CREEDS AND RULES OF FAITH

The three-level ministry, effective as it was in uniting local proto-orthodox Christian communities in the face of theological rivals and persecution, was not the only important development in the second and third centuries. The proto-orthodox Christians tried to state in a brief form the consensus of what they regarded as essentials of the teaching of the apostles. The process of creating statements of belief went on simultaneously with the rise of the three-level ministry and, as we shall see later in this chapter, with the creation of a canon of scripture.

From early in the history of the Jesus Movement, believers sought for ways to sum up who Jesus was. The earliest statements of belief were often brief, although not simple. For instance, Paul wrote that "Jesus Christ is Lord" (Phil 2:11). In Matthew 16:16, Peter declared to Jesus, "You are the Christ, Son of the Living God." The brevity of such statements of belief left them open to widely differing interpretations. Many rival Christian groups could accept that Jesus was Lord or the Christ, as long as that was understood in their way. Sometimes proto-orthodox leaders recommended that their followers not listen to the rival views. For instance, Ignatius of Antioch praised the Christians at Ephesus because "you no longer listen to anyone, except one who speaks truthfully about Jesus Christ" (Ignatius, *Letter to the Ephesians*, c. 6 in *The Apostolic Fathers*, vol. 1, edited and translated by Bart D. Ehrman, LCL 24 [Cambridge, MA, and London, 2003], p. 227). But in the lively religious atmosphere of the first and second centuries, such a block-your-ears approach to rival views had limited success. Because those who try to refute an opposing view need a clear grasp of their own view of the issue, controversy often sharpens the way beliefs are described. Some proto-orthodox Christian writers and local churches experimented with brief statements about what they believed, especially on the points that separated them from their main second-century rivals, the many kinds of gnostic Christians. The importance of statements of belief should not be overlooked. For centuries, most Christians, who were illiterate, knew the stories about Jesus and the interpretations attached to them primarily because they heard them read aloud in services, interpreted in sermons, and, in later times, depicted in art. If such people memorized a brief statement of belief, they might be "inoculated" against the ideas of other Christian groups.

Proto-orthodox Christians had various ways to sum up their consensus on important beliefs. Sometimes proto-orthodox writers incorporated into their works a "rule of faith," whose structure and wording were not fixed and could vary according to the author's circumstances. In his letter to the Christians at Smyrna, Ignatius of Antioch wrote a summary of his beliefs about Jesus that was clearly aimed against the Christians in that town who denied Jesus' physical reality. Note how he used the word "truly" to counter the view that Jesus only "appeared" to be human. "For I know that you have been made complete in a faith that cannot be moved—as if you were nailed to the cross of the Lord Jesus Christ in both flesh and spirit—and that you have been established in love by the blood of Christ. You are fully convinced about our Lord, that he was truly from the family of David according to the flesh, Son of God according to the will and power of God, truly born from a virgin, and baptized by John that all righteousness might be fulfilled by him. In the time of Pontius Pilate and the tetrarch Herod, he was truly nailed for us in the flesh...so that through his resurrection he might eternally lift up the standard for his holy and faithful ones, whether among Jews or Gentiles, in the body of his church" (Ignatius, *Letter to the Smyrnaeans*, c. 1, in *The Apostolic Fathers*, vol. 1, edited and translated by Bart D. Ehrman, LCL 24 [Cambridge, MA, and London, 2003], p. 297).

Some congregations also adopted statements of belief, called "creeds" because the Latin statements of belief began with the Latin word "credo," which means "I believe." The creeds are sometimes called "baptismal creeds" because they were often used at baptism, when converts fully committed themselves and when congregations fully accepted the converts. Because the converts decisively rejected their former lives and chose new lives at baptism, they needed to know what they were accepting. These creeds were more precise and fixed in their wording than the looser "rules of faith." They expressed the widely held consensus of proto-orthodox belief. Their repetition over decades gave the creeds a kind of authority that discouraged tampering with their words. In some places, the men and women preparing for baptism were told the exact words of the local church's creed, which they memorized and recited publicly just before baptism.

Most proto-orthodox Christian congregations probably had their own baptismal creed, often prized because it had been used for a long time. A creed might differ in some words from the creeds of other churches but usually had the same features. Creeds were generally Trinitarian in structure, moving from statements about the Father to statements about the Son to statements about the Holy Spirit, with other matters added at the end. When Rufinus of Aquileia commented on the creed of Aquileia, he compared it with what is called the "Old Roman Creed" (composed about 180): "I believe in God the Father Almighty and in Christ Jesus, his only son, our Lord who was born of the Holy Spirit and the Virgin Mary; who was crucified under Pontius Pilate and was buried and the third day rose from the dead; he ascended into heaven and sits on the right hand of the Father, whence he will come to judge the living and the dead; and [I believe] in the Holy Spirit; the holy church; the remission of sins; the resurrection of the flesh; [the life everlasting]" (Rufinus of Aquileia, *Commentary on the Apostles' Creed* in NPNF, second series, vol. 3, pp. 541–563). The western baptismal creeds of the fourth through sixth centuries were adapted from the Old Roman Creed. In the eastern churches after the fourth century, the ordinary baptismal creed was the one approved at the Council of Constantinople (381), which was heavily dependent on the Creed of the Council of Nicaea (325).

The creation of creeds gave an opportunity to all proto-orthodox Christians to memorize a brief summary of their faith, which could help them recognize and shun other views. The creeds, in conjunction with the three-level ministry, contributed to the stability of the communities that used them, especially by erecting a barrier of proto-orthodox consensus against other religious views.

THE CANON OF SCRIPTURE

It can be an idea that takes some time to absorb: The collection of writings called the "New Testament" did not exist in its present form during the first three or four centuries. Christians living in the first and second centuries had no single written thing called a "New Testament." For them, the "scriptures" were the Jewish Bible, which they usually read in the Greek translation called the "Septuagint." When the early Christians adopted the Septuagint as *their* sacred book and defended their theological views by quoting from it, Jews abandoned the Septuagint. Some Jews made new Greek translations, and others used only the documents written in Hebrew and Aramaic as their scriptures. The proto-orthodox Christians kept the Septuagint as their Old Testament.

The history of the formation of the New Testament is quite different from the formation of the Old Testament. For a generation or two after Jesus' death, his teachings circulated in oral forms. Beginning about 70 and perhaps earlier, a few Christians began to collect in written form the teachings of Jesus to which they had access, although the written documents did not put a sudden end to oral transmission. Competing groups within the wider Jesus Movement promoted their views by composing gospels, letters, sermons, apocalypses, and other texts, which were attributed to apostles or early Christian figures. Some of the documents were written to promote competing theological ideas. Some are difficult to put into a category because they seem to have been pious historical fiction written to satisfy curiosity about such things as Jesus' childhood.

During the second and third centuries, the swirl of texts attributed to apostles and other great figures of the early days posed a serious problem for believers of every sort. What written texts were to be accepted as a basis for belief? In response, proto-orthodox Christians began the long, messy task of gaining a consensus among themselves about those documents that they regarded as authoritative in the same way that they regarded the Old Testament as authoritative. An accepted list of scripture is called a "canon," from a Greek word meaning "a straight rod," a kind of yardstick by which things could be measured. In part, the proto-orthodox Christians may have been reacting against Marcion (died about 160), who created his own canon, which consisted of ten letters of Paul and a shortened version of Luke. In part, they were excluding from their churches the many texts of their Christian rivals.

The New Testament is an anthology, that is, a gathering of documents that were originally composed by different authors in different times, places, and circumstances. Perhaps ten or twelve different authors wrote the documents that were eventually included in the New Testament, which in its final form consisted of four gospels, one acts of the apostles, twenty-one letters, and an apocalypse, a total of twenty-seven documents. It would have been convenient for modern historians, theologians, and believers if some official pronouncement, perhaps by a council of bishops, had determined the table of contents of the New Testament. But that did *not* happen. The agreement on the canon of a New Testament was not a single event but rather a process carried out by mostly anonymous Christians who came to a consensus about which writings were authoritative for them.

By the middle of the second century, a "New Testament" was emerging, although it was not yet what you can buy in a modern bookstore. Irenaeus of Lyons (about 180) was the first writer to use the term "New Testament," which he placed on the same footing as the "Old Testament." But he did not state precisely what he included in that New Testament or why he accepted some documents and rejected others. No ancient source stated clearly all the principles on which some documents were accepted as authoritative and others were rejected.

However, from scattered statements in the writings of proto-orthodox Christians of the second, third, and fourth centuries, we can determine how some documents were included and others excluded. There was not one decisive criterion for inclusion. Instead, indicators of acceptability, often overlapping one another, converged. In light of the importance given to a connection to the apostolic tradition, it is no surprise that the proto-orthodox Christians expected that their sacred documents would be linked somehow to the apostles. In practice, that could not be a decisive matter because many Christian groups claimed that an apostle had composed their documents. To further complicate the link to the apostles, some of the proto-orthodox Christians' favorite texts, including Mark's gospel, Luke's gospel, and Luke's Acts, did not claim to be by apostles. As a second principle of inclusion and exclusion, proto-orthodox Christians expected that an acceptable document would agree more or less with what they already believed. The document had to be in harmony with the creeds of prestigious churches and with the traditional teaching of the bishops. That requirement eliminated many gnostic texts, which claimed apostles as authors but contradicted the proto-orthodox consensus on belief. A third criterion for inclusion or exclusion was whether the document had been cited approvingly by reliable "fathers" or had been read publicly in the oldest churches, especially those that could claim to have been founded by an apostle. If such churches used a document for official teaching or in public worship, there was a strong presumption of its authority. Bishops, who had a major say in what would be read in their liturgical assemblies, had a great part in the process of including some documents and excluding others. The process of choosing some written documents and excluding others took several centuries to complete. Many gnostic texts were rejected easily, both for their obvious contradictions to the proto-orthodox consensus and for their often mysterious style of writing. But the proto-orthodox Christians disagreed among themselves about some documents that were acceptable in their teaching, widely read, and relatively old. For instance, the *Teaching of the Twelve Apostles* (the *Didache*), the *First Letter of Clement*, the *Epistle of Barnabas*, and Hermas'

Shepherd were widely read for spiritual uplift or for the instruction of new converts. Although in some places and times there were proto-orthodox Christians who regarded those texts as valuable, none of them finally gained entry to the canon of scripture. Some proto-orthodox Christians had doubts about documents that were eventually included in the canon. For instance, Bishop Eusebius of Caesarea (260–339), who was quite interested in the scriptures of his day, accepted the authority of the Epistle to the Hebrews but reported that the Roman Church did not think the letter was by Paul. Eusebius himself had hesitations about including the Revelation of John, although the proto-orthodox consensus eventually accepted it.

There is no need to exaggerate the uncertainties and differences of opinion among proto-orthodox Christians about the documents they accepted. By the later second century, a consensus had developed among them about the *core* of a New Testament, which included the four canonical gospels and the letters of Paul. For instance, the Muratorian Fragment, probably written at Rome about 200, throws considerable light on canon-making and on the canon at that time in that place. It is called "Muratorian" from its eighteenth-century discoverer, Lodovico Muratori, and it is called a "Fragment" because the first page is missing. The Muratorian Fragment began with a partial sentence referring to Mark's gospel. It said that Luke's gospel was the "third," so the gospels of Matthew and Mark must have been treated on the missing page. The unknown author of the Fragment has a sort of New Testament (not yet the canonical New Testament) that consists of the gospels of Matthew, Mark, Luke, and John, Luke's Acts of the Apostles, thirteen letters of Paul (he warns readers against two other letters he says were forged in Paul's name), the letter of Jude, two out of the three canonical letters of John, and the Apocalypse of John. Thus, of the twenty-seven documents that were eventually included in the New Testament, the author of the Muratorian Fragment accepted twenty-two. He did omit five: the letter to the Hebrews, the letter of James, the third letter of John, and the first and second letters of Peter. The author approved "The Wisdom written by the Friends of Solomon" that was not finally received

into the New Testament canon. He wrote approvingly of the "Apocalypse of Peter," although he conceded that "some of our friends will not have it read in church." Some second-century Christians regarded the book called the *Shepherd*, written by a visionary named "Hermas," as authoritative. The author of the Muratorian Fragment used the criterion of apostolic connection to eliminate Hermas' *Shepherd*. He knew that Hermas lived in the mid-second century and had made no claim to a direct link to the apostles. The author regarded the *Shepherd* as so pious and orthodox that Christians could read it privately for their own edification but should not read it publicly in church. The Fragment ended with the rejection of some gnostic texts and some texts associated with Marcion of Sinope. On the one hand, the Muratorian Fragment is a snapshot of the as-yet-incomplete process that created the New Testament. On the other hand, it shows that about 200 the proto-orthodox consensus had embraced the guts of a New Testament, especially four gospels and Paul's letters. But differences of opinion persisted for a long time about some documents, including the Apocalypse of John, the Letter to the Hebrews, the letter of James, and some of the other letters in the back of a modern New Testament.

A letter of Bishop Athanasius of Alexandria (died 373) listed for the first time the canon of the New Testament exactly as it is today. In his *Life of Constantine* (3.18), Eusebius wrote that the Council of Nicaea (325) settled long-standing disputes about determining the date on which the festival of Easter should occur. The Pascha, as it was called in Greek, was to be observed on the first Sunday after the first full moon after the spring equinox, which was fixed at March 21. As a consequence, the date of Easter was different every year, as it still is. Some bishops apparently could not calculate the correct date. The powerful bishops of Alexandria customarily informed the Egyptian bishops in the villages scattered along the Nile River what the date of Easter was in any given year. They took the occasion to instruct the bishops on other matters. In his Easter Letter of 367, Bishop Athanasius sent to the bishops of Egypt a list of the New Testament books, which corresponds for the first

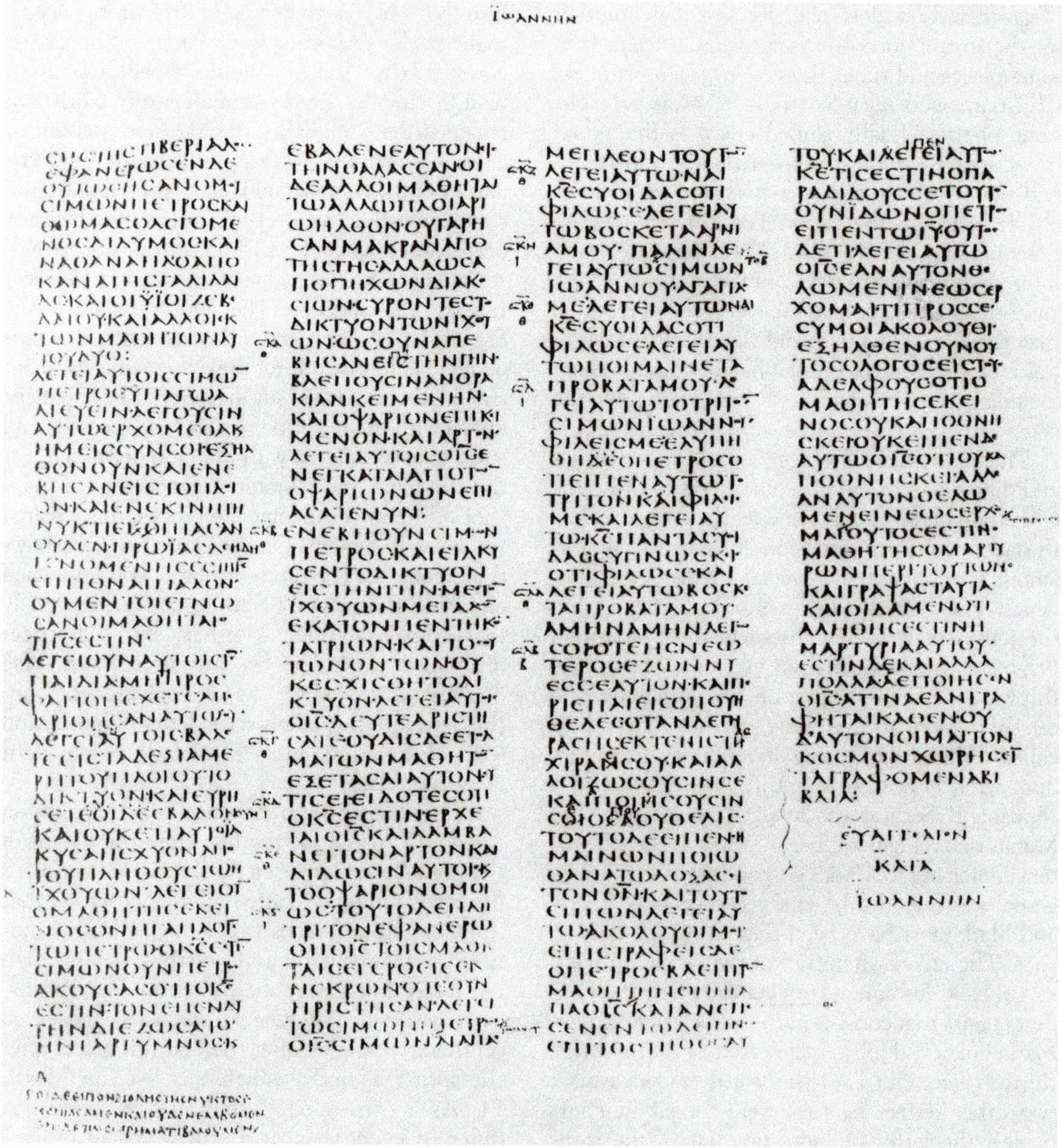

Figure 6.1 The Codex Sinaiticus. Written in the mid-fourth century, the "Bible of Sinai" may be the oldest surviving Bible. It was discovered in St. Catherine's Monastery on Mount Sinai in the nineteenth century. The codex contained both the Old and New Testaments in Greek. The manuscript also included the Epistle of Barnabas and the Shepherd by Hermas, which indicates that even around 350, the canon of scripture was fluid. In 1933 the British government and people bought the manuscript that had belonged to the Russian Czar, from the Bolsheviks. It is now in the British Library. *(HIP / Art Resource, NY)*

time exactly to the twenty-seven items in the New Testament canon. He also listed twenty-two books that he recognized as comprising the Old Testament canon. Athanasius did not suddenly invent this canonical list—he was repeating what was accepted at Alexandria and elsewhere. But his need to specify the canon probably indicated that there was still uncertainty about the precise list of authoritative documents. His list of the canonical books probably had no official standing outside his regional church, but it reveals a crucial moment when one important church regarded the canon in its modern form as complete. In three church councils, one at Hippo (393) and two at Carthage (397 and 419), Bishop Augustine of Hippo reaffirmed the modern canon of the New Testament. When Jerome (about 346–420) revised the competing Latin translations of the New Testament, he included only books in the consensus. As his Latin version of the New Testament, called the "Vulgate," gained acceptance, the books it contained were regarded in the west as the "New Testament." By the middle to late fourth century, the debate over the canon was virtually settled, although regional views and even personal preferences persisted in adding books, at least for a while.

In spite of the hesitations, by the later second century proto-orthodox Christians had agreed on the core of a canon that gradually distinguished their churches from those of their rivals and gave them a common basis on which to construct their theologies and to model their practices.

During the second century, proto-orthodox Christian communities had gradually separated themselves into a distinct group within the Jesus Movement. No one ordered the changes, no one planned them. But a consensus developed among like-minded Christians. They organized around the threefold ministry of one bishop, multiple elders, and multiple deacons. They began to state in "rules of faith" and brief creeds what they believed. They moved in fits and starts toward an agreed-upon canon of scripture. Proto-orthodox Christian communities were taking on what we may call a "shape," a set of institutions, attitudes, and internal arrangements that persisted for more than a thousand years, in some churches to modern times.

A CASE STUDY: THE NEW PROPHECY

The proto-orthodox consensus about bishop, creed, and scriptural canon did not end debate even among the proto-orthodox themselves. A voluntary consensus can have built-in seeds of dissent. Proto-orthodox Christians experienced divisions among themselves, a recurring fact that has persisted into modern times. Some proto-orthodox Christians resisted the consolidation around bishop, creed, and canon. For instance, the confessors who had bravely survived persecution claimed a special status and authority that occasionally clashed with those of the bishops. In the early third century, Hippolytus noted that a confessor who had been in actual chains for the Lord's name was accorded the honor of being a presbyter or a deacon without a laying-on of hands. But if such a confessor was chosen bishop, then he needed a laying-on of hands as any bishop did (*Apostolic Tradition*, c. 9). At Carthage in the 250s, confessors issued letters reconciling other Christians who had lapsed during persecution. Some confessors imposed no penance on those they reconciled. Bishop Cyprian of Carthage opposed their right to reconcile without suitable penance. He thought they should allow the bishops to impose penances. He warned the confessors not to fall into arrogance and defy the bishops. The disagreement was heated.

I shall describe one important division within the proto-orthodox Christian group, but there were many. First- and second-century Christian sources respectfully mentioned living prophets and prophetesses. But in the later second century, the livelier forms of spirit possession, such as speaking in tongues, had become rarer, were, in fact, dying out, but had not yet disappeared. In particular, ecstatic (literally "to stand outside oneself") prophecy fell out of favor in proto-orthodox Christian communities, probably because it was so disruptive. But the common belief that the Holy Spirit picked out individuals to receive spiritual gifts had the potential to threaten the as-yet-immature consensus about bishop, creed, and canon. Some prophets and prophetesses clashed with the emerging authority of bishops when they claimed to bypass their authority and speak directly from the Spirit.

Montanus (active in the second half of the second century) lived in Phrygia in Asia Minor, territory where there had been Christian churches in some towns for more than one hundred years. Perhaps to discredit Montanus, his enemies said that before he converted to Christianity he had been a priest in the violent, bloody worship of the goddess Cybele. In about 170 (the date is uncertain), he began to prophesy in an unconscious, ecstatic manner, that is, he acted as if a spirit had seized him, taken over his mind, and spoke through his mouth. He was joined by two prophetesses, Maximilla and Priscilla, who were co-leaders of the New Prophecy, as supporters called the movement. Opponents called it the "Phrygian heresy." Only in the fourth century was the group called "Montanist," after its early leading figure. Montanus may have believed that he was the Paraclete (the "Comforter" or "Advocate") or the spokesman for the Paraclete, which Jesus had promised to the disciples in John 14:25–26: "I have said these things to you while I am still with you. But the Advocate, the Holy Spirit, whom the Father will send in my name, will teach you everything, and remind you of all that I have said to you."

When Montanus, Priscilla, and Maximilla began to prophesy in their out-of-body way, proto-orthodox Christian communities in Asia Minor experienced a great stir. Some people welcomed what they thought was a new outpouring of the Spirit, and others opposed it. The followers of the New Prophecy were proto-orthodox Christians, who did not reject the ordinary beliefs of their fellow Christians. They shared with other proto-orthodox Christians an opposition to gnostic forms of thought. The New Prophets were literalists in reading the scriptures. They believed there would be a real second coming of Christ (which they thought was very near), followed by a real resurrection of the dead. Most of their views fit well within the emerging proto-orthodox consensus of belief. The new aspect of the message of the New Prophets was about how Christians should prepare for Jesus' return. The prophets wanted a return to the early days of Christianity (as they imagined them), by then more than a century in the past, when strict moral behavior, the visible manifestations of the Spirit, and the vivid expectation of Jesus' return were intertwined. By Montanus' day

different Christian groups dealt with the delay of the Jesus' second coming in their own ways. Most gnostic Christians, for whom salvation was an individual journey of escape from matter and ignorance of self, rejected the very notion of a second coming of Jesus. Many other Christians continued to believe that Jesus would ultimately return but did not concern themselves much with when it would happen. But then, as now, some Christians thought that they saw in their own day the signs of Jesus' return. The New Prophets' ardent hopes for Jesus' imminent return, coupled with their claims that the spirit of prophecy spoke through them, provoked significant divisions within some second-century churches.

The followers of the New Prophecy claimed that God's Spirit was speaking again through their prophets, whose revelations legitimately completed the Law, the Old Testament prophets, and the gospels. The sayings of Priscilla, Maximilla, and Montanus were collected, probably in imitation of the Old Testament prophets such as Isaiah and Jeremiah, who had entire biblical books devoted to their utterances. The collections of prophecies do not survive, but proto-orthodox Christian critics sometimes quoted them in order to refute them. The following prophecies give some of the flavor of the New Prophecy.

1) Christ (or the Spirit) was reported to have said through the ecstatic Montanus: "Lo, the man is as a lyre [a musical instrument], and I fly over him as a pick [the instrument to pluck the strings of the lyre]. The man sleepeth, while I watch. Lo, it is the Lord that distracteth the hearts of men and giveth the heart to men" (Epiphanius, *Panarion*, 48.3.11, in *The Panarion of Epiphanius of Salamis: Books II and III (Sects 47–80, De Fide)*, translated by Frank Williams, Nag Hammadi and Manichaen Studies, vol. xxxvi [Leiden, New York, Cologne, 1994], pp. 9–10).

2) In another prophecy, Montanus said: "I am the Lord God, the Almighty, dwelling in man." And in another place, "Neither angel nor ambassador, but I the Lord, God the Father, have come" (Epiphanius, *Panarion*, translated by Frank Williams, 48.11.1, p. 16; 48.11.9, p. 17).

3) The prophetess Maximilla said: "Hearken not unto me but hearken unto Christ" and "After

me will be no prophet more, but the consummation [the end of the world]..." (Epiphanius, *Panarion*, translated by Frank Williams, 48.12.4, p. 17; 48.2.4, p. 7).

4) The prophetess Priscilla predicted the descent of the New Jerusalem at a place in Asia Minor near the little towns of Tymion and Pepouza: "Christ came to me dressed in a white robe in the form of a woman, imbued me with wisdom, and revealed to me that this place [Pepouza] is holy, and that Jerusalem will descend from heaven there" (Epiphanius, *Panarion*, translated by Frank Williams, 49.1.3, p. 21).

5) When Christian bishops and their communities began to reject the New Prophecy, Maximilla spoke thus in the name of her Spirit: "I am driven as a wolf from the sheep. I am not a wolf. I am word and spirit and power" (An anonymous opponent of Montanism quoted by Eusebius, EH 5.16.17).

In the history of Christianity, persecution almost always led to or intensified the conviction that the end of the world was very near. In the later second century, there were some bloody local persecutions of Christians in Asia Minor, where the New Prophecy originated. In preparation for the world's end and the last judgment, the prophets announced the need for rigorous self-denial, including severe fasting and sexual abstinence that apparently went beyond that required in other proto-orthodox congregations. In response to the prophets' utterances, some followers abandoned their jobs and families to wait for Christ's return near the little towns of Pepouza and Tymion. The followers of the New Prophecy shared with other Christians a deep admiration for the martyrs who bravely died for their faith. An unidentified prophet emphasized the desirability of martyrdom: "Do not hope to die in bed...or in languishing fevers, but in martyrdom, so that he [that is, Jesus] who suffered for you may be glorified" (Quoted in Robert M. Grant, *Second Century Christianity: A Collection of Fragments*, second edition [Louisville and London, 2003], p. 42). Some followers of the New Prophecy perhaps provoked the Roman authorities into killing them so as to hasten Jesus' return. When Montanus, Priscilla, and Maximilla died, they were buried at Pepouza, which remained the center for the Montanist Christians

until the tombs and bones were destroyed under the Emperor Justinian in the sixth century.

The New Prophets, at least in the beginning, were proto-orthodox Christians in almost every way, but they became "schismatics," that is, people whose behavior produced a schism, literally a "division," in many Christian communities. They shared the beliefs and rituals of the proto-orthodox Christians but went further in accepting an ecstatic style of prophecy, a vivid expectation of Jesus' return, a really strict ascetic discipline, and the prominence of women. By the mid-second century, none of these was within the general proto-orthodox consensus. The New Prophecy had widespread support or at least tolerance because many proto-orthodox Christians thought prophecy was possible and desirable. But others disagreed. The prophets raised a vital question: Could there be a third revelation, a third testament, to take its place alongside the Old Testament and the emerging New Testament? Proto-orthodox Christians lined up on both sides because the prophets seemed to have a case. First, there had been prophets in the Old Testament and in the New Testament. Why not now? Second, some proto-orthodox Christians admired stern self-denial, to which Montanist Christians were very devoted. Third, many proto-orthodox Christians admired martyrs who imitated Jesus in a literal way: The New Prophecy produced martyrs. The defenders of the prophets quoted Matthew 23:29–32 against their opponents: "Woe to you, scribes and Pharisees, hypocrites! For you build the tombs of the prophets and decorate the graves of the righteous, and you say, 'If we had lived in the days of our ancestors, we would not have taken part with them in shedding the blood of the prophets.' Thus you testify against yourselves that you are descendants of those who murdered the prophets. Fill up, then, the measure of your ancestors." Many proto-orthodox Christians were reluctant to be seen as "prophet-slayers" who tried to silence the Spirit of God.

After a period of hesitation, the bishops in Asia Minor opposed the New Prophecy. They did not deny that the Spirit *might* choose to speak through living people but not through these people. Theological disagreements among Christians have often been conducted in an atmosphere of ridicule or vicious personal attacks. An opponent is thought to be not just wrong but, in fact, evil.

There is a Latin phrase for such an attitude, *odium theologicum* ("theological hatred"). Opponents of the prophets attacked not only the ecstatic *way* that they prophesied but also their personal character. They asked where Montanus' prophecy came from: "Was he possessed by a Holy Spirit or Satan?" A group of bishops once tried to exorcize Maximilla on grounds that an evil spirit spoke through her. Her supporters prevented them.

The New Prophecy set in motion an important institution in Christian history. Across Asia Minor and soon elsewhere, bishops met to deal with the challenge to their authority posed by the New Prophecy. Meetings of bishops, called "councils" in Latin and "synods" in Greek, became the ordinary way for proto-orthodox and later orthodox Christian communities to settle disputes about belief and discipline, although they did not always succeed. The bishops in Asia Minor rejected the New Prophecy and expelled its followers from their communion. But its appeal continued among some segments of the rank-and-file. The New Prophecy spread to North Africa, where the great Tertullian was sympathetic to it. He might even have left proto-orthodox Christianity to join a prophetic group in about 208, although that is not certain. At Rome, opinion was divided over the New Prophecy. In Gaul, where many Christians were emigrants from Asia Minor, the prophets and their martyrs were viewed favorably. Montanist congregations survived for at least three centuries, but they were decisively outside the proto-orthodox consensus.

The emergence of a distinct proto-orthodox Christian consensus that was shared by a loose federation of churches was neither quick nor simple, but it had firmed up by about 200. Other forms of Christianity continued, but the proto-orthodox Christians more and more constituted the main line of development, even though they were prone to split among themselves, as the New Prophecy vividly showed.

FURTHER READING

Ancient Sources

Ron Cameron, ed., (the Westminster Press, 1982), *The Other Gospels: Non-Canonical Gospel Texts*, edited by A

manageable selection of translations and explanations of sixteen gospels or gospel fragments.

Bart D. Ehrman, *Lost Scriptures: Books That Did Not Make It into the New Testament* (Oxford and New York, 2003). A rich collection of translated non-canonical gospels, acts, epistles, apocalypses, and ancient efforts to list canonical books of the New Testament.

J. K. Elliott, ed. (Oxford, 1993) *The Apocryphal New Testament*, has 747 pages devoted to Christian writings that were not received into the canon of the New Testament.

Andrew Louth, ed., The *Didache* in *Early Christian Writings*, translated by the editor (Harmondsworth, 1987), pp. 191–199. A brief but crucial document for the study of early Christianity.

Maxwell Staniforth, trans., Ignatius of Antioch, *The Epistles of Ignatius*, revised translation, with introductions and new editorial material by Andrew Louth (Harmondsworth, 1987), pp. 53–112. Full of insights about early second-century Christianity.

Alistair Stewart-Sykes, trans., Hippolytus, *On the Apostolic Tradition*, an English version with introduction and commentary (Crestwood, NY, 2001). A difficult text that gives important insights into many facets of Christianity in the early third century.

Modern Works

Roger Gryson, *The Ministry of Women in the Early Church*, translated by Jean Laporte and Mary Louise Hall (Collegeville, MN, 1976).

Ronald E. Heine, *The Montanist Oracles and Testimonia*, North American Patristic Society, Patristic Monograph Series 14 (Macon, GA, 1989). A collection of 148 ancient and medieval documents that refer to Montanism.

J. N. D. Kelly, *Early Christian Creeds*, third edition (1972). A thorough, demanding treatment of the emergence and development of early Christian statements of belief.

Kevin Madigan and Carolyn Osiek ed., trans., *Ordained Women in the Early Church: A Documentary History*, edited and translated by (Baltimore and London, 2005). In this book you can read in translation the complex sources on deaconesses in early Christianity.

Bruce M. Metzger, *The Canon of the New Testament: Its Origin, Development and Significance* (Oxford, 1987). An excellent treatment of the processes by which the canon of scripture came into existence. Metzger translated the Muratorian Fragment on pp. 305–307.

Christine Trevett, *Montanism: Gender, Authority and the New Prophecy* (Cambridge, 1996).

CHAPTER 7

Roman Society and the Christians

Between the first and third centuries, competing forms of Christianity struggled against one another, primarily with written and spoken words. In contrast, Roman officeholders and urban mobs inflicted real violence against Christians. Countless modern books, films, and sermons have found a theme in the Roman persecution of the Christians. But the history of persecution is more complicated than it might seem. Pressure against Christians came from at least two directions. On the one hand, the Roman state came to regard the Christians as an illegal, politically subversive group that should be forced to conform or be repressed. On the other hand, some pagans and Jews disliked Christian behavior and views so much that they denounced Christians to the authorities or attacked them in mob violence.

ROMAN LAW AND THE CHRISTIANS

In Roman history, the legal proceedings against Christians were exceptions. The Roman authorities normally practiced religious toleration but not because they valued religious freedom of the sort expressed in the first amendment of the United States Constitution. They tolerated their subjects' religions for practical reasons, primarily because toleration helped them to govern their huge empire, which embraced many ethnic groups, languages, and religions. The Roman authorities were not tolerant of everything in other people's cults. They dealt harshly with those that encouraged resistance to Roman rule, such as that of the Celtic druids or that of the Jews who rebelled in 66–70 and 132–135. They also suppressed or forced changes in religions that did things that the authorities regarded as seriously wrong, such as human sacrifice. The Roman magistrates tried, not successfully in the long run, to prevent Roman citizens from participating in religious practices that seemed to them immoral or barbaric, such as the sexually explicit worship of some mother goddesses, although the native worshippers of such goddesses were left alone. But these exceptions to religious tolerance were unusual. The Roman authorities allowed the vast majority of their citizens and subjects to worship as they wished. Why did the Christians become an exception to the policy of religious toleration? Why were they liable to severe punishment and even death? The answers are not simple.

Before the mid-third century, no law survives that forbade Christianity to exist. Some scholars have argued that the attitudes of the Roman magistrates put the Christians in legal danger. Magistrates expected to be obeyed, especially by the millions of subjects who had been incorporated into the empire by conquest. Most Christians were subjects, not citizens. Their refusal to worship when told to do so could infuriate the magistrates who dealt with them. The Roman governor Pliny expressed that view in about 112 when he told the Emperor Trajan (98–117) that even if the Christians he uncovered in northern Asia Minor had committed no crime, they deserved punishment for their "unbending stubbornness" and "obstinacy." They had dared to refuse to obey when Pliny told them to worship the gods. When Roman magistrates arrested, interrogated, tortured, and executed Christians they were acting legally. The refusal to worship when commanded to do so was perhaps the single most important reason that brought the legal wrath of Roman magistrates down on those who admitted to the *nomen christianum* ("Christian name").

Political and religious developments also influenced the legal persecution of Christians. For centuries, the inhabitants of Syria, Egypt, and Asia Minor had honored their rulers as gods. After the Romans conquered them, they transferred their traditional ruler-worship to Roman emperors. They honored them as they had honored their earlier god-kings, with such things as temples, statues, inscriptions full of praise, and the slaughtering of animals in sacrifice. The Romans, who had lived for about five hundred years in a republic with annually elected magistrates, had no tradition of worshipping their rulers. At first, they were reluctant to promote this "cult of the emperor." But it began to seem useful to give subjects an opportunity to express in a public way their gratitude for the stability, peace, and prosperity that the empire brought them. The assassinated Julius Caesar was deified—made a god—by the Roman Senate in 44 BCE. In the first and second centuries CE, the Roman authorities encouraged the worship of the emperor (or his *genius*, which was his life force or protective spirit) together with the goddess Roma, who was the personification of Rome. Important local people joined priesthoods, which organized celebrations on such occasions as the emperor's birthday or the anniversary of the date when he assumed imperial power. The cult of Roma and the emperor was tolerant: A person could honor as many or as few other gods as he or she chose. But it was not wise to refuse openly to participate in the cult of Roma and the emperor. Christians were monotheists, many of whom were unwilling to join in the expanding worship of emperors. At least some were proud of their defiance. That was a dangerous choice that had terrible consequences.

When the Christians refused to worship the gods and especially the emperor, the authorities suspected that they posed a political threat. As they were on so many issues, Christians were divided among themselves on how they should regard the Roman Empire. The dominant view expressed in proto-orthodox Christian writings was decidedly non-revolutionary. In the four canonical gospels, Jesus was never depicted as attacking the Roman state. In the Synoptic Gospels, he told his followers to pay their taxes and to render to Caesar that which was Caesar's (Mt 22:15–22;

Mk 12:13–17; Lk 20:20–22). The Roman authorities could be alarmed when Christians talked of a "Kingdom of God" that was coming soon, but some Christians took pains to explain that the kingdom was a spiritual thing that was no threat to Rome. For instance, the early second-century Christian writer Hegesippus reported an encounter that the Emperor Domitian (81–96) had with two grandnephews of Jesus, who were apparently humble farmers. "When asked about Christ and His Kingdom, its nature, and the place and time of its appearance, they replied that it was not of the world nor earthly, but heavenly and angelic; that it would appear at the end of the world, when he would come in glory and judge the living and the dead, and render unto every man according to his conduct." The emperor saw no threat in such a non-political kingdom: "...after this, Domitian in no way condemned them, but despised them as men of no importance [and] let them go free...." (EH 3.20, altered). Repeatedly Christian writers encouraged their readers to be loyal, or at least submissive, to their rulers. In his letter to the Christians at Rome (13:1–7), Paul justified obedience to rulers because they were part of the plan of God from whom they held their power.

But other Christians thought differently about the Roman Empire. The Christian expectation that Jesus would return soon to establish the Kingdom of God was sometimes expressed in violent political rhetoric, especially while Roman magistrates were arresting, torturing, and executing Christians. Some Christians wrote and probably talked eagerly about the fiery end of the world, when their unbelieving neighbors would be destroyed and the city of Rome itself would become a deserted wasteland. That rhetoric occasionally peeks out of Christian texts. The author of the Second Letter of Peter (3:12) encouraged believers to keep up hope for the end of the world. He wrote that they ought to be "waiting for and hastening the coming of the day of God, because of which the heavens will be set ablaze and dissolved, and the elements will melt with fire." The Book of Revelation, which was probably written during a persecution in later first-century Asia Minor, expressed strong, rebellious views. The visionary John heard an angel's voice exulting in a long passage that "Babylon the great [a Jewish and Christian code phrase for the city of Rome] has fallen," "has become a dwelling place of demons, a haunt of every foul spirit" (Rev 18). The suspicions of the authorities were strengthened by the knowledge that Roman officials had executed the Jewish founder of the Christians.

THE "CROWD" AND THE CHRISTIANS

The Christians also suffered occasionally from mob violence, which was illegal but difficult to control. The religious cults of the ancient Mediterranean world were tolerant of one another and generally did not require their converts to abandon all other gods to worship only their gods. For instance, the native Roman religion had no desire to make converts—there were no missionaries trying to turn the whole world to the worship of Jupiter Optimus Maximus, the chief Roman god. The Roman elite believed that every ethnic group had its own gods who ought to be honored with their traditional forms of worship. Only Jews and Christians rejected that tolerance of other gods, sometimes openly despising other religions and, especially in the case of the Christians, aspiring to convert all mankind to their monotheistic beliefs, which excluded the worship of other gods. That view provoked many ordinary pagans to hatred and occasionally to violence against Christians and Jews.

Christian beliefs and behavior also aroused popular disfavor. For the first two centuries of their existence, Christians were a tiny subdivided minority of the empire's population, yet they believed that their experience of Jesus made them the culmination of God's plan. They claimed that the entire purpose of the universe was expressed in them. They saw themselves as a separate people, whose true homeland was not in this world. They were proud to be different from the people around them. They consciously cut themselves off from ordinary life, the "world" as they called it, and in return they were accused of "hatred of mankind." The anonymous author of the *Epistle to Diognetus* expressed the Christian sense of alienation in a mild, conciliatory form: "For Christians are no different from other people in terms of their country, language, or customs. Nowhere do they inhabit

cities of their own, use a strange dialect, or live life out of the ordinary.... They inhabit both Greek and barbarian cities.... They live in their respective countries, but only as resident aliens; they participate in all things as citizens, they endure all things as foreigners. Every foreign territory is a homeland for them, every homeland foreign territory.... They live on earth but participate in the life of heaven" (*Epistle to Diognetus*, c. 5 in *The Apostolic Fathers*, vol. 2, edited and translated by Bart D. Ehrman, LCL 124 [London and New York, 2003], pp. 139–141).

The Christian sense of alienation from the society around them could lead to actions that annoyed their pagan neighbors. The Christians required their converts from paganism to abandon, even to hate, their ancestral gods. Christians equated the pagan gods with demons or denied that they existed at all. In return, worshippers of the Greek and Roman gods called Christians "atheists." The Christian rejection of the gods posed a significant threat to the basic structures of Greco-Roman society. The modern Western separation of religion from other aspects of life did not exist. Religion was intertwined with every public and private aspect of life, from the small statues in household shrines to the magnificent, publicly supported temples that stood in the center of every city. The Christians' pagan neighbors were sure that such atheists made the gods angry when they refused to maintain the proper relationship between the gods and their worshippers, which was called the *pax deorum* ("peace of the gods"). They were sure that angry and neglected gods sought vengeance. The pagan masses sometimes blamed the atheist Christians for natural disasters that were interpreted as signs of the gods' wrath. As Tertullian wrote: "...they think the Christians [are] the cause of every public disaster, of every affliction with which the people are visited. If the Tiber rises as high as the city walls, if the Nile does not send its waters up over the fields, if the heavens give no rains, if there is an earthquake, if there is famine or pestilence, right away the cry is: 'Away with the Christians to the lion!'" (Tertullian, *Apology*, 40.2, in ANF, vol. 3, p. 47). Other Christian behaviors also aroused popular suspicion. Some Christians refused to participate in the public life of the cities in which they lived and in the army because each of those areas of life was intertwined with the pagan gods. Christian meetings, which were held under cover of darkness and closed to outsiders, also roused suspicions. Some non-Christians suspected that what went on was hideous immorality such as cannibalism (the Christians did claim to eat the flesh and drink the blood of somebody) or incest (even husbands and wives called each other "brother" and "sister") or sexual orgies. Fronto (about 100–about 166), a well-known rhetorician, tutor to the future Emperor Marcus Aurelius (161–180), and holder of the consulship, highest civilian office in the state, painted a lurid picture of what even an educated Roman imagined about the bizarre goings-on in the secret meetings of the Christians:

> An infant covered over with flour, in order to deceive the unwary, is placed before him who is to be stained with their rites: this infant is slain by the young pupil....Thirstily—O horror!— they lick up its blood; eagerly they divide its limbs. By this victim they are pledged together; with this consciousness of wickedness they are bound to mutual silence....On a solemn day they assemble at the feast, with all their children, sisters, mothers, people of every sex and of every age. There, after much feasting, when the fellowship has grown warm, and the fervor of incestuous lust has grown hot with drunkenness, a dog that has been tied to the lamp stand is provoked by throwing a small piece of food.... And thus the visible light being overturned and extinguished in the shameless darkness, the connections of abominable lust involve them in the uncertainty of fate. (Fronto, quoted by Minucius Felix, *Octavius*, 9, in ANF, vol. 4, pp. 177–178, altered)

The relations between Greco-Roman society and the Christian movement were not static: They evolved significantly between the first and third centuries. The official and the popular objections to Christianity could operate separately or could intertwine. In either case, Christians were vulnerable to persecution. For clarity, I shall divide the evolution of persecution into phases, although reality was not so neat.

THE FIRST PHASE OF PERSECUTION (ABOUT 29–ABOUT 250)

During its first three or four decades, Christianity was a sect within Judaism. Because the first-century Roman authorities probably could not distinguish the Jewish Christians from other Jews, they treated them like other Jews. The Romans granted Judaism special status because it was an ancient national religion with numerous adherents. In Judea itself, the ultimately unsuccessful Roman policy was to respect the sensitive feelings of the Jews about their holy city of Jerusalem and its Temple. Because strict Jews would not participate in the worship of the emperor and Roma, the Romans sensibly allowed the Jews to offer a daily sacrifice in their Temple on behalf of the emperor. In the synagogues of the Diaspora prayers were offered for the emperors. The Roman authorities generally protected the Jews from their pagan fellow citizens, with whom they sometimes had conflicts. When the Jews rebelled in 66 and again in 132, social relations between Jews and their pagan neighbors were soured even further. But after the Romans had decisively defeated the Jewish rebels, they permitted the Jewish religion to reconstitute itself and continued to protect it. However, the Romans sporadically discouraged conversion to Judaism.

The Jewish followers of Jesus enjoyed Roman tolerance for as long as they appeared to be another sect of Jews. Luke emphasized repeatedly in his Acts that the Roman authorities were fair to Paul and his fellow missionaries. But the Roman tolerance in the early days did not mean that the Jewish Christians were at peace. The Roman authorities agreed that this dissident sect within Judaism was primarily the responsibility of the Jewish authorities, who did try to repress it. There were outbreaks of Jewish violence against Jewish-Christians. For instance, in Acts 9:1–2, Luke wrote that before Paul's conversion, the high priest at Jerusalem had authorized him to arrest Jewish Christians at Damascus. In the 40s, 50s, and 60s, some Jews jailed, beat, stoned, and killed leading Jewish-Christians, including Stephen (Acts 6:8–8:1); James, the brother of John, killed in about 42 (Acts 12:1–3); and James, the brother of the Lord, killed in 62. Paul wrote that "[f]ive times I have received from the Jews the forty lashes minus one" (2 Cor 11:24). But as long as the Jewish Christians were within Judaism, the Romans treated them no better and no worse than other Jews. That was an unstable situation for at least two reasons. Judaism was rejecting Jewish Christians, and gentile Christian converts were splitting away from Jewish Christianity. By the second half of the first century, Christians were becoming visible to the Roman authorities as a separate and unauthorized religion.

As the Christians converted increasing numbers of gentiles, many ties to contemporary Judaism gradually faded away. The Roman authorities no longer saw them as a sect within Judaism. People who were at the same time gentiles and Christians must have appeared peculiar to Roman magistrates because they did not fit into the usual categories: They were neither a traditional religion nor an identifiable people. They were not entitled to special treatment. They were not even entitled to the ordinary tolerance given to other established religions. When the Christians no longer appeared to be Jews, they became vulnerable to attack by Roman magistrates.

Nero and the Christians

The first significant clash with the Roman state took place in the city of Rome itself, but only there and in special circumstances. In 64, a massive fire destroyed a large part of the city. Rumors spread that the Emperor Nero (54–68) caused the fire in order to clear the ground for his grandiose building plans. In a search for someone to blame, Nero singled out the Christians at Rome, who must have been both an identifiable and unpopular group. The Roman historian Tacitus (died about 120), writing about fifty years after the fire, asserted that the Christians' unpopularity made them a target to blame.

> …Nero substituted as culprits, and punished with the utmost refinements of cruelty, a class of men, loathed for their vices, whom the crowd styled Christians. Christus, the founder of the name, had undergone the death penalty in the reign of Tiberius, by sentence of the procurator

Pontius Pilate, and the pernicious superstition was checked for a moment, only to break out once more, not merely in Judea, the home of the disease, but in the capital itself where all things horrible or shameful in the world collect and find a vogue. First, then, the confessed members of the sect were arrested; next, on their disclosures, vast numbers were convicted, not so much on the count of arson as for hatred of the human race. And derision accompanied their end: they were covered with wild beasts' skins and torn to death by dogs; or they were fastened on crosses, and, when daylight failed, were burned to serve as lamps by night. (Tacitus, *Annales* 15.44, translated by John Jackson, *Tacitus in Five Volumes*, LCL [London and New York, 1937], vol. 5, pp. 283–285, altered)

Tacitus' account makes clear that he, like many Greeks and Romans, disliked the Christians, who were suspected of immoral and anti-social behavior—"hatred of mankind." In blaming the Christians, Nero took advantage of the widespread view that such secretive, immoral, and rebellious people might well have started a fire. These suspicions, shared by magistrates and ordinary pagans, formed the background against which later legal prosecutions and mob attacks took place.

Pliny and the Christians

Nero's attack on the Christians in 64 took place only in the city of Rome and ended quickly, but it might have implanted a negative view of Christians in the minds of many Roman officials. One magistrate wrote an informative letter about his encounter with Christians. Pliny the Younger (about 61–about 112), a sophisticated Roman writer, was sent to govern the province of Bithynia-Pontus, an area in northern Turkey along the Black Sea. When Christians were denounced to him he began to take action. But as the number of accusations grew he became unsure whether what he was doing was legally correct. He wrote to the Emperor Trajan (98–117) for advice: "Till I hear from you, I have adopted the following course towards those who have been brought before me as Christians. First I have asked them if they were Christians. If they confessed that they were, I repeated my question a second and a third time, accompanying it with threats of punishment. If they still persisted in their statements, I ordered them to be taken out [and executed]. For I was in no doubt that, whatever it was to which they were confessing, they had merited some punishment by their stubbornness and unbending obstinacy." He sent Christians who were Roman citizens to Rome for their punishment. Pliny's letter did not mention any popular violence against Christians, but he might have heard rumors about illicit behavior because he assured the emperor that Christians ate "harmless, ordinary food" at their meetings. But his proceedings against Christians incited some pagans to settle scores with Christians by sending him lots of names of suspects. "An anonymous notebook was presented with many names in it. Those who denied that they were or ever had been Christians I thought should be released, provided that they called on the gods in my presence, and offered incense and wine to your statue (which I had expressly brought in with the images of the gods for that very purpose), and, above all, if they renounced Christ, which no true Christian, I am told, can be made to do." Some Christians were overwhelmed with terror and obeyed Pliny's order to sacrifice to the emperor and other gods. Some suspects said that they used to be Christians but no longer were. One declared that he had given up the religion twenty-five years earlier. After they offered incense and wine to the emperor's statue and the images of the gods and publicly renounced Christ, Pliny was satisfied that they were not Christians and freed them. As the numbers of accused grew, Pliny became alarmed and stopped what he was doing. "I have therefore postponed any further examination and hastened to consult you. The question seems to me to be worthy of your consideration, especially in view of the number of persons endangered; for a great many individuals of every age and class, both men and women, are being brought to trial" (Pliny, *Letters*, 10.96, translated by Betty Radice, Pliny, *Letters and Panegyricus*, vol. 2, LCL 59 [Cambridge and London, 1969], p. 291, altered).

The Emperor Trajan wrote a brief, businesslike reply. "You have followed the right course of procedure ... in your examination of the cases of persons charged with being Christians, for it is impossible to lay down a general rule.... *These people must not be hunted out* [my italics]; if they are brought before you and the charge against them is proved, they must be punished, but in the case of anyone who denies that he is a Christian, and makes it clear that he is not by offering prayers to our gods, he is to be pardoned as a result of his repentance however suspicious his past conduct may be. But pamphlets circulated anonymously must play no part in any accusation. They create the worst sort of precedent and are quite out of keeping with the spirit of our age" (Pliny, *Letters*, 10.97, in Radice, *Pliny*, vol. 2, LCL 59, pp. 291–293, altered). Before about 250, most Roman officials took Trajan's advice and rarely hunted for Christians or accepted anonymous accusations against them. During that long period, the full power of the Roman state was never directed in a systematic way against the Christians. When a local magistrate became aware of Christians, he might ignore the matter, but he might also punish them severely (and legally) with imprisonment, torture, and even execution.

The persecutions had a deep influence on Christians, who developed their own way to talk about their fellow believers who suffered official prosecution, popular violence, or both. If believers held firm, they were called "martyrs," which means "witness" in Greek. They became heroes to their fellow Christians because they had imitated Christ, the model martyr. Many admirers were sure that the Holy Spirit granted them the gifts of visions and prophecies while they were imprisoned as well as the strength to endure. Their deaths were called a "second baptism," no longer in water but in their own blood. They were thought to go directly to heaven, whereas ordinary Christians awaited the final resurrection in their graves. Some martyrs were remembered in written accounts and honored at their burial places on the anniversary of their death, which was described as their heavenly birthday. The martyrs gained a central position in Christian admiration and imagination. Some other Christians were tortured, imprisoned, and lost their property but were eventually released. They were also martyrs who had bravely witnessed, but they were commonly called in Latin "confessors" because they had "confessed the name" of Jesus (see Mt 10:32–33) at great personal cost. After their release, the confessors were often influential in their churches, sometimes rivaling the authority of the bishops and presbyters. Finally, if a believer submitted to his tormenters and sacrificed, Christians said he or she lapsed ("slipped or fell") or became an apostate ("one who turns away").

Persecution at Lyons and Vienne

In the summer of 177, an attack fueled by popular hatred broke out at Lyons and Vienne in the Rhône River valley in Gaul. Local factors probably provoked the violence, but they are unknown to us. After the persecution ended, the survivors sent a long letter to "the brethren throughout Asia and Phrygia, who hold the same faith and hope of redemption" (all quotations are from "The Letter of the Churches of Lyons and Vienne" in NPNF, second series, vol. 1, pp. 212–219). The violence at Lyons and Vienne began when Christians, many of whom were Greek-speaking emigrants from Asia Minor, were "shut out from houses and baths and markets...." Pagans attacked them with "blows and draggings and robberies and stonings, and imprisonments, and all things which an infuriated mob delight in inflicting on enemies and opponents." Such mob violence quickly drew the attention of the Roman authorities, who intervened to restore order. Their intervention did not end the attack on the Christians, who were now subject to legal punishments. During the account of the legal proceedings, the hatred of the local pagans for the Christians was always in the background. Soldiers rounded up the most zealous Christians, on whom the two churches depended. Not all the arrested Christians reacted in the same way: "Some were clearly ready to become our first martyrs, and finished their confession with all eagerness." About ten others "appeared unprepared and untrained, still weak, and unable to endure so great a conflict." They lapsed and worshipped the gods. Some Christians were prosperous enough to have servants, who were arrested and confirmed under threat of torture the dark suspicions that their Christian masters ate human flesh and had sexual intercourse with close relatives, even their mothers. At that news, even sympathetic pagans turned hostile.

The Roman prefect set out to break the will of the resisters by brutal torture. They were whipped, beaten, and stretched on the rack, and as a last resort, red-hot bronze plates were pressed against the tenderest parts of their bodies. Some were strangled in prison, and others died of their wounds. The crowd was especially enraged at Bishop Pothinus of Lyons, more than ninety years old and ill with breathing difficulties: "When he was brought by the soldiers to the tribunal, accompanied by the civil magistrates and a multitude who shouted against him in every manner as if he were Christ himself, he gave a noble witness. Being asked by the governor, Who was the God of the Christians, he replied: 'If you are worthy, you will know.' Then he was dragged away harshly, and received blows of every kind. Those near him struck him with their hands and feet, regardless of his age; and those at a distance hurled at him whatever they could get; all of them thinking that they would be guilty of great wickedness and impiety if any possible abuse were omitted. For thus they thought to avenge their own gods. Scarcely able to breathe, he was thrown into prison, and died after two days."

The letter then turned from the prison and the courtroom to the amphitheater, where the torments of the Christians were made a public spectacle. As Pliny had done about sixty years earlier, the Roman authorities at Lyons and Vienne consulted the emperor, who was the Stoic philosopher Marcus Aurelius (161–180): "For Caesar commanded that they should be put to death, but that any who might deny the faith should be set free." August 1 was a major festival day on which the governor was expected to provide public entertainment. He decided to save some expenses by using the condemned Christians in the public games. In obedience to the emperor's instructions, he "beheaded those who appeared to possess Roman citizenship, but he sent the others to the wild beasts." "They endured again the customary running of the gauntlet and the violence of the wild beasts, and everything which the furious people called for or desired, and at last, the iron chair in which their bodies being roasted, filled them with their fumes.... But [the slave girl] Blandina was suspended on a stake and exposed to be devoured by the wild beasts that should attack her. And because she appeared as if she was hanging on a cross, and because of her earnest prayers, she inspired the [Christian] combatants with great zeal. For they looked on her in her conflict, and beheld with their outward eyes, in the form of their sister, him who was crucified for them." Over the next few days, the final act of the persecution was played out in the amphitheater at Lyons. The slave girl Blandina and the fifteen-year-old Ponticus had refused to yield. The crowd was infuriated at them, and in order to force them to swear by the gods the authorities intensified their sufferings. Young Ponticus died under the torments. "But the blessed Blandina was last of all....And after the scourging, after the wild beasts, and after the roasting seat, she was finally enclosed in a net and thrown before a bull. And having being tossed about by the animal, but feeling none of the things which were happening to her on account of her hope and firm hold upon what had been entrusted to her, and her communion with Christ, she also was sacrificed [that is, died]. And the pagans themselves confessed that never among them had a woman endured so many and such terrible tortures." Some pagans at Lyons and Vienne knew that Christians treasured the bodies of the martyrs, which they believed would be glorified in a future resurrection of the dead. The authorities took measures to prevent the Christians from recovering the bodies for burial. "For they cast to the dogs those who had died of strangling in the prison, carefully guarding them by night and day, lest anyone should be buried by us. And they exposed the remains left by the wild beasts and by fire, mangled and charred, and placed the heads of the others by their bodies, and guarded them in like manner from burial...." The surviving Christians wanted to bury the martyrs' bodies, but they could not steal them at night, bribe the guards, or get any powerful pagan to intervene on their behalf. After six days in the open air, "the bodies of the martyrs...were afterward burned and reduced to ashes and swept into the river Rhône by the wicked men, so that no trace of them might appear on the earth." The author of the account attributed the burning of the bodies to a pagan desire to thwart the hope of resurrection.

The letter reporting the persecution mentioned ten martyrs by name: the slave Blandina and her owner; the young Ponticus; Vettius Epagathus, a prominent citizen; Alexander, a doctor who had come from Phrygia in Asia Minor; Attalus, an emigrant from Asia Minor and a Roman citizen; Sanctus, a deacon of the church of Vienne; Maturus, "though newly baptized, a noble athlete"; Biblis, a woman who at first apostatized [I think the word is 'apostasized'] and then infuriated her captors by confessing the Name of Jesus; and Pothinus, the elderly bishop. The account mentioned other unnamed people who were strangled in prison or died of their wounds. (It also acknowledged at least ten apostates, who sacrificed to the gods.) Although we do not have an exact number, perhaps forty or fifty Christians were killed. The fury died down— we do not know why—and the Christian communities at Lyons and Vienne survived. Within a few years, the influential theologian and anti-gnostic writer Irenaeus succeeded Pothinus as bishop of Lyons. He may be the anonymous author of the letter that reveals so much about the interplay between popular hatred and official legal proceedings that shaped persecution in many places besides the Rhône valley.

Between about 29 and about 250, the sufferings of the martyrs and the confessors were traumatic events in the history of individual Christian communities. They provided many Christians with powerful models of how they ought to act, even if in reality many Christians wavered or gave in when persecution came. Tertullian argued that the bravery of the martyrs even attracted the favorable attention of at least some pagans. He wrote to the Roman proconsul of Carthage that "Your cruelty is our glory....For all who witness the noble patience of its martyrs,...are inflamed with desire to examine the matter in question; and as soon as they come to know the truth, they straightway enrol themselves its disciples" (Tertullian, *Ad Scapulam*, 5, in ANF, vol. 3, pp. 107–108). In his *Apology*, Tertullian made a similar observation: "Nor does your cruelty, however exquisite, get you anything....The oftener we are mowed down by you, the more in number we grow; the blood of Christians is seed" (Tertullian, *Apology*, 50.13, in ANF, vol. 3, p. 55).

Attacks from neighbors and legal prosecutions from magistrates posed a moral problem for believers. What were they to do if they were attacked? Gnostic Christians were divided about martyrdom. Some accepted the goodness of martyrdom as an imitation of Christ. Others were hostile to the willingness of the unenlightened Christians to accept or even seek martyrdom. The anonymous author of the *Testimony of Truth*, who saw no virtue in accepting or seeking death, wrote that "the foolish—thinking [in] their heart [that] if they confess, 'We are Christians,' in word only (but) not with power, while giving themselves over to ignorance, to a human death, not knowing where they are going nor who Christ is, thinking that they will live, when they are (really) in error—hasten toward the principalities and the authorities. They fall into their clutches because of the ignorance that is in them. For (if) only words which bear testimony were effecting salvation, the whole world would endure this thing [and] be saved. [But it is in this way that they [drew] error to themselves. [...they do] not [know] that they [will destroy] themselves. If the [Father were to] desire a [human] sacrifice, he would become [vainglorious]" (*The Testimony of Truth*, 31.24–32.20, translated by S. Giversen and B. A. Pearson in *The Nag Hammadi Library in English*, third edition, edited by James Robinson [New York, 1988], pp. 450–451). Some gnostic Christians said that it made no difference if one worshipped the pagan gods because it was only one's body that made the gestures of worship. The real inner "I" could hold the gods in contempt while the outer shell, the body, poured wine or offered incense before the idols. It is not surprising that gnostics produced few martyrs—at least that is what their proto-orthodox Christian opponents charged. For instance, Tertullian wrote that when some fearful Catholic Christians faced persecution, the gnostic arguments against accepting martyrdom appealed to them. Tertullian compared the Valentinians, a prominent gnostic Christian group, with scorpions whose "poison" weakened the resolve of ordinary Christians to resist persecution: "When, therefore faith is greatly agitated, and the Church is burning...then the Gnostics break out, then the Valentinians creep forth, then all the opponents of martyrdom bubble up.... For because

they know [that] many [Christians are] simple and also inexperienced, and weak moreover...they perceive that they [the weak Christians] are never to be approached more than when fear has opened the entrance to the soul, especially when some display of ferocity has already crowned the faith of martyrs" (Tertullian, *Scorpiace*, 1, in ANF, vol. 3, p. 633).

Some Christians welcomed their own sufferings as a way to encourage Jesus to come quickly. Origen reported that the pagan critic Celsus, who wrote about 178, complained that Christians provoked the wrath of rulers, which brought on them suffering and tortures and even death (Origen, *Contra Celsum*, 8:65, in ANF, vol. 4, p. 664, altered). Tertullian recorded the exasperation of a Roman magistrate in Asia Minor who was faced with the Christians of a province voluntarily appearing before him. He executed some but told the others that if they wanted so badly to die they could jump off cliffs or hang themselves (Tertullian, *Ad Scapulam*, 5.1, in ANF, vol. 3, pp. 107–108).

Proto-orthodox Christians valued martyrdom as a special way of imitating Christ, the innocent victim of evil men. But bishops advised their followers not to seek martyrdom or to provoke the authorities. They approved escape if it could be done without religious compromise, citing Jesus' saying: "...and you will be hated by all because of my name. But the one who endures to the end will be saved. When they persecute you in one town, flee to the next; for truly I tell you, you will not have gone through all the towns of Israel before the Son of Man comes" (Mt 10:22–23). The author of the account of the martyrdom of Bishop Polycarp of Smyrna offered a warning about the dangers of seeking martyrdom. A Christian named "Quintus," who had voluntarily given himself up and had encouraged others to do so, lapsed when he faced the beasts. The author drew the lesson that such results were the reason "why we [the bishops, perhaps] do not approve of those who choose to come forward in persecution. That was not what the Gospel taught" (*The Martyrdom of Polycarp*, c. 4). But when a proto-orthodox Christian was confronted with the choice of worshipping the emperor and the gods or enduring death, the bishops advised that the proper choice was martyrdom, although in reality not all made that choice.

Roman society saw nothing wrong with cruel public punishments. High Roman magistrates, including emperors, were expected to provide expensive public games that pleased the crowds by torturing and killing in painful ways criminals, captured barbarians, and animals. Because the Roman populace enjoyed the public spectacle of suffering, blood, and death, the penalties that Christians faced for defiance were horrible. In reality, many frightened Christians sacrificed to the gods and later, when calm returned, sought reconciliation with their congregation. In spite of the many lapsed Christians, there were enough examples of heroic resistance to provide the Christians with encouragement in times of pressure.

Before 250, persecutions were sporadic in time and place, depending in some instances on the attitudes of local Roman officials, who varied in their willingness to prosecute, and in other instances on the attitudes of the local people, who had varying degrees of antipathy to Christians. Such occasional and scattered attacks were usually not severe enough to threaten the existence of Christianity itself, although some local communities were devastated. For almost two centuries, denunciations of individual Christians to the Roman authorities or mob violence against Christians set the legal machinery in motion. From 29 to about 250, there were many local attacks, but by twentieth- and twenty-first-century standards of slaughter, their consequences were modest.

THE SECOND PHASE OF PERSECUTION (250–260)

Until about 250, the empire and the Christian movement existed in an uneasy truce, broken by sporadic local mob violence and occasional official legal proceedings. There were no state-sponsored, systematic attempts to stop the spread of Christianity or to wipe it out. After 250, some Roman emperors tried to destroy Christianity in a systematic way. That change in policy was probably linked to the decline of the empire's prosperity and stability, to the fears aroused by the decline of traditional pagan cults, and to the rise in Christian numbers and visibility in society. For more than two hundred years, the empire enjoyed what has

been called the "Pax Romana" ("Roman Peace"), during which economic prosperity and urban life flourished around the Mediterranean Sea. It was surely not a perfect era, but it was the best that the Roman Empire was ever to have. After about 235, the empire suffered interconnected disasters. The orderly procedures for choosing emperors broke down. Generals contending for the emperorship waged destructive civil wars. Between 235 and 284, about fifty generals, with the backing of their armies, claimed to be emperor. The Senate at Rome recognized twenty-six of them as emperors. Only one of the twenty-six died a non-violent death. Most died in battle or were assassinated by their own junior officers. The political breakdown was worsened by serious barbarian invasions that penetrated deep into Roman territory. Steep inflation, periodic famines, and the outbreak of infectious diseases increased the empire's woes. Cities, the heart of Greco-Roman life, shrank. The total population of the empire probably shrank as well.

These disasters shocked the empire's rulers and intellectuals. In modern times, the disruptions might be explained in rationalistic terms by referring to economics or political science. But in the third century, the most natural explanations were religious. Rome had prospered for a thousand years under the protection of its traditional gods. The thousandth anniversary of the founding of the city of Rome was celebrated in 248, even as the calamities that threatened to destroy the state and social order were accelerating. The mounting disasters seemed to prove that the gods were angry. Two emperors decided that one way to regain the favor of the gods was to make everyone worship them. When such "general sacrifices" were ordered, Christians stuck out like a sore thumb because many would not worship the gods. Refusal to sacrifice was a serious crime because the person was thought to be purposely endangering the already fragile welfare of the empire by angering the gods. When faced with pain and death many Christians did sacrifice, although others refused and took the severe consequences.

The Emperor Decius (249–251)

In 250, the Emperor Decius ordered a general sacrifice. Each adult was to offer incense or wine to the gods and was to receive a certificate, called a *libellus* ("little book"), about forty of which survive from Egypt. This *libellus* is typical: "To the commission chosen to superintend the sacrifices in the village of Alexander's Isle. From Aurelius Diogenes, son of Satobous of the village of Alexander's Isle, aged 72 years, with a scar on the right eyebrow. I have always sacrificed to the gods, and now in your presence in accordance with the edict I have made sacrifice and poured a libation..." (J. R. Knipfing, "The Libelli of the Decian Persecution," *Harvard Theological Review* 16 [1923], p. 363, as cited in *A New Eusebius*, edited by J. Stevenson, revised with additional documents by W. H. C. Frend [London, 1987], p. 214). Decius' general sacrifice was probably not aimed specifically at Christians, but it certainly shone a bright light on them as the only major group to refuse.

Because Christians had just passed through about thirty years when even local persecutions were rare, they were taken by surprise when Decius ordered the general sacrifice. Bishop Dionysius of Alexandria (died 264/265) wrote a letter about what happened in that great city, which was home to many kinds of Christians. For about a year before Decius issued his edict, an Alexandrian Christian-hater had been agitating the pagan masses, who were eager to settle scores with the Christians or just to steal their possessions. Decius' edict gave a legal justification to the mob violence. Bishop Dionysius reported that anti-Christian rioting and looting of Alexandrian Christian homes and businesses intensified. In the face of beatings, torture, the threat of economic ruin, and death, large numbers of Christians "lapsed" (EH 6.41). After Decius' order, the events at Alexandria were repeated in many places. Some frightened Christians, including bishops, presbyters, deacons, and property owners, sacrificed to the gods. Others bribed their way out of sacrificing or bought a *libellus* or just ran away. If Decius had not been killed in battle in 251, the official crackdown might have had greater success. After his death, serious troubles for the empire reasserted themselves, and the persecution stopped temporarily.

The Emperor Valerian (253–260)

In response to military defeats and severe financial problems, the Emperor Valerian decided in 257 to attack Christians because he believed they were offensive to the gods and disloyal to the empire. As a bonus, he confiscated their property for the bankrupt imperial treasury. Unlike Decius' general sacrifice, this sacrifice was certainly directed at Christians. The anti-Christian purge was carefully thought out. At first, bishops, presbyters, and deacons were ordered to sacrifice or suffer exile. Ordinary Christians were forbidden to assemble for Christian worship. Within a year, measures intensified. Cyprian, bishop of Carthage (248–258), who was later executed during the persecution, wrote that "Valerian had sent a prescript to the Senate, to the effect that bishops and presbyters and deacons should immediately be punished [executed]; but that senators, and men of importance, and Roman knights should lose their dignity and moreover be deprived of their property; and if,... they should persist in being Christians, they also should lose their heads; but that matrons should be deprived of their property, and sent into banishment. Moreover, people of Caesar's household, whoever of them had either confessed before, or should now confess, should have their property confiscated, and should be sent in chains by assignment to Caesar's estates" (Cyprian, Letter 80, in ANF, vol. 5, p. 408). Before Valerian could fully implement his plans, he died in captivity of Rome's longtime enemy, the Persians: He was skinned and stuffed and used as a foot stool by the Persian King of Kings. Gallienus (253–268), Valerian's son and co-emperor, ended the persecution and restored to the bishops the churches and cemeteries that had been confiscated (EH 7:13). In subsequent decades, some emperors might have intended to strike at Christians, but short reigns and severe military, political, and financial problems prevented it.

In the decades of peace (260–303) after the end of empirewide persecution, Christians grew in numbers and in visibility. Some areas of the Near East and North Africa might have had Christian majorities. There were certainly villages of Christians in Egypt and Asia Minor. Christians were found in all classes and most occupations. Even a small number of aristocrats and intellectuals were Christian. The forty-three years of peace would be shattered by an outbreak of severe, state-sponsored persecution early in the fourth century, a topic to be treated in chapter 10.

FURTHER READING

Ancient Sources

Herbert Musurillo, *The Acts of the Christian Martyrs* (Oxford, 1972), gathered twenty-eight accounts of martyrs that he believed were written before the fourth century. Especially illuminating are the *Martyrdom of Polycarp* (pp. 2–21), the aged bishop of Smyrna who was killed in the second century, and the *Letter of the Churches of Lyons and Vienne* (pp. 62–85), which informed other Christians about a persecution in those cities in 177. *The Martyrdom of Saints Felicity and Perpetua,* in Musurillo, pp. 106–131, is especially interesting because it is based in part on the diary that Perpetua wrote in prison. For a vivid source on the late third- and early fourth-century persecutions, written by a contemporary, read Eusebius, *The Ecclesiastical History,* books 8–10.

Modern Works

Everett Ferguson, ed., *Church and State in the Early Church,* with introductions by the editor, *Studies in Early Christianity,* vol. 7 (New York, 1993), especially pp. 1–224, reprints important articles on the causes and consequences of persecution. The journal *Christian History,* vol. 9, part 3 (1990), devoted a clearly written issue to persecutions in early Christianity.

W. H. C. Frend, *Martyrdom and Persecution in the Early Church: A Study of a Conflict from the Maccabees to Donatus* (Oxford, 1965). A classic treatment of the origins and consequences of the Jewish and Christian willingness to resist religious persecution.

CHAPTER 8

Christian Intellectuals

In spite of mob violence and official prosecutions, the interactions between Christians and the Greco-Roman world before the fourth century were not entirely negative. Although some Christians had rejected the secular world and waited eagerly for its destruction, other Christians sought to come to terms with those aspects of the society around them that they thought were compatible with their religion. Some educated Christians entered into a dialogue with Greco-Roman culture, in which they defended Christianity from the charges that provoked popular and official violence. They accepted some elements of Greek and Roman culture but rejected others. Those Christian writers are often called "apologists," from the Greek word *apologia*, which in the study of rhetoric was a speech in defense of something or someone.

Greco-Roman culture, which traced its roots back to the poet Homer in the eighth century BCE, was rich in literary, artistic, and philosophical achievements. As in most complex societies, there developed a division between high and low versions of Greco-Roman culture. An elite possessed the "high" culture, which had to be learned in schools at considerable expenditure of time and money. To understand the educational aims of the "high" version of Greco-Roman culture, imagine that you spent years in school and tens of thousands of dollars to learn to speak and write English exactly as Shakespeare or Chaucer did (and you looked down on people who could not do that). Educated Greek speakers generally idealized the language of Pericles' Athens in the fifth century BCE, and educated Latin speakers idealized the Latin of the period of the Emperor Augustus (37 BCE–14 CE) and his early successors. The educated elite admired the rhetoricians who had mastered the complex

literary education because they were learned and eloquent people who could think, speak, and write in languages that were increasingly different from ordinary Greek and Latin. The educated elite held high positions in the empire's government, and their opinions carried great weight in the highest circles of society.

There was also a "low" version of Greco-Roman culture. In the first, second, and third centuries CE, there were many pagans, Jews, and Christians who could read, but that did not make them intellectuals or give them access to the higher versions of their culture. There is a modern myth that early Christianity was a religion of slaves. Because there were so many slaves in the ancient world, there surely were many slaves who were Christians. But many second- and third-century Christians seem to have belonged to what we might roughly describe as the lower-middle groups in society, many illiterate, some literate but surely not educated in the upper-class way. Thus, the cultural gap in Greco-Roman society was wide, and most Christians—in fact, most people—were on the low side of it.

Not only was high culture unattainable for most Christians, but they also had religious reasons to dislike it. It is probably significant that the word "philosophy" appeared only once in the New Testament and then in a decidedly negative way. The Letter to the Colossians, 2:8, admonished: "See to it that no one takes you captive through philosophy and empty deceit...." The North African Tertullian (died about 220), who had a good rhetorician's education, was critical of the effect that he thought secular learning had on Christianity. In particular he accused philosophy of being a cause of heresy: "Indeed heresies [he had in mind forms of gnostic Christianity] are themselves instigated by philosophy. From this source came the 'Aeons'... in the system of Valentinus, who was of Plato's school. From the same source [philosophy] came Marcion's better god, with all his tranquility: he came of the Stoics. Then, again, the opinion that the soul dies is held by the Epicureans.... What indeed has Athens to do with Jerusalem? What concord is there between Academy [the school of Plato] and the Church? What [concord] between heretics and Christians?... Away with all attempts to produce a mottled Christianity of Stoic, Platonic, and dialectic composition! We want no curious disputation after possessing Christ Jesus, no further inquiry after enjoying the gospel! With our faith, we desire no further belief" (Tertullian, *On Prescription against Heretics*, c. 7, in ANF, vol. 3, p. 246, altered). Because of their financial circumstances, social origins, and negative view of high culture, the majority of Christians were poorly equipped to answer their educated critics in ways that would be respected.

But there were also Christians who saw value in putting forth a rational defense of Christianity. For instance, the First Letter of Peter, 3:15–16, recommended to its readers that they "[a]lways be ready to make your defense to anyone who demands from you an accounting for the hope that is in you; yet do it with gentleness and reverence." Luke reported that at Athens, the center of Greek philosophical thought, Paul had adapted his message to the educated Greek pagans in front of him (Acts 17:22–31). He sought common ground with his audience by emphasizing things that many intelligent pagans would have accepted, especially that there is one God who created and still governs the world and whom humans naturally seek. He took a swipe at popular religion's devotion to statues, about which educated Greeks had their own doubts: "Since we are God's offspring, we ought not to think that the deity is like gold, or silver, or stone, an image formed by the art and imagination of mortals." In his speech to the Athenians, Paul did not mention Jesus by name but alluded to him, to the judgment of the world, and to his resurrection (Acts 17:30–31). Luke wrote that when Paul mentioned resurrection from the dead he lost the favor of many in the audience, who thought it was a ridiculous idea.

Within a century of Jesus' death, a small number of people with a Greco-Roman higher education began to convert to Christianity. Some used their education to defend Christianity in documents we call "apologies." We know of about ten formal defenses of Christianity written during the second and third centuries. Most apologists wrote in Greek. The earliest was Quadratus of Athens (about 129), whose apology is lost, but a quotation from it claims that he knew people whom Jesus had healed or raised from the dead. Two other apologies that do not survive are those by Melito of Sardis (second half of the second century) and Apollinaris of Hierapolis (middle of the second century). Aristides of Athens (second century) wrote the earliest surviving apology; Justin Martyr (about 100–about 165) wrote two surviving apologies; Tatian (active about 160), a student of Justin from beyond the eastern border of the empire, wrote not so much a defense of Christianity as a harsh attack on paganism called *Against the Greeks*; Athenagoras of Athens (about 177) addressed an apology to the Emperor Marcus Aurelius and his son Commodus; Theophilus, bishop of Antioch (late second century) wrote to a man named "Autolycus," with whom he discussed Christianity; an anonymous author wrote the *Epistle to Diognetus* (second or third century); and Origen (about 185–251) composed *Against Celsus* in response to a written attack by a pagan author named "Celsus," who was active in the 170s. Two early apologists wrote in Latin. Minucius Felix (late second or early third century) wrote a dialogue called *Octavius*, and the fiery Tertullian wrote at least three apologies. The pioneering apologists of the second and third centuries had an impact within Christianity far beyond their small numbers because they opened a dialogue with the surrounding culture.

Christians suffered as a result of criticism from ordinary people and from intellectuals. The apologists tried in their individual ways to counter the negative views about their religion. Certain topics reappear in the apologies because they were hot issues of the times. The apologists asserted that Christians were loyal subjects of the emperor. They denied that Christians were guilty of cannibalism, incest, and atheism. The apologists tried to influence their intellectual equals, the educated elite who shared in the popular dislike of Christianity but also had complaints against the Christians that were more intellectual in nature. Educated pagans disliked what they saw as arrogant Christian claims to have superior knowledge. They saw the Christians as uneducated people who pretended to know more and better things than the educated elite. Celsus, who wrote the first extensive attack on Christianity, really disliked the lower-class Christians whose teaching undermined the authority of fathers, masters, teachers, and educated people like himself. "We see, indeed, in private houses workers in wool and leather, and laundry-workers, and persons of the most uninstructed and rustic character, not daring to utter a word in the presence of their elders and wiser masters; but when they get hold of children privately and certain women as ignorant as themselves, they pour forth wonderful statements, to the effect that they ought not to give heed to their father and to their teachers, but should obey them; that the former [that is, fathers and teachers] are foolish and stupid, and neither know nor can perform anything that is really good, being preoccupied with empty trifles; they alone know how men ought to live, and that, if the children obey them, they will both be happy themselves, and will make their home happy also. And while thus speaking, if they see one of the instructors of youth approaching, or one of the more intelligent class, or even the father himself, the more timid among them become afraid while the bolder incite the children to throw off the yoke, whispering that in the presence of father and teacher they neither will nor can explain to them any good thing, seeing they turn away with aversion from the silliness and stupidity of such persons as being totally corrupt, and far advanced in wickedness and such as would inflict punishment on the children; but, that if they wish (to avail themselves of their aid), they must leave father and their instructors, and go with the women and their play fellows to the women's apartments or to the leather shop or to the fuller's shop, that they may attain to perfection" (Origen, *Contra Celsum*, 3.55, in ANF, vol. 4, p. 486).

Because intellectuals were educated in a culture that had a deep reverence for what was old in religion, they also scorned Christianity for its recent appearance during the reign of the Emperor Tiberius (14–37 CE). They wanted to know why God had waited so long before intervening on Earth. Some intellectuals who knew something about specific Christian beliefs found them ridiculous—for instance, that God would become human or that bodies would rise from the dead. The educated critics also charged that there was not much original in Christianity, which, they said, borrowed from other religions that also had "sons of god," sacred washings, and ritual meals.

Because the apologists wanted favorable treatment for their religion, they were usually reasonable, trying to build bridges to the aspects of Greek and Roman civilization they saw as good, although they were highly critical of the aspects they thought were immoral or idolatrous. The apologists addressed their works not to the illiterate pagan masses but rather to educated intellectuals and government bureaucrats or to the emperor himself. Emperors did routinely receive petitions and written pleas from their subjects concerning all sorts of issues. It is possible that some apologists actually delivered their works to the emperor or to his secretaries who had responsibility for letters and petitions. But there is no evidence that emperors and their officials read or responded to them. In a society where the emperor was increasingly the central figure, the apologists never threatened political rebellion or recommended disloyalty. The main exception was Tatian, who seems to have hated every aspect of Greco-Roman society. The real audience for the apologists' works may have been other Christians, who needed help to defend their beliefs against intellectual arguments.

Some apologists acknowledged that there were good aspects of Greco-Roman culture but not necessarily what modern people value. Since the Italian Renaissance of the fifteenth and sixteenth centuries, Greco-Roman literature and art have been widely admired in Western culture. Museums are proud of their collections of Greek and Roman art. Tourists flock to such archaeological sites as the Parthenon (the Temple of Athena in Athens) and the physical remains of Roman temples, amphitheaters, and aqueducts. But the early Christian apologists never wrote that they saw anything good in the visual arts—that was understandable because statues, paintings, and many fine buildings were connected to the pagan gods. The apologists were also wary of the ancient literature that used to be at the heart of high-class education in Western Europe and America. Some modern students study Latin, and a few still study ancient Greek. Colleges still teach in the original languages or in translations the poems of Homer and Virgil, the Greek tragedies and comedies, and the speeches of Cicero. But the Christian apologists rarely praised Greek or Roman literature because it was often concerned with the myths of the gods, whose behavior the apologists thought was immoral or irrational. The apologists were wary of philosophy but found some common ground with certain Greek philosophers, mostly Stoics and Platonists, who taught such things as the immortality of the soul, the need for ethical behavior, and the need to control the body's desires. In short, the apologists wrote positively only about those aspects of Greco-Roman culture that seemed compatible with their Christian beliefs.

JUSTIN MARTYR (ABOUT 100–ABOUT 165)

Justin, who died a martyr's death at Rome, was an early and influential apologist. He was a Greek-speaker from Samaria, a territory in modern Israel, who wrote two apologies, one addressed to the Emperor Antoninus Pius (138–161), his two sons, the Roman Senate, and the Roman people, and the other to the Romans. Because Christians were criticized not only by pagans but also by Jews, Justin also wrote an apologetic work aimed at Jews, the *Dialogue with Trypho*, which was composed in the form of a discussion with a learned Jew named "Trypho" about Jewish-Christian relations and especially about the proper interpretation of the prophets of the Hebrew scriptures. An account of Justin's trial and execution at Rome in about 165 also survives.

Justin was born a Greco-Roman pagan. He studied philosophy, which he thought was primarily a search for God. In his *Dialogue with Trypho*, he described, perhaps in an idealized way, his travels among the philosophical schools of his day. He first approached a Stoic philosopher but left him when the philosopher admitted that he knew nothing

about God and did not think such knowledge was necessary. He next approached an Aristotelian philosopher but left because the man was too eager to demand his fee. He then approached a Pythagorean philosopher, who insisted that Justin first learn about music, astronomy, and geometry as preparations for the study of philosophy. When Justin admitted his ignorance of those subjects, the Pythagorean sent him away. Looking back, Justin admitted that he did not want to invest the time necessary to meet the Pythagorean educational ideal. "In my helpless condition, it occurred to me to have a meeting with the Platonists, for their fame was great. I thereupon spent as much of my time as possible with one who had recently settled in our city, a wise man, holding a high position among the Platonists. And I progressed, and made the greatest improvement daily. And the perception of immaterial things quite overpowered me, and the contemplation of ideas furnished my mind with wings, so that in a little while I supposed that I had become wise; and such was my stupidity, I expected immediately to look upon God, for this is the purpose of Plato's philosophy (Justin, *Dialogue with Trypho*, c. 2, ANF, vol. 1, p. 195, altered). To find solitude, Justin used to go to a deserted field near the sea. One day he met an old man with whom he began talking about Platonic philosophy. The man gradually demolished Plato's arguments about the ability of a living person to see God, about the uncreated nature of the world, and other key Platonic ideas. When Justin was reduced to a state of confusion, the old man recommended to him that he read the Hebrew prophets, who were inspired by the Holy Spirit to foretell events that were now taking place. "The prophets both glorified the Creator, the God and Father of all things, and proclaimed His Son, the Christ [sent] by Him" (Justin, *Dialogue with Trypho*, c. 7, ANF, vol. 1, p. 198). The old man then left, never to be seen by Justin again. "But immediately a flame was kindled in my soul; and a love of the prophets and of those men who are friends of Christ possessed me; and while revolving the old man's words in my mind, I found this philosophy [Christianity] alone to be safe and profitable.... for this reason, I am a philosopher" (Justin, *Dialogue with Trypho*, c. 8, ANF, vol. 1, p. 198, altered).

After Justin converted to Christianity, he went to the city of Rome, as so many ambitious people did, and opened a philosophical school above a bath. There were many rival philosophical schools, but in his school Justin taught what he saw as the highest philosophy, Christianity. He was not a member of the Roman clergy, and his school probably had no official standing with the local proto-orthodox church. His students probably included interested pagans, catechumens preparing for baptism, and baptized Christians who wanted a deeper knowledge of their faith.

Justin's *First Apology*, which fills about fifty pages in English translation, contains many arguments that other apologists later used. It represents an educated Christian's response to popular hostility, criticism from educated people, and official legal prosecution. Justin began by pleading to the Emperor Antoninus Pius for fairness, a virtue that the Romans valued. He argued that it was unjust to prosecute Christians only for the Name, that is, just for admitting they were Christians. He asked the authorities to investigate specific charges and to punish Christians only if they committed actual crimes.

Justin then described in positive terms the beliefs and especially the behavior of Christians. He hinted darkly that gnostic Christians engaged in sexual orgies and perversions but not his kind of Christians. (He identified with what we call "proto-orthodox Christians.") "All who take their opinions from these men [he has just criticized gnostics, including Simon Magus and Marcion] are...called Christians, just as also those who do not agree with the philosophers in their doctrines have in common with them the name of philosophers.... And whether they [the gnostic Christians] perpetrate those fabulous and shameful deeds—the upsetting of the lamp and promiscuous intercourse, and eating human flesh—we do not know; but we do know that they are neither persecuted nor put to death by you, at least on account of their opinions" (Justin, *First Apology*, c. 26, ANF, vol. 1, p. 172). He argued that contrary to the rumors, his Christians were sexually pure, self-disciplined, generous, honest, and peaceful. They paid their taxes. He stressed that their political loyalty was genuine in spite of their refusal to sacrifice to the emperor: "[w]hence to God alone we render worship, but in other things we gladly serve you, acknowledging you as kings and rulers of men, and praying that with your kingly power you be found to possess also sound judgment" (Justin, *First Apology*, c. 17, ANF, vol. 1, p. 168). He argued that the Christians' willingness to accept death was a proof of their sincerity. He asked why immoral people would be willing to endure death if they could escape by a few words addressed to the pagan magistrates. His argument for toleration, like that of most apologists, was that Christians were politically loyal and personally moral; in fact, they were good citizens.

Justin then turned his pen against popular paganism. He could expect some agreement from his educated audience because for centuries Greek and Roman intellectuals had mocked much in popular religion. Many educated pagans were, in fact, monotheists of a hazy sort, convinced that behind the many gods and goddesses of popular belief there was one divine power. Justin also drew on the Jewish tradition of criticizing paganism. Justin mocked the irrationality of worshipping idols made of stone, wood, silver, or gold that had to be guarded from thieves—what sort of gods could be stolen? He argued that much of popular paganism was sexually immoral. He claimed that the Greek myths, which inspired the finest of Greek art and literature, told filthy stories about the gods. Those immoral myths had counterparts in the behavior of pagans, whom he accused of committing infanticide by the abandonment of children, prostitution, and all sorts of things widely regarded as immoral. He declared that Christianity was morally superior to paganism. He also argued that Christianity made more sense in its clear assertion of one God. This must have been the sort of Christian talk that irritated the pagan-in-the-street, but Justin was not writing for them but rather for the political and intellectual elite, who had their own doubts about ordinary Greco-Roman religion. Many high-minded pagans might have agreed with much that Justin wrote.

In their debates with Jews about whether Jesus was the Messiah, Christians relied heavily on the argument that the Hebrew prophets foretold events in Jesus' life. Justin must have thought that even when trying to convince educated pagans, the argument based on prophecy was a useful intellectual weapon. Some Greeks and Romans knew something about the Jewish scriptures, which were believed to be so old that Moses predated Plato, which he did, and that Plato borrowed ideas from Moses, which he did not. Even for pagans, an argument from prophecy might carry some weight because their society was full of oracles, fortunetellers, and prophets. Justin quoted Old Testament texts that he thought foretold such events as Jesus' birth to a virgin, his suffering, his death, and his resurrection. He argued that contemporary events such as the destruction of Jerusalem and the conversion of gentiles to Christ were also foretold. But it is doubtful that such an argument from prophecy would be decisive for pagan intellectuals, who had at most a superficial acquaintance with the Greek Old Testament and had no reason to give any special authority to the prophets of the Jews. But the argument from prophecy was useful to Christians themselves who in the second century still had ongoing debates with Jews. The argument from prophecy armed them for those disputes, which might have been a reason why Justin stated it in detail.

Some in Justin's intended audience of intelligent pagans knew a great deal about the rich religious mix of the Roman Empire and wondered something like, "What's new in this Christian mish-mash?" Educated critics pointed to the fact that much in Christianity was also in other religions. The followers of Mithras had sacred meals; the Greek heroes, such as Heracles, were called the sons of the god Zeus; other cults had purifying washings—baptisms of a sort. To defend the uniqueness of Christianity, Justin explained away such similarities as wily tricks of demons, who had read and understood the Old Testament prophecies. The demons introduced future Christian practices into rival religions so as to confuse pagans and weak Christians into believing that Christianity was not much different from other religions. Justin argued that, clever as they were, the demons had failed to foresee the unique feature of Christianity, the crucifixion of Jesus, which separated Christianity from its demonic "imitators."

Most early Christian writers were reluctant to tell outsiders about the "mysteries" of their religion, perhaps because they feared they would be ridiculed. Some apologists took readers to the door of the Christian assemblies but did not tell them what happened inside. That silence fed the suspicions of outsiders that something shameful went on in the predawn or after-dark meetings of the Christians. Justin was unusual in that he opened the door to assure his readers that Christians did nothing immoral or anti-social. He is the most informative source about how baptism and the Eucharist were carried out in the middle of the second century. Justin's descriptions of baptism and the Eucharist can be found in chapter 9 of this book. They are worth reading for the unique, detailed information they provide.

Justin's *First Apology* is an important work in the history of proto-orthodox Christianity, in part because in it he argued that Christians could take and use all that was good in the created world. From its origins, the Christian movement generally had a low opinion of the world, which included Greco-Roman education, art, literature, and philosophy. But Paul once expressed a different idea that had a great future ahead of it. In his letter to the Christians at Philippi he wrote, "Finally, beloved, whatever is true, whatever is honorable, whatever is just, whatever is pure, whatever is pleasing, whatever is commendable, if there is any excellence and if there is anything worthy of praise, think about these things" (Phil 4:8). Unlike the vast majority of his fellow Christians, Justin, who had been educated in high culture, saw not just evil in the culture around him (although he saw plenty of that) but also some good. Justin developed an influential theory—a theology, really—that tried to explain why there were good things even among non-Christians. He took a clue from the prologue to John's gospel, where Christ was called the "Word" ("In the beginning was the word...."), which in Greek is *logos*. Justin argued that the Word, the Divine Logos, had been active in the created world even before it became flesh in Jesus. The Word/Logos had planted in Greco-Roman and Jewish culture some things that were true or good. In particular, the Logos had inspired the Hebrew prophets and even the "good" pagan philosophers, especially Plato, who taught things that were compatible with Christian belief and ethical behavior. Because the Logos was the source for everything good or true, whether in the pagan or Jewish traditions, Christians could claim those good things as theirs. Justin even declared that all good people who lived by reason (another meaning of the complex word "logos") before the Logos appeared in Jesus had been Christians without knowing it: "But lest some should...for the undermining of what we teach, maintain that we say that Christ was born one hundred and fifty years ago...and should cry out against us as though all men who were born before Him were not accountable—let us anticipate and solve the difficulty. We have been taught that Christ is the first-born of God, and we have declared that He is the Word [Logos] of whom every race of men were partakers. And they who have lived with the *Logos* are Christians, even though they have been thought atheists..." (Justin, *First Apology*, c. 46, ANF, vol. 1, p. 178). But Justin argued that there was no substitute for Christianity, which was better than the Hebrew prophets and the good Greek philosophers because the Logos had been present only partially in them but in its entirety in Jesus. Hence, Justin thought that Christians were in a position to judge the surrounding culture, rejecting its evil aspects and claiming as their own its true and good things. This was a revolutionary idea in a religion that usually held the world at arm's length.

ORIGEN (ABOUT 185–251)

Alexandria was one of the great cities of the ancient world, large, rich, and religiously diverse, with vibrant Jewish, pagan, and Christian groups. Reliable evidence for the presence of proto-orthodox Christians in Alexandria appears only in the later second century. Clement (about 160–215), who taught and wrote in Alexandria, may have been, like Justin at Rome, the teacher in a private school that taught Christianity as the true philosophy. His younger contemporary Origen was the most important Christian thinker between Paul in the first century and Augustine in the fifth century. Origen left extensive writings, including commentaries on scripture, sermons, and treatises on a variety of subjects. In his writings, he occasionally referred to his own life and times. In addition,

Eusebius of Caesarea wrote something like a biography of Origen, as a consequence of which we know more about him than about any other Christian who lived before the fourth century (EH 6). He was born in Egypt to a Christian family. He had an excellent secular education in Greek literature and philosophy. Although there were no Christian schools for the education of young people, he had a religious education within his family, encouraged by his father, who had him memorize scripture. After his father's martyrdom in 202, Origen taught to support his mother and six brothers. The bishop of Alexandria asked the eighteen-year-old Origen to head the catechetical school, that is, the school that provided elementary religious and moral instruction to the people who were preparing for baptism.

It would have been difficult for a bright, well-educated man like Origen to avoid contact with rival forms of Christianity. For instance, early in his career a rich gnostic Christian lady welcomed him into her household and offered financial support. He went there for a while, but he refused to pray with her gnostic Christian chaplain named "Paul" (EH 6.2). From his youth Origen was an ascetic, that is, he chose to live with the minimum in clothing, food, sleep, and other physical comforts. Chapter 16 of this book quotes Eusebius of Caesarea's description of Origen's rigorous life of voluntary self-denial. Eusebius reported that Origen had himself castrated perhaps in response to Jesus' saying (Mt 19:12): "It is not everyone who can accept what I have said, but only those to whom it is granted. There are eunuchs born that way from their mother's womb, there are eunuchs made so by men and there are eunuchs who have made themselves that way for the sake of the kingdom of heaven. Let anyone accept this who can." Eusebius wrote that Origen chose castration so that he could discuss religious matters with women without suspicion of sexual immorality (EH 6:8). Modern scholars are divided as to whether the castration actually occurred.

Origen eventually gave up the catechetical school with its elementary instruction and opened a private school for advanced religious study, as Justin Martyr had done at Rome about seventy years earlier. Such private schools, run by philosophers of every sort, were a common feature of the intellectual life of the Greco-Roman world. Origen stood in the tradition of Christian thought laid out by Justin Martyr and Clement of Alexandria, that encouraged the use of all in secular culture that was compatible with proto-orthodox Christianity. He taught secular subjects in his school but regarded them as a preparation for the study of the scriptures. For most of his life, he was not a member of the clergy. He was a private teacher who lived frugally from the sale of his secular books, the fees of students, and the gifts of admirers. As he grew older, his reputation among Christians was high. He was the most prominent Christian intellectual of his generation. Once when he was in Palestine, he was invited to preach before the bishops, an unusual honor because he was not yet ordained to the clergy. The pagan Empress Julia Mammea invited him to meet with her. Even non-Christian intellectuals acknowledged that he was a learned man. He acted occasionally as a consultant to bishops, who asked him to carry on formal debates with heretics. In the course of his life, he visited such places as Rome, Athens, Palestine, Asia Minor, and Arabia. He was eventually ordained a presbyter in Palestine. When he was about forty he had a serious conflict with the bishop of Alexandria, who criticized him for his castration, for preaching while unordained, and for accepting ordination as a presbyter in Palestine instead of in Alexandria. The Alexandrian bishop might have been jealous of Origen's eminence, but in any case, in about 234 forty-nine-year-old Origen moved permanently to Caesarea in Palestine, where the bishop was a friendly patron.

Although he was an eminent teacher, Origen was reluctant to write anything. But in his forties he began to do so with the financial support of Ambrose, a wealthy educated man whom he had converted from Valentinian gnostic Christianity. Ambrose paid for stenographers to whom Origen dictated (most ancient writers dictated their works) and for female scribes who multiplied copies of his works. Origen produced the huge output of approximately six thousand scrolls. His prodigious energy earned him the nickname "Adamantius," from the Greek word for the hardest metal.

For most of Origen's adult life, Christianity enjoyed relative peace under the later emperors of the Severan dynasty, who were interested in all sorts of religions. The overthrow of the Severan emperors in 235, when Origen was about fifty years old, ended the Christians' peace. The new emperor, Maximinus (235–238), and his successors had to deal with the deteriorating condition of the empire. Maximinus attacked Christianity directly and forcefully. Origen fled to Asia Minor to wait out the persecution, which ended with the emperor's death in 238. Origen was later arrested in Decius' persecution (250–251), tortured, but eventually released and thus was a confessor. As a result of his mistreatment in prison, he died at Tyre shortly thereafter. His tomb was still visible when the crusaders arrived in the twelfth century.

Origen and the Scriptures

Origen's biography tells us a great deal about Christianity in the third century. But he is especially remembered for his intellectual achievements, above all in the study of the scriptures. Origen was aware that the very words of the Old Testament were in some doubt. Scribes wrote by hand every copy of the Old Testament (and the New Testament and indeed every ancient document). They depended on the accuracy of the document in front of them. They could add their own mistakes as they copied long, complex, or strange documents. Long before Origen's lifetime, Christians used as their Old Testament the Septuagint that had been translated into Greek in Egypt in the third century BCE. In some passages, the Septuagint did not agree with the Hebrew documents that Jews were using in Origen's day. For instance, Origen knew that in the Septuagint, Isaiah 7:14 declared that a virgin (*parthenos*) would bring forth a child, whereas the Hebrew text used by contemporary Jews declared that a young girl (*almah*) would have a child. In such a situation, there could be no assurance among Christians they had the accurate words of the Old Testament. Origen also realized that there could be no religious debate with Jews on the basis of scripture unless both sides agreed that the words were accurate. Origen became the first textual critic of the Bible, the first to try in a systematic way to determine the words of the Old Testament, a massive task. A Jewish Christian taught him Hebrew, a rare achievement among gentile Christians, although Origen may never have become fluent in the language. Over a period of twenty years, he put together a huge book (estimated at six thousand pages), called the *Hexapla* ("Sixfold Bible"). In six parallel columns, he copied the scriptures in Hebrew and four Greek translations. In the first column, he placed the Hebrew text; in the second column, he placed a Greek transliteration of the Hebrew so that a Greek speaker could pronounce the Hebrew words; in the third column, he placed a very literal translation from Hebrew into Greek that had been made about 130 by Aquila, a convert to Judaism; in the fourth column, he placed a translation into Greek by Symmachus (late second century); in the fifth column, he placed the Septuagint, the Greek translation used by the proto-orthodox Christians; and in the sixth column, he placed a late second-century Greek translation by Theodotion, who might have been a Jewish Christian. As a result, the Old Testament was written out five times in parallel columns that could be compared. As he carried out this huge task, he carefully drew attention with special marks to the many variations among the columns of text. In later centuries, Jerome and other biblical scholars consulted the *Hexapla* at Caesarea. There was probably never more than one copy of this massive work, and it does not survive.

Because Origen regarded the scriptures as the revelation of God, he wanted to determine the exact words—hence his *Hexapla*. But he also wanted to know what those words meant. Origen was a tireless interpreter of the scriptures, about which he wrote voluminously. The interpretation of scripture is often called "exegesis," and the interpreter is often called an "exegete"; both words derived from a Greek word meaning "to explain or interpret." His techniques for exegesis had a lasting influence on later generations. Origen's efforts to understand the meaning of scripture provide us an opportunity to discuss the important question of how early Christian scholars interpreted scripture. Educated Christians did not regard the scriptures as simple or clear. They often thought that the scriptures, under seemingly simple words, presented a major intellectual challenge. Some exegetes compared the scriptures with a vast, almost impenetra-

ble forest. To avoid being lost, those who entered the forest needed an experienced guide, who was the exegete or interpreter. Others thought that God had purposely expressed his revelation in ways that were difficult to understand so as to stimulate the thought of the interpreter. Origen believed that God had concealed important spiritual meanings beneath the surface of the scriptural words. His task, and that of any interpreter, was to discover those spiritual meanings. Not just anyone could interpret the scriptures without the danger of serious error. The skilled Christian interpreter needed long experience, detailed familiarity with the words of the scriptures, methods to draw out the hidden meanings, and even inspiration by the Holy Spirit to do it correctly. To put it briefly, Origen thought that the interpretation of scripture belonged to an elite of Christians. Bishops and presbyters might— or might not—belong to that elite.

The way scriptures were interpreted led to significant theological consequences. Gnostic Christian teachers, who believed that their secret knowledge enabled them to find the deep meanings beneath the simple biblical words, had been the pioneers of formal biblical interpretation. Origen attempted to counter the biblical interpretations of the gnostics because he feared that if no one did, the gnostic views would prevail: "But even now the heterodox [heretics], with a pretense of knowledge, are rising up against the holy Church of Christ and are bringing compositions in many books, announcing an interpretation of the texts both of the Gospels and of the apostles. If we are silent and do not set up the true and sound teachings...they will prevail over inquisitive souls which, in the lack of saving nourishment, hasten to foods that are forbidden and are truly unclean and abominable" (Origen, Commentary on John, 5:8, in *Commentary on the Gospel According to John, Books 1–10*, translated by Ronald E. Heine, FOC, vol. 80 [Washington, DC, 1989], p. 166). When some gnostic Christians read the Old Testament literally, they created an unflattering portrait of the Creator-God, whom they depicted as petty, vindictive, cruel, and a liar—perhaps not even the real God. Marcion of Sinope had gathered numerous followers, in part by insisting that a literal reading of the Old Testament showed that the God described there did not act as if he was Jesus' loving Father. Some proto-orthodox Christians favored a literal reading of the scriptures, in which the words meant simply what they said. Origen knew such people and criticized them (and they criticized him). He thought those who kept to a literal approach taught that God did such unjust things that they drove intelligent Christians from the Church.

Origen and other interpreters tried to defend God against his critics by interpreting the scriptures in figurative rather than literal ways. They began their interpretative efforts with the assumption that the "real" meaning of the scripture could never be unworthy of God by depicting him in a negative light and could never deviate from the rule of faith, that is, the core of beliefs of the Church. If the literal meaning of a biblical text seemed unworthy of God or contradictory to the rule of faith, the proto-orthodox Christians interpreted it so as to make it uplifting, useful, and orthodox. By the third century, interpreters, among whom Origen stood out, had mastered ways to find what they regarded as the true meanings hidden in the scriptures.

The canon of the New Testament was still in its formative stages during Origen's career. But he accepted as authoritative the four gospels, fourteen letters of Paul, Acts of the Apostles, I Peter, I John, Jude, and Revelation. He quoted occasionally from documents that were eventually excluded from the accepted books, such as the Protoevangelium of James and the Gospel of Peter. Christians had thought a great deal about how the Old Covenant, represented in the Old Testament, related to the New Covenant created by Jesus. For instance some argued that the Old Testament was imperfect, the New Testament perfect. Others argued that God revealed things in the Old Testament in a veiled way that he revealed clearly in the New Testament. Still others held that the true meaning of events and people in the Old Testament became clear only in the light of the New Testament. Origen built on those comparisons by using a method of interpretation that modern scholars call "typology," in which people and events in the Old Testament were explained as foreshadowings of people and events in the New Testament. The interpreters thought that the Old Testament was always about

Christ but that became clear only after Christ came. Origen did not invent typology, which went back to the earliest days of Christianity. One example will do. Genesis, chapters 16–21, told the relatively long story of Abraham's quest for a male heir. Because his wife Sarah was sterile, with her permission he impregnated her slave Hagar, who gave birth to Ishmael. God eventually granted the aged Abraham and the aged Sarah a son, Isaac. In Galatians 4:21–30, Paul found in the story of Abraham, Sarah, and Hagar a deeper meaning. He wrote that the two women represented the two covenants with God. Hagar the slave woman represented the first covenant of the Mosaic Law, and Sarah the wife represented the second covenant of freedom in Christ. Paul found other meanings as well. The slave woman represented the earthly Jerusalem, and the wife represented the heavenly Jerusalem. Paul concluded by telling the Galatians, "So then, friends, we are children not of the slave but of the free woman." For other instances where the writers interpreted Old Testament people and events as foreshadowing the reality that was revealed in Jesus, look at I Peter (3:20–21) and the Letter to the Hebrews (especially chapters 9–10).

Typology almost always involved a comparison of the Old Testament and the New Testament. Origen also used the interpretive tool called "allegory," where one thing in a biblical account stands for another. Pagan scholars, especially at Alexandria in Origen's native Egypt, had used allegory to reinterpret the myths of the gods when they seemed at a literal level to be ridiculous or immoral. Philo and other Jews living in the Diaspora had used allegory to explain things in the Hebrew scriptures that seemed barbarous. The writers of the gospels also wrote that Jesus used figurative and allegorical language. In Matthew (13:1–9 and 13:18–23), Jesus told a story that would be easily understood in an agricultural region such as Galilee. A man sowing seed cast it rather carelessly on all sorts of ground: on a path, on rocky ground, among thorns, but also on good soil. Jesus' disciples did not know what the parable meant, so he explained it to them privately. It turned out that the simple agricultural story was not really about the sowing of seed at all. It was an allegory about how different people reacted to hearing God's word (the seed). Each realistic agricultural detail stood for something more spiritual:

> When anyone hears the word of the kingdom and does not understand it, the evil one comes and snatches away what is sown in the heart: this is what was sown on the path. As for what was sown on rocky ground, this is the one who hears the word and immediately receives it with joy; yet such a person has no root, but endures only for a while, and when trouble or persecution arises on account of the word, that person immediately falls away. As for what was sown among thorns, this is the one who hears the word, but the cares of the world and the lure of wealth choke the word, and it yields nothing. But as for what was sown on good soil, this is the one who hears the word and understands it, who indeed bears fruit and yields, in one case a hundredfold, in another sixty, and in another thirty.

Jesus told other parables, some of which had an allegorical explanation attached (Mt 13:24–30), but most had no explanation. But what if every biblical story might really be an allegory? Later interpreters tried their pens and intelligence at allegorizing almost any story in either testament. To many modern people, the allegories seem forced, but they were apparently useful and satisfying to ancient Christians. Allegory allowed the interpreter to find a deeper spiritual meaning where none appeared at the literal level. Allegory was a powerful intellectual tool that could find spiritual meaning in a dull genealogy or a shocking story of slaughter. For instance, the Old Testament book called the "Song of Solomon" or the "Song of Songs" or the "Canticle of Canticles" is a celebration of the physical love between a man and woman. Incidentally, God is never mentioned in it. Perhaps it was composed to be sung at a wedding. If the Song of Songs was made into a modern film, it might raise controversy if shown on prime-time television! Yet, there it was in the Hebrew scriptures. In line with Jewish practices, Origen recommended that the Song not be revealed to simple Christian believers. Some Jewish scholars allegorized it to make God the husband and Israel the wife. Origen was the first Christian interpreter to interpret the Song as an allegory in which the husband is actually Christ

and the wife is actually his Church. An allegorical interpretation turned a somewhat spicy poem into a rich meditation on the relation of God to his beloved Israel, or to his Church or even, as some suggested, to an individual soul.

Origen assumed there were different levels of meaning in each biblical text or even in each biblical word. There could be two meanings, literal and spiritual, or even three meanings, a literal meaning, a moral meaning, and a spiritual meaning. The literal meaning of a biblical text was just the beginning. Interpreters were usually more eager to go beyond the literal meaning to find the deeper, more important meanings of scripture. Origen did not invent the two-level or three-level method of interpretation, but he used it extensively. He wanted especially to refute literalists like some gnostic Christians and the Jews who, from his point of view, stressed the least significant meaning of the Bible, which was the literal one.

Many people might be satisfied with the literal meaning of the Old and New Testaments, but educated interpreters, using sophisticated techniques such as typology, allegory, and levels of meaning, pursued the mysteries hidden under the biblical words. Some of the brightest Christians, among whom Origen was outstanding, labored to find satisfying, orthodox interpretations of the scriptures.

While he was trying to determine the words of the Old Testament, Origen was also producing commentaries on virtually every book of the Old and New Testaments—sometimes three commentaries on the same book. His scriptural commentaries influenced the understanding of the Bible for centuries. In addition to his lifelong attention to the words and deeper meaning of the scriptures, Origen wrote works addressed to contemporary needs or doubts. Their titles are revealing: *On Prayer, On Resurrection,* and *On Martyrdom.* When he lived at Caesarea in Palestine, he preached regularly during public worship services. About 280 sermons survive. Much of Origen's written work had an apologetic aspect, defending proto-orthodox Christianity against gnostic, Jewish, and pagan critics. In the late 240s, Origen's friend and patron Ambrose brought to his attention Celsus' book called *The True Word,* an extensive and sophisticated attack on Christianity, written about seventy years earlier. Origen had never heard of the book and, after some hesitation, agreed to respond.

He wrote the longest, most sophisticated apologetic work of the ancient Church in his book *Against Celsus*, which takes up 508 pages in Henry Chadwick's translation.

Origen the Theologian

In ordinary life, there is often a distinction between "faith" and "theology." Faith usually comes first. It is what people believe. For instance, some Christians might believe that the scriptures are without errors or that in the Eucharist, the bread and wine really become Jesus' body and blood. But throughout history, faith has presented intellectual problems that many ordinary believers are not able to solve. Theology is the effort to draw out the implications of faith, to create coherent intellectual systems based on faith, and to make Christianity comprehensible to the culture of a specific time and place. Some of the earliest Christian theologians were gnostics, who were skilled at creating complex theological systems. But certainly Paul of Tarsus, Irenaeus of Lyons (115–202), Tertullian of Carthage (about 160–220), and Clement of Alexandria (160–215) were theologians who wrote about the faith that they largely shared with their fellow believers. In their surviving writings, they tried to turn that shared faith into a theology or theologies. In addition to being a scholar of broad learning and remarkable energy, Origen was a creative theologian. It is important to pause here to clarify a view that Origen shared with many other Christian thinkers. There was stream of esoteric or secretive Christian thinking that went back to the first century and remained strong in later centuries. Paul was thought to be expressing that idea when he told the Corinthians that he fed them only milk because they were not spiritual people, but when he dealt with mature or spiritual people he fed them solid food (1 Cor 2:6–3:3). Later proto-orthodox thinkers divided believers between a large group of simple Christians and a smaller group of mature Christians. Fear motivated the simple Christians, who were weighed down by worldly concerns. Love for God motivated the mature Christians, who had separated from worldly concerns, often by

self-denial and devotion to scripture reading. The simple Christians were members of the Church but were thought incapable of understanding the deeper mysteries of the scriptures. In fact, some mysteries had to be kept from them.

Origen wrote a daring synthesis of Christian theology, called *On First Principles (Peri Archōn)*, which attempted to refute gnostic Christians, especially the followers of Valentinus, while answering their questions about where evil, matter, and human unhappiness originated. He wanted to show that a mature proto-orthodox Christian could be a true gnostic, that is, "one who knows," as opposed to the false gnostics, whom he opposed as heretics. He knew that his undertaking would be criticized by many of his fellow simple Christians. He probably never intended that they have access to it. Origen asserted that he accepted the Church's beliefs as they were expressed in creeds and the rule of faith, "But I hope to be a man of the Church. I hope to be addressed not by the name of some heresiarch [the term for the founder of a heresy] but by the name of Christ. I hope to have his name, which is blessed upon the earth. I desire, both in deed and in thought, both to be and to be called a Christian" (Origen, Homily on Luke 16.6, in *Origen: Homilies on Luke: Fragments on Luke*, translated by Joseph T. Lienhard, FOC, vol. 94 [Washington, DC, 1996], pp. 67–68). But the traditional creeds were brief and said nothing about many topics, on which Origen felt free to speculate and to seek the inner meaning of the scriptures. He carefully qualified his views and did not insist that they were true. Yet, his *On First Principles* shocked his contemporaries and succeeding generations of Christian thinkers. I cannot do justice to the complexity of the book, but here are some points to give the flavor of it. *On First Principles* had a huge topic, embracing all that happened before creation, in the created world, and after the created world would cease to exist. The unapproachable, indescribable God had created a realm of purely spiritual beings, each of whom had free will. They chose to rebel, with varying degrees of guilt, as a consequence of which there are different kinds of people and different kinds of angels and demons. Only the Christ-Spirit remained loyal to God. As a consequence of that rebellion, the material universe in which humans live was created. Unlike many gnostic Christians, Origen denied that the created world was evil. Although flawed, it shares in the goodness and order of its creator. The universe also has a good purpose. God created it as an educative tool to restore the fallen spirits to their former happy state. Because God respects free will and forces no one, the fallen spirits must voluntarily choose to repent. The world's evils and suffering are part of God's providential plan because they cause thinking beings, whether they want to or not, to realize their dependence on God and to acknowledge his preeminence. Creatures move up and down a scale of perfection according to the choices they make. Origen speculated that across endless time and maybe even across successive creations all the fallen spirits would return to God by their own free choice—perhaps even Satan could be saved. The Christ-Spirit was the force for restoration in the universe. That Christ-Spirit came in a special, intense way in the man Jesus to trick and crush the demons. Not everyone can perceive that—only the mature Christians. Origen interpreted figuratively much of early Christian imagery—heaven, hell, resurrection, second coming, millennial rule. He called literal-minded Christians "judaizers" because he thought that they paid too much attention to the literal words of scripture at the expense of the inner meaning.

In spite of his massive contribution to the study of the Bible and his status as a confessor for the faith, Origen became a controversial figure in the fourth and fifth centuries. In the many decades since Origen had died, theological views had evolved. Some of his views came to seem wrong, dangerous, even heretical. Some of his *theological* views were even condemned at councils. His most controversial works, including *On First Principles*, were no longer copied or were revised to make them more orthodox. But he had many followers, and his works, translated into Latin and other languages, influenced the intellectual history of Christianity for centuries.

Although we have no evidence that Christian intellectuals influenced any emperor or high official or prevented any persecution, they were important for at least three reasons. First, they might actually have written for their fellow proto-orthodox

Christians, many of whom must have been bothered by criticisms from pagans, Jews, and other kinds of Christians but were unable to formulate a response on their own. The Christian readers of an apologist might find a response to criticism directed at them. Second, the apologists opened a dialogue with Greco-Roman society that was to have immense success in the future. Within a few centuries the Christian Church had embraced many, but not all, aspects of that society and was embraced by that society. Finally, the apologists contributed to the development of theology. In their efforts to make Christianity appear reasonable and to defend its beliefs against ridicule or refutation, they tackled such thorny issues as the relation of God to the created world, the relation of Jesus to God, the relation of faith to reason, the role of Christians in Greco-Roman society, and the proper ways to interpret scripture. They set directions in which Christian theology developed. Later generations of Christians thought that some of the early intellectuals' theological ideas were inadequate—heretical even—which perhaps explains why the apologies survive in so few copies. For instance, on the thorny issue of Jesus' relationship to the Father, Justin Martyr referred once to Jesus as a "second god" (*Dialogue with Trypho*, 129.1), which implied that Jesus was subordinate to the Father, a view that roused great controversy in the fourth century. But in the second and third centuries, before such doctrines as the nature of the Trinity had been worked out in detail, the apologists were probably reflecting widely held views among the proto-orthodox Christians of their day.

The trail blazed by the apologists points to a contrast to Judaism's path of development. In the first century, Judaism was to some degree a missionary religion with enough appeal to make some converts, who were called "proselytes," and to gather some sympathizers, who were called "God-fearers." The crushing Roman defeats of the Jews in 73 and 135 led the religious leaders of Judaism to rethink their stance toward the outside world. They survived in part by choosing to separate as much as they could from that world. For instance, as the Greek translation of the Old Testament (the Septuagint) became the version that the Christians used, the Jewish leaders rejected it in favor of the Hebrew version, or, in the Greek-speaking Diaspora, Jewish translators made new Greek translations for Greek-speaking Jews. Even though the Roman emperors tried to prevent or limit conversion to Judaism, it remained possible, but in the later Roman Empire leading rabbis themselves made conversion more difficult and even discouraged it. Judaism survived—along with Christianity it is only living religion from the Greco-Roman world—but in a self-isolated form. In part under the influence of the apologists, Christianity did not reject Greco-Roman culture but rather adopted some parts while rejecting others. This was an important step toward the Christianization of the empire in the fourth and fifth centuries.

FURTHER READING

Ancient Sources

You can enter the debate between Celsus and Origen from two directions. You can read Origen's refutation of Celsus in Henry Chadwick's translation of Origen's *Contra Celsum* (Cambridge, 1953). But you can also focus on Celsus' arguments against Christianity in *Celsus on the True Doctrine: A Discourse against the Christians*, translated by R. Joseph Hoffmann (New York, 1987), where Hoffmann could reconstruct Celsus' views because Origen quoted and paraphrased so many of them. See:

Origen's *On First Principles (Peri Archōn)*, a challenging work, is translated by G. W. Butterworth, *Origen: On First Principles* (London, 1936, and reprinted several times).

Leslie William Barnard, Justin, *The First Apology in Saint Justin Martyr: The First and Second Apologies*, with introduction and notes by the translator by ACW no. 56 (New York, 1997), pp. 23–72 and notes pp. 103–186.

Eusebius, *Ecclesiastical History*, book 6, has an account of Origen's life written about two generations after his death.

Andrew Louth, ed., *The Epistle to Diognetus*, in *Early Christian Writings*, translated by Maxwell Staniforth, revised by the editor (London, 1987), pp. 137–151, is a brief, calm, positive defense of Christianity written by an anonymous second-century Christian.

Modern Works

Robert M. Grant, *Greek Apologists of the Second Century* (Philadelphia, 1988).

Robert M. Grant, with David Tracy, *A Short History of the Interpretation of the Bible*, second edition (Philadelphia, 1984), especially pp. 3–82, treats early Christian forms of biblical interpretation.

Joseph Wilson Trigg, *Origen: The Bible and Philosophy in the Third-Century Church* (Atlanta, 1983), and Joseph W. Trigg, *Origen*, in the Early Church Fathers series (London and New York, 1998), where there are translated examples of Origen's interpretation of scripture.

CHAPTER 9

Proto-Orthodox Christian Communities in the Third Century

Some people think of the history of Christianity as primarily the history of theology. But Christians did not spend most of their time arguing about, thinking about, and accepting or rejecting abstract beliefs. They lived in communities that shared not only beliefs but also such elements as organization, building styles, art, and ways of worship. Many kinds of Christians were active in the third century but this chapter is about the proto-orthodox Christians who lived in independent communities shaped by the office of the bishop, the emerging canon of scripture, and their creeds. By the third century, such churches, especially the larger ones about which we have some sources, were complicated. They had developed ways to preserve themselves, to attract new members, to protect their values, and to sharpen the differences between them and the outside world. You can visualize third-century proto-orthodox Christian communities as three concentric circles. In the innermost circle were the people who were full members, the baptized faithful. Two groups were in the second circle: the unbaptized catechumens ("those under instruction") who were seeking entry to the inner circle and the baptized penitents who had been expelled from the inner circle and were trying to get back in. The huge third circle held the non-believers (pagans and Jews), the former Christians (apostates), and the unacceptable Christians (heretics). There was significant diversity among third-century proto-orthodox churches, but a brief look at the internal arrangements of the communities about which we know something is enlightening.

THE BAPTIZED FAITHFUL

The baptized faithful filled the inner circle of every church. They were called the "laity," from a Greek word meaning "the people" (*laos*). Most of the laity seem to have been married people who worked for a living and raised families, but even within that group distinctions developed. A few laypeople, including widows, virgins, and male ascetics, chose a life of self-denial. Already in the First Letter to Timothy 5:3–16, "real" widows had a special place in the community, which was encouraged to support poor widows over sixty, who were expected to devote themselves to prayer and works of charity. In the middle of the third century, Bishop Cornelius of Rome (251–253) wrote that his church supported fifteen hundred widows and distressed persons (EH 6.43). In the late fourth century, John Chrysostom ("the Golden-Mouthed") estimated that there were three thousand widows and virgins supported by the church at Antioch (John Chrysostom, Homily 66.3 on Matthew, NPNF, first series, vol. 10, p. 407).

The most important distinction within the community of the baptized faithful was that between the laypeople and their religious leaders, who were called "clergy," that is, the bishops, presbyters and deacons, and lesser functionaries. In the hundreds of small proto-orthodox Christian communities scattered around the Roman Empire, many of the clergy in the second and third centuries must, like the leather-worker Paul, have had jobs to support themselves. But in large communities, a professional clergy was emerging whose members were supported by the offerings of the faithful, which were distributed to them by the bishop. Bishop Cornelius gave us a rare glimpse of the body of clergy that had developed by 250 at Rome, a large church. He noted that there was one bishop, forty-six presbyters, seven deacons, seven subdeacons, forty-two acolytes, and a total of fifty-two exorcists, readers, and doorkeepers (EH 6.43).

THE CATECHUMENS ("THOSE UNDER INSTRUCTION")

By the third century, there were church members who had been born into Christian families. But converts remained perhaps the most important source of growth. The way outsiders were integrated into the community had changed since the earliest days. Some first-century evidence suggests that admission to the just-forming Christian communities was "easy," perhaps prompted by the desire to reach as many people as possible before the Lord returned. For instance, Luke wrote that on the road to Gaza the evangelist Philip encountered an Ethiopian eunuch who was returning from worship at Jerusalem. The eunuch was reading the prophet Isaiah 53:7–8 ("Like a sheep he was led to the slaughter...."), which Philip explained was a prophecy about Jesus. After Philip told the eunuch more about Jesus, the eunuch believed and said, "Look, here is some water! What is to prevent me from being baptized?" Philip baptized him then and there (Acts 8:26–40). But as Christ's second coming receded and Christian communities were forced to organize for an indefinite future, some leaders perceived a negative side to such quick conversions. Churches gained members whose commitment was superficial or who were heretics or who renounced Christianity when faced with persecution or even with social disapproval. By about 200, many Christian communities were beginning to insist on testing non-Christian adults before admitting them to baptism. Those who wished to convert were held for a time in what I have called the "second circle." The *Apostolic Tradition* written by Hippolytus (about 170–about 236) tells a great deal about the barriers that had been put up to prevent quick baptism. Hippolytus was a presbyter of the Roman church and an important theological thinker who clashed with two Roman bishops. He

became the bishop of a schismatic group at Rome. Hippolytus was troubled by changes in worship introduced by those he called "ignorant men," perhaps the bishop and presbyters of the Roman church with whom he had a falling-out. In 235, the Roman Emperor Maximin (235–238) sent both Hippolytus and Bishop Pontian of Rome into exile on the island of Sardinia. The two men, who died soon, may have been reconciled during their sufferings because when Maximin's persecution ended, Bishop Fabian (236–250) brought both bodies back to Rome, where they were buried on the same day, August 13. In later centuries, Hippolytus was regarded as a martyr.

In his *Apostolic Tradition*, Hippolytus laid out a vivid verbal picture of the diverse sorts of people who might want to become catechumens (in his terminology, they wanted "to hear the word"). He also described the measures taken by the important Christian community at Rome to receive some as catechumens and to reject others: "Those who come to hear the word for the first time should first be brought to the teachers in the house, before the people come in. And they [the teachers] should enquire concerning the reason why they have turned to the faith. And those [Christians] who brought them shall bear witness whether they have the ability to hear the word" (Hippolytus, *The Apostolic Tradition*, c. 15, in *On the Apostolic Tradition*, an English version with introduction and commentary by Alistair Stewart-Sykes [Crestwood, NY, 2001], pp. 97–98). Hippolytus anticipated that the preliminary inquiry would reveal people whom the community was unwilling to allow to hear the word. Some prospective converts were rejected outright, including those who committed unspeakable sexual sins, magicians who were not even to be considered for acceptance, and those possessed by a demon, who were not allowed to hear the word until they were freed by the church's exorcists. If soldiers executed anyone or took the military oath, which was pagan in content, they were rejected. Other prospective converts had to change the way that they earned their living before they could hear the word. A pimp should stop or be rejected. Painters or carvers of pagan idols and pagan priests should stop or be rejected. Actors, charioteers, gladiators, or those in related professions should stop or be rejected. Hippolytus was lenient toward some who might have been rejected. People who taught children worldly (probably pagan) knowledge should stop. But if they had no other way to make a living, they could be forgiven. Hippolytus was sympathetic toward slave women who were at the mercy of their owners' sexual demands. A slave-concubine could hear the word if she had reared her children and had been monogamous with her owner. On the other hand, a man with a concubine had to marry properly (not necessarily the concubine) or be rejected. This is just a selection of the many people whom Hippolytus thought were unfit to be accepted as catechumens because of their occupations and moral behavior (Hippolytus, *The Apostolic Tradition*, c. 16).

If those who wanted to hear the word were judged to be worthy—and there must have been many of them—they became catechumens. From one perspective, the unbaptized catechumens were Christians or at least Christians-in-the-making. They had one foot in the church with the other in the "world." They had begun the transition from the world of sin but had not yet been admitted to the tight world of the baptized faithful. For instance, Hippolytus allowed catechumens to attend the assembly when the scriptures were read and the sermon was given, but they were told to leave when the "mysteries" (that is, the Eucharist) were performed. Only the baptized could participate in or even witness the Eucharist. The catechumens could not give or receive the kiss of peace because their kiss was not yet pure. They could not take part in the religious meals of the baptized faithful.

When the bishop and elders thought that a catechumen had been sufficiently tested, which according to Hippolytus might take as long as three years, they would admit him or her to baptism. The weeks before the baptism were filled with instruction and exorcisms (remember those fifty-two exorcists in the Roman church about 250) because all non-baptized persons were thought to be in the grip of evil powers. After the catechumens were accepted for baptism, they were told the exact words of the local church's creed, which in some places they memorized and recited at their baptism. The bishop, assisted by his presbyters

and deacons/deaconesses, baptized the catechumens early on Sunday morning, perhaps at Easter or Pentecost, which were preferred days for baptism in later centuries. After the baptism, the new members were admitted to the innermost circle of the community, that of the baptized faithful.

PENITENTS, APOSTATES, EXCOMMUNICATES

The movement of people was not entirely one way, from non-believer to catechumen to baptized believer. Some catechumens and baptized faithful chose to leave Christian churches for what must have been a wide variety of reasons. Those who stayed in the church scornfully called those who left "apostates" ("those who turn away"). Other catechumens and baptized faithful were expelled for moral and theological faults that the community thought were intolerable. If apostates or excommunicated persons tried to come back, the church might grant them the status of penitents, which was another subgroup within many church congregations.

Christians saw conversion as the pivotal moment in a person's life. They thought that those who believed in the Christian message, repented for their sins, and were baptized were freed from all prior sin and given a fresh start. They had put away the old self and put on a new self (Eph 4:22–24) and were a new creation (Gal 6:15). The "saints," as Paul called baptized believers, were expected to avoid serious sin after they had been baptized. Reality turned out to be different. Some baptized faithful committed serious sins. We need to be clear. The baptized Christians who committed "ordinary" sins, such as committing petty theft or telling lies or gossiping, were told to confess their sin to God and to seek the advice of the bishop or a presbyter about what they should do. Ordinarily they were counseled to repent sincerely and then to give alms to the needy, to pray, and to fast.

But proto-orthodox Christians regarded a few sins as so serious, so deadly, that a consensus grew that these sins had to have significant public consequences, perhaps even expulsion from the community. The really serious lapses included such things as apostasy (the renunciation of Christianity), idolatry (the worship of idols), sexual sins, and murder. It was not just moral lapses that led to expulsion. Heresy could also lead to excommunication. In the mid-second century, when Marcion explained to the Roman clergy his theological views about the distinction between the Good God of the gospels and the Just God of the Jewish scriptures, he was formally expelled from the Roman church.

But what if an apostate or expelled sinner wanted to return to the church? Opinions and practices varied. Christians generally believed that all members had repented when they were baptized. During the second and third centuries, Christians debated among themselves whether any baptized person who committed a really serious sin, for which he was expelled, could ever be granted a *second* repentance and then be readmitted to the congregation. Some rigorous believers who opposed any second repentance relied on texts in the evolving New Testament that seemed to point to a category of unforgivable sins. "And I tell you, every one of men's sins and blasphemies will be forgiven, but blasphemy against the Spirit will not be forgiven. And anyone who says a word against the Son of Man will be forgiven; but let anyone speak against the Holy Spirit and he will not be forgiven either in this world or in the next" (Mt 12:31–32). "If anybody sees his brother commit a sin that is not a deadly sin, he has only to pray to God and God will give life to the sinner—not those who commit a deadly sin; for there is a sin that is death and I will not say that you must pray about that" (1 John 5:16–17). "As for those people who were once brought into the light, and tasted the gift from heaven, and received a share of the Holy Spirit and appreciated the good message of God and the powers of the world to come, and yet in spite of this have fallen away—it is impossible for them to be renewed a second time. They cannot be repentant if they have willfully crucified the Son of God and openly mocked him" (Heb 6:4). "If, after we have been given knowledge of the truth, we should deliberately commit any sins, then there is no longer any sacrifice for them" (Heb 10:26).

There were also defenders of a more "liberal" but still strict view who argued that a second repentance was possible. Hermas, who lived at Rome

in the first half of the second century and whose brother was Bishop Pius (died 154), wrote a long book called *The Shepherd*. Hermas, who claimed to speak on the basis of visions, argued that after the repentance that preceded baptism, a second repentance was allowed, but only one. Those were the stark choices among proto-orthodox Christians, either *no* opportunity to reenter the community or *one* opportunity to do so.

Circumstances in the third century sharpened the issues surrounding the repentance of serious sinners. The harsh government-sponsored persecutions of Decius and Valerian pushed many Christians to "lapse," that is, to commit the deadly sins of apostasy and idol worship. In a pattern repeated often, when a persecution ended, many of the "lapsed" sought reconciliation with their churches. The sheer numbers of lapsed seeking readmission forced bishops, who were struggling to gain supervision of such matters, to find a solution. After Decius' persecution died down in North Africa in 251, Bishop Cyprian of Carthage turned to a council of fellow bishops to decide how to deal with the lapsed who sought to return: "... when the persecution died down and opportunity offered for us to convene together, there gathered in Council a generous number of bishops who had been preserved safe and unharmed thanks to their own staunch faith and the protection of the Lord. Scriptural passages were produced, in a lengthy debate, on both sides of the issue and eventually we arrived at a balanced and moderate decision.... On the one hand, hopes for reconciliation and for admission to communion were not to be denied altogether to the lapsed, for there was the danger that in their despair they might fall away even further, and finding themselves shut out from the Church, they might follow the ways of the world and start living no better than pagans. But on the other hand, the strictness of the gospel teachings ought not be so relaxed that the fallen should be allowed to come rushing forward to communion pell-mell. Rather they should undergo prolonged penitence, and with grief and tears beg for indulgence from the Father; their various cases should be scrutinized individually, along with their personal attitudes and the special pressures under which they may have acted" (Cyprian, Letter 55, 6.1,

The Letters of St. Cyprian of Carthage, translated and annotated by G. W. Clarke, ACW 46 [New York and Mahwah, NJ, 1986), pp. 35–36, altered). Bishop Cornelius of Rome agreed with the North African bishops' decision to allow one reconciliation to the lapsed after they had submitted to a long period of demanding penance.

The second repentance was strict and difficult. Many Christians thought that sincere inner repentance was not just a matter of saying words. Real repentance had to be seen as well as heard. The once-in-a-lifetime opportunity to do penance was public, long-lasting, and intentionally humiliating. There were traditional ways to show outwardly that one repented inwardly. The penitents were expected to shed tears, to wear sackcloth, to put ashes on their heads, to ask the congregation publicly for forgiveness, and, in general, to accept humiliation. The example of Natalius, which took place between 202 and 217, is a vivid account of what third-century penance looked like. Natalius had been a confessor, that is, he had suffered for the Name but had not died. When the Roman church was divided over a theological issue, Natalius agreed to let one faction—the losing faction, as it turned out—ordain him as bishop. In his opponents' eyes, Natalius had committed the deadly sin of introducing a split, a schism, into the church. His sin was especially serious because many must have respected him for his suffering: "So Natalius was persuaded by them to take the title of bishop at a salary, and to be paid by them one hundred and fifty denarii a month. When, therefore, he became one of them, he was frequently admonished by the Lord in visions. For our compassionate God and Lord, Jesus Christ, did not wish that a witness to his suffering should perish outside the Church. But when he paid less regard to the visions, being ensnared by having the first place among them, and by the desire for tainted money which destroys many, he was finally scourged by the holy angels, and suffered serious punishment the whole night long; insomuch that he rose at dawn, put on sackcloth, covered himself with ashes, and with all haste prostrated himself in tears before Zephyrinus the bishop; and, rolling at the feet not only of the clergy but also of the laity, he moved with his tears the compassionate Church of the mer-

ciful Christ. And though he used much entreaty and showed the bruises from the beating he had received [the marks of the whipping the angels gave him], scarcely was he taken back into communion" (EH 5.28, altered). In the most elaborate recorded form of penance, which did not exist in most churches, a council at Ancyra in Asia Minor (314) was concerned with the rush of clergy and laity who sought readmission to the church after the end of the persecutions associated with the Emperor Diocletian and his allied emperors. The bishops at Ancyra issued nine canons to deal with the various degrees of apostasy and guilt. Guilty presbyters could no longer offer the Eucharist, preach, or perform any priestly function, but they could sit with the other presbyters. Deacons who had lapsed were denied their functions but could keep their rank. Many penitents were required to pass through stages of reconciliation over the course of five years. For a year, they were "hearers" who stood at the back of the church. For three years, they were "prostrators" who joined the congregation but knelt or were flat on the ground. For a year, they were "standers" who stood with the congregation but were denied communion of the bread and wine. During their period of penance, they wore sackcloth and ashes, fasted severely, and begged the clergy and laity to pray for them. When the bishop and presbyters decided that the penitent had shown sincere repentance in word and deed, the bishop readmitted him or her to the body of the faithful on the Thursday before Easter. The situation at Ancyra may have been unusual, but because public penance everywhere demanded so much, some who committed a serious sin might never seek to return to the church. They became apostates.

Thus, in the second and third centuries, proto-orthodox Christian churches were internally complex. The core of the congregation was made up of the baptized faithful, who in turn were divided into major and minor clergy (who were distributed from the bishop down to doorkeepers and gravediggers) and laity (who were divided among married people, widows, virgins, and ascetics). The core group had at its edges, so to speak, the catechumens who sought entry and the penitents who sought re-entry.

CHRISTIAN BUILDINGS BEFORE CONSTANTINE

The Christians did not live on a cloud without material needs. They used buildings; they were sometimes attracted and sometimes repelled by the art of the Greco-Roman world; and they developed their ways of group worship, called "liturgy." During the first three centuries, there was no central authority among the churches to impose standards about architecture, art, and worship. As a result, there was variation in proto-orthodox Christian practices across the vastness of the Roman Empire, but the shared practices were strong. Because the conversion of the Emperor Constantine in the early fourth century had such important consequences for the Christians, his reign will be the end point for this chapter. But even after Constantine's turn to Christianity, there was massive continuity of the Christian communal life that had developed between the first and early fourth centuries.

The gods of the state enjoyed the magnificent temples that we associate with Greece and Rome. Some private, voluntary religions had wealthy patrons or other resources to provide them with respectable places to gather and worship. Like other voluntary religious groups, Christian congregations also needed some place to gather for such events as worship, the instruction of catechumens, and their group meals. But financial and legal constraints prevented Christians from having impressive buildings before the fourth century, when the resources of Christian emperors and rich members made such buildings possible and growing congregations made them necessary.

Not much evidence about pre-fourth-century churches survives. The letters of Paul and Luke's Acts occasionally remarked on the sorts of places where Paul preached and Christians worshipped. At Ephesus, Paul used, perhaps rented, the lecture hall of a teacher named "Tyrannus" (Acts 19:9). Paul also indicated that Christians met in the private homes of well-to-do converts. For example, he passed on the greetings of "Aquila and Prisca, together with the church in their house..." (1 Cor 16:19). At Corinth, which is relatively well documented, Luke's Acts and Paul's letters imply the existence of five or six house churches in the 50s and 60s. The owner of the house probably continued to live there, making it available to fellow Christians for their meetings. Between the first and fourth centuries, there must have been hundreds, perhaps thousands of such "house churches" across the Roman Empire. But archaeologists have never identified a simple house church. That is understandable. If such a structure were unearthed today, how would we know it served for Christian worship because few or no changes were made to accommodate the occasional Christian meeting in the dining room or courtyard of an ordinary dwelling place?

House churches had their limitations. They were sufficient for a few dozen members or maybe more, but when congregations got larger, other arrangements had to be made. The pace of change in church architecture varied by region and by the size and financial resources of each congregation. In some instances, the ownership of the house might pass to the congregation by sale or gift. The building became more "church" than "house." In such a case, the house might be renovated—walls ripped out and new rooms added—to meet the needs of a medium-sized congregation.

By a remarkable stroke of luck, one renovated Christian house church has been excavated at Dura-Europos, a small city on the eastern border of the Roman Empire, in present-day Iraq. For centuries, the Roman Empire had fought wars on its eastern frontier against the Persian Empire. During one of the border wars, Dura-Europos was under siege. In order to strengthen the city's defenses, the authorities buried buildings that were close to the walls. The defense of the city failed, and in 256 it was overrun and subsequently abandoned—it became a sort of time capsule. Between 1922 and 1937, archaeologists from France and Yale University excavated the site, where they found the remains of the buildings that had been buried along the walls. There were thirteen temples, dedicated to various Greek, Roman, and local gods. There were also private houses that had been reconfigured to serve as places of worship, including a house turned into a Mithraeum for the worship of the god Mithras, two adjoining houses that had been combined to make a fine synagogue with impressive wall paintings, and a Christian "house church," the only one ever surely identified.

The church at Dura had originally been a private house, which was adapted between 241 and 256 to the use of a small Christian congregation. From the street, it probably looked like other private houses, but internal alterations made it a church. The main assembly hall, which was created by combining two rooms, could accommodate approximately sixty-five to seventy-five people. There was a raised platform at the one end of the room where perhaps the bishop and presbyters sat during services. The house church also had a room set aside specifically for baptisms. In the baptistery, two columns supported a plaster canopy decorated with blue sky and stars that was over the basin in which baptisms took place. The basin was approximately five feet by three feet and about three feet deep, probably not deep enough for full immersion, so baptism may have been carried out by pouring water on the candidate, who stood in the font. The baptistery's walls were decorated with biblical scenes that illustrated such themes as hope and deliverance. The wall behind the font had a scene of the Good Shepherd with a ram across his shoulders as well as a small depiction of Adam, Eve, and the serpent. On other walls in the baptistery, there were paintings of the women at Jesus' tomb, Jesus and Peter walking on water, Jesus healing a paralytic, the Samaritan woman at the well, and David and Goliath. The wall paintings in the baptistery at Dura-Europos have the earliest datable depictions of Jesus, where he is portrayed as a young man without a beard. There may have been a second floor on which the bishop or presbyter lived, but it does not survive.

In many small towns, churches that had been adapted from private houses continued to be used. But during the Great Peace (about 260–303) that preceded Diocletian's persecution, some prosperous urban congregations outgrew their house churches and began to build larger structures that were publicly identifiable as churches, although we do not know what they looked like because we have only brief written references. Eusebius wrote that in his youth, in the later third century, the Christians had peace and respect from their pagan neighbors and rulers. One sign of that happy time was the growth of congregations and the building of churches: "And how could one fully describe those assemblies thronged with countless people, and the multitudes that gathered together in every city, and the famed gatherings in the places of prayer, by reason of which they were no longer satisfied with the buildings of olden times, and would erect from the foundation churches of spacious dimensions throughout all the cities?" (EH 8.1, altered). The central architectural feature of the new churches was a room large enough for the congregation to assemble, with adjoining rooms for such events as baptism and the teaching of catechumens.

By the third century, many Christian communities owned not only church buildings but also cemeteries. In general, pagans, Jews, and Christians were concerned about the respectable burial of their loved ones, which is fortunate for us because much of what we know about the ancient world comes from tomb inscriptions and the graves themselves. Christians shared the concern for proper burial, which they regarded as a pious act. They also believed that living and dead Christians continued to be members of the same Body of Christ. To promote decent burials, Roman law allowed people to form burial societies, comparable with an insurance arrangement in which individuals contributed small amounts of money regularly to a common fund, so that at death each member would receive a proper burial. Christian congregations might have found it useful to appear to be burial societies, which would have given them some protective covering from inquisitive magistrates. In about 202, the Roman Bishop Zephyrinus put the former slave Callistus, who succeeded as bishop of Rome from about 217 to 222, in charge of a Christian cemetery in the catacombs on the Appian Way. This is the first evidence of a congregation owning a cemetery. Eventually, many congregations had aboveground and below-ground cemeteries, in which the Christian dead were grouped with their own, often near the graves of the local congregation's heroes, the martyrs, or maybe just one martyr. Christians met in the cemeteries to commemorate the dead. For example, in 156, Bishop Polycarp of Smyrna was martyred by burning. The remarkable account of his death recorded that "we afterwards took up his bones, as being more precious than the most exquisite jewels, and more purified than gold, and deposited them in a fitting place, where, when we gather together as opportunity is allowed us, the Lord shall grant us to celebrate the anniversary of his martyrdom...." (*The Martyrdom of Polycarp*, c. 18, ANF, vol. 1, p. 43, altered).

By 200, some Christians had adopted the practice of having a meal, called a *refrigerium* ("refreshment"), at or near the tomb of a dead loved one or of a martyr on the anniversary of the person's death. Poor Christians might be invited to share in the meal or might receive a gift of food afterward. The meal, perhaps consisting of foods that had symbolic significance for Christians, such as bread, fish, and wine, was eaten very close to, perhaps on top of, the gravestone. In some cemeteries, a special building, called a *martyrium*, was placed over the grave of a martyr to mark it out and to shelter from the weather the Christians who gathered to eat on the anniversary day of the martyr's death. The best-preserved and most famous Christian cemeteries were those in the catacombs at Rome, which will be discussed later. Thus, even before Constantine's conversion, Christian congregations possessed property, including their churches, their cemeteries, and their memorials to the martyrs. To judge from the church at Dura-Europos and the catacombs at Rome, third-century Christians decorated their buildings with paintings of religious scenes and religious symbols.

CHRISTIAN ART BEFORE CONSTANTINE

The early Christians were a secretive group, both because of fear of attack and because of their view of themselves as aliens in a sinful, doomed world. Like many such groups, they developed uses of ordinary words and objects that were meaningful only to them. These included symbols whose meaning was known primarily to believers. A well-known special Christian image is that of the fish, based on the fact that the spelling of the Greek word for "fish"—IXTHUS—could stand for the first letters of the words "Jesus Christ, Son of God, Savior." There is no convincing evidence of distinctive Christian art before about 180. That does not mean that the earliest Christians had no art in their homes, their house churches, or for their personal adornment. But if they did have art during the first century and

a half, they probably bought it in the market just as their pagan neighbors did. Even if archaeologists found a ring or a decorated lamp owned by a first- or early second-century Christian, they might not be able to tell from the object itself that the owner was Christian. After about 180, some Christians began to use existing artistic motifs to which they gave a Christian interpretation. For instance, Clement of Alexandria (about 160–215) gave advice to the relatively sophisticated Christians of the great city of Alexandria in Egypt. He did not forbid Alexandrian Christians to wear jewelry, but he recommended that from the wide variety of images that was for sale in the market, they should choose symbols compatible with Christianity. Rings were a common personal adornment, both for practical and aesthetic purposes. Almost everyone who owned property, including Christians, had a ring with a distinct seal on it, which they used to mark possessions, to seal jars of valuable wine or olive oil, and to indicate that letters were authentic. Clement did not approve of a Christian having a ring with a pagan god or an erotic picture carved into it. He encouraged Christians to use symbols that could be given a Christian interpretation. He told his readers, "let our seals be either a dove, or a fish, or a ship scudding before the wind, or a musical lyre..., or a ship's anchor,..., and if there is a person fishing [on the seal], he [the owner of the seal] will remember the apostles, and the children drawn out of the water [of baptism]" (Clement of Alexandria, *The Instructor (Paedagogus)*, 3.11, ANF, vol. 2, pp. 285–286, altered).

As they were in other matters, Christians were divided in their attitudes toward art. Some art forms that were admired in pagan circles were absolutely forbidden. For instance, early Christians never created statues in the round, which were too similar to the hated idols of the gods. Some strict Christians criticized the use of any personal jewelry, paintings, and sculptures that were carved on the surface of stone, metal, wood, or ivory. But others permitted a restrained use of art for personal adornment and religious expression. In the long run, the second group won the argument, and Christians used art, eventually creating magnificent art to carry their message and especially to adorn their churches and to enrich their liturgy.

In addition to the wall paintings in the baptistery of the house church at Dura-Europos, the best-preserved Christian art from before the reign of Constantine is found in the catacombs of the city of Rome. Our popular culture makes the catacombs more mysterious than they should be. They took their name from a place called *ad catacumbas* ("near the hollow places"), a district in Rome with a large underground cemetery. Eventually, all underground burial places were called "catacombs." They were created to meet a practical need. By the standards of ancient cities, Rome had a huge population, in the hundreds of thousands. Finding places to bury the unending supply of the dead was a major problem. Rich, powerful people built the expensive above-ground tombs that still line the Roman roads that flow out of the city. But most people in the city of Rome could not afford such luxury. They were buried in underground passages cut into the relatively soft stone that lay under the city. The catacombs were businesses, where people bought places for their dead from the entrepreneurs, called *fossores* ("diggers") who dug the burial galleries and chambers. Over the course of three or four centuries, miles of galleries were created to hold hundreds of thousands of the dead. Contrary to a widely held opinion, the catacombs were not exclusively Christian. There were all sorts of catacombs. Many pagans were buried in the catacombs. Roman Jews buried their dead in their own catacombs. Some catacomb burial places belonged to families, where master, mistress, children, servants, and slaves were buried together. Christians also used the catacombs extensively for their dead. Over time, the Roman church bought or received as gifts many catacombs where Christians were buried. In the catacomb of San Callistos, owned by the Roman church, seven third-century bishops of Rome were buried in what is called the "Crypt of the Popes." In 384, Pope Damasus was the sixteenth and last bishop to be buried there.

Many ancient people thought it wrong to send their beloved dead into the ground anonymously. They often put the person's name and sometimes a lot more on the covering to the grave. The burial niches in the walls and the larger chambers in the pagan, Jewish, and Christian catacombs were decorated with paintings and inscriptions. Between

Figure 9.1 Burial Niches in the Catacomb of San Callisto. Over the course of three or four centuries, miles of tunnels were dug around and under the city of Rome for burials. The dead were placed in niches such as those visible in this illustration, and each niche was sealed by stone or terracotta (all the coverings and the bodies are gone in this part of the catacombs). The Catacomb of San Callisto belonged to the Roman church since about 217. *(Erich Lessing / Art Resource, NY)*

the late second and the early fifth centuries, the Christian art in the catacombs stressed peace, security, and deliverance of the dead from harm. For instance, in the early Christian catacomb of Domitilla, the artists represented such "salvation stories" as Daniel standing safe between two lions, Noah welcoming the returning dove that revealed the end of the flood, and the good shepherd holding on his shoulders the sheep that had been lost. In other Christian catacombs, there were representations that suggested but usually did not realistically show the Lord's Supper and baptism, which were the hopeful rituals of salvation. Often, especially on the stone or terracotta slabs that closed

Figure 9.2 Crypt of the Popes. In the Catacomb of San Callisto, an area was set apart for burial of the bishops of Rome. Between 236 and 283, seven bishops of Rome were buried in the crypt, and other bishops were buried elsewhere.

the burial niches in the walls, the art was heavily symbolic but again stressed security and deliverance for the holy dead. For instance, the carving of an anchor, a dove, a ship, an olive branch, vines, and bunches of grapes referred to biblical stories or to widely understood symbols of peace and safety. Christians periodically entered the catacombs to share a meal with their dead and to offer the Eucharist. The living who looked at the art were reassured about their fate after death.

The suffering of Christ and of believers was not a common theme in the catacomb art. Although simple crosses are commonly depicted, the crucifixion as the representation of Christ's suffering and redemptive work is not found in the first three centuries of Christian art. The earliest surviving clear

representation of Christ crucified between the two criminals (Mt 27:38; Mk 15:27; Lk 23:32; John 19:18) is on the bronze doors of the early fifth-century church of Santa Sabina in Rome.

Although some prominent Christian figures disapproved of the use of art for religious purposes, the catacombs and the house church at Dura-Europos show that others, including many ordinary, anonymous believers, wanted to represent their religion in visual ways. They won the argument. Christians experimented with the forms and the content of art during the first three centuries, borrowing images from the world around them but changing them by giving them a Christian meaning.

WORSHIP BEFORE CONSTANTINE

In the first three centuries, there must have been considerable regional variation in how proto-orthodox Christians worshipped. However, they shared a common framework built around the meal of bread and wine, which already had a stable pattern by the second half of the first century, according to Paul (1 Cor 11:23–26) and the Synoptic Gospels (Mt 26:26–29; Mk 14:22–25; Lk 22:14–20). During the second and third centuries, the tendency for worship services to follow a general structure intensified. As a result of repetition over many decades, both clergy and laity expected a Eucharist (or a baptism or even a group meal) to unfold in a certain way, although the details were not rigidly fixed. The presiding clergyman, ordinarily the bishop, could improvise the wording of the prayers and maybe other things as well, but he improvised within traditional boundaries. Improvisation has its potential problems. Some people are skillful at it and others are not; an improvised prayer might be too long, too short, or too gnostic. Hippolytus described a situation in the early third century when patterns of worship were hardening, although there was still room for creativity. Hippolytus had written down some Eucharistic prayers as models, but he told his readers not to think that they were mandatory: "When the bishop gives thanks in accordance with what was said above it is not absolutely incumbent on him that he recite the identical words...as though performing a set declamatory exercise! In giving thanks to God let each pray according to his ability. If he has the ability to pray easily in a sophisticated manner then that is good. If someone, when he prays, offers a simple prayer do not seek to prevent him, only he must pray in an orthodox manner" (Hippolytus, *The Apostolic Tradition*, 9.3–5, in *On the Apostolic Tradition*, p. 92, altered). Although between the first and fourth centuries each Eucharist or baptism could differ in details from every other one, there developed unwritten rules and expectations that eventually led to the creation of rituals recorded in written service books in the fourth and fifth centuries.

Baptism

Proto-orthodox Christians and other kinds of Christians shared the practice of baptism, by which converts were washed of their sins, "illuminated" or "enlightened," and admitted to the ranks of the baptized faithful. Over time, baptism grew more elaborate in its symbolism and prayers. By about 200, churches were accepting new members in a process that modern scholars have described as "Christian initiation," a term that emphasizes that we can still call the process "baptism" so long as we do not imagine that the entire business consisted of a few minutes in which water and prayers welcomed the new member.

There are some documents that allow us to trace in a general way that process of baptismal elaboration. The early second-century *Didache*, perhaps written for a church in Palestine or Syria, opened with a sermon on the "Way of Life and the Way of Death" that would have been appropriate for people about to be baptized. It then noted that "But with respect to baptism, baptize as follows. Having said all these things in advance [the sermon on the way of life and the way of death], baptize in the name of the Father and of the Son and of the Holy Spirit, in running water. But if you do not have running water, baptize in some other water. And if you cannot baptize in cold water, use warm. But if you have neither, pour water on the head three times in the name of the Father and Son and Holy Spirit. But both the one baptizing and the one being baptized should fast before the baptism, along with some others if they can. But command the one being baptized to fast one or two

days in advance" (*Didache*, c. 7, in *The Apostolic Fathers*, vol. 1, edited and translated by Bart D. Ehrman, LCL 24 [Cambridge, MA, and London, 2003], p. 429).

Three or four decades later Justin Martyr described the way people were baptized at Rome. "I will also relate the manner in which we dedicated ourselves to God when we were made new through Christ....As many as are persuaded and believe that what we teach and say is true, and try to live accordingly, are instructed to pray and ask God with fasting for the remission of their past sins, while we pray and fast with them. Then they are brought by us where there is water, and are reborn in the same manner in which we ourselves were reborn. For, in the name of God, the Father and Lord of the universe, and of our Savior Jesus Christ, and of the Holy Spirit, they then receive the washing with water.... And this washing is called illumination, because they who learn these things are illuminated in their understandings. And he who is illuminated is washed in the name of Jesus Christ, who was crucified under Pontius Pilate, and in the name of the Holy Spirit, who through the prophets foretold all things about Jesus" (Justin, *First Apology*, c. 61, ANF, vol. 1, p. 183, altered).

About sixty years after Justin wrote, Hippolytus described in his *Apostolic Tradition* what he thought were the traditional worship practices, which he called "apostolic." His account shows that at Rome the steps by which a person became a Christian had grown more elaborate, in part to test the candidate's worthiness and in part to emphasize the seriousness of conversion. Hippolytus described the distinct stages of progress toward baptism. As we have seen, those who asked to join were questioned about their occupations and their sins, some of which made them ineligible even to begin the process. Those judged worthy "to hear the word" became catechumens, and for as long as three years they were instructed and exorcised, and their behavior was observed: The catechumens lived through a time of testing. When they were judged ready for baptism, which usually took place on a Sunday, they bathed on Thursday. They, and other Christians who wished to support them, fasted on Friday and Saturday. The bishop exorcised the catechumens on Saturday to drive out demons. The catechumens spent Saturday night and Sunday before dawn in an all-night vigil during which they heard the reading of scripture and religious instruction. Hippolytus described the baptism that took place early Sunday morning ("at cockcrow"). The clergy prayed over the water to be used at the baptism. After taking off their clothes, the catechumens said aloud, "I renounce you Satan, and all your service and all your works"; the catechumens were then anointed with an "oil of exorcism" to drive out evil spirits. When the catechumens entered the water, the baptizer placed his hand on each candidate's head and asked three questions based on the creed. After each answer of "I believe," the candidate was immersed in water. As the baptized people emerged from the water, they had a new status, that of "neophyte" ("newborn Christian"). A presbyter anointed each neophyte with the "oil of thanksgiving." The neophytes dried off, put on a white garment to symbolize their new state of purity, and were led into the church assembly. In the presence of the baptized faithful, the bishop laid hands on each neophyte's head, prayed, and poured oil on the head to "sign" or "seal" the person. For the first time, the newly baptized were allowed to pray with fellow baptized Christians. They received and gave the kiss of peace, a sign of fellowship. For the first time, the neophytes saw the Eucharist, at which they ate the bread and drank the wine. They also drank from a cup of water and milk mixed with honey, symbolizing that they had entered the land flowing with milk and honey (see Ex 3:8) (Hippolytus, *Apostolic Tradition*, c. 21). Thus, by the third century, Christian communities baptized new members in ceremonies that added symbolic actions and complex prayers to the core practice of baptizing in water while invoking the names of Father, Son, and Holy Spirit.

Eucharist

An individual was baptized only once, although some groups, such as the North African Donatists, rebaptized other Christians who joined them. Ordinary baptized Christians probably rarely or never saw a baptism other than their own, which took place away from the assembly of the baptized faithful. The Lord's Supper or the Eucharist was the repeated event that sharpened believers' sense of belonging to a community. When Paul and the authors of the gospels of Mark, Matthew, and Luke wrote in the second half of the first century the Eucharist already had a structure. Writing to the Corinthian Christians about 51, Paul provided the earliest description of the Lord's Supper: "For I received from the Lord what I also handed on to you, that the Lord Jesus on the night when he was betrayed took a loaf of bread, and when he had given thanks, he broke it and said, 'This is my body that is for you. Do this in remembrance of me.' In the same way he took the cup also, after supper, saying, 'This cup is the new covenant in my blood. Do this, as often as you drink it, in remembrance of me.' For as often you eat this bread and drink the cup, you proclaim the Lord's death until he comes" (1 Cor 11:23–26; compare Mt 26:26–28; Mk 14:22–25; Lk 22:15–20).

The baptized faithful were the only ones allowed to share in the Eucharist. As the *Didache* declared, "No one is to eat or drink of your Eucharist but those who have been baptized in the Name of the Lord; for the Lord's own saying applies here, 'Give not that which is holy unto dogs'" (*Didache*, c. 9). The *Didache* organized the Eucharist as a dialogue between the presiding person and the congregation: "And with respect to the thanksgiving meal [literally: "eucharist"], you shall give thanks as follows. First, with respect to the cup: 'We give you thanks, our Father, for the holy vine of David, your child, which you made known to us through Jesus your child. To you be the glory forever.' And with respect to the fragment of bread: 'We give you thanks, Our Father, for the life and knowledge that you made known to us through Jesus your child. To you be the glory forever. As this fragment of bread was scattered upon the mountains and was gathered to become one, so may your Church be gathered together from the ends of the earth into your kingdom. For the glory and the power are yours through Jesus Christ forever" (*Didache*, c. 9, *The Apostolic Fathers*, vol. 1, edited and translated by Bart D. Ehrman, LCL 24 [Cambridge, MA, and London, 2003], p. 431). The *Didache* also contained three prayers of thanksgiving to God to be said after the Eucharistic meal.

In his *First Apology*, written about a half-century after the *Didache*, Justin Martyr provided two revealing descriptions of the Eucharist, perhaps because he wanted to assure his pagan readers that ugly rumors about what went on at Christian worship were untrue. He first described the Eucharist that followed baptism, which was the first that the neophytes had ever seen (Justin, *First Apology*, c. 65). Justin also described an ordinary Sunday assembly that included a Eucharist. Justin called the presiding clergyman the "ruler of the brethren," but he was clearly the bishop: "c. 66. And this food is called among us Eucharist, of which no one is allowed to partake but the person who believes that the things which we teach are true, and who has been washed with the washing that is for the remission of sins, and for rebirth, and who is living as Christ commanded. For we do not receive these things as common bread or common drink; but in like manner as Jesus Christ our Savior having been made flesh by the Word of God, had both flesh and blood for our salvation, so likewise we have been taught that the food which is blessed by the prayer of His word, and from which our blood and flesh are nourished by transmutation, is the flesh and blood of that Jesus who was made flesh. The apostles, in the memoirs composed by them, which are called Gospels, have delivered to us what was commanded to them; that Jesus took bread and when he had given thanks said: 'This do you in remembrance of Me, this is my body'; and in the same way, having taken the cup and given thanks, He said: 'This is my blood'; and gave it to them alone. c. 67.... And on the day called Sunday, all who live in cities or in the country gather together in one place and the memoirs of the apostles or the writings of the prophets are read, as long as time permits. Then when the reader has finished, the one who presides verbally instructs and exhorts us to the imitation of these good things. Then we all rise together and pray; and...when our prayer is ended, bread and wine and water are brought, and the one who presides offers prayers and thanksgivings to the best of his ability, and the people assent, saying the Amen; and there is a distribution to each and a participation of that over which thanks have been given, and to those who are absent a portion is sent by the deacons. And those who are well-to-do and willing give what each thinks fit; and what is collected is deposited with the one who presides, who cares for the orphans and widows, and those who, through sickness or any other cause, are in want, and those who are in bonds, and the strangers who sojourn among us, and in a word he takes care of all who are in need" (Justin, *The First Apology*, c. 66–67, ANF, vol. 1, pp. 185–186, altered).

The faithful gathered at least every week for a holy meal, for instruction through scripture and sermon, and for mutual charity. Only the baptized faithful could participate in the Eucharist itself. The Eucharist was a powerful promoter of a sense of solidarity, of specialness, of being God's chosen people.

Ordination

Baptism and the Eucharist were the central liturgical practices of early Christians. But there were other occasions when patterns of recurring religious activity emerged. Bishops, presbyters, and deacons died. To replace them in an orderly way, Christians developed the process of ordination. The *Didache*, chapter 15, told readers to appoint bishops and deacons but gave no instructions on how the choosing was done. Perhaps because Justin was writing a defense addressed to an emperor, not a complete church manual, he wrote almost nothing about church leaders. But as the distinction between clergy and laity sharpened, the process of making a layman into a clergyman, which was the purpose of ordination, received its own expression in liturgy. Accounts in Acts were taken as the basic model: "While they were worshipping the Lord and fasting, the Holy Spirit said: 'Set apart for me Barnabas and Saul for the work to which I have called them.' Then after fasting and praying they laid their hands on them and sent them off" (Acts 13:2–3). By the second century, bishops had gained the right to ordain a presbyter or deacon, that is, lay their hands on the candidate with accompanying prayers. Only bishops could ordain other bishops. Hippolytus described the ways that men were given the status of clergy in the early third century. "All the people" chose the bishop, although we do not know how the "election" worked. But Hippolytus described the laying-on of hands that made a man a bishop: "And when he has been named and found pleasing to all, let the people come together with the presbyters, and any bishops who are present, on the Lord's day. When all give their consent they lay hands on him and the presbytery stands in silence. And all shall keep silence, praying in their heart for the descent of the Holy Spirit. After this, at the request of all, one of the bishops who is present, laying a hand on him who is being ordained bishop shall pray thus" (*Apostolic Tradition*, c. 2, in *On the Apostolic Tradition*, pp. 56–57). The ordaining bishop's prayer asked God that the new bishop receive the power that God gave to Jesus and that he in turn bestowed on the apostles. The prayer then asked that God grant the new bishop, "whom you have chosen," the ability to minister blamelessly to the flock and to God. The prayer then asked God to grant the powers that the bishop was thought to acquire from the Holy Spirit: "And let him have the power of high priesthood, to forgive sins according to your command, to assign duties according to your command, to loose every tie according to the power which you gave to the apostles, to please you in gentleness and with a pure heart, offering you the scent of sweetness" (*Apostolic Tradition*, c. 3, in *On the Apostolic Tradition*, p. 61).

Hippolytus then described how a bishop laid on his hands and prayed to make a man a presbyter or a deacon. Prestigious and spirit-filled confessors, who had "been in chains for the sake of the Name of the Lord," were accorded the honor of the diaconate or the presbyterate without a laying-on of hands. But if a confessor was chosen bishop, he needed the usual ordination by other bishops. Hippolytus was careful to insist that some Church members who had a special status were not ordained but were "appointed." For instance, the bishop appointed a reader by giving him a book but did not lay hands on him. The subdeacon, who assisted the deacon, was not ordained. A virgin did not receive an imposition of hands because her personal choice made her a virgin. Widows were not ordained but rather were appointed to the order of widows. Charismatics, who claimed a direct gift from the Holy Spirit, were neither appointed nor ordained. Instead, they were to be tested with a touch of skepticism: "If somebody appears to have received the gift of healing or revelation a hand is not laid on

him for the facts of the matter will reveal whether he has spoken the truth" (*Apostolic Tradition*, c. 14, in *On the Apostolic Tradition*, p. 96).

Not surprisingly, over the course of two centuries, Christian worship had changed, although the core of baptism and the Lord's Supper were always recognizable. There was a general movement toward more structure, more symbolic actions, more prayers, and more control of the event by the bishop and presbyters. There was also a tendency for important regional bishoprics, such as Rome, Alexandria, Milan, and Carthage, to influence the liturgical practices of their less important neighboring bishoprics. Sometimes lesser bishops borrowed practices that they saw in the important churches; sometimes the bishops of the important churches actively encouraged bishops within their sphere of influence to imitate their liturgy. Liturgical "families" that shared liturgical prayers and practices emerged. Generations of repetition made the regional liturgies a mark of local pride and identity.

Christian Customs

Baptism, Eucharist, and ordination were major events that became permanent features of Christian personal and community life. But if a group lasts long enough, as Christianity did, it often develops ways of doing things that separate it from rivals or from non-members of the group. In modern times, for instance, members of Masonic lodges recognize one another by their secret handshake and the decals on their automobiles. Members of college fraternities and sororities have their Greek letters as a short-hand way of saying, "You and I are brothers/sisters." Muslims observe Friday as their holy day, Jews observe Saturday, and Christians Sunday. The distinct days of worship are effective reminders every week that each group is separate from the others. The early Christians developed practices that set them off from outsiders and helped them recognize one another. Some sources reveal bits and pieces of information on the customs that early Christians adopted, but we would probably be amazed if we could see the full range of those specials ways of living. No single community had all of them, and there were probably customs that are not recorded. Here are some important customs that shaped Christian identity and separateness.

The sign of the cross. The most common special Christian sign was that of the cross, a reminder of Jesus' saving death. Justin Martyr wrote that the shape of the cross was found purposely all through the universe, for example, in anchors, plows, the masts of ships, and the human body with arms outstretched (Justin, *First Apology,* c. 55). Christians used the cross in all sorts of situations. They made the sign of the cross on their foreheads or on objects to drive away the ever-present demons. Christians also drew or scratched the cross on the gravestones of their dead. They wore rings and jewelry that had crosses on them or had an image that could be interpreted as a cross. For a long time, non-Christians did not know what the cross meant to Christians.

Fasting. Jews, Christians, and some pagans placed a high value on fasting, which was the elimination or reduction of food for a period of time. Many Jews and Christians thought that fasting prepared the mind for holy things, expressed inward repentance in an outward way, and strengthened self-control. They also believed that God was more inclined to listen to the prayers of fasters. The Hebrew scriptures approved fasting that was undertaken for such reasons as mourning for the dead (1 Sam 31:13), calling on God's aid after a military defeat (Judges 20:26), showing repentance (Joel 2:15), or preparing for the Day of Atonement (Lev 16:29–34). By the first century, pious Jews fasted every Monday and Thursday. Jesus accepted fasting as a first-century Jew would (Mt 6:16–18). For instance, he fasted for forty days in the desert before beginning his ministry. Likewise Luke said that Paul fasted before he was baptized (Acts 9:9). Second- and third-century Christians fasted on many occasions. In some places, they fasted two days every week, but they chose days that emphasized their growing alienation from their Jewish origins. The *Didache* warned its Christian audience, "Do not keep your fasts with the hypocrites! For they fast on Monday and Thursday; but you should fast on Wednesday and Friday" (*Didache*, c. 8, in *The Apostolic Fathers*, vol. 1, edited and translated by Bart D. Ehrman, LCL 24 [Cambridge, MA, and London, 2003], p. 429). Justin wrote that in preparation for baptism,

the catechumens, the clergy, and others fasted for a day or two. There was fasting before the ordination of clergy. In some communities, there was fasting for one, two, or three days before Easter, a practice that eventually grew into the forty-day fast of Lent. In addition to the fasts expected of all proto-orthodox Christians, some subgroups fasted more often or more intensely. For example, widows who belonged to the order of widows were encouraged to fast voluntarily; people undergoing penance were required to fast as a sign of their sincerity; some Christians, called "ascetics," embraced a strict way of life that demanded voluntary and severe fasting. The details of fasting became more uniform by the fourth century, but Christians were fasters from the beginning.

Meals. Christians did not just fast. They also had their own customs about meals. Already in the 50s there was a special meal at Corinth, although Paul was annoyed at the behavior of Corinthian Christians during the group meal: "So then, my brothers and sisters, when you come together to eat, wait for one another. If you are hungry, eat at home, so that when you come together, it will not be for your condemnation" (1 Cor 11:33–34). Originally the Eucharist took place within a meal, but at an early date the meal and the Eucharist separated. A meal that was called "agape" (usually translated "love feast") benefited widows and the poor members of the church by providing them with food. As noted earlier, Christians also ate meals, called *refrigeria*, in cemeteries and catacombs with dead members of their family or with martyrs. There are scenes of such meals in the art of the catacombs. The many occasions for eating together strengthened group bonds, expressed solidarity, and sharpened the sense of us against outsiders because non-members could not participate in the Christian meals.

Prayer. In addition to liturgy, which was increasingly formal, Christians prayed privately and personally. Because such prayer was private, we shall never know exactly what it looked and sounded like. But some early Christian writers gave advice about personal prayer, which developed its own patterns. The *Didache* told its readers: "...as the Lord commanded in his gospel, you should pray as follows." It then gave the version of the

Lord's Prayer from Mt 6:9–13 and added, "Pray like this three times a day" (*Didache*, c. 8, in *The Apostolic Fathers*, vol. 1, edited and translated by Bart D. Ehrman, LCL 24 [Cambridge, MA, and London, 2003], pp. 429–431). By the later second century, Christians were encouraged to pray when they awoke in the morning, at the third, sixth, and ninth hours of the day, at bedtime, and once during the night. Clement of Alexandria recommended that the morning prayer should be said facing the sunrise in the east, a common practice for prayer in the ancient world (Clement of Alexandria, *The Stromata or Miscellanies*, 7.7, in ANF, vol. 2, p. 535). Christians prayed on other occasions, including before or after they ate. There were also habitual postures for prayer, which Christians thought appropriate to the intention of the prayer. The commonest posture, shared with Jews and pagans, was standing with arms raised and palms up—the so-called Orans posture, from a Latin word meaning "one who prays," often depicted in art, including paintings in the catacombs. But if the person praying wanted to express humility or repentance, he or she might kneel or lie prostrate on the ground.

Veils and tattoos. Some customs were local or short-lived. For instance, Tertullian recommended that Christian virgins wear veils, just as married women did. He might have had some local success in North Africa, but there was resistance. Augustine of Hippo recorded that in North Africa in the fifth century, some people had a cross tattooed on their foreheads, which surely set them off from pagans and Jews (Tertullian, *On the Veiling of Virgins (De Virginibus Velandis)*, in ANF, vol. 4, pp. 27–39); on the tattooing of a cross on the forehead see F. van der Meer, *Augustine the Bishop*, translated by Brian Battershaw and G. R. Lamb (London and New York, 1961), p. 355.

Between the first and early fourth centuries, the proto-orthodox Christians developed a sturdy organization, supported by the three-level ministry, the almost completed canon of scripture, and the creeds that expressed in a brief way central beliefs that every member could understand. They also experimented in the development of their own architecture, art, liturgical practices, patterns of behavior, and customs, which, taken together, made up a "way of life" that was not uniform everywhere but that enabled such Christians to recognize one another and to recognize who were "outsiders."

FURTHER READING

Ancient Sources

Trans. by Leslie William Barnard, Justin, *The First Apology*, especially chapters 61–67 on Christian liturgy, in *St. Justin Martyr: The First and Second Apologies*, by ACW 56 (New York and Mahwah, NJ, 1997), pp. 66–72 and pp. 171–185, for a commentary on Justin's document.

Andrew Louth, ed., *The Didache*, in *Early Christian Writings*, translated by Maxwell Staniforth; revised translation by the editor (Harmondsworth, England, 1987), pp. 187–199.

Alistair Stewart-Sykes, trans., Hippolytus, *The Apostolic Tradition*, (Crestwood, NY, 2001). The detailed commentary in this translation helps the reader understand the document.

Modern Works

Paul F. Bradshaw, *Early Christian Worship: A Basic Introduction to Ideas and Practices* (Collegeville, MN, 1996). A brief, informative introduction to early forms of worship.

Louis Duchesne, *Christian Worship: Its Origins and Evolution*, fifth edition, translated by M. L. McClure (London, 1927). In spite of its age, this book provides a wealth of information on the development of all aspects of liturgy up to the ninth century.

Thomas Finn, *From Death to Rebirth: Ritual and Conversion in Antiquity* (Mahwah, NJ, 1997). Christian conversion and baptism in the context of ancient paganism and Judaism.

Wayne Meeks, *The First Urban Christians: The Social World of the Apostle Paul*, second edition (New Haven, 2003). An interesting, challenging treatment of the world in which Paul traveled, preached, and organized churches.

Robert Milburn, *Early Christian Art and Architecture* (Aldershot, England, 1988). A manageable, interesting introduction to the art of early Christians down to the sixth century.

Graydon F. Snyder, *Ante Pacem: Archaeological Evidence of Church Life before Constantine* (Macon, GA, 1985). A careful introduction to the Christian art, inscriptions, and buildings of the period before Constantine.

L. Michael White, *The Social Origins of Christian Architecture: Volume I: Building God's House in the Roman World: Architectural Adaptation among Pagans, Jews and Christians*, Harvard Theological Studies 42 (Baltimore, MD, 1990).

PART III

✠

The Creation of a
Christian Empire

Timeline of Later Christianity

280 CE/AD	320 CE/AD	360 CE/AD	400 CE/AD	440 CE/AD	480 CE/AD	520 CE/AD	560 CE/AD

▼ 284 Diocletian became emperor

▼ about 301 King Tiradates of Armenia converted to Christianity

▼ 303 Diocletian launched the Great persecution

▼ 305 Diocletian retired, persecution in the western empire ceased

▼ 311 The dying Emperor Galerius granted toleration to Christians

▼ 312 Constantine's victory at the Milvian Bridge ended the Great persecution

▼ 312 The Donatist Schism began in North Africa

▼ 313 Emperors Constantine I and Licinius granted full toleration and reparations to Christians in the "Edict of Milan"

▼ 319 The Arian/Trinitarian Controversy broke out in Alexandria

▼ 324 Constantine I defeated Licinius and controlled the entire empire

▼ 325 Council of Nicaea, May to June

▼ 328 Athanasius chosen bishop of Alexandria

▼ 330 Constantine I dedicated "New Rome" or "Constantinople"

▼ 337 Constantine I died on May 22

▼ 361–363 Julian converted from Christianity to paganism and tried to reverse Christian advances

▼ 378 Emperor Valens killed in Roman defeat at Adrianople

▼ 379 Theodosius I became emperor

▼ 380 Theodosius I made Nicene Orthodox Chrisianity the legal religion of the empire

▼ 381 Council of Constantinople

▼ 385 Bishop Ambrose and Senator Symmachus clashed over the Altar of Victory in the Senate house

▼ 391 Theodosius I issued laws against pagan cults, especially sacrifices to the gods

▼ 392 Theodosius I issued laws against Christian heretics

▼ 395 Theodosius I died

▼ 431 The Council of Ephesus rejected Nestorius' emphasis on the two natures of Christ

▼ 440-460 Pope Leo I

▼ 451 Council of Chalcedon rejected the Monophysite ("One Nature") theology of Christ

529 Justinian closed the philosophical schools at Athens ▼

CHAPTER 10

Diocletian, the Great Persecution, and the Conversion of Constantine

The persecutions of the mid-third century failed to prevent the spread of Christianity. In the years of peace (260–303), Christians grew in numbers and in visibility within Greco-Roman society. Around 300, Christians might be forgiven for believing that their troubles with the Roman state were over, but they were not. By the early fourth century, Christianity remained divided, but the dominant form called itself "orthodox" ("right believing") and "catholic" ("universal"). I shall use those terms hereafter unless the context calls for more precision.

THE EMPEROR DIOCLETIAN (RULED 284–305)

In spite of the serious disorders of the third century, the Roman Empire did not collapse. In fact, it survived about two hundred years in the west and twelve hundred years in the east. But the political and military recovery of the empire led to profound changes, including a sudden end to the four decades of peace for the Christians. The Emperor Diocletian, a great figure in Roman history, was a tough general from the Balkans who restored stability by reorganizing the empire on openly dictatorial lines. He was a conservative man who distrusted new, non-Roman religions. For example, he ordered death by burning for Manichees, who believed in a form of gnosticism preached by Mani (216–272/277), who had lived in Persia, Rome's traditional military enemy. Like many preceding emperors, Diocletian believed that Christians were disloyal, disrupted social unity, and displeased the gods. In 303, when he had ruled for about eighteen

years, he launched the so-called Great Persecution against the Christians. We know many details about that persecution because literate Christians, including Eusebius (about 260–about 337) and Lactantius (about 250–about 325), lived through it and recorded it in detail. In his work on *The Deaths of the Persecuting Emperors*, Lactantius reported that when Diocletian was participating in an official ceremony, the pagan priests could not read the entrails of the animals because Christians who were present made the sign of the cross to ward off demons. In fury, Diocletian ordered a purge of Christians from his court and from the army. That purge eventually spread to the entire empire. On 22 February 303, soldiers destroyed the bishop's church at Nicomedia, which could be seen from Diocletian's palace—the fact that the building was obvious is a sign of the effect of the years of peace. On 23 February 303, Diocletian ordered that the Christian scriptures be confiscated and burned, that all church buildings be destroyed, and that church meetings be prohibited. On 24 February 303, Christians were stripped of legal rights, such as that of making a will or defending themselves in court. Diocletian thought that two fires in his palace were Christian assassination attempts. A rebellion of Christians in Syria, the first such rebellion on record, confirmed Diocletian's belief that Christians were dangerous. The intensity of the persecution grew. He ordered that all clergy be arrested and imprisoned. His previous measures had avoided killing people, but that changed. Two hundred sixty-eight Christians were executed at Nicomedia. In a measure reminiscent of his predecessors Decius and Valerian, Diocletian ordered

123

all the inhabitants of the empire to sacrifice to the gods. Those who refused were tortured, maimed by blinding in one eye and by cutting the hamstring tendon in one leg, enslaved, or, for flagrant violators, publicly executed.

Diocletian set in motion the most determined, long-lasting, and sophisticated persecution in Roman history. Yet, the persecution failed to wipe out Christians. Why? The Roman state lacked the means to carry out a purge on a scale sufficient to obliterate Christianity. Thousands of confessors were imprisoned, tortured, maimed, and enslaved. But by modern standards of butchery, the number of martyrs was modest. For instance, Eusebius, an eyewitness, recorded only ninety-seven deaths in Palestine, which had a relatively high percentage of Christians. A change in the attitude of some pagans toward Christians also blunted the effectiveness of the persecution. By the early fourth century, Christians were no longer a small, foreign sect. They had pagan friends and relatives who might disapprove of their eccentricities but who did not want torture or death as the remedy. Some Roman officials were eager to attack Christians, but others dragged their feet as the measures became harsher. That was especially true in the west, where the senior emperor, Constantius Chlorus (father of the Emperor Constantine), was willing to burn scriptures but did not encourage the execution of Christians. There were few martyrs west of Italy.

Circumstances within the Christian community itself had also changed in the decades since the persecutions of the Emperors Decius and Valerian. When those persecutions broke out, many Christians were unprepared. There were relatively few martyrs. And crucially, there was no significant Christian resistance. In ways we cannot see because there are almost no sources, between 260 and 300 Christianity had spread from cities into the countrysides of Egypt, North Africa, and Asia Minor. Rural peasants, whether they were pagan or Christian, were near the bottom of the Roman social hierarchy, heavily taxed, oppressed, controlled, and generally pushed around by their social betters. Like pagan peasants, some Christian peasants hated the Roman state for social and economic reasons, to which they now added religious persecution. Some of them, notably

in North Africa, had an immense respect for the martyrs who resisted the hated state. Some rural Christians were prepared to resist and die, unlike their city brethren, who often were not. In these new circumstances, persecution had costs for the government. Disorder cut tax collection and grain production, especially because Christianity happened to be rooted in the crucial grain-producing regions of Egypt and North Africa.

The politics of choosing emperors also became tied up with the persecution of Christians. When the Emperor Diocletian retired in 305, he tried to arrange an orderly succession to the emperorship, but his plan failed. Civil war followed. Some of the rival generals supported Christianity, and others opposed it. The Emperor Galerius (305–311) was an eager persecutor. Constantine, another claimant to be emperor, was favorable to Christians. When Constantine defeated his main western rival, Maxentius, in 312, he inaugurated a new phase in the interaction of the Roman state and the Christians. Christianity received toleration, quickly followed by official favor and support that lasted in varied forms from the fourth to the eighteenth or nineteenth centuries.

CONSTANTINE (RULED 306–337)

In 400, the position of Catholic Christianity in Greco-Roman society was remarkably different than it had been in 300, so different that the change can be called a revolution. The Roman Emperor Constantine was a central figure in that transformation because he set in motion a process that changed the course of Christian and imperial development. At the core of the revolution was Constantine's grant of legal toleration and then imperial favor to the Christians who had been harshly persecuted by other emperors. Under Constantine's fourth-century successors, the official treatment of the "orthodox" form of Christianity grew more favorable and that of its rivals—heretics, pagans, and Jews—less favorable. The processes that Constantine set in motion reached an important stage about sixty-five years later when the Emperor Theodosius I (379–395) made orthodox Christianity the official religion of the Roman Empire.

In the Greek Orthodox Church, Saint Constantine is remembered in the liturgy on 21 May. In the west, he was regarded until the thirteenth century as a model Christian ruler, who ended persecutions and began the conversion of the empire. But since the thirteenth century, Constantine has also been a controversial figure in the west. Some of those who were unhappy with the state of Christianity in their time traced the beginning of what they saw as problems to Constantine. The difference of opinion persists in modern times: Historians and theologians continue to debate especially about two issues. Was Constantine's conversion sincere, and were the consequences of his conversion positive, negative, or mixed for Christianity? But whatever the answers, Constantine keeps his important place in the history of Christianity.

By 300, Jesus was more distant in time from his living followers than George Washington is from us. In its 270 years of existence, the Christian movement had not spread like wildfire, but it had grown to be a significant element in the empire's population. It had outlasted serious persecutions in the mid-third century and had grown in numbers during the period of peace between 260 and 303. Precise population figures for the ancient world are rare, but it seems likely that about 300, Christians constituted 10–15 percent of the empire's population. For purposes of comparison, the U.S. Census reported that in 2000 people identifying themselves as African Americans made up about 12.3 percent of the U.S. population, and those identifying themselves as Hispanics made up 12.5 percent. Both groups are numerically minorities, but like the early fourth-century Christians they are culturally and politically significant minorities. But the modest numbers of Christians do not tell the whole story. The orthodox Christians were a tough group, with their sturdy structure of local congregations organized around a three-level ministry, sacred writings, brief creeds, their sense of belonging to a universal church, and their suspicion of some aspects of Greco-Roman life. Even so, it was not inevitable that Christianity would become the dominant religion of the Roman Empire. Christians could have remained a minority in the Roman world, similar to what happened to the Jews, also a tough group

whom the Roman rulers tolerated grudgingly but prevented from making significant numbers of converts. Or Christianity could have developed in the Roman Empire as it later did in the Muslim world, where Christians became a permanent, more or less tolerated (and restricted) minority. Events and decisions associated with Constantine were central to Christianity's success in the later Roman Empire and in the societies that succeeded the empire, down to the present day.

There may have been emperors in the 200s who were interested in Christianity. An unreliable source says that the Emperor Alexander Severus (222–235) had a statue of Christ in his private chapel along with those of Alexander the Great and Abraham. The church historian Eusebius thought that the Emperor Philip the Arab (244–249) was a Christian. But Constantine made decisions that turned out to be permanent for Christianity. It is sometimes said that Constantine "converted" the Roman Empire, but that is inaccurate. A sweeping change in Greco-Roman society's religions was so fundamental that it required a long time to take place. Constantine set in motion a process of Christianization that turned out to be irreversible. At first, he granted toleration to the Christians (311–324), that is, he gave them the same legal rights as other religions but no more. That toleration tilted to open favor after Constantine had defeated his last rival emperor and was in firm control of the entire empire (324–337). Christianity became the family religion of Constantine's sons, who continued to favor it actively (337–361). But it was only in 380 that the Emperor Theodosius I made orthodox Catholic Christianity the official religion of the Roman state. Even then there were significant groups of dissenters, including followers of the traditional Greek and Roman gods, Christians who were regarded as heretics by the dominant group, and substantial numbers of Jews. Even Theodosius' law was not in itself an end but rather a beginning of centuries of effort to transform official favor into a church that penetrated deep into ordinary Greco-Roman society.

In order to comprehend the relations of rulers to religion before modern times, you have to recognize that before the eighteenth century there were not many atheists, that is, people who denied the existence of gods or a God, and not many agnostics, that is, people who were unsure if there were gods or a God. Virtually everyone believed that unseen powers, some good and some evil, were active in human life. In the Greco-Roman world, the good and evil spirits were thought to be numerous and everywhere. In a universe visualized as having a heaven, an earth, and an underworld, there were no firm barriers that prevented coming and going from the upper world of good spirits and from the lower world of evil spirits to the Earth, where humans lived. The spiritual beings helped or hurt humans. Sophisticated thinkers, such as Augustine of Hippo, accepted that God worked in mysterious ways, but most people, including most Christians, thought that the gods or God aided in practical, material ways those who pleased them and punished in practical, material ways those who displeased them. Consequently, sensible people, including sensible rulers, took religion seriously and tried to please the gods.

Even the persecuting emperors probably believed that the Christian God existed. The God was not the problem, but his stubborn followers were. The Emperor Diocletian's intense persecution of Christians was continued by Galerius, his fiercely anti-Christian successor. In 311, Galerius fell ill with what may have been stomach cancer. He concluded that he had angered some god, probably the Christian God, whose followers he had been attacking. On his deathbed, Galerius issued an edict of toleration that expressed some traditional Roman ideas about religion. Galerius first defended persecution by saying that he was trying to restore all things "in accordance with the ancient laws and public order of the Romans." He accused the Christians of abandoning the good old ways: "they had been possessed of such self-will and seized with such folly that...they made for themselves and were observing laws merely in accordance with their own disposition and as each one wished, and were assembling various multitudes in various places." In spite of his government's efforts, Galerius admitted, the Christians had endured. But as a result of the disruptions caused by persecution "they [the Christians] were neither paying the worship due to the gods of heaven nor honouring the god of the Christians." The dying emperor con-

ceded defeat and granted "[t]hat Christians may exist again and build the houses in which they used to assemble, always provided that they do nothing contrary to order...." Remarkably, he asked them to pray for him: "...they will be bound to beseech their own god for our welfare, and that of the state, and their own...." (EH 8:17). For the first time in Roman history, Christianity was legally tolerated, although Galerius granted it no special favors and certainly did not make it the religion of the empire. When Galerius died in 311, his policy of toleration lapsed, but the precedent had been set. To understand what happened next, we need to turn briefly to Roman politics.

The Roman Empire never developed a successful long-term way to decide peacefully who the next emperor would be, especially when the dead emperor left no strong male heir. In theory, the Senate, which was regarded as a repository of wisdom and experience, confirmed the best candidate for the position. When there was no clear successor, rival armies supported their generals in periodic outbreaks of civil war. In civil wars, the Senate was ordinarily compelled to approve the general who seemed most dangerous to them. In the late third century, the Emperor Diocletian tried to create an orderly method of succession, called the "Tetrarchy," the "rule of four." He divided the empire into eastern and western parts, each ruled by a co-emperor with the title of "augustus." Each of those halves was divided in half, with a junior emperor, called a "caesar," to assist each augustus. Diocletian planned that when an augustus left his position, the caesar would be promoted, and a new caesar would be chosen. But when Diocletian gave up power in 305, his political experiment of two augusti and two caesares failed. In 312–313, two civil wars broke out. In the west Constantine fought Maxentius, and in the east Licinius fought Maximin Daia. In order to cement an alliance against their respective rivals, Licinius married Constantine's sister.

Faithful to traditions that went back to the origins of the Roman state, each contender for the emperorship tried to strengthen his armies by seeking supernatural aid. Apparently no one had full confidence in the traditional gods, and so they turned to new ones. For example, Constantine's rival Maxentius consulted a collection of prophecies, the Sybilline books, which said that an enemy of Rome would die (it turned out to be him). Constantine also chose a heavenly patron, the God of the Christians (more precisely, as we shall see later, Constantine believed that the Christian God chose him). He might have had some loose family connections with Christianity. Between 293 and 306, his father, Constantius Chlorus, had ruled Gaul, Britain, and Spain. When Diocletian's persecution began, Constantius Chlorus was willing to destroy Christian buildings and burn copies of the scriptures but hesitated to execute people. In addition, Constantine had a half-sister, a daughter of Constantius Chlorus, who was named "Anastasia," which meant "resurrection" in Greek and might point to Christian influences in his father's family. In any case, Constantine believed that the God of the Christians became his patron in the civil war.

There are three roughly contemporary Christian stories about how the Christian God became Constantine's protector. About 317, Bishop Eusebius of Caesarea wrote that Constantine fought with the aid of God, was victorious, and to commemorate the victory set up at Rome a statue of himself holding a cross (EH 9:9). In 320, about eight years after the victory over Maxentius, Lactantius, the Christian tutor of Constantine's son Crispus, wrote that Constantine had a dream in which he was told to inscribe on his men's shields a special sign, the Greek letters *chi* (X) and *rho* (R), which are the first letters of the word "Christ" in Greek. This image was called the "Labarum," which became the Christian symbol used by the Constantinian dynasty on coins, battle standards, and in art. Many years after the victory, Eusebius of Caesarea wrote a biography of Constantine in which he told a third version of how Constantine placed his army under Christ's protection. Eusebius says he heard the story from Constantine's lips: "He said that about noon, when day was already beginning to decline, he saw with his own eyes the trophy of a cross of light in the heavens, above the sun, and bearing the inscription, CONQUER BY THIS. At this sight he himself was struck with amazement, and his whole army also…witnessed the miracle. He said that he was unsure what the vision meant. And while he continued to ponder and reason on

its meaning, night suddenly came on; then in his sleep the Christ of God appeared to him with the same sign which he had seen in the heavens, and commanded him to make a likeness of that sign, and to use it as a safeguard in all engagements with his enemies" (Eusebius, *The Life of Constantine*, bk. 1. c. 28–29, NPNF, second series, vol. 1, p. 490, altered). To complicate the picture, an anonymous pagan orator delivering a panegyric, which is a speech in praise of someone, reported a vision in which the god Apollo and the goddess Victory appeared to Constantine, offering him long life and victory. Scholars have spilled much ink over these four accounts, which are difficult to reconcile. But some basic assertions seem clear. Constantine, like his enemies, sought divine aid. During the third century, many pagans adopted a somewhat loose form of monotheism. They tended to believe that behind the crowd of gods, goddess, and other spirits, there was a dominant god. Many identified that chief god with the Unconquered Sun God (Sol Invictus). The Emperor Aurelian (270–275) promoted the worship of the Unconquered Sun. There were priests and a fine temple in Rome dedicated to the Sun God. The other gods continued to receive their traditional worship, but the Sun God had a special place in Roman life until the adoption of Christianity. Constantine was at first devoted to the Unconquered Sun God, who might be represented by the god Apollo. Constantine may have had just one sun-related vision, to which a pagan orator gave his interpretation and the Christians gave theirs. Whatever happened, Constantine came to believe that the Christian God came to him and chose him. (Think of Paul, who also thought God chose him to be the apostle to the gentiles.) On 28 October 312, Constantine won a stunning victory over his rival Maxentius near the Milvian Bridge over the Tiber River. At that point, he was not a Christian but was probably a vague monotheist who honored the Unconquered Sun God. He believed that his victory was due to the God of the Christians, who had picked him out for special favor. He wanted to repay his new patron God for victory. He concluded that he should favor his patron God's people, the Christians.

Licinius, Constantine's brother-in-law and ally at the time, also sought divine help. The Christian writer Lactantius wrote that before Licinius' decisive victory over his eastern rival Maximin Daia, he had a dream in which a heavenly being told him to have his army offer a certain prayer to God. Licinius distributed written copies to his officers: "Supreme God, we beseech you; Holy God, we beseech you; to you we commend all justice, to you we commend our safety; to you we commend our empire. Through you we live, through you we are victorious and happy. Supreme Holy God hear our prayers: to you we stretch forth our weapons. Hear, Holy Highest God" (Lactantius, *On the Deaths of the Persecutors*, c. 46, ANF, vol. 7, p. 319). With its vague appeal to the "Supreme Holy God," this prayer is not openly Christian, but Christians could interpret it in a Christian way. Pagan soldiers, who probably made up the majority of the troops, could also recite it with no problem.

After Constantine and Licinius had won their respective victories, they divided the empire between them, Constantine taking the western half and Licinius the eastern. They met at Milan in 313 when Constantine's sister married Licinius. They worked out a policy, traditionally called the "Edict of Milan," which granted toleration to all religions, including the Christians. "When I Constantine Augustus and I Licinius Augustus had come under happy auspices to Milan...we resolved to make such decrees as should secure respect and reverence for the Deity; namely, to grant both to the Christians and to all the free choice of following whatever form of worship they pleased, to the intent that all the divine and heavenly powers...might be favorable to us and all those living under our authority....we have granted to these same Christians free and unrestricted authority to observe their own form of worship....authority has been given to others also, who wish to follow their own observance and form of worship...so that each one may have authority to choose and observe whatever form he pleases. This has been done by us, to the intent that we should not seem to have detracted in any way from any rite or form of worship" (EH 10:5, altered). Constantine and Licinius also ordered measures to reverse the damage done to the Christians during a decade of persecution. Churches, cemeteries, and other property confiscated from Christians should be given back at no cost. The imperial treasury would reimburse those who had purchased the confiscated property.

In 313, neither Constantine nor Licinius was Christian. Over the next few years, their religious policies developed in opposite directions. Constantine grew more favorable to Christians, invited Christian bishops to his court as advisers, issued laws favorable to Christians, made lavish gifts to Christian churches, and chose a Christian tutor for his children. After about 317, he identified more openly with the Christians, for instance, by putting on some coins the Christian symbols of the cross and the Labarum, although until about 324 he continued to issue coins with the image of the Unconquered Sun. In contrast, Licinius moved away from toleration of Christianity and back to the traditional gods. Both emperors abandoned the general toleration that the edict of Milan had announced as they prepared for the civil war to come. Constantine began to criticize and pressure pagans and to favor Christians openly. Licinius began to persecute Christians in the east, whom he saw as Constantine's allies. As a sign of how entangled Christianity and imperial politics had become in the decade since the Great Persecution ended, Licinius rallied his followers by openly championing the traditional gods, while Constantine rallied his followers by claiming to be the agent of the Christian God. In 324, Constantine defeated Licinius at a battle in modern western Turkey and gained control of the undivided empire. His victory strengthened his conviction that the Christian God was a mighty god whose patronage was well worth having.

After 324, Constantine openly supported Christianity, a move that had huge consequences. We could leave it at that because the consequences of imperial favor will be treated in subsequent chapters. But scholars and others have been interested in Constantine's motives. Why in about a decade did he move from paganism through tolerance to favor and eventually to membership in the church? Some historians have said that he was influenced primarily by politics, that he perceived Christians as useful allies. Such an explanation does not entirely fit the world in which he lived. Most fourth-century Christians were not pacifists, but they were not a warlike minority either. There was no clear political or military profit from favoring them. Such a political explanation presupposes a sort of religious skepticism that exists in modern times but that did not generally exist in late antiquity. Some historians argue that Constantine was a syncretist ("one who combines"), that is, a person who mixes together religious ideas and practices that were originally separate. From their point of view, Constantine wanted to add the powerful Christian God to his personal religion without rejecting other gods, especially the Unconquered Sun. Finally, some historians say that he genuinely came to believe. I think he was a syncretist who over a relatively short time, perhaps five years, became a believer. Constantine was convinced that the Christian God had helped him at a crucial point in his life. During the rest of his life, continuing military and political success strengthened that conviction. He wanted to repay his victory-bringing God, which he did by favoring his Christian followers. At the beginning, he was hazy on what the Christians believed. But Christians joined his court, bishops became his advisers, and his mother Helena became a pious Christian. Constantine became more knowledgeable and eventually became a convert.

Constantine was a brutal ruler when he felt he had to be. He had his wife Fausta and eldest son Crispus executed for reasons not clear to us. But he was personally puritanical. For instance, there is no record of mistresses or illegitimate children. He admired Christian chastity, honesty, self-denial, and bravery under persecution. But most importantly, he continued to be victorious with the aid of the Christian God who had given him his special symbol, the Labarum. Even when he joined the church, he remained a catechumen who postponed baptism—but so did many upper-class men in the fourth century. His delay in seeking baptism made sense in light of Christian penitential sternness. To protect the Roman state and to keep personal power, emperors had to do things that were sinful in the eyes of the church. The strict church still demanded from serious sinners severe penance, which was permitted only once. To be an emperor and to be baptized seemed incompatible, a view that changed during the next century.

Figure 10.1 Colossal Marble Head of the Emperor Constantine (306–337). Roman emperors built on a large scale. They also exalted themselves with much-larger-than-life statues. This marble head and a marble hand are all that survive from an approximately thirty-foot statue in Rome. Constantine has his gaze fixed on the heavens, perhaps to emphasize his relationship to God. Orthodox Christianity had allied itself to a powerful institution, the Roman Empire, and to powerful rulers, the emperors. *(Scala / Art Resource, NY)*

Constantine planned to retire at some point and to be baptized in the Jordan River, at the spot where tradition said John the Baptist had baptized Christ. In 337, Constantine fell ill unexpectedly at the imperial city of Nicomedia. When he knew he was dying, he took off the purple robes of an emperor, was baptized, and died in the white robes of a newly baptized person. He had prepared his burial place in the city he had founded, called "New Rome" or "Constantinople." In the Church of the Holy Apostles there were twelve cenotaphs ("empty tombs") for the twelve apostles, and he was buried among them as the thirteenth apostle.

FURTHER READING

Ancient Sources

Averil Cameron and Stuart G. Hall Eusebius, *Life of Constantine*, with an introduction, and commentary by the translator, (Oxford, 1999). A rich contemporary account, slanted toward praising Constantine but full of important information.

P. R. Coleman-Norton, *Roman State & Christian Church* (London, 1966), vol. 1, pp. 17–215. A rich selection of translated sources with good explanations on the Great Persecution and religious policies of Constantine.

J. L. Creed, ed., Lactantius, *De mortibus persecutorum (On the Deaths of the Persecutors)*, with an English translation by the editor, (Oxford and New York, 1984).

J. Stevenson, *A New Eusebius: Documents Illustrating the History of the Church to AD 337*, revised by W. H. C. Frend (London, 1987), pp. 317–370. Translations of many fourth-century documents by and about Constantine.

Modern Works

Timothy D. Barnes, *Constantine and Eusebius* (Cambridge, MA, 1981). An important treatment of the Emperor Constantine and his historian, Eusebius.

Averil Cameron, *The Later Roman Empire, AD 284–430* (Cambridge, MA, 1993). A brief introduction to the Roman Empire in its Christian phase.

Hal Drake, *Constantine and the Bishops: The Politics of Intolerance* (Baltimore, MD, 2000).

A. H. M. Jones, *Constantine and the Conversion of Europe* (1948; reprinted Toronto, 1994). A brief book that untangles the civil wars and imperial politics that accompanied Constantine's conversion.

CHAPTER 11

The Christian Empire and the Imperial Church

Constantine's conversion was personal, but it had a major public impact because he was the unrestricted ruler of the empire. He and his sons ruled for about forty-five years (317–361). It is hard for us to understand what it meant for a Roman emperor to become a Christian without some knowledge of what it meant to be a Roman emperor. From about 509 BCE, the traditional date for the expulsion of its last king, Rome had been a republic in which power was shared among assemblies of male citizens, magistrates usually elected for one-year terms, and the Senate, which was a body of elders and former high magistrates. In 27 BCE, a young general named "Octavian" won a civil war and emerged as the sole ruler, the first emperor (27 BCE–14 CE). The Roman Senate gave him a new name, "Augustus," which eventually became the title of every emperor. The still-powerful Roman aristocracy preferred a republic, so Augustus claimed to be "restoring" the republic rather than ending it. He allowed traditional political institutions to continue. Magistrates were still elected annually, the Senate still deliberated, and the assemblies still met, but they were under his control. Between the first and fourth centuries, successive emperors took more and more power into their own hands. The institutions of the republic withered in the face of the emperor's growing authority. By Constantine's day, more than three hundred years after Augustus, emperors were military dictators who had no effective legal limits on their power. They controlled the armies, directed the bureaucracy, made laws on their own authority, spent the money of the state as they saw fit, and acted more or less as they wished. The only practical checks on their power were self-restraint, a lack of resources, the inefficiency and corruption of the bureaucracy, rebellions, assassination, or natural death.

In the pre-Christian phase of the Roman Empire (about 27 BCE–313 CE), the emperor's vast power was justified partly in religious terms. The emperor held the office of pontifex maximus, the highest priest of the state religion, which authorized him to supervise the state cults. Ceremonies that became more elaborate over time made clear that the emperor claimed a status above that of ordinary humans. He dressed in a distinctive color, purple; people who came into his presence prostrated themselves on the ground; his closest advisers stood in his presence while he sat; and everything connected with him was given the adjective "sacred." When the empire was still pagan, many of the emperor's subjects regarded him as a living god or at least a god after death. When Constantine became a Christian, he could no longer claim to be a god himself, but his Christian subjects were willing to regard him and his successors as rulers chosen by their God. In 336, on the thirtieth anniversary of Constantine's accession to the emperorship, Bishop Eusebius of Caesarea delivered an effusive speech in the presence of the imperial court. Because Eusebius had lived through the horrible persecutions of Diocletian, Galerius, and Licinius, his enthusiasm for Constantine is understandable. He was deeply grateful for the changes Constantine brought about for orthodox Christianity. But Eusebius' oration reveals more than gratitude. He laid out a theological view that placed Constantine within the framework of God's plans: The emperor's conversion was a consequence of God's providence. Eusebius drew elaborate parallels between the Divine Word (which became human in Jesus Christ) and the Emperor Constantine. The emperor was the Divine Word's friend, imitator, and collaborator in the work of salvation. This is just a sample of the speech, which must have gone on for hours: "This only begotten Word of God reigns, from ages which had no beginning, to infinite and endless ages, the partner of his Father's kingdom. And (our emperor)..., who derives the source of imperial authority from above, and is strong in the power of his sacred title, has controlled the empire of the world for a long period of years. Again, that Preserver of the universe [the Word] puts order into these heavens and earth...consistent with his Father's will. In the same way our emperor, whom he [the Word] loves, brings those whom he rules on earth to the only begotten Word and Savior and makes them fit subjects of his kingdom. And as he who is the common Savior of mankind...drives far away from his flock...those apostate spirits [devils] which once flew through the airy tracts above this earth, and fastened on the souls of men; so his friend [Constantine], graced by his heavenly favor with victory over all his foes, subdues and punishes the open adversaries of the truth in accordance with the usages of war. He who is the pre-existent Word, the Preserver of all things, imparts to his followers the seeds of true wisdom and salvation, makes them truly wise, and enlightens and gives them understanding in the knowledge of the Father's kingdom. Our emperor, his friend, acting as interpreter for the Word of God, aims at recalling the whole human race to the knowledge of God; proclaiming clearly in the ears of all, and declaring with a powerful voice the laws of truth and godliness to all who dwell on the earth. The universal Savior opens the heavenly gates of his Father's kingdom to those whose are going there from this world. Our emperor, striving to follow his Divine example, having purged his earthly dominion from every stain of impious error, invites each holy and pious worshipper within his imperial mansions, earnestly desiring to save with all its crew that mighty vessel [the Roman Empire] of which he is the appointed pilot" (Eusebius, *The Oration of Eusebius Pamphilus in Praise of the Emperor Constantine Pronounced on the Thirtieth Anniversary of His Reign*, 2.1–5, in NPNF, second series, vol. 1, p. 583, altered).

As Eusebius' oration shows, even after emperors became Christians, they kept a central role in religion: Constantine was a mediator between the Divine Word and the world. The conviction that the Christian emperor had a special relationship with God never lost its appeal, especially in the Greek-speaking east. But experience modified somewhat the views of later Christian thinkers. They continued to see the emperor as God's chosen representative on Earth, but *only* if he was orthodox in belief. Some bishops, especially in the west, resisted even orthodox emperors whom they regarded as overstepping their rights when they intervened too forcefully in the church's affairs. But if an emperor was orthodox, he had great influence inside the church. It does not go too far to say that during the fourth and fifth centuries the orthodox emperor became the leading member of the church, although he was not free to do anything he wanted in the matter of religion.

Not every kind of Christianity enjoyed imperial toleration. Constantine and his sons used their resources to strengthen the position of orthodox catholic Christianity. Because they held great political power and controlled tremendous wealth, their patronage had important consequences. For instance, they used their wealth to change the architectural and artistic settings in which Christian worship took place. In comparison with the publicly supported pagan temples, the Christian churches of the later third and early fourth centuries, often nothing more than reconfigured houses, must have seemed shabby. The emperors and empresses had the resources to bestow impressive buildings on their favored religion. For instance, Constantine built large, ornate churches at sites that had importance for Christians, including the Church of the Nativity in Bethlehem, the Holy Sepulcher (Christ's Tomb) in Jerusalem, and the churches at Rome over the burial places of Peter and of Paul. Other wealthy Christians imitated the emperors by building churches, monasteries, and hospitals in cities and on their country estates. Buildings needed furnishings. Most Christian clergy believed that God wanted awe-inspiring ceremonies and magnificent liturgical objects in his worship. Emperors, bishops, and wealthy lay-people gave fine copies of the scriptures, tapestries, candelabra, chalices, mosaics, sacred images (icons), clerical vestments, and the wide range of expensive liturgical things that are so valued in modern museums. Within a human lifetime, the Christians gained buildings and objects devoted to worship that were as magnificent as the temples of the pagan gods. Sometimes, but not often, the pagan temples themselves were taken over for Christian use. More often the pagan temples were abandoned, looted for their stonework, or even demolished.

Constantine also founded a new city that was to have an important role in the history of ancient Christianity. The city of Rome was associated with the most respected political traditions and pagan religious sites of the empire, but it was located far from the dangerous borders where military threats from barbarians were growing. Beginning in the late third century, the emperors abandoned the city of Rome as their residence for places more useful for military reasons. In 324, Constantine began to build a new city on the site of a small Greek city called "Byzantion." In 330, Constantine dedicated the new imperial capital, which was officially called "New Rome" but often called "Constantinople" ("Constantine's City"), which is the modern Istanbul in Turkey. The city had a splendid location for military needs and commerce, situated on a peninsula that jutted out into the Bosporus, the waterway that drained the Black Sea into the Aegean Sea. The site was protected on three sides by water and on the western, landward side by massive walls and ditches that were built later. Constantine gave his New Rome the features of the Old Rome, including its own seven hills, Senate, forum, palaces, and impressive art, some of it seized from ancient temples and sacred places. Constantine probably had military and commercial considerations uppermost in his mind, but New Rome was free of the pagan associations of Old Rome. He did not destroy the existing pagan temples, but he began a process of church-building and other measures that eventually made it a Christian city. In Constantinople, he and his successors built churches, not temples, and supported Christian ascetics, not pagan Vestal Virgins. He built his burial church, that of the Twelve Apostles, in Constantinople. The city became the center of the Eastern Roman or Byzantine Empire and of the Greek Orthodox Church. For many centuries, it was the largest, richest Christian city in the world.

Imperial gifts were important to Christianity, but so was the reshaping of Roman law in its favor. As the power of emperors had grown, they had become the source of law itself. They needed no one's permission to issue an edict. The sixth-century Emperor Justinian asserted in his textbook for law students that the Roman people had conferred all law-making power on the emperor. As he put it, what seemed good to the emperor had the force of law (*Institutes*, 1.2.6). In practice, emperors usually had sophisticated jurists to advise them and to draft and interpret their edicts. The first Christian emperors began the long tradition of enacting Christian-inspired laws. For instance, Constantine made Sunday a special day on which no law courts sat. He also forbade the punishment of branding on the face because each person was made in the image of God. An accumulating body of laws integrated Christian beliefs, organizations, and clergy on a favored basis into Roman society.

The later Roman Empire had severe economic problems and an insatiable need for income. Successive emperors resorted to such measures as heavy taxes on land, confiscations, and forced labor without pay. The emperors also required many peasant farmers and people employed in vital occupations such as shipping and soldiering to remain in their jobs. In a move toward a caste system, their sons were sometimes forced to follow in their fathers' occupations. Men of wealth were forced to join the curia ("town council") of their city. The members of the curia, called *curiales*, were responsible for collecting local taxes. If they fell short, they had to make it up out of their wealth—sometimes a sure way to impoverishment. Tax collectors could be brutal in carrying out their duties. Aristocrats protected themselves, but poor and middle-class people were sometimes oppressed terribly by the strong-arm tactics that were used to meet the financial needs of the Roman army and bureaucracy. In such a world, emperors granted valuable financial privileges to churches and to orthodox Christian clergy.

Because Christian churches in the pagan empire had no legal standing, they could not securely possess their buildings and cemeteries. They could not securely accept a gift or a legacy given in a Christian's will. The Christian emperors issued laws that recognized churches as legal corporations that could own property, receive gifts and legacies, and build up endowments. As a result, some important churches became rich, and even the poor churches had secure possession of whatever property they owned. The emperors favored the Christian clergy as well, treating them as God's servants whose acts of worship brought divine favor on the state and the emperor. For that reason, they granted the clergy "privileges," which were exemptions from laws that bound everyone else. A comparable modern "privilege" is the exemption from taxation that American states and the federal government grant to schools, hospitals, and churches. Those institutions do not have to pay some of the taxes that they would otherwise pay if they were treated under the laws that apply to ordinary citizens and institutions. Imperial laws eliminated or at least lightened burdens for clergy, who were exempted from degrading forced labor, from the harshest forms of taxation, and from mandatory service as *curiales* (they still paid some taxes).

In the Christian empire, bishops rose in social stature and legal position. In a tradition going back to Paul (1 Cor 6:1–8), Christians had often asked their bishops to settle disputes among them. Christian emperors legalized that practice by granting some judicial powers to bishops, for instance, the legal right to certify the freeing of slaves by their masters. The bishops' courts were popular because they were probably faster, cheaper, fairer, and less corrupt than the secular courts. In a society where political authority ordinarily flowed downward from the emperor, fourth- and fifth-century Christian congregations still had a role in choosing their bishops. Some bishops defended local interests against the imperial bureaucracy because they represented local people, especially ordinary people, in way that few others could.

The economic and legal privileges of the clergy attracted to clerical careers men who were not particularly pious but sought personal advantages. Some men sought ordination to the clergy as a way to escape the burdens of taxation or membership on the town council—emperors tried to stop or at least limit that so as to prevent taxpayers from avoiding their financial duties. Some men sought ordination to share in the growing prestige that surrounded the higher clergy. Jerome (331–420), who lived at Rome in the 380s, was a skilled satirist. He may have overstated the situation, but his sharp descriptions point to what could happen in such a prosperous church as that at Rome. He mocked clergy who became angry when their meals were not good enough. He scorned clerics who sought the friendship of rich women for the gifts and legacies they could give. He satirized rich widows who pretended piety but lived in luxury, extravagantly dressed and carried in litters, surrounded by eunuchs and slaves and flattered by priests and deacons. In rare circumstances, the desire for church offices could lead to actual violence. Jerome's friend and patron, Pope Damasus (366–384), had been chosen in a disputed election and in an atmosphere of violence that left dozens of his opponents dead.

Constantine and his successors favored lay Christians in the bureaucracy and the army, the pillars on which the late empire stood. At first they proceeded slowly because there was a strong pagan presence in both institutions. It was particularly dangerous to alienate the army. Ability also sometimes outweighed religion. Skilled or trusted pagans continued to be appointed to high bureaucratic and military positions when they were good at them. Eventually both the army and the bureaucracy became Christian strongholds.

JULIAN THE "APOSTATE" (361–363)

The efforts of Constantine and his sons had spotty results and did not sweep away other religions. In particular, paganism in its complex forms was not dead in the mid-fourth century. Many people of all classes retained emotional and religious attachments to the traditional gods. They wanted to honor them with traditional sacrifices. Even some Christians wavered when military defeats at the hands of barbarians and of Persians called into question the power of the Christian God. There are signs of a pagan revival in the middle of the fourth century, when some new shrines of the gods were built or existing shrines refurbished. The traditional religion(s) were so deeply rooted in the structures of the state and the lives of its inhabitants that resistance to the spread of Christianity—sometimes called a "pagan reaction"—was probably inevitable.

Pagan hopes were raised briefly when the last ruler from the Constantinian dynasty converted from Christianity to paganism. Julian, called "the Apostate" by his Christian enemies, was emperor for eighteen months during 361 to 363. When Julian's uncle Constantine I had died in 337, Julian's father, uncle, brother, and three cousins were murdered to eliminate rivals for imperial power. Julian, who was only five or six, and his half-brother Gallus were spared because they were too young to pose a threat. Julian hated his cousin Constantius (337–361), whom he blamed for his family's massacre. The young Julian was held in exile in Asia Minor, where he received an excellent education in Greek literature and philosophy, in addition to a Christian education. He even had a minor clerical office as a reader in church. When he was in his late teen years, he was allowed to study with pagan rhetoricians and philosophers who still had intellectual prestige. In 351, at age twenty, his love of ancient literature and neo-Platonic philosophy led him to convert secretly to the old religion, which he called "Hellenism," the religion of the Hellenes or Greeks. For his safety, he hid his feelings and religious beliefs for about a decade. He attended Christian church services, even as he was honoring the gods in secret. The Emperor Constantius had no sons. When Constans (337–350), his last brother, was killed in 350, Constantius sought help to rule the vast empire that was reunited in his hands. He married his sister Helena to Julian, who was one of his few adult male relatives, and in 355 made the twenty-four-year-old Julian a subordinate ruler, a caesar, with authority in the west. When Julian was sent to defend Gaul, he defeated some Germanic barbarians along the Rhine. His troops, who were disgruntled with Constantius, mutinied at Paris in 360 and declared that Julian was augustus, that is, co-emperor with Constantius. Civil war, that curse of Roman politics, was beginning. Julian began to move his troops east for a confrontation with his cousin, but Constantius died unexpectedly at age forty-four in November 361. Julian was sole emperor.

Now free to do so, Julian openly professed his allegiance to the old gods. He and his supporters in the army sacrificed oxen in public and performed other pagan rituals to assert the new situation. He rallied supporters who wanted to halt or turn back the advance of Christianity. He probably wanted to destroy it and restore the honor of the pagan gods. Julian hated Christianity, which he regarded as superstitious and vulgar. He once ridiculed Christians as people who hissed when they thought they were in the presence of demons and frequently made the sign of the cross. What one emperor had given, another emperor might be able to take away. Julian reversed the direction of imperial favor. He restored sacrifices to the traditional gods, and he paid for exuberant public pagan religious ceremonies. He stripped Christian churches and clergy of the economic and legal privileges that had flowed to them since the time of Constantine. He expelled Christians from his court. Because Julian was offended that Christians taught the pagan literature he loved so much but did not believe in the myths that often shaped it, he prohibited them from teaching classical literature. In spite of his hostility to Christianity, he did not dare to persecute it on a large scale because by the 360s there were too many Christians. He adopted a policy of toleration. "...we ought to persuade and instruct men, not by blows, or insults, or bodily violence....I admonish those who are zealous for the true religion [Hellenism] not to injure the communities of the Galilaeans [Julian's term for Christians] or attack or insult them....we ought to pity rather than hate men who in matters of the greatest importance are in such an evil situation. For in very truth the greatest of all blessings is reverence for the gods, as, on the other hand, irreverence is the greatest of all evils. It follows that those who have turned aside from the gods to corpses and relics [Julian's view of Christ and the martyrs] pay this as their penalty" (Julian, Letter 41 in *The Works of the Emperor Julian*, in three volumes with an English translation by Wilmer Cave Wright, LCL [London and New York, 1923], vol. 3, p. 135, altered). Julian's toleration had hidden motives. He knew the catholic Christians had deep divisions among themselves, arising out thirty-five years of bitter disagreements over the relationship of the Son to the Father, often called the "Arian" or "Trinitarian Controversy," to be treated in chapter 13. During those years, the winners in the theological quarrels called upon Constantine and then his sons to depose and exile their opponents, who were usually bishops. Ammianus Marcellinus (about 330–395), a pagan historian, commented that Julian knew "that no wild beasts are such enemies to mankind as are most of the Christians in their deadly hatred of one another" (*Ammianus Marcellinus*, 22.5.3–4, with an English translation by John Rolfe, in three volumes, LCL [London and Cambridge, MA, 1940], vol. 3, pp. 203–205). Julian's predecessor, Constantius, who had favored Arian Christianity, exiled opposing bishops. Julian hoped to whip up turmoil in Christian ranks by allowing the exiled bishops to return to claim a church where another bishop presided. In his last months, when things were not going as he wished, he did not punish anti-Christian riots in Asia Minor and in the Near East. He sporadically confiscated the property of churches, for example, at Edessa. He burned the bodies of some martyrs. But there was no full-scale persecution of Christians.

Julian knew that if he was to revive paganism, he needed to do more than criticize and disrupt Christianity. He took steps to restore the pagan temples, priesthoods, and sacrifices, which had fallen on hard economic times, especially in the eastern parts of the empire where Christianity was growing rapidly. After almost fifty years of rule by Christian emperors, many pagans were discouraged. For instance, when Julian arrived at Apollo's oracle at Daphne, near Antioch, he found the temple more or less destitute. None of the traditional accompaniments to worship was there for Apollo's festival—no incense, no sacrificial food, and, above all, no animals to offer to the god. The temple priest told Julian that the city of Antioch, which used to contribute to the festival, had provided nothing. The priest brought from his own house a goose to offer to Apollo. When Julian tried to consult Apollo's oracle at Daphne he was told it no longer spoke because the body of the Christian martyr Babylas had been buried nearby. Julian ordered Babylas to be taken back to his original burial place. Soon thereafter, the temple of Apollo burned to the ground. Julian suspected Christian arson and turned his fury on the Christian churches of Antioch.

Even though Julian hated Christianity, he grudgingly admired its organization and charitable activities. He tried to implant in Hellenism some aspects of Christianity. Julian lamented that Hellenism had no central organization, did not address the widespread social misery of the lower classes, and had no coherent intellectual defense for the sacrifices to the images of the gods. Julian also regretted that Christian charitable acts were effective in winning adherents: "Why do we [the pagans] not observe that it is their benevolence to strangers, their care for the graves of the dead and the pretended holiness of their lives that have done most to increase atheism [that is, Christianity]? I believe that we ought really and truly to practice every one of these virtues" (Julian, Letter 22 in *The Works*, vol. 3, p. 69). He provided funds so that pagan temples, like Christian churches, could give aid to the poor and to strangers. He tried to make pagan priests behave more like Christian clergy. He commanded them to lead morally purer lives with no attendance at the theater and taverns, no hanging around with actresses (who were generally thought to be prostitutes), and no reading of erotic books. He even had to tell the priests that they should not allow their wives, children, and servants to be Christians! Julian thought he could find allies among the Jews, whose situation had deteriorated under his Christian predecessors. He began to subsidize the rebuilding of the Jewish Temple in Jerusalem as a way to win Jewish support for his cause. A disaster at Jerusalem on 19 May 363, perhaps an earthquake, put a stop to the work of rebuilding. Christians regarded it as a heavenly sign, but many Jews and pagans saw it as a bad omen for the future.

Julian could not devote all his energy to the restoration of traditional religion. Like so many emperors before him, he had to defend the eastern border, which was threatened by the Persian Empire. He led an army into Persian territory with some early successes, but on 26 June 363, in modern Iraq he was killed in battle. Julian had ruled only about eighteen months as emperor before death overtook him at age thirty-two. The retreating army chose a Christian officer, Jovian (363–364), to be emperor. The death of Julian probably eliminated the last chance for traditional paganism to reassert itself. There was another brief pagan reaction between 392 and 394 when Eugenius, a nominal Christian who sought pagan support for his rebellion, tried to seize the imperial title. Pagan hopes quickly faded when Eugenius was defeated and executed at the orders of Emperor Theodosius. After Julian's reign, subsequent emperors restored (and increased) Christian legal, social, and political privileges. There was no organized pagan church that might have presented a united front against the deeply entrenched, well-organized, and aggressive Christians. Julian and the pagan counterattacks against Christianity turned out to be minor impediments to the spread of the religion.

THE DYNASTY OF THEODOSIUS (379–455)

In 379, a general from Spain, Theodosius I (379–395), became emperor. He was an able ruler and, more important, committed to orthodox Christianity. Even though Christian emperors (except for Julian) had ruled since the early fourth century, the rivals to orthodox Christianity, including pagans, heretics, and Jews, were numerous, tenacious, and diverse. Theodosius and his dynasty hardened their stance toward the rivals. The policies toward each group need to be treated separately.

Pagans in the Christian Empire

Christians had a strong sense that it was God's will that their religion replace paganism, which they scorned as old-fashioned, outmoded and, of course, wrong. They were convinced that paganism should and would disappear. Although emperors from Constantine's dynasty had undermined the worship of the traditional gods by both words and deeds, none of them dared to outlaw it because many aristocrats, bureaucrats, soldiers, and ordinary people remained pagan. Some Christians believed that the pagan gods and their followers deserved no toleration. Such people advocated the

expulsion of the old gods by force if that was necessary. About 346/48, Firmicius Maternus, a pagan who had converted to Christianity, addressed his *On the Error of the Profane Religions* to Constantine's sons, Constantius I and Constans. In violent words he encouraged them to use their legal power to destroy paganism. He told them that God wanted the emperors to save the pagans, whether the pagans wanted saving or not. He encouraged them to seize the treasures of the temples for their own use and even to destroy the temples. Firmicius quoted Deuteronomy 13:6–10 to emphasize that God hated the worship of idols and threatened horrible punishments for idol worshipers. He assured the emperors that if they suppressed paganism God would grant them victory, wealth, peace, prosperity, as well as personal health and long life. Firmicius Maternus expressed an extreme form of anti-paganism that was never implemented.

But the emperors shared with many other Christians the view that paganism would eventually disappear. Sometimes Christian emperors took symbolic actions to discourage paganism. For instance, Constantine publicly criticized the pagans for clinging to outmoded and backward ways, but he did not cease to tolerate them. Later Christian emperors refused to participate in the pagan rituals that for more than a thousand years had been thought to support the state. For instance, the Emperor Gratian (375–383) stopped using the venerable pagan title "pontifex maximus." Some emperors took practical actions that struck at the stability of paganism, denying imperial favor to the traditional pagan cults or directing imperial wrath against them. They confiscated some temple endowments, closed some temples, and withdrew financial and legal privileges from others. By the 380s, the times had changed so much in favor of Christians that Theodosius and then his successors felt free to legislate vigorously against paganism. Theodosius' decrees were a decisive turning point in the history of Greco-Roman paganism. He forbade any Christian to return to paganism, to be an apostate, as Julian and others were. Christians especially hated pagan blood sacrifice, which was the age-old practice of slaying animals in honor of the gods. Such bloody sacrifices were the heart of pagan religious worship, as they had been of worship in the Jewish Temple before it was destroyed in 70. In 391, Theodosius prohibited blood sacrifices (*Codex Theodosianus*, XVI.10.10). He imposed heavy fines on imperial officials who practiced forbidden rituals or went to temples in order to worship. In 394, Theodosius confiscated the endowments of the six Vestal Virgins, who for perhaps a thousand years had guarded the symbolic hearth fire of Rome. In about 407 or 408, the emperors Arcadius and Honorius, sons of Theodosius, issued a law that was sweeping in its attack on the visible signs of paganism. "1. If any images stand even now in the temples and shrines, and if they have received, or do now receive, the worship of the pagans anywhere, they shall be torn from their foundations....2. The buildings themselves of the temples which are situated in cities or towns or outside the towns shall be seized for public use. Altars shall be destroyed in all places, and all temples situated on Our landholdings shall be transferred to suitable uses....3. It shall not be permitted at all to hold convivial banquets in honor of sacrilegious rites...or to celebrate any solemn ceremony. We grant to bishops also of such places the right to use ecclesiastical power to prohibit such practices...." (*Codex Theodosianus*, XVI.10.19 in *The Theodosian Code and Novels and the Sirmondian Constitutions*, translated by Clyde Pharr [Princeton, NJ, 1952], p. 475, altered). In an especially strong sign of the withdrawal of imperial favor, the Emperor Justinian (527–565) closed the pagan philosophical schools at Athens in 529, ending an educational tradition that went back in various forms almost a thousand years to Plato and Aristotle.

The thundering imperial laws against pagans and other religious dissenters must be placed in context. Imperial laws could be dead letters, the expression of a wish; the emperor could be reaffirming his position as a Christian ruler or his willingness to satisfy the demands of a Christian pressure group. The laws were repeated often because enforcement was difficult or even intentionally lax. Powerful patrons protected the pagans (or heretics or Jews), bribes quieted down local officials, and vigorous enforcement occasionally provoked serious resistance. But the laws were there if anyone wanted to enforce them against pagans. Relying on the emperor's laws, some bishops organized campaigns against paganism in their cities and the surrounding countryside. In one instance in Gaul, Bishop Martin of Tours (372–397) demolished a temple and cut down a sacred pine tree that was close to the shrine. His biographer boasted that Martin constructed a church or monastery wherever he destroyed a pagan shrine. Unauthorized, illegal violence also broke out, especially in the east. Christian mobs, often reinforced by monks, smashed the idols and demolished the temples of the gods, and in extreme cases killed prominent pagans. In 415, a Christian mob at Alexandria killed the influential female pagan philosopher, mathematician, and astronomer named "Hypatia." Some Christians argued that the gods' inability to stop or punish the destruction of their statues and their temples proved that they were powerless. Many disheartened pagan believers gave up and converted. But others retaliated. Pagans occasionally killed clergy and monks, either by assassination or in pitched battles. In many cities and villages, especially in the east, this violent struggle between Christians and pagans played itself out in the later fourth and early fifth centuries. As any sensible rulers would, the Christian emperors opposed mob violence, but they generally favored the Christian side, which had the weight of law supporting it. Pagan victories were few, and the combination of legal and financial pressure, punctuated by popular violence, eroded the visible presence and prestige of the old gods in Greco-Roman society. The public buildings and public rituals of the pagans were especially vulnerable to legal and popular attack. Some pagans continued to worship in secret; others ignored or defied the laws because they were protected by powerful people; others were of such low status that they rarely drew the interest of officials.

Sometimes the Christian-pagan struggle was more dignified. In the later fourth century, the Roman Senate remained a prominent stronghold of traditional paganism. Some senators were Christian, but many senators from distinguished families upheld the religious traditions of the Roman past. After the failure of Julian's plans to restore Hellenism, intelligent, upper-class pagans realized that they could not turn back the clock. Some pleaded for toleration, as the Christian apologists had in the second and third centuries.

They had no more success than the apologists did. A controversy over the Statue and Altar of Victory tells us a great deal. In 29 BCE, the emperor Augustus had placed a statue of the goddess Victory, along with an altar for sacrifices to her, in the building where the Roman Senate met. For more than 350 years, the meetings of the Senate had begun with sacrifices to Victory on her altar. The Christian Emperor Constantius removed the Altar of Victory in 357, an action that was an important symbolic break with the pagan Roman past. The Emperor Julian restored the altar in 361. The Emperor Gratian (375–383) ordered it to be removed again in 382. On that occasion, a leading pagan senator, Symmachus, wrote a plea to the Emperors Theodosius, Arcadius, and Valentinian to put the Altar of Victory back in the Senate house. In the rhetorical style of the time, Symmachus wrote as if Rome itself were pleading for toleration of its traditional religious ways: "Excellent princes, fathers of your country, respect my years to which pious rites have brought me. Let me use the ancestral ceremonies, for I do not repent of them. Let me live after my own fashion, for I am free. This worship subdued the world to my laws, these sacred rites repelled Hannibal from the walls...." Symmachus then made his personal plea to the emperors: "We ask then for peace for the gods of our fathers and of our country. It is proper that all worship should be considered as one. We look on the same stars, the sky is common [to us all], the same world surrounds us. What difference does it make by what pains each seeks the truth? We cannot attain to so great a secret by one road...." (Symmachus, *Relatio*, in NPNF, second series, vol. 10, p. 415, altered).

In reply to Symmachus, Bishop Ambrose of Milan (374–397) wrote to the Emperor Valentinian (375–392), a boy of about thirteen in whose territories the city of Rome was situated, to prevent the restoration of the Altar of Victory. He mocked the weakness of the old gods who, he said, could not defend Rome from its enemies. In particular, he had Rome itself attack the blood sacrifices, which so offended Christians. "She [Rome] speaks with other words. 'Why do you daily stain me with the useless blood of the harmless herd? Trophies of victory depend not on the entrails of the flocks, but on the strength of those who fight....Why

do you bring forward the rites of our ancestors? I hate the rites of a Nero'" (Ambrose, Letter 18, in NPNF, second series, vol. 10, p. 417). The Altar of Victory was restored only briefly under the nominally Christian but pro-pagan Emperor Eugenius (392–394). The toleration of paganism for which Symmachus pleaded was not granted. There were no widespread, officially sanctioned bloodbaths of pagans, but paganism faded, pushed by the legal and financial pressure of the empire and by the disapproval and occasional violence of the increasingly confident Christians.

After about 400, many of the old religious *beliefs* survived, but they were in a sense "beheaded." Of course, they were not actually beheaded, but paganism was gradually deprived of its intellectual leadership and official support. Public funds and privileges were withdrawn; temple endowments were confiscated; pagan priesthoods were impoverished or ceased to function; the local campaigns to destroy statues and temples continued; and the important Roman aristocratic families who had supported paganism converted one by one to Christianity, often led to the new religion by their female members. Functioning temples, pagan priesthoods, and public pagan sacrifices probably became extinct during the early fifth century. The last reservoirs of pagan belief and practice were at the bottom and the top of imperial society. In the countryside, where Christianity lacked the resources to put permanent churches and resident clergy, some traditional rituals and beliefs survived. Near the top of society, there were occasional scandals when prominent people, such as senators, imperial officials, lawyers, teachers, and intellectuals, were discovered to be practicing the old religion in secret. For instance, in 529 and again in 546 the sternly orthodox Emperor Justinian punished high-ranking persons who were pagans. Paganism's disappearance took a long time. Some scholars believe it never entirely died out. But it ceased to be a significant force in society during the fifth century.

Christian Heretics in the Christian Empire

Emperors did not extend their favor to every kind of Christian. Only catholic/orthodox Christians were the recipients of imperial patronage. During the fourth and fifth centuries, other kinds of Christians continued to be rivals to orthodox Christianity. But a distinction must be made between "old" and "new" heresies. The "old" heretical Christian groups that survived from the pre-Constantinian period, such as the many gnostic Christian groups, Marcionites, and Montanists, were by the fourth century generally separated from orthodox Christianity by visible barriers. They frequently had their own forms of leadership, liturgies, customs, beliefs, and revered documents that differed significantly from those of orthodox Christians. Most fourth-century orthodox Christians could see that the followers of the "old heresies" were not orthodox Christians.

Emperors explicitly excluded the "old heresies" from the privileges granted to the catholic Christians. Imperial laws also penalized them. Their possession of churches was insecure; their rights to make a will, to inherit, or to give testimony in court were curtailed; they were forbidden to meet. They were usually not put to death for their religious beliefs. These traditional heresies were not expanding and never had a chance to become the religion of the Christian empire. Over time, legal disfavor, economic pressure, and some violence led to the decline of most and even the disappearance of some. But others survived for centuries by keeping out of sight, by settling in isolated areas, and by conforming when they had to.

But there were also "new" heresies in the fourth and fifth centuries that arose *among catholic Christians themselves* who split over the relation of the Son to the Father (the Trinitarian Controversy) and the relation of the divine nature to the human nature in Jesus (the dispute over the Incarnation). The "new" Christian religious rivals in the fourth and fifth centuries looked very much alike. They shared virtually all aspects of church life, including the same forms of clergy, liturgy, buildings, doctrine, and scriptures. Whether a bishop did or did not accept the equality of the Father and the Son, most of what went on in his church was unaffected. Fourth-century contemporaries could not have known which theological view would prevail among the disputing catholic Christians. Political considerations led to the rise and to the fall of rival religious views. Christian emperors in

the fourth and fifth centuries favored some forms of orthodox Christianity and repressed others. In the east, Constantius (337–361) favored bishops who would not accept the equality of the Father and the Son (anti-Nicenes), while in the west his brother Constans (337–350) favored bishops who accepted the equality of Father and Son (pro-Nicene). Emperors funneled their legal favor and financial gifts to the group with which they agreed and penalized the other groups as heretics.

In 380, Theodosius made catholic Nicene Christianity the only legal form of Christianity in the empire. In his decree, the issue that took most attention was the relation of the Father, Son, and Spirit. Theodosius enacted into law the Trinitarian view that the three persons were fully equal. He did not accept as catholic Christians the followers of the "old" and "new" heresies. He used as the standard of orthodoxy the teaching of the bishops of Rome and Alexandria, two churches associated with St. Peter. "It is Our Will that all the peoples who are ruled by the administration of Our Clemency shall practice that religion which the divine Peter the Apostle transmitted to the Romans....It is evident that this is the religion that is followed by the Pontiff Damasus [Pope from 366 to 384] and by Peter, Bishop of Alexandria...; that is, according to the apostolic discipline and the teaching of the gospel, we shall believe in the single Deity of the Father, the Son, and the Holy Spirit, under the concept of equal majesty and of the Holy Trinity. We command that those persons who follow this rule shall embrace the name of Catholic Christians. The rest, however, whom We adjudge demented and insane, shall sustain the infamy of heretical dogmas, their meeting places shall not receive the name of churches, and they shall be smitten first by divine vengeance and secondly by the retribution of Our own initiative...." (*Codex Theodosianus* XVI 1.2 in *The Theodosian Code*, p. 440, altered). In other laws, Theodosius decreed that old and new Christian heretics were to be denied the financial, social, and legal privileges that were to go exclusively to orthodox catholic Christians who accepted the creed of Nicaea. The dissident Christian groups survived for generations or centuries, but they lived under the threat and sometimes the reality that the laws would be enforced against them.

Jews in the Christian Empire

The Christian emperors wanted to eliminate pagans and Christian heretics by applying financial, legal, and social pressure and sometimes force. That aim was not entirely fulfilled, but over many decades pagans and heretics moved to the margins of society and some groups even to extinction. The policy toward the numerous Jews in the Roman world was different. Neither the imperial government nor the bishops aimed to eliminate them. The Roman Empire, in both its pagan and its Christian phases, had a troubled history with the Jews. But after the failure of the Jewish rebellions of 66–73 and 132–135, a compromise developed. The Romans permitted the Jews to worship and to live according to their own traditions, provided they remained peaceful. But even during the pagan period of imperial history, there was some popular dislike of Judaism—a modern scholar has called it "Judeophobia," which means "fear of Jews." Some pre-Christian imperial laws discouraged the conversion of gentiles to Judaism by forbidding circumcision. Such measures were not vigorously enforced, but they point to a policy that can be described as the simultaneous toleration and containment of Judaism. After the failure of the Jewish War of 66–70, the Roman authorities wanted to deal with a Jewish leader who could speak for much of Judaism. They recognized, maybe even created, the patriarch (*ha-Nasi*, literally "the Prince") of the Jews as the political and religious head of the Jews within the empire. The patriarchs, who were descended from the important Pharisee teacher Hillel (first century BCE), eventually settled at Tiberias in Palestine. The imperial authorities wanted the patriarch to take a leading role in Jewish affairs all over the empire. They granted the patriarchs legal privileges, money, and land to strengthen their hand in dealing with their fellow Jews. The Roman rulers authorized the patriarch to nominate all officers in synagogues as well as to send out representatives to maintain contact with Diaspora communities and to collect taxes owed to the patriarch. The patriarch exercised such religious duties as determining the religious calendar for Jews in the Roman Empire. The patriarch could also expel Jews from membership if they had some-

how offended. For reasons that are not clear, the patriarchate went into a decline in the early fifth century. When the last patriarch died without a male heir, the hereditary line died out. The Roman Emperor Theodosius II (408–450) abolished the patriarchate of the Jews in 429. The numerous Jewish communities maintained their identity and distinctiveness from the world around them but no longer had a central leadership.

When the Roman Empire became legally Christian, the status of the Jews remained the same in some ways and changed in others. Christian emperors issued many laws concerning the Jews, who remained legally tolerated, free to worship, to live, and to work where they wished. Judaism retained its own institutions and ways, such as the patriarch of the Jews (until 429), synagogues, charities, kosher butchers, and academies for the study of Torah. There were no obligatory ghettos, although Jews often chose to live near one another for religious and cultural reasons. Forced conversion of Jews to Christianity was illegal, and Jewish personal property and synagogues were given the same protection as those of other Roman subjects. But there were boundaries that bishops, emperors, and Christian opinion would not allow Jews to cross. The Jews were increasingly, to use a modern term, second-class citizens with rights but hemmed in by restrictions that did not apply to everyone. Intermarriage between Christians and Jews was forbidden; Jews could not convert their Christian slaves to Judaism; Jews could not build new synagogues without permission, although they could repair existing ones; and Jews were forbidden to hold positions of authority over Christians. Because Jews were forbidden to make converts, they survived through the children born to them.

The legal rights of Jews had a grudging and negative aspect to them. At the popular level, there was between Jews and Christians a love-hate relationship whose intensity and extent we cannot measure precisely. On the one hand, Christian writers between the second and the fifth centuries reported that some Christians kept ties with Judaism. At Antioch in the 380s, John Chrysostom preached against Christians, whom he called "judaizers" because they participated in Jewish religious festivals, danced when the Jews celebrated their out-of-doors holidays, went to synagogues to add solemnity to oaths, and went to rabbis for blessings, healings, and magical amulets. In spite of the laws against conversion, some Christians became Jews. Such Christians obviously found something attractive in Judaism. On the other hand, harsh talk against Jews was common. Sporadic violence grew as well, including the destruction of synagogues.

The long-standing Greco-Roman dislike of Judaism was reinforced by the Christian theological conviction that Judaism had been superseded by Christianity and that the stubborn blindness of the Jews prevented them from seeing the truth of the Christian view. Even when defending the Jews' legal rights, Christian emperors issued laws that used harsh language about them. There was also a stream of sermons and tracts that attacked Judaism, often in inflammatory ways. Dislike occasionally burst into violence when, for instance, a Jew circumcised his male Christian slaves or married a Christian woman who then converted to Judaism. The occasional voluntary (and illegal) conversions of Christians to Judaism might lead to violent Christian reactions. Public Christian festivals, when large crowds gathered, were dangerous times for Jews (and pagans) because emotions ran high. Local conflicts, whose exact details we generally do not know, could lead to rioting and to the destruction of synagogues. Roman law demanded that those who destroyed a synagogue pay its rebuilding, but Christian bishops and monks sometimes refused. The interplay of the moderate position of the emperors and the sterner views of many bishops played out at Milan in the 380s. At Callinicum on the eastern frontier, a Christian mob including some monks destroyed a church used by Valentinian gnostic Christians and a synagogue. In accordance with the law, the Emperor Theodosius ordered the local bishop to punish the rioters and to pay for the repair of both buildings. Ambrose (374–397), the powerful, articulate bishop of Milan, preached a sermon in Theodosius' presence. He said that the use of church resources to repair buildings used by heretics or Jews was wrong. He made a veiled threat that he might not in the future offer the Eucharist in the emperor's presence. Theodosius relented, and the bishop at Callinicum did not pay for the rebuilding.

The Jews, who were numerous and well organized in many cities, were not passive in the hostilities.

In 315, Constantine issued a mandate that forbade Jews to throw stones at or otherwise attack apostates, that is, Jews who had become Christians. Christian writers reported Jewish attacks on Christians and their churches. A Jewish rebellion in 351, during which churches and clergy were attacked, and the brief Jewish alliance with Julian the Apostate (361–363) helped to sour already tense Jewish-Christian relations. Many Romans suspected that Jews sympathized with and even supported Rome's Persian enemies, which fueled the cycle of hostility. In the sixth and seventh centuries, some rulers, including the Emperors Justinian (529–565) and Heraclius (610–641), as well as the Germanic Visigothic kings in Spain who had replaced Roman emperors there, promoted forcible conversions, but bishops usually disapproved. However, the bishops welcomed conversions brought about by social pressure, preaching, and even financial inducements. In spite of it all, Judaism survived in the Roman Empire, remained a rival of Christianity in the Middle Ages, and remains a significant religion in the modern Western world.

In about a century (roughly 320–420), the legal, social, economic, cultural, and demographic position of catholic Christianity had been radically transformed. The Christian emperors favored it at the expense of all rivals while at the same time seeking to direct it for their political needs, especially their desire for unity within their empire. By 420, perhaps the majority of the empire's inhabitants had become catholic Christians. But the new situation did not lead to internal harmony or peace within the church. Quite the contrary, the church's freedom probably intensified theological struggles, which have been mentioned only in passing in this chapter but will be taken up in chapters 13 and 14.

FURTHER READING

Ancient Sources

For one of John Chrysostom's sermons against "judaizing," Christians, see "Against the Jews Oration I" in Wendy Mayer and Pauline Allen, *John Chrysostom* (London and New York, 2000), pp. 148–167.

Paul R. Coleman-Norton, *Roman State and Christian Church: A Collection of Documents to A.D. 535* (London, 1966).

A collection of 652 translated documents on the relations of the Roman state to the Christian church, to Christian heretics, to pagans, and to Jews down to the reign of the Emperor Justinian (died 565).

The Emperor Julian's letters in volume 3 of *The Works of the Emperor Julian*, with an English translation by Wilmer Cave Wright, LCL (London and New York, 1923). Read Julian's pungent comments on fourth-century Christianity and his ambitious although unsuccessful plans to revive paganism.

Clarence Forbes, trans., ed., *Firmicius Maternus: The Error of the Pagan Religions*, ACW 37 (New York, 1970). Firmicius Maternus was a fourth-century Christian writer who argued that the sons of Constantine should root out paganism with no mercy.

Ramsay MacMullen and Eugene Lane, editors, *Paganism and Christianity, 100–425 C.E.: A Sourcebook* (Minneapolis, MN, 1992).

Severus of Minorca, *Letter on the Conversion of the Jews*, edited and translated by Scott Bradbury (Oxford, 1996). A detailed account of the conversion of Jews on the island of Minorca in 418 CE.

Modern Works

G. W. Bowersock, *Julian the Apostate* (Cambridge, MA, 1978). A brief, clear introduction to the complex character of Julian.

G. W. Bowersock, Peter Brown, and Oleg Grabar, *Late Antiquity: A Guide to the Postclassical World*, eds., (Cambridge, MA, and London, 1999), especially the essays by Béatrice Caseau, "Sacred Landscapes," and Richard Lim. "Christian Triumph and Controversy."

A. H. M. Jones, *The Later Roman Empire, 284–602* (Norman, OK, 1964), volume 2, pp. 873–985. A richly detailed description of many aspects of church life and organization between the fourth and the sixth centuries.

Ramsey MacMullen, *Christianizing the Roman Empire, A.D. 100–400* (New Haven, 1984). A brief introduction to the complex processes that are wrapped up in the seemingly simple word "conversion."

Peter Schäfer, *Judeophobia: Attitudes toward Jews in the Ancient World* (Cambridge, MA, 1997). An examination of the sympathy with and opposition to Judaism in the Greco-Roman world.

CHAPTER 12

The Government of the Church

The emergence of a Christian empire challenged the traditional ways in which proto-orthodox Christians had made decisions about behavior and belief. Ecclesiology is the branch of theology that tries to answer the question "What is the church?" As with so many things, Christians differed about the way churches should be organized. Jewish Christians had their ways, and the wide array of gnostic and other Christian groups had their distinctive ways, about which few sources survive. Proto-orthodox Christians did not generally write separate works directly on ecclesiology, although in about 251 Cyprian of Carthage wrote a treatise, *On the Unity of the Catholic Church*, but he was unusual. Because there were competing and overlapping views about the nature and organization of the church, some Christian writers, councils of bishops, and emperors did comment on organizational matters, such as who had the right to make decisions about proper behavior, orthodox belief, church finances, and membership. During the first six centuries, there are at least five identifiable broad patterns of church governance that can only be sketched in this chapter. One pattern laid stress on the authority of the local bishop; a second pattern emphasized the authority of bishops acting together in councils; a third pattern emphasized the harmonious cooperation of five important bishops, later called "patriarchs"; a fourth pattern stressed the unique position of the bishop of Rome; and a fifth pattern looked to the God-chosen emperor for leadership in the church. Much of the time the patterns of governance coexisted peacefully, but at other times they were in conflict. In antiquity, none of the patterns of governance decisively ousted the others within the larger church.

THE LOCAL BISHOP

The collection of texts that eventually made up the New Testament presented no single organizational pattern for churches. At Jerusalem, the early organization resembled the governing structure of a synagogue. A leading figure and a group of elders led the Jerusalem church, a pattern that probably lasted until the Romans destroyed it along with the city in 135. In contrast, Paul's churches seem to have been organized around people claiming inspiration from the Holy Spirit. As Jesus' second coming receded into the future, his followers were forced by circumstances to organize themselves somehow. In terms that are perhaps too simple, they moved away from the loose Pauline structure toward the more settled Jerusalem structure. During the second century, many proto-orthodox Christians gathered in local congregations headed by a bishop, who was assisted by presbyters and deacons (and deaconesses in some areas of the eastern Mediterranean). Theology and practice bolstered the dominant position of the bishop. His supporters regarded him as the living successor to the apostles, whose position he held and whose teaching he proclaimed in his corner of the world. He was or at least could be chosen by the laity and clergy of his church. In practice, he tried to control all important aspects of his congregation's life. In his local church, he was the chief preacher, teacher, liturgical figure, and dispenser of discipline. He created clergy by laying on his hands. He admitted new members at baptism. He presided over the Eucharist. He expelled those guilty of serious sin and oversaw the public penance and reconciliation of those who repented. He handled finances, paid the clergy's salaries, distributed charity, and sometimes supported the ill, the old, the widowed, and the orphaned from the members' gifts, which were his to distribute.

Although a man elected bishop needed other bishops, often three, to consecrate him, after he was in charge of the local church he needed no one's permission to carry out his many tasks. The bishop's authority was not always unchallenged, especially if he was perceived as negligent, inadequate for the tasks he had to carry out, theologically out of step, or a public sinner. A bishop sometimes had a falling out with his presbyters or with important members of his congregation. Confessors and charismatics who claimed direct access to the Holy Spirit sometimes challenged the bishop's authority over them. Other bishops might intervene to mediate or in extreme cases to depose the troublesome bishop. On a day-to-day basis, local congregations, of which there were eventually hundreds, were self-contained and self-governing. Even after Constantine's conversion, the local bishop remained the central figure of his particular church

THE BISHOPS IN COUNCIL

The strong local character of churches was balanced by the desire to be "universal" or to be "whole" across time and space, which is what the word "catholic" meant in Greek. Proto-orthodox and orthodox Christians had a conviction that their church transcended the individual congregations in which they experienced their religious lives. They thought of themselves as belonging to the worldwide Body of Christ or to God's People. They were proud that they had fellow believers "everywhere" and often criticized gnostic and other Christian opponents because they had followers only in specific places. In concrete ways, bishops and their congregations behaved as if they belonged to a universal church. They participated in a complex web of contacts that stretched across the Roman Empire and eventually beyond its borders. For instance, bishops kept in touch with one another through letters and messengers. Churches sent expressions of sympathy and sometimes practical aid in the form of money to near or distant congregations that experienced persecution. Wherever Christian travelers went, they could expect hospitality from fellow believers, although they often needed a letter of introduction from their bishop to weed out freeloaders, excommunicated people, and heretics.

A local bishop usually wanted to be in agreement with other bishops on important matters. When bishops began to gather in small or medium-sized groups to treat matters of discipline and belief that transcended the boundaries of any local congregation, they created a second pattern of church government, that of bishops meeting in a council. The biblical precedent for councils was Luke's report of the meeting about 49 CE where Paul and Barnabas discussed with James, the apostles, and the elders at Jerusalem the conditions under which gentiles could be accepted as followers of Jesus (Acts 15). James stated the decision in words from which a theology of collective decisions could be derived: "For it has seemed good to the Holy Spirit and to us...." (Acts 15:28). The theology that developed to justify the authority of councils was that each bishop was a successor to the apostles and had the inspiration of the Holy Spirit. When bishops met in councils, they pooled that inspiration and represented the traditional beliefs of their churches. The ideal outcome of a council was a unanimous decision, which was interpreted as confirming the presence of the Holy Spirit. Bishop Cyprian of Carthage endorsed that view: "The authority of the bishops forms a unity, of which each holds his part in its totality" (Cyprian, *The Unity of the Catholic Church (De ecclesiae catholicae unitate)*, c. 5 in De Lapsis and De Ecclesiae Catholicae Unitate, text and translation by Maurice Bénevot [Oxford, 1971], p. 65).

The pattern of governance by councils emerged in response to specific historical developments. In the middle of the second century, bishops in Asia Minor met to decide on a common policy toward the prophet Montanus and the prophetesses Priscilla and Maximilla, whose claim that the Holy Spirit was speaking through them divided churches. Within twenty or thirty years, councils were widely accepted as a way to deal with disputed matters of all sorts. For instance, in the 190s a controversy erupted about when to celebrate Easter. Relying on traditions they believed went back to the Apostle John, the proto-orthodox churches in Asia Minor celebrated Easter on the same day—whatever day of the week that was—that the Jews celebrated Passover. Most other churches always celebrated Easter on a Sunday. The discrepancy seemed bothersome enough to require major regional consultations among bishops. "So then, synods and assemblages of bishops came together, and unanimously drew up in letters an ecclesiastical decree for the faithful everywhere, to the effect that the mystery of the Lord's resurrection from the dead should never be celebrated on any day other than the Lord's day...." (EH 5.23). Before Constantine's conversion, the governance by bishops meeting in a council had taken deep root, but it grew stronger under the Christian empire. The Council of Nicaea (325) was the largest gathering of bishops up to that time. After the council, Constantine wrote to urge the church at Alexandria to heal its divisions by accepting the council's decision that the Son was of the same substance as the Father. In his defense of the authority of the Council of Nicaea to make such a decision, Constantine summarized a theological justification for the authority of councils of bishops: "...more than three hundred bishops remarkable for their moderation and intellectual keenness were unanimous in their confirmation of one and the same faith....For that which has commended itself to the judgment of three hundred bishops cannot be other than the doctrine of God; seeing that the Holy Spirit dwelling in the minds of so many dignified persons has effectually enlightened them respecting the Divine will (Socrates, *Ecclesiastical History*, I.9 in NPNF, second series, vol. 2, pp. 13–14).

Serious theological disputes and the encouragement and financial support of successive Christian emperors led to fourth- and fifth-century councils that were larger than ever before. Between the fourth and sixth centuries, the roads and sea lanes of the empire were busy with bishops and their entourages going to and returning from councils. Approximately 460 bishops participated at the Council of Chalcedon (451), which was the largest gathering of bishops in the ancient church. Even though most councils were small and local, they represented an important view of how the church should be governed by the collective decisions of bishops.

Before the empire embraced Christianity, a council of bishops had few means to carry out its decisions, especially against bishops who chose to defy it. Force was never used against defiant bishops, probably because it was not available. Moral pressure and excommunication often brought the resisters to agree. If the defiant bishop and his church (or his faction of supporters within the local church) ignored the council, a schism occurred. The opponents refused communion with one another. But in the Christian empire, the emperor could, if he wished, put his authority behind conciliar decisions, that is, he could make them legally enforceable. Then those bishops who refused to obey a council of their fellow bishops might be deposed and exiled.

Between the fourth and sixth centuries, church law and custom approved several kinds of councils. On rare occasions, an emperor summoned an empirewide council, which, if later generations accepted it as authoritative, was called "ecumenical" from the Greek word *oikumene*, which generally meant "the whole civilized world" but in Christian language meant something like "the entire household of the people of God." The Roman Catholic and Orthodox churches accept seven councils as ecumenical. Some Protestant churches tend to emphasize the first four councils, but others give little or no authority to councils: Nicaea (325), Constantinople (381), Ephesus (431), Chalcedon (451), Constantinople (553), Constantinople (680–681), and Nicaea (787). The bishops of a Roman province might also meet in a council under the direction of the metropolitan bishop, who governed the church in the chief city of the province (the metropolis or "mother city"). A local bishop could also meet in a council with his own clergy. Finally, some councils were summoned for specific purposes and did not fit into any of the traditional categories.

The bishops in a council believed that they could rule on virtually any issue. They formulated disciplinary decisions, which are called "canons," and theological decisions. They sat as judges to hear thorny legal issues such as the disputed election of a bishop, the appeal of a clergyman against a decision of his bishop, and the appeal of a bishop against a decision of his metropolitan bishop or another council. The twenty influential canons issued at the Council of Nicaea (325) illustrate the wide variety of matters that a council might take up. The Nicene canons treated such issues as the conditions under which eunuchs could be admitted to the clergy; how soon a recently baptized pagan could be made a presbyter or bishop; which women, if any, could live in the house of a clergyman; how many bishops had to participate in the consecration of a new bishop; the need for every bishop to respect an excommunication imposed by any other bishop; how frequently bishops should meet in councils; the authority of the bishop of Alexandria and the bishop of Rome in their respective territories; how heretics and schismatics who wanted to join the catholic Church should be received; how a man wanting to be a presbyter should be examined; how to deal with a person who lapsed during persecution and was then ordained to the clergy by a bishop unaware of the circumstances; how a dying excommunicated person who asked for reconciliation and the Eucharist should be treated; whether bishops, priests, and deacons could move from one city to another, presumably seeking better positions; whether a bishop should ordain or accept a clergyman who belonged to another bishop's church; whether a clergyman should loan money at interest; and whether worshippers ought to pray in a standing position on the Lord's Day and on Pentecost. When bishops disputed about belief or discipline, each side appealed to the past, whether to documents they considered authoritative or to long-standing customs. Beginning in the fourth century, they also appealed to the canons of Nicaea, which took on an aura of great authority. The canons of many councils were gradually gathered into collections that formed a law specifically for the church, called the "canon law."

Governance by councils of bishops had problems of which contemporaries were aware. Gregory of Nazianzus (about 313–about 390), who resigned as bishop of Constantinople because he was discouraged by ecclesiastical intrigue, wrote with some exaggeration "...my inclination is to avoid all assemblies of bishops, because I have never seen any council come to a good end, nor turn out to be a solution of evils. On the contrary, it usually increases them. You always find there love of con-

tention and love of power....and, while sitting in judgement on others, a man [a bishop] might well be convicted of ill-doing himself long before he should put down the ill-doings of his opponents...." (Gregory of Nazianzus, Letter 130, quoted in *Creeds, Councils and Controversies*, edited by James Stevenson, revised with additional documents by W. H. C. Frend [London, 1989], pp. 118–119).

In the heated atmosphere of theological controversy between the fourth and sixth centuries, councils sometimes contradicted one another. They issued "improved" creeds that were more divisive than unifying. Councils were occasionally unruly and even violent meetings that did not achieve the unanimity that was thought to indicate the presence of the Holy Spirit. Councils sometimes yielded to the emperor's pressure to reach a consensus, but such politically inspired theological agreements had a way of unraveling over time. Councils could also undermine the basic unit of church government, the local bishopric. The travel to and from councils was expensive. Bishops were away from their congregations for extended periods of time. In spite of the problems, councils of bishops remained an important pattern of governance by which local churches, regional churches, the church in the empire, and the churches beyond the empire's borders tried, sometimes successfully and sometimes unsuccessfully, to settle internal disagreements about belief and discipline.

THE APOSTOLIC BISHOPRICS

Alongside the more or less independent local bishops and the more or less equal bishops in a council, a third pattern of church organization stressed the superior authority of the bishops of a few important bishoprics. From one point of view, all bishops were successors of the apostles and for that reason equal. But reality sometimes modifies theology. Most proto-orthodox Christian congregations were small with few resources. Many bishops had a limited education that handicapped them in dealing with subtle and potentially explosive theological and disciplinary questions. As early as the second century, some bishops stood out from others by the size of their congregations, by the number of their clergy, by their church's wealth, and above all by

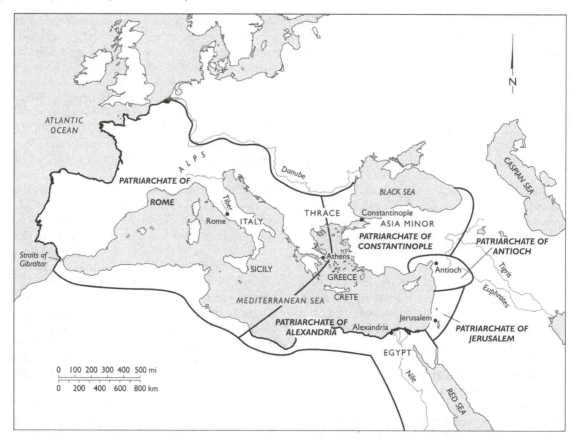

Figure 12.1 The Five Patriarchates about 600 CE. About 600, a generation before the Arab Muslim conquests, the five patriarchates were already dealing with internal problems. The patriarchate of Rome was mostly in the hands of Germanic kings who paid little attention to the bishop of Rome. The patriarchates of Alexandria, Jerusalem, Antioch, and Constantinople were bitterly divided between pro- and anti-Chalcedonian churches.

their claim that their church had been founded by the apostles. Over the course of time, the bishops of a few important cities began to provide intellectual, liturgical, and organizational leadership to the smaller bishoprics in their regions. During the fourth and fifth centuries, the bishops of Rome, Constantinople, Alexandria, Antioch, and Jerusalem gained extensive authority over the churches in their surrounding regions. It was only in the sixth century that they were formally called "patriarchs," but the authority of those bishops was evident even before the title "patriarch" was applied to them. The Council of Nicaea (canon 6) supported the authority of the bishop of Alexandria

over Egypt, the authority of the bishop of Rome, and the authority of the bishop of Antioch. Canon 7 ordered that Jerusalem should be "honored." Constantinople had not been founded when Nicaea met in 325, but during the fourth century it became an important place because it was the residence of the emperor, the seat of his government, and a populous, rich city. However, its standing in the developing hierarchy of bishoprics was low or at least ambiguous. By the late fourth century, Constantinople's position in the larger church was formally changed to fit with its imperial status. The Council of Constantinople (381) declared that the bishop of Constantinople should have "honor" just

Figure 12.2 Peter and Paul. Sometime in the fourth century, the sepulcher of a child named Assellus was decorated with a carving of Peter and Paul. The Roman church based its claim to authority on Christ's words to Peter, but Paul was often cited as a second source of authority. Both apostles were thought to be buried under Roman churches.
(Erich Lessing / Art Resource, NY)

after the bishop of Rome because, as the council declared, Constantinople is the New Rome (canon 3). The Emperor Justinian I (524–565) formally ratified the "Pentarchy" ("rule of five") in one of his laws (novella 123, ch. 3), where he referred to "patriarchs of old Rome and Constantinople and Alexandria and Antioch and Jerusalem." Three of the patriarchs presided over churches that claimed a tie to the Apostle Peter: Rome (where Peter was believed to have been martyred and buried), Antioch (which claimed Peter as its first bishop before he went to Rome), and Alexandria (which claimed Peter's "son" Mark as its founder; see 1 Peter 5:13). The fourth patriarchate, Constantinople, owed its prominence to its position after 330 as the imperial capital. The fifth patriarchate, Jerusalem, was hallowed by its associations with the origins of Christianity but was a small and relatively insignificant city when compared with the other four. There was no standard "job description" for patri-

archs. Their ability to exert effective power varied. In general, the patriarchs did such things as ordain the metropolitan bishops in their regions, summon and preside at councils of their bishops, hear appeals from clergy in their regions, and give advice and orders to local bishops, whose behavior they sought to supervise. A patriarch supported by a council of his many bishops was important in church governance and expressed the theological, cultural, and regional diversity that marked both the church and the empire. The bishops of Alexandria exerted strong, almost dictatorial, control over the bishops of Egypt and Libya. The bishops of Rome were in relatively firm control of Italy from Rome southward and claimed wide influence over the entire western portion of the empire. The other leading bishops had looser control in their regions.

The patriarchal pattern of church governance functioned best when the patriarchs treated one another with respect and cooperated with one another and with the emperor. They kept in touch. For instance, they consulted by letters and embassies about major issues. They informed one another of their election, sought advice from one another about problems, and expressed joy for one another's victories and sympathy for one another's troubles. Occasionally the four eastern patriarchs met at councils or at the imperial court, but the bishop of Rome almost never went east. Instead he sent two or three clergy as his representatives to the eastern councils. The patriarchs generally accepted as normal that their regions differed in liturgy and customs, but they wanted to agree on matters of belief. The ideal of patriarchal harmony worked only some of the time. In the vigorous theological debates that marked the later Roman Empire, the patriarchs sometimes disagreed and struggled against one another, each relying on his bishops and his supporters at the imperial court.

In later Roman culture, the public expression of hierarchy and dignity was a well-developed art. Every important person in the emperor's court had his proper place. An observer could tell a great deal from where a dignitary stood, what he wore, and how he was addressed. In the Christian empire, all bishops were given a place in that hierarchical system. The five most important bishops stood at the top of the hierarchy of ecclesiastical honor, which usually determined where they or their representatives sat at councils, marched in processions, and the like. After 381, the official hierarchy of honor among the chief bishops was, from top to bottom, Rome, Constantinople, Alexandria, Antioch, and Jerusalem. Emperors dutifully sought the patriarchs' opinions and prized their approval of church-related matters—sometimes they prized it so much that they demanded it.

After the 630s, the patriarchal pattern of governance suffered grave damage when Muslim armies captured Antioch, Jerusalem, and Alexandria. The patriarchs of those cities continued to function, as they do today. They continued to correspond with one another, to attend councils when they could, and to share their opinions on important theological matters. But they lived in a hostile environment with shrinking congregations, diminishing resources, and without the support of the Roman emperor. Only the patriarchs of Rome and Constantinople retained their independence within the Roman Empire. As often happens in a system that has only two poles, the Roman and Constantinopolitan bishops began to act more like rivals than like colleagues. But the patriarchal system, in an expanded form, has remained to the present day the ideal governing pattern of the family of Orthodox churches centered in the Balkans and Eastern Europe.

THE BISHOP OF ROME

A fourth pattern of church governance was centered on the bishop of Rome, who also had a place in the other patterns. He presided over the bishopric of Rome just as any local bishop presided over his diocese. Like any metropolitan bishop, he held councils with his bishops to settle disputes, to treat disciplinary matters, and occasionally to render a judgment on theological questions. He was eventually regarded as the patriarch of the west, in fact, the only patriarch in the west. He supervised or tried to supervise a zone of authority, including Italy, parts of the Balkans, North Africa, Spain, Gaul, and Britain, that was considerably larger than any of the other four.

In some ways the leading bishops were more or less equals, in spite of the differences in the honor due them. But beginning in the later fourth century the bishops of Rome claimed a position in the governance of the church that was broader than that of the other important bishops. Because all orthodox Christians agreed that the Roman bishops were the direct successors of the Apostles Paul and Peter, their right to be first in honor was not controversial, but their efforts to extend their practical authority across the entire church, especially to act as judges and to issue commands, were resisted.

The roots of the Roman bishop's claim to a special place in the church went deep into the past. Long before Constantine's conversion, the church at Rome and its bishops stood out among the churches. Some theological factors and some practical factors contributed to that preeminence. In the life-and-death struggle against gnostic Christianity, proto-orthodox Christians had defended the idea that their bishops could trace a public, historical continuity with Christ's apostles. Thus, every bishop was regarded as "apostolic" in the sense that he succeeded the apostles and taught or should teach what they had taught. Most bishops could not name their church's founding apostle and had to claim succession from the apostles as a group. But the doctrine of apostolic succession put the bishop at Rome in a special light. He presided over the *only* church in the western part of the empire that had a plausible claim to direct contact with Jesus' apostles. His main western rivals—the bishop of Carthage in North Africa and the bishop of Milan in northern Italy—were important regional leaders but never claimed direct foundation by an apostle. In fact, it was widely accepted that all the churches in the western parts of the empire had been converted *from* Rome, so that the Roman church was regarded as the mother church of all western churches. The Roman church was not just the only apostolic foundation in the west. It could name its founding apostles, Peter and Paul, whom all proto-orthodox Christians, wherever they lived, regarded as the greatest apostles. Furthermore, in a religion where martyrs were revered, the Roman church had in its possession the mortal remains of those two apostles who, it was believed, had died as martyrs in Rome. At least since the second century, pilgrims came to visit their burial places, Peter on the Vatican Hill, and Paul on the Ostian Way. Some modern scholars and religious leaders doubt or deny that Peter and Paul were the founders of the Roman church, but no one in the ancient church did so.

The Roman church's distinctive apostolic credentials were strengthened when it gained a reputation for strict orthodoxy in the numerous theological debates of the fourth and fifth centuries. Many of the important eastern bishops occasionally found themselves on the losing side in the long-running, ever-shifting disagreements over the nature of the Trinity and of the God-man Christ (to be treated in chapters 13 and 14). The Roman church was generally on the winning side. Roman bishops argued that they preserved apostolic teaching and exercised apostolic authority in a unique way. In a two-word phrase that was heavy with theological claims, the Roman church began to call itself simply the "Apostolic See"

(*Apostolica Sedes*), in which *sedes* was the Latin word for "chair," referring to the chair in which Peter sat to teach.

The Roman church's assertion of a special role within the entire church was supported by practical realities. Its religious prestige was magnified by its geographical and political position. For centuries the city of Rome was the seat of the imperial government, and even after the emperors no longer lived there, the city remained the symbolic center of the Roman Empire. By the third century at the latest, the number of Christians at Rome was large, although just a minor fraction of the great city's overall population. Prominent Christians (and lots of humbler ones) from all over the empire visited Rome, in part to see the great city and in part to visit the Roman church and its martyrs' shrines. The Roman church also had a reputation for generosity. It received visiting Christians warmly and sent donations of money to those imprisoned for the faith and to far-off brethren in need. Bishop Dionysius of Corinth (about 170) wrote a letter to Bishop Soter of Rome (166–175) in which he praised the customary generosity of the Roman church. "For this has been your custom from the beginning: to do good in various ways to all the brethren, and to send supplies to many churches in every city: sometimes relieving the poverty of the needy, at other times making provision, by the supplies which you have been in the habit of sending from the beginning, for brethren in the mines; and thus as Romans you observe the hereditary custom of Romans, which your blessed bishop Soter has not only maintained, but even advanced, by providing in abundance the help that is distributed for the use of the saints, and by exhorting with blessed words, as a loving father his children, the brethren who come up [to Rome]" (EH 4.23, altered).

When Constantine legalized Christianity in the early fourth century, the Roman church was already acknowledged as the first among churches in honor and prestige. But that position of honor did not automatically give its bishop a right to give commands to other churches outside of central and southern Italy, especially to the important apostolic sees such as Jerusalem, Antioch, or Alexandria, which supervised the bishops in their regions.

During the later fourth and fifth centuries, some vigorous, talented Roman bishops began to claim more than their church's traditional honor. They began to assert a right to exercise St. Peter's jurisdiction in the here-and-now, that is, they argued and acted as if the bishop of Rome had a position not merely of honor but of authority over the other churches. They stressed that they were Peter's heirs and that as his heirs they inherited the power and promises that Christ made to Peter. On the basis of Matthew 16:13–20, they asserted that they succeeded to Peter's position as the rock on which the church was built and that they possessed the keys to the kingdom of heaven. On the basis of John 21:15–17, they said that they had Peter's responsibility to feed the sheep and lambs of Christ's entire flock. In short, the later fourth- and fifth-century popes argued that they exercised Peter's ministry. Peter lived on in the Roman bishops who were his heirs and successors. In a sermon, Pope Leo I (440–461) explained that although he was personally weak and unworthy, the living authority of St. Peter, the founder of the Roman church, strengthened him: "Although, therefore, dearly beloved, we be found both weak and slothful in fulfilling the duties of our office, because, whatever devoted and vigorous action we desire to do, we are hindered by the frailty of our very condition; yet having the unceasing favor of the Almighty and perpetual Priest [Christ], who being like us and yet equal with the Father, brought down his Godhead even to things human, and raised His Manhood even to things Divine, we worthily and piously rejoice over His arrangement of things, whereby, though He has delegated the care of his sheep to many shepherds [bishops], yet He has not Himself abandoned the guardianship of His beloved flock. And from His overruling and eternal protection we have received the support of the Apostles' aid also, which assuredly does not cease from its operation; and the strength of the foundation, on which the whole superstructure of the Church is reared, is not weakened by the weight of the temple that rests upon it. For the solidity of that faith which was praised in the chief of the Apostles [Peter] is perpetual: and as that remains which Peter believed in Christ, so that remains which Christ instituted in Peter. For when…the Lord had asked the disciples whom they believed Him to be amid

the various opinions that were held, and the blessed Peter had replied, saying, 'Thou art the Christ, the Son of he Living God,' the Lord says, 'Blessed art thou, Simon Bar-Jona, because flesh and blood hath not revealed it to thee but my Father, which is in heaven. And I say to thee, that thou art Peter, and upon this rock will I build my church, and the gates of Hades shall not prevail against it. And I will give unto thee the keys of the kingdom of heaven. And whatsoever thou shalt bind on earth, shall be bound in heaven; and whatsoever thou shalt loose on earth, shall be loosed also in heaven'" [Mt 16:13–19] (Leo I, *Homily* III.2, NPNF, second series, vol. 12, p. 117, altered).

The fourth- and fifth-century popes also drew on Paul, the other apostle of Rome, to claim a duty to care for all the churches. They applied to themselves a passage in Paul's second letter to the Corinthians, 11:28 ("I am under daily pressure because of my anxiety for all the churches"). In the papal conception of church governance, the bishop of Rome was not just one bishop among all the others or one among the five leading bishops. He had churchwide responsibilities and churchwide rights. It was not just popes who thought so. At the Council of Chalcedon (451), the representatives of Pope Leo I presented a document called his *Tome*, which laid out his view of the relation of the divine and human natures in Jesus Christ. The bishops at the council, who were entirely from the east, began to chant "Peter speaks through Leo."

From the later fourth century onward, successive popes repeated the theme of Peter's (and their) responsibility and authority that exceeded those of other bishops. They did more than claim a position: They sought to impose it. One papal letter will have to stand for many. In a pattern that reappeared often, a bishop (in this instance, Himerius of Tarragona in Spain) sent a letter to a pope (in this instance, Damasus I [366–384]) for guidance on a series of issues. Damasus died before he could respond, and his successor, Pope Siricius (384–399), answered Himerius in a long letter. Siricius set the tone early in his letter by putting his responses in the context of his succession to Peter. "And since we must assume the labors and responsibilities of him [Peter] whose honor we have assumed, by God's grace,…we will not deny you a full reply to each detail of your inquiry, as the Lord deigns to inspire us. For in view of our office we have no right to...keep silence, since it is our duty more than anyone's to be zealous for the Christian faith. We bear the burdens of all who are heavy laden; nay, rather, the blessed apostle Peter bears them in us and protects and watches over us, his heirs, in all the care of his ministry" (Siricius, letter 1, in James T. Shotwell and Louise Ropes Loomis, *The See of Peter* [New York and Oxford, 1927], p. 699).

As a practical matter, the bishop of Rome in the ancient church did not have an administrative staff sufficient to intervene regularly in the hundreds of bishoprics in the Roman Empire. Furthermore, the other leading bishops, who accepted that he had the first place of honor, would not generally allow the bishop of Rome to decide practical matters of appointments or finances or judicial decisions within their spheres of influence. But the fourth- and fifth-century popes argued that at the very least all *majores causae*, that is, all really important church matters, must be referred to them for judgment. Some clergy did appeal to the bishop of Rome, especially from churches in the west, but occasionally from those in the east. A bishop, abbot, or other clergyman who received an unfavorable decision in Milan, Carthage, Alexandria, Constantinople, or elsewhere welcomed the opportunity to make his case again before a council at Rome. In 445, the Emperor Valentinian III ratified in Roman civil law the Roman church's right to act as a court of appeals in church matters. "It is certain that for us and our Empire the only defence is in the favor of the God of heaven; and to deserve it our first care is to support the Christian faith and its venerable religion. Inasmuch then as the primacy of the Apostolic See is assured by the merit of St. Peter, prince of the episcopate, by the rank of the city of Rome, and also by the authority of a sacred Synod. Let not presumption endeavor to attempt anything contrary to the See. For then finally will the peace of the churches be everywhere maintained, if the whole body acknowledges its ruler [the Roman Church]. [Valentinian then related complaints from Pope Leo I about the independent and, in his view, outrageous actions of Bishop Hilary of Arles]....we decree by this perpetual edict that it shall not be lawful for the bishops of Gaul or of the other prov-inces, contrary to ancient custom, to do anything without the authority of the venerable Pope of the Eternal City; and whatsoever the authority of the Apostolic See has enacted, or may hereafter enact, shall be the law for all. So that, if any bishop summoned to trial before the Pope of Rome shall neglect to attend, he shall be compelled to appear by the Governor of the Province...." (*Constitutio Valentiniani III*, in B. J. Kidd, *Documents Illustrative of the History of the Church*, vol. 2 [London and New York, 1923], pp. 282–283, altered).

In addition to welcoming formal appeals that asked for their advice or their judgment, fourth- and fifth-century popes actively sought to intervene in a wide range of matters, especially inside their western zone of influence. Pope Siricius and his successors encouraged other bishops to consult them about disputed matters of liturgy, discipline, and finances. The popes then responded in formal letters, called "decretals," which answered the questions with an air of authority. Sometimes a pope sought the advice of a council of his own central Italian bishops before formulating a decretal letter. At other times, a pope might act on his own, in his capacity as successor of Peter. He was asserting his claim to a unique authority because he was acting without the participation of a council, without the agreement of other prominent bishops, and without the permission of an emperor. The written records of appeals, inquiries, and papal replies were preserved in the papal archives as prec-edents for future decisions. The papal decretal let-ters, along with the canons of councils, were a major component in the formation of western canon law, which enshrined the papal understanding of how the church should be governed.

THE EMPEROR

The fifth pattern of church governance had no sup-port in the pre-Constantinian church, when emper-ors were pagans, but it was prominent in Christian societies for more than fifteen hundred years after Constantine's conversion. Most modern Christians would not favor it. As chapter 1 has already demon-strated, whether the Roman state was a republic, a pagan empire, or a Christian empire, one constant concern of public religious policy was the careful maintenance of favorable relationships with the gods or with God. Constantine's conversion modified the details but not the substance of that perennial concern. Constantine's Christian subjects refused to regard him as a god—the second-, third-, and early fourth-century martyrs had died rather than worship the emperors. But they generally believed that God chose every orthodox Christian emperor to be the (or perhaps "a") leader of the church just as God chose him to be the leader of society. The Christian emperors, like their third-century pagan predecessors, were immersed in ceremonies, gestures, and words that emphasized their remoteness from and superiority to ordinary humans. The militarized Christian Roman Empire, ruled by an awesome heaven-connected autocrat who was theoretically all-powerful, survived until 476 in the west and until 1453 in the east.

Because there had never been a Christian emperor before Constantine, no one at the time knew how a Christian emperor should behave in religious matters. Constantine set many precedents that made succeeding emperors powerful within the church, just as they were in every aspect of late Roman life. He preserved the Roman

Figure 12.3 Emperor Justinian I, Bishop Maximian of Ravenna, and Attendants. About 547, the Church of St. Vitale in Ravenna was decorated with fine mosaics. In this scene, Justinian carries a loaf of bread for the Eucharist. He stands at the center of the scene, dressed in purple robes and purple shoes, with a crown and other jewelry and with a halo behind his head. The clergy to his left and the soldiers to his right may symbolize the main supports of his regime. *(Cameraphoto Arte, Venice / Art Resource, NY)*

tradition of concern for the state's religion, which he redirected toward Christianity. In the long pagan phase of Roman history, a good emperor was expected to be generous to the gods in the expectation that they would be favorable to him and the state. Constantine continued that tradition but gave imperial wealth and legal privileges to God's servants, who were now the Christian clergy, and to God's houses, which were now the Christian churches. Constantine also took an active interest in the church's internal life. He tried to settle theological disagreements among Christians because he thought they might anger God, who could withdraw his favor. He also knew from experience that such disagreements set citizen against citizen, sometimes to the point of violence.

Constantine accepted and even strengthened the traditional forms of church governance, especially councils, to settle ecclesiastical disputes. He set an important precedent when he transferred a council from Ancyra in central Asia Minor to Nicaea (325). Thereafter, emperors, not bishops or patriarchs or popes, summoned all ecumenical councils up to II Nicaea (787). Constantine attended some of the meetings of the bishops at Nicaea and participated in the debates. The effect of Constantine's presence was great because only a few years earlier Constantine's pagan predecessors had arrested some of the bishops who now sat in the imperial hall at Nicaea, still carrying on their bodies the signs of torture and mutilation. Bishop Eusebius of Caesarea described the emperor's entrance into the Council of Nicaea: "As soon, then, as the whole assembly had seated themselves with becoming orderliness, a general silence prevailed, in expectation of the emperor's arrival. And first, three of his immediate family entered in succession, then others also preceded his approach, not of soldiers or guards who usually accompanied him, but only friends in the faith [Christian members of the imperial court]. And now, all rising at the signal which indicated the emperor's entrance, at last he himself proceeded through the midst of the assembly, like some heavenly messenger of God, clothed in garments which glittered as it were with rays of light, reflecting the glowing radiance of a purple robe, and adorned with the brilliant splendor of gold and precious stones. Such was the

external appearance of his person; and with regard to his mind, it was evident that he was distinguished by piety and godly fear. This was indicated by his down-cast eyes, the blush on his face, and his gait. For the rest of his personal excellences, he surpassed all present in height of stature and beauty of form, as well as in majestic dignity of appearance, and invincible strength and vigor.... As soon as he had advanced to the upper end of the seats, at first he remained standing, and when a low chair of wrought gold had been set for him, he waited until the bishops had beckoned to him, and then sat down, and after him the whole assembly did the same" (Eusebius, *The Life of Constantine*, 3.11, NPNF, second series, vol. 1, p. 522, altered).

Constantine embraced the view that God chose him to protect the church. On one occasion, Constantine was reported to have said that the bishops were in charge of those inside the church, but he was the "bishop of those outside." But Constantine and successive emperors did not rely only on councils to get what they wanted. They intervened directly in church affairs that in earlier times would have been handled by local bishops or by councils or would have been untreated because no one had authority. Christians who were divided over doctrine—and there was a lot of that among catholic Christians between the fourth and sixth centuries—grew accustomed to appealing to the emperor, who could endorse the views of one side and remove from their bishoprics the adherents of the other side. When Constantine died in 337, he was buried in the Church of the Holy Apostles in Constantinople. The placement of his tomb within that church tells a great deal about his self-view. Twelve cenotaphs (literally "empty tombs") or inscribed pillars for the twelve apostles were set up in the church, with Constantine buried in their midst. In his own view, he was the thirteenth apostle. There was some truth in that self-evaluation. From a historical point of view, he had made possible the conversion of more people than had all the apostles combined.

The emperor's important position in the church was not based solely on raw power and secular politics—although both were present. A respectable theology supported a Christian emperor's claim to a leading position in the church. Christians were convinced that no one became emperor by chance: God wanted that person to be emperor. When God chose an emperor, he expected him to carry out the divine will on Earth. Some scriptural texts seemed to support that view. In the Old Testament, the kings of Israel and Judah had a direct dependence on Yahweh, who chose them, rewarded them, punished them, and deposed them if they sinned. In the Synoptic Gospels, Christ had ratified obedience to secular rulers by telling his followers to render to Caesar what belongs to Caesar (Mt 22:15–22; Mk 12:13–17; Lk 20:22–25). Paul had treated the pagan rulers of his day with respect, even attributing to them a position in God's plan. In his letter to the Romans, 13:1–9, he exhorted his fellow believers: "Let every person be subject to the governing authorities; for there is no authority except from God, and those authorities that exist have been instituted by God. Therefore whoever resists authority resists what God has appointed and those who resist will incur judgment." He told his fellow Christians to give taxes, respect, and honor to those to whom they owed them. When the emperor was himself a Christian, the biblical words took on an even stronger meaning. Constantine and successive emperors were the patrons to whom the bishops found it difficult—although not impossible—to say "no."

Occasionally the emperor's position in the church was criticized or resisted. The traditions of independent governance by local bishops, by councils, and by leading bishops often clashed with imperial intervention, especially if the emperor was too aggressive in his claims or was regarded by many as a heretic. In 355, the Arian Emperor Constantius expressed his strong views on the emperor's role in church governance to bishops at Milan who resisted his efforts to have them condemn Athanasius of Alexandria, the defender of the Creed of Nicaea. He is reported to have said, "What I will is to be considered a canon. For when I make such pronouncements, the bishops of Syria put up with it. Obey therefore or you will go into banishment" (Athanasius, *History of the Arians*, c. 33, cited in *Creeds, Councils and Controversies*, p. 32). In his tract *Against Constantius*, Bishop Hilary of Poitiers (about 315–about 367) called the reigning Christian emperor "anti-Christ" and

linked him with Nero and Decius, who had been persecuting pagan emperors. Bishops, monks, and ordinary believers sometimes successfully resisted emperors who tried too openly or too autocratically to dictate theology. But the religious conviction that Roman emperors had a central place in God's plan for the church was rarely challenged directly. The imperial pattern of church governance, supported by theology, imperial power, and imperial wealth, assured that Christian emperors would have a leading role in the church. But between about 400 and 600, the eastern and western parts of the empire developed in different ways that led to important differences in the position of the emperor in the churches of each area.

THE EASTERN EMPIRE: CONTINUITY

The eastern part of the Roman Empire, often called by modern historians the "Byzantine Empire," was severely pressed by migrating peoples and by Muslim armies. But the empire survived in the east, although it lost a great deal of territory. The prominence of imperial authority within the church intensified. Emperors enacted laws that touched directly on church matters. For instance, the sixteenth book of the Theodosian Law Code, issued in 438, was devoted to the church, including such diverse matters as its finances, its organization, its personnel, and even its beliefs. Eastern bishops continued to meet in councils, but the decisions of councils often needed the emperor's assent to become effective. The emperor continued to have an aura of the priestly and the sacred around him. We must be clear that he was not regarded as a priest in the strict sense of that word. He could not perform the central priestly act, which was the consecration of the bread and wine. But he was not regarded as a mere layman either. Christian subjects regarded the late Roman and Byzantine emperors as unique human beings who stood between layman and priest, in fact, between earth and heaven. In the elaborate Byzantine court ceremonies, the emperor was consciously cast in Christ's image. For instance, at the Eucharist, he was the only nonclergyman allowed into the most sacred area of the church, the sanctuary at the church's front. The Byzantine Church and people embraced the imperial pattern of governance even more tightly as they saw themselves under endless attack by barbarians, Muslims, and even Latin Christians, whom they regarded as heretics or at least schismatics.

An emperor was a powerful rival to the local, conciliar, patriarchal, and papal patterns of church governance. However, he could not replace the other patterns and usually did not wish to do so. Cooperation between the emperor and the bishops was the ideal. The system worked well in the east as long as councils and important bishops respected the emperor's rights and responsibilities and he respected theirs. But there were boundaries that an emperor was unwise to cross. For the imperial pattern of governance to function, eastern Christians had to regard the emperor as orthodox in his beliefs. If some important interest group(s), such as the bishop of Constantinople or the monks or significant numbers of ordinary people, thought that an emperor had deviated from the traditional faith, he could expect fierce opposition. The emperors retained their extensive, but not absolute, control of the Byzantine Church until there were no more emperors after 1453.

THE WESTERN EMPIRE: DISCONTINUITY

In the western parts of the empire, the power of the emperor in the church slowly eroded. Bishop Ambrose of Milan (373/374–397) set important precedents that were later used to limit imperial power within the western church. For instance, in 390 the citizens of Thessalonika in Greece killed several imperial officials. The Emperor Theodosius I (379–395) ordered a massacre in Thessalonika to punish the city. Bishop Ambrose strongly disapproved and forcefully reminded the emperor, not publicly but in a private letter, that like any other Christian he was subject to the moral law and to church discipline for sin. Paulinus, author of the *Life of Ambrose*, wrote that "When the bishop learnt what had happened [the massacre at Thessalonika], he refused the emperor admission to the cathedral, nor would he pronounce him fit to sit in the

congregation or to receive the Sacraments until he had done public penance. When the Emperor objected that David had committed both adultery and murder, his [Ambrose's] reply was: 'As you imitated him [David] in his transgression, imitate him in his amendment.' The Emperor took these words so much to heart that he did not shrink even from public penance; and the effect of his making amends was to give the bishop a second victory" (Paulinus, *Life of Ambrose*, c. 24 in F. R. Hoare, *The Western Fathers* [New York, 1954], pp. 167–168, altered). In the context of the time, Ambrose took a dangerous step. He could have been deposed, exiled, or even executed for denying the emperor communion. Instead he successfully invoked religious sanctions for a sin committed by an orthodox emperor, who agreed to perform public penance.

Historical developments that had nothing to do with religion also decreased the emperor's importance in the western church. Between 378 and 476, Roman political power in the western part of the empire dramatically weakened and then disappeared. During that crucial century, Germanic chiefs and their followers conquered Roman territory in Britain, Gaul, Spain, and Italy. After 476, there were no more emperors living in the west. The emperors at Constantinople never gave up their claim to rule the western parts of the empire but were so preoccupied with their desperate efforts to preserve the eastern half of the empire against its attackers that they were only sporadically able to exercise any power in the west, including power within the church. If the emperors had retained effective control over the west, the history of the western churches might have been quite different, closer to the state church of Byzantium. But the emperors lost the west.

The bishops of Rome, liberated by the weakening of the emperors in the west, asserted frequently their jurisdiction within the wider church, based on their succession to St. Peter. But they paid a price for their freedom from imperial control. Emperors had protected as well as directed the church. The Germanic conquests in the west undermined not only imperial control but also the effectiveness (but not the theology) of the papal pattern of church governance. Although the situation differed by region, each Germanic conquest eliminated or reduced the bishop of Rome's ability to function within his patriarchate. The Germanic invaders of Britain were pagans who created small kingdoms from which Christianity vanished until missionaries from Rome and Ireland reintroduced it in the late sixth and seventh centuries. The Visigoths in Spain, the Vandals in North Africa, the Burgundians in Gaul, and the Lombards in Italy were Arian Christians, that is, heretics in the eyes of their catholic Christian subjects. The Arian Germanic kings had no incentive to pay attention to papal advice, threats, or claims of jurisdiction. Some Germanic kings, notably those of the Franks in Gaul, eventually converted to catholic Christianity (about 500), but in their churches the king and his bishops managed things without outside interference, including that of the bishop of Rome. The sixth-century Frankish kings corresponded occasionally and respectfully with the popes but allowed them no significant influence in the Frankish churches.

The most dangerous moments for the papacy came after 568, when the Lombards, some of whom were Arian Christians and others Germanic pagans, invaded the Italian peninsula and almost conquered the city of Rome. The emperors at Constantinople wanted to keep the city for symbolic and political reasons, but they could not or would not divert adequate resources to the defense of Italy. They did manage to keep control of Rome and a few other places on the coast. The popes of the sixth century were loyal Roman subjects, although they protested vigorously if the emperor infringed on what they regarded as the rights and dignity of St. Peter. In spite of Lombard attacks, plague, famine, and other disruptions, the popes solemnly and frequently repeated the Petrine doctrine, that is, that they had primacy of honor *and* of jurisdiction in the entire church, even though their effective power usually did not reach much beyond central Italy.

Bishops as individuals, as participants in councils, and as supporters arranged around their patriarchs were always important in the governance of the church. The bishop of Rome claimed a special, if not sharply defined, role in the governance of the church. But if I were pressed to identify the most influential person in the church from the fourth century to the sixth century (and in the east, far later than that), I would point to the Roman emperor. His position in the governance of the church was supported by a theology that placed the Roman Empire in a prominent position in God's plan for the human race. The emperor's influence was magnified because he had access to wealth, power, and force. He controlled two of the three pillars of Roman society—the army and the bureaucracy—and he almost dominated the third pillar, the church. He was an important factor in the shaping of theology but did not have a free hand because bishops, monks, and laypeople thwarted him on occasion when they thought he was in error.

The power of the Roman emperor in church governance may seem odd to a twenty-first century reader. But even into relatively modern times Christian rulers of all sorts have often had a leading role in church government. For instance, in his "Address to the Christian Nobility of the German Nation" (1520), Martin Luther called on the lay rulers, but not the ordinary person in the street, to undertake reform of the church in their territories on the grounds that as Christians who held political power, they had a right and a duty to do so. Constantine would have understood. There were important proponents of the divine right of kings in Western Europe at least to the French Revolution (1789). Until the Bolshevik Revolution of 1917, the Russian czar (the title is derived from the word "Caesar," a title of Roman emperors) exercised a control over the Russian Orthodox Church that a late Roman emperor would have recognized and perhaps envied for its scope. The queen of England is still "Defender of the Faith and Head of the Church of England," a title that does not mean much now but once did.

By 600, roughly the date at which the ancient church was changing in recognizable ways into the medieval church, the issue of governance in the church remained contested. Individual bishops continued to lead their local churches. When conditions were favorable, they met in councils, often under the control of Germanic kings or Byzantine emperors, at which they still handled a wide range of matters. The patriarchs continued to supervise their patriarchates and to correspond with one another in the search for unity. The bishops of Rome repeated over and over their claim to be more than patriarchs, to sit in the "Apostolic See" with a responsibility for and authority over all the churches. The emperors at Constantinople continued to exert great influence in the churches within their territories. But no single pattern of church governance had ousted the others. There is still no agreement among Christians about the structure of authority within the church.

FURTHER READING

Ancient Sources

Maurice Bévenot, trans., Cyprian, *The Unity of the Catholic Church* in *De Lapsis and De Ecclesiae Catholicae Unitate*, (Oxford, 1971), pp. 56–99. A good document to get a feel for church problems and Cyprian's solutions. *The Lapsed (De Lapsis)* in the same book, pp. 2–55, is also worth reading.

James T. Shotwell and Louise Ropes Loomis, *The See of Peter* (New York, 1927; reprinted 1991). A rich collection of translated sources from the first to fourth centuries concerning the papacy.

Modern Works

Geoffrey Barraclough, *The Medieval Papacy* (New York, 1968), especially pp. 13–37.

William J. La Due, *The Chair of Peter: A History of the Papacy* (Maryknoll, NY, 1999).

Eamon Duffy, *Saints and Sinners: A History of the Popes* (New Haven, 1997), pp. 1–36. A quick look at the early bishops of Rome.

Robert Eno, *The Rise of the Papacy* (Wilmington, DE, 1990).

Timothy (Kallistos) Ware, *The Orthodox Church*, new edition (London, 1993), pp. 18–47. A readable view of how the modern Orthodox churches regard the structures of ecclesiastical authority.

CHAPTER 13

The Trinitarian Controversy

Christianity's place in Greco-Roman society changed profoundly as it went from a persecuted group at the beginning of the fourth century to the official religion of the Roman Empire at the end of the century. As the Christian empire developed, theological issues increasingly became matters of concern not only to churchmen but also to emperors. During the same period that the Roman Empire and the Christian church were moving toward an alliance that was new to both, severe theological disputes, often described in a sort of shorthand as the Trinitarian Controversy and the Christological Controversy, broke out.

Some modern readers who expect that ancient Christians were concerned about the same religious issues that they are can often be puzzled when they learn about the theological debates of the fourth and fifth centuries or, for that matter, those of the second and third centuries. The sixteenth-century Protestant Reformation and the Catholic response to it laid out issues, some of which still divide western Christians. (Eastern Christians have generally been less interested in the western theological debates.) Ancient Christians debated the issues of *their* time. They were especially concerned to understand the status of the being sometimes called the "Son of God" and at other times the "Word of God." How did the Son/Word relate to God? They disagreed on the answer. That question and others like it led to major disruptions *within Catholic Christianity* during the fourth, fifth, and later centuries.

At times, modern people are also surprised at how much written material survives from the first six centuries of the history of Christianity. From the first to the fourth centuries, dozens of authors and hundreds of documents survive. The amount of the surviving writing can be misleading. The act of writing implied an education, a major expense in time and money. In the written work, we hear mostly—not always—the voices of an educated, male Christian elite. Women, slaves, the uneducated in general appear rarely in the surviving written sources. Aside from archaeology, which occasionally illuminates the subliterate groups, we must work with what we have, with the awareness that there is so much we do not know. During the fourth, fifth, and sixth centuries, writing exploded as men with good educations in rhetoric and philosophy became Christians, many of whom became bishops. Hundreds of authors, thousands of documents, and tens of thousands of pages in Greek, Latin, Syriac, Armenian, and other languages throw light, inadequate as it may be, into all sorts of dark corners. The disputes over the Trinity and subsequently over the nature(s) of Christ, which were complex and technical, filled letters, treatises, conciliar decisions, histories, creeds, and imperial laws.

Theological debates are important in the history of Christianity, but the reader should recall that simultaneously with those sometimes bitter debates catholic Christianity was both displacing paganism and heresies and marginalizing Judaism. Even as intellectuals, bishops, and emperors debated serious questions, orthodox Christianity was developing distinctive forms of art, architecture, literature, and liturgy. A reader must balance the advance of Christianity along a broad front with the seemingly unending internal dissent among fourth- and fifth-century catholic Christians. Many fourth- and fifth-century bishops, especially those living in the eastern part of the empire, were caught up in the ebb and flow of views about the Trinity and the later debates about the nature(s) of Christ. But some bishops and many presbyters, deacons, monks, nuns, and laypeople must have gone on living their religious lives without much disruption.

Sometimes the history of theology is written as if theological doctrines developed in a pure realm that did not touch the grubby earth. When modern readers are introduced to the theological debates of the fourth and fifth centuries, they are sometimes shocked by the atmosphere in which they took place. Those debates were not carried on by calm scholars sitting in their manuscript-lined studies. From one perspective, the story is one of misunderstandings, vicious personal attacks, distortions, violence, bribes, mutual excommunication, intervention by emperors, and the deposition and exile of bishops and others who lost in the struggle. From another perspective, the story is one of theological creativity that has shaped Christian beliefs for about fifteen centuries.

Historical reasons explain in part why fourth- and fifth-century theological disagreements shook both church and empire. First, Christians were prone to split from one another over differences in belief and behavior. They still are. A quick look at the telephone directory of a large American city will reveal hundreds of churches espousing a wide range of beliefs as well as having different kinds of church officers, architectural and artistic choices, preferences in music, preaching styles, and the like. The tendency to split goes back to the beginning. Paul's letters and the gospels preserve signs of disagreement and mutual rejection among the earliest Christians. Even when—or *especially* when—the orthodox Christians had become the main Christian tradition inside the Christian empire, the impulse to disagree over belief and customs did not disappear. Second, some disputed topics in theology were regarded as important enough to draw in all sorts of participants, ranging from rock-throwers in the street, to monks, to bishops, to the emperor himself. Third, church politics—the competition for prestige, positions, wealth, and influence—intensified theological disagreements. As important bishops struggled to protect or enlarge their spheres of influence, conflicts flared that had almost no direct theological content but that intensified the existing theological disputes. For instance, a successful charge of heresy could damage a rival church's prestige and its claim to a high position in the evolving church structures. Fourth, the outcome of a theological quarrel often had significant consequences in the here-and-now. The Roman emperor, as God's chosen ruler, was thought to be responsible for the stability of the empire and the purity of orthodox belief. Many emperors were sincerely concerned about theological matters. Some were even competent theologians and participated in the intellectual debates, a precedent set by Constantine at the Council of Nicaea (325). All theological parties sought the emperor's support by whatever means they could find. They reminded him that his personal welfare, the welfare of his dynasty, and of the empire depended on the favor of God; they tried to convince him of the correctness of their view; they sought supporters among important people at the imperial court to whom they might give bribes; and they vigorously blackened their opponents' reputations, sometimes charging them with the serious political crime of disloyalty to the emperor. Some emperors were not inclined to take sides in theological disagreements, but they could not ignore for long the political consequences of theological disagreements that divided the empire's elites and sometimes stirred up ordinary people. The theological party that won the emperor's approval was favored with legal privileges, subsidies, and bishoprics. The losing party faced legal and financial problems and the exile of its leaders. Because the consequences of losing a theological argument could be so severe, the quarrels were all the more fierce. There was a lot at stake.

But practical reasons for the ferocity that often accompanied theological debate must be balanced against the background of deeply- held religious beliefs. Fourth- and fifth-century Christians did not regard theological beliefs as mere matters of opinion, as many modern people do. They generally believed that correct (or incorrect) belief had serious real-world consequences for individuals and for society. They were convinced that right belief and correct behavior were more than matters of life and death. They were matters of eternal salvation and damnation. For that reason, they often regarded their opponents not merely as wrong but as intentionally wrong, even evil. Efforts at compromise often but not always failed in such an atmosphere.

SCHISMS

There were degrees of division among orthodox Christians. Sometimes they split from one another over disciplinary matters, which were not exactly theological but often had theological implications. The word "discipline" refers to the many practical details of managing a church. For instance, modern churches have quite varied practices, that is, they have varied forms of discipline, on such issues as how their clergy are trained, hired, and fired; how old a person should be before ordination; whether stained glass windows or other decorations are permissible in church; whether the presiding clergyman should wear special liturgical clothing at services; and who should be admitted to the church's Eucharist. The point is that churches generally have their own ways of doing things, their discipline, which can occasionally lead to internal disagreement. If the disagreement grows heated enough, one faction might split off to form a new congregation, perhaps more or less identical in belief and behavior with the former congregation but differing in some matter(s) of practice, that is, in discipline. If a division involves primarily discipline, it is usually called a "schism," which means in Greek a "split" or "rip." A schism tore the unity of a church or group of churches. The most dramatic public expression of a schism was that one group of Christians would not share the Eucharistic meal with another group of Christians. Contemporaries often hoped that a schism could be mended, especially if the disagreement was not rooted in deeply held beliefs.

The processes that led to schisms were at work already in pre-fourth-century churches. For instance, in the second century, there was a threat of schism between the churches in Asia Minor and most other churches over the day of the week on which Easter should be celebrated (EH 5.23–25). The persecutions in the third century provoked widespread disagreements over discipline. Many who lapsed during persecution wanted to be readmitted to the churches. Proto-orthodox Christians generally agreed that weakness in persecution, especially when it led to the worship of the hated idols, was a terrible sin. Few believed that the lapsed could simply come back to the church with no consequences. What was to be the discipline governing their treatment? Some churches were split internally between rigorists whose vision of a pure church led them to refuse any reconciliation for the lapsed and those with a vision of a church composed of both saints and sinners that led them to readmit the lapsed after the imposition of disciplinary measures that included strict public penance. The schismatic churches were often indistinguishable from the proto-orthodox churches in such things as belief, liturgy, and organization, but they rejected communion with those churches whose discipline they regarded as too lax.

No rigorist schism convinced the majority of Christians to follow it, although some schisms survived for a long time. For instance, Novatian, a Roman presbyter of the mid-third century, objected when his church allowed those who had lapsed during Decius' persecution to be readmitted to the church even after they had performed severe public penance. When Novatian was not elected Roman bishop, he received consecration as a counterbishop of Rome and created what he called a "virgin church," that is, a church untainted by what he regarded as laxity in discipline. His followers called themselves "the pure." Even some proto-orthodox Christians grudgingly admired the rigorism and sincerity of the Novationists, who survived until the 700s as a strict, although small group.

One schism stands out for its staying power. Constantine, who expected that Christianity would be a unifying force in his empire, learned in 312 that the Catholic Christians in North Africa were bitterly divided. In the last months of the Great Persecution, a serious schism had broken out in Carthage when one party of clergy accused another party of clergy of handing over the scriptures to the Roman persecutors. Members of the rigorist group, called "Donatists" from their leader Donatus the Great (313–355), broke off communion with members of the other group, whom they scornfully called *traditores* ("those who hand over").

THE ORIGINS OF THE TRINITARIAN CONTROVERSY

Schisms were rooted primarily in disagreements about discipline, but they often became more theological as opponents tried to justify their views. In the early fourth century, disagreements directly about theology led to bitter strife among catholic Christians, who debated about differing views of the preexistent Word of God, in particular whether the Word was equal to or subordinate to the Father or, to put it another way, whether the Word of God had been created or had always been with God. Out of those debates the orthodox doctrine of the Trinity was defined.

The fifty or so sacred books in the Old and New Testaments, to which Christians gave authority, had been written by different people, in different times, for different purposes, and with different viewpoints. In a centuries-long effort, some of the best minds among Christians tried to integrate the "data" in the Old and New Testaments into systems of belief, which we may call "theologies." But it was not easy to create coherent theology out of them. Some texts in the Old and New Testaments seemed to say that the Son and the Father were identical; some texts seemed to say that God had adopted Jesus, perhaps at his baptism, and made him divine; some texts seemed to say that the Word/Son was subordinate or inferior to the Father. There was a persistent tension in Christian belief between the desire to affirm the oneness of God and at the same time to affirm the threeness of God. As you read about the Trinitarian Controversy, keep in mind this simplified statement of the underlying issue at stake: Should God be understood as absolutely one and alone or as three, a Father, a Son, and a Spirit? Then, as now, many believers were content not to probe too deeply or to seek precise explanations of the one and the three that they read about in scripture, confessed in creeds, sang about in hymns, and invoked in baptisms. But it was difficult to avoid the tension.

Christianity's Jewish roots stressed the oneness of God. The sacred books of the Jews, claimed by Christians as their Old Testament, taught a strict monotheism: There is only one God. In morning and evening devotions in the Temple and in the synagogue service, Jews recited (and still recite) the prayer called the "Shema," which began "Hear O Israel, the Lord is our God, the Lord is One" (Deut 6:41). Orthodox Christians also said that they were monotheists. The Christian apologists mocked the many gods of their pagan rivals. By the fourth century, orthodox Christianity had developed its own collection of sacred books, the New Testament. Some New Testament texts talked about God not just as one but also as three. For instance, Christians baptized their converts in the threefold name of Father, Son, and Spirit (Mt 28:19). They also composed written creeds that were structured around declarations about the Father, then the Son, and then the Spirit. Between about 180 and 200, Tertullian in Latin (*Against Praxeas*, 3) and Theophilus of Antioch in Greek (*Apology to Autolycus*, 2:15) used the word "Trinity" to express the belief that God was one but also three.

Precise definitions of how the one and the three were related were difficult to formulate. The scriptural references, which we may call the "data" out of which theology would be created, were diverse. Some scriptural texts referred only to the Father and Son, with no mention of the Spirit. For instance, Paul greeted the Galatians "Grace to you and peace from God our Father and the Lord Jesus Christ...." (Gal 1:3). Other scriptural texts referred to a Father, a Son, and a Holy Spirit (Mt 28:19). Some Christians did try to understand how God could be one and three. For instance, in the third century a man named "Sabellius" defended the oneness of God by making the Son and the Spirit "modes" or temporary manifestations of God. Sabellius apparently argued that there were no permanently existing and separate divine persons. Instead, when the one God wanted to communicate with humans he took on the mode of the Father, the Son, or Spirit. When a mode was no longer needed it was reabsorbed into the one God. Sabellius' views, often called "modalism," were eventually rejected, even though they may have reflected the view of many believers.

The long-standing uncertainty about how the Son related to the Father exploded in Egypt in the early fourth century. (The relationship of the Spirit to the Father and to the Son was not seriously raised until the middle and later fourth century.) Around

318, Bishop Alexander of Alexandria (312–328) supported publicly the view that the Word of God/Son and the Father were co-eternal, that is, they were equally eternal. Arius (about 260–336), a respected senior presbyter of the Alexandrian church, protested against his bishop's view. Because Arius emphasized the oneness of God, he taught that the Word of God, who was enfleshed in Jesus, was subordinate to or less than the Father. Arius praised the Son as the first and greatest of creatures. He conceded that the Son could be called "God" but denied that he was God in the same way that the Father was God. At the heart of his theology, Arius insisted that the Son was a *created* being who was neither eternal nor equal to the Father. Arius used clear, bold language—slogans really—such as "There was a time when He [the Son] was not" and "He [the Son] did not exist before he was born." Arius' views often did not diminish the Christians' traditional reverence for the Word. Many of those who agreed with some version of Arius' views still regarded Christ as worthy of worship and still baptized in the name of the Father, Son, and Spirit. But his strong statement of the subordinationist position drew many into the debate.

In the traditional pattern of dealing with serious matters, Bishop Alexander convened a synod of about one hundred Egyptian bishops who excluded Arius and his followers from communion. However, after Arius had raised so clearly the thorny issue of the Son's relation to the Father, it did not go away. For at least three generations, the churches of the empire, especially in the east, were embroiled in what has been called the "Arian Controversy," named for Arius, although it is more correctly called the "Trinitarian Controversy." Bishops, clergy, and many laypeople were confronted with a diversity of views about the relation of the Word or Son of God to the Father.

When Constantine gained control of the eastern half of the empire in 324, he was distressed to learn that the mighty church of Alexandria was divided bitterly over the relation of the Son to the Father. He sent a trusted adviser, Bishop Ossius of Cordoba, to get the opponents to reconcile. He also sent substantial letters to Bishop Alexander and to Arius in which he referred to their differences over the relation of the Son to the Father

as "unprofitable," the sort of thing that people with too much time on their hands bring up. He encouraged them not to discuss such matters, to stop arguing and make up! Constantine did not yet understand the importance of the debate to the participants, but he would soon learn. When his efforts to reconcile the combatants failed, he summoned a council to meet in 325 in the imperial palace at Nicaea in Asia Minor. The emperor provided the bishops with subsidies and the use of the imperial transport system to encourage their presence. The number of bishops at the Council of Nicaea was later said to be 318, the same as the number of Abraham's servants (Gen 14:14), but that was probably a symbolic number. There were certainly about 220 bishops at the council, almost entirely Greek-speakers from the eastern half of the empire. There were perhaps five bishops from the west. Bishop Sylvester of Rome, who did not attend, was represented by two presbyters.

At Nicaea, the divisions among the bishops soon became clear. Some bishops agreed with Arius that the Son was created; some bishops vehemently disagreed with Arius; and a middle group of bishops, perhaps the largest, sought compromise. The bishops had a difficult time finding precise words to describe the relation between the Father and the Son. Many wanted to exclude Arius' view that the Son was a created being, subordinate to the Father, while at the same time they did not want to endorse the opposite view that the Son was so equal to the Father that he was absorbed into him. That seemed close to Sabellius' view that the one God had temporary modes, which were merely called "Father, Son, and Spirit." Constantine participated in the proceedings. Eusebius, who was also present, recorded that the emperor suggested that the Greek term *homoousios* ("of the same substance") could describe the relationship of the Father and the Son. Some bishops thought that it was a bad precedent to use the word *homoousios*, which was not in the scriptures, to describe something as crucial as the relation of Son and Father. Some bishops objected that *homoousios* opened the way to a view of divine oneness with which Sabellius could have agreed. But they did not prevail. The Council of Nicaea issued a creed that was intended to reject Arius' views and settle the matter, although the controversy did not end for decades. The Nicene Creed declared that "[w]e believe in one God, the Father Almighty, maker of all things visible and invisible; and in one Lord Jesus Christ, the Son of God, the only-begotten of his Father, of the substance of the Father, God of God, Light of Light, true God of true God, begotten, not made, being of the same substance [homoousios] with the Father. By whom all things were made, both which are in heaven and on the earth. Who for us men and for our salvation came down and was incarnate, and was made man. He suffered, and the third day rose again, and ascended into heaven. He shall come again to judge both the living and the dead. And [we believe] in the Holy Spirit" (*The Nicene Creed* [325] in NPNF, second series, vol. 14, p. 3, altered). The council then added to the creed condemnations of the views of Arius and his followers. "And whoever shall say that there was a time when the Son of God was not, or that before he was begotten he was not, or that he was made of things that were not, or that he is of a different substance or essence [from the Father] or that he is a creature, or subject to change...—all that say so, the Catholic and Apostolic Church anathematizes." Unanimity at a council was regarded as a sign of the Holy Spirit's presence. The Council of Nicaea almost achieved unanimity, although later events show that many bishops had serious reservations that they did not express at the time. Constantine exiled temporarily two bishops who refused to agree to the creed and two other bishops who accepted the creed but refused to accept the condemnation of Arius' views. Arius was also exiled but was readmitted to communion in 335.

Later generations revered the Council of Nicaea as special, as an authoritative ecumenical ("universal") council. It came to be called the "Great Council" whose decisions should not be changed. But in 325, the participants could not have foreseen that. They had gathered to treat a contemporary issue that was splitting the church. During Constantine's lifetime, the Creed of Nicaea prevailed. But almost immediately after he died in 337, controversy that lasted for more than forty years broke out again. The western Latin-speaking bishops, who were less speculative in their theology than the eastern Greek-speaking bishops, generally favored the theology of Nicaea. But many serious Christians did not agree that the Son and the Father were so equal as to be "of the same substance." That kind of relationship posed intellectual problems. Some bishops, especially eastern bishops who emphasized the distinction among Father, Son, and Spirit, thought that the Nicene Creed was dangerously close to Sabellianism. If two things are "of the same substance," then are they really just the same thing? Is the Son merely a temporary manifestation of God? If so, at some point did the Son not exist, and will the Son eventually "disappear" into God and lose an independent existence? The controversy over Arius' views spread quickly from Alexandria to other churches in the east. Athanasius, who had attended the Council of Nicaea as Bishop Alexander's deacon, emerged in later years as the main defender of the Creed of Nicaea. As Bishop of Alexandria (328–373), he proved to be a man of energy and bravery, with powerful verbal and literary skills. His opponents accused him, with some justification, of violence, trouble-making, and arrogance. By the 350s, he was an unwavering defender of the Creed of Nicaea.

Church politics intertwined with the heated theological debate. Those who favored a subordinate status for the Son found support among some eastern bishops who resented the growing power of the bishops of Alexandria. In 335, a council of bishops at Tyre in modern Lebanon deposed Athanasius for something like conduct unbecoming a bishop, including a charge of murdering a presbyter—later disproved when the "dead" presbyter was produced alive. Imperial politics also stirred the waters. Athanasius' unwavering support of Nicaea annoyed the Emperor Constantius (337–361), who supported an anti-Nicene theology, called "Homoian," which asserted that the Son was "like" the Father. Constantius wanted some flexibility to settle the theological dispute, which was disrupting the peace of the empire. He thought that strict adherence to the Nicene Creed was an impediment to church unity. But Athanasius was not the man from whom one could expect flexibility. Athanasius was repeatedly deposed, exiled, and restored to the bishopric of Alexandria. At one point when he was hunted by the imperial secret police, he hid in the Egyptian desert among the monks, many of whom were strong allies. He spent in exile about fifteen of his forty-five years as bishop of Alexandria.

It is a mistake to think that the disputes that swirled around the Creed of Nicaea were just political. They were also profoundly theological. They went to the heart of Christianity. A clear picture of the participants' views is difficult to get. Both the supporters and the opponents of the Nicene Creed disagreed among themselves. One broad group can be called "pro-Nicene" because they believed that the Son was "of the same essence" (*homoousios*) as the Father, he was equal to the Father; he was "true God of true God," as the Creed of Nicaea said. They believed that Jesus was God without having to qualify that word. Another broad group was "anti-Nicene," which contained diverse views, although they shared the general outlook that the Son was subordinate to the Father in some way(s). For instance, some more radical thinkers, who were close to Arius' view, argued that the Son was actually "unlike" (*anomoios*) the Father. The bishops at the Council of Sirmium (357) issued a creed reflecting the views of those Anomoians. "There is no question that the Father is greater. No one can doubt that the Father is greater than the Son in honor, dignity, splendor, majesty and in the very name of Father, as the Son Himself testifies, 'He Who sent Me is greater than I.' And no one is ignorant that it is Catholic doctrine that there are two persons of Father and Son; and that the Father is greater, and that the Son is subordinated to the Father, together with all things which the Father has subjected to Him [the Son], and that the Father has no beginning and is invisible, immortal and impassible, but that the Son has been begotten from the Father...." (*The Creed of Sirmium* [357], in Hilary of Poitiers, *On the Synods*, c. 11 in NPNF, second series, vol. 9, pp. 6–7, altered). Other anti-Nicenes argued that the Son was not God in a strict sense of that word but rather was "like" (*homoios*) the Father. Their views attracted many who did not want a more precise statement of belief that would provoke controversy. An important party of bishops added one Greek letter ("iota") to the word *homoousios*, making it *homoiousios*, which meant "of a similar substance." The Homoiousians argued

that the Son was like the Father with respect to his substance. For about forty years (340–381), pro- and anti-Nicene advocates wrote against one another, gathered in councils to condemn one another and to issue what they regarded as better creeds. They also sought imperial support to penalize and depose their opponents. The period was marked by frequent comings and goings of bishops. There were more than a dozen important councils during Constantius' reign (337–361), and about eighteen creeds were issued with the intent of settling the matter. The pagan historian Ammianus Marcellinus complained that under the Emperor Constantius the imperial transport system was overburdened with bishops going to and coming from councils at public expense (*History*, XXI, 16.18).

Although the Trinitarian Controversy was complicated and often expressed in philosophical language that used Greek and Latin words in subtle ways, it aroused some interest among ordinary Christian clergy and laypeople. Constantinople was a large, sophisticated city, some of whose inhabitants were fascinated by theology. Bishop Gregory of Nyssa described the situation at Constantinople in a sermon, *On the Deity of the Son and the Holy Spirit*: "If in this city you ask anyone for change, he will discuss with you whether the Son is begotten or unbegotten. If you ask about the quality of bread, you will receive the answer that 'the Father is greater, the Son is less.' If you suggest that a bath is desirable, you will be told that 'there was nothing before the Son was created'" (As quoted in W. H. C. Frend, *The Early Church* [Philadelphia, 1982], pp. 174–175).

The tendency of ancient Christianity to divide by regions is also visible in the Trinitarian Controversy. The western bishops, usually led by the bishops of Rome, were generally but not always supporters of the pro-Nicene position. Many eastern bishops were opposed to or at least uneasy with the Nicene solution to the problem of how God could be one and three. In a region of central Turkey called "Cappadocia," three remarkable bishops, who were also important theologians—Basil of Caesarea (330–379), his brother Gregory of Nyssa (about 340–about 395), and Gregory of Nazianzus (about 329–390)—prepared the ground for the intellectual victory of the pro-Nicene view of the Trinity. In letters, treatises, sermons, and personal alliances with like-minded bishops, they defended and developed the pro-Nicene position that the Son shares his substance (*ousia*) with the Father. They also vigorously supported the appointment of bishops who agreed with them because that was the surest way to build a party. In his old age, Athanasius was willing to agree that the views of the Cappadocians were close enough to his own *homoousian* views that they could be allies against the anti-Nicenes, especially the Anomoians, who openly subordinated the Son to the Father.

The alliance of the Cappadocian bishops and their allies with Athanasius and his allies laid a strong basis for the acceptance of Trinitarian theology along the lines of the Nicene Creed. But in the Christian empire, it was probably inevitable that theological debates would intertwine with political developments. The competing theological parties sought support from the emperors. Two of Constantine's sons and successors, Constantine II (337–340) and Constans (337–350), were pro-Nicenes. His third son, Constantius (337–361), who had inherited the eastern part of the empire and gained control of the entire empire after his brothers died, favored an anti-Nicene theology. During his reign, imperial favor flowed to anti-Nicene groups, especially the Homoians. But the unpredictability of war had an influence on theological outcomes. In 378 at Adrianople, just west of Constantinople, the anti-Nicene Emperor Valens was killed in battle with the Germanic Visigoths. The surviving emperor in the west, Gratian (375–383), was only nineteen and inexperienced. In that dangerous military moment, he appointed Theodosius, a successful general in his early thirties, to be emperor in the east. Theodosius I (379–395) eventually stabilized the military situation and changed the religious situation decisively as well. In 380, he declared catholic Christianity, in its pro-Nicene form, to be the official religion of the empire. He provided a capsule version of pro-Nicene belief: "we shall believe in the single Deity of the Father, Son, and the Holy Spirit, under the concept of equal majesty and of the Holy Trinity" (*Codex Theodosianus*, XVI,1.2 in *The Theodosian Code and Novels and Sirmondian Constitutions*, translated by Clyde Pharr [Princeton, NJ, 1952], p. 440). He also summoned the Council of Constantinople (381), which was later regarded as the second ecumenical council, at which about 150 bishops, all from the eastern part of the empire, reaffirmed that the Son and the Father were of the same substance (*homoousios*). The Council of Constantinople issued a creed, which is often called the "Nicene-Constantinopolitan Creed" or simply the "Nicene Creed," which is recited at the Eucharistic service of some modern churches. The Council of Constantinople also treated the relation of the Spirit to the Father and the Son, which had been a minor matter fifty-six years earlier at the Council of Nicaea.

The Holy Spirit

The relation of the Son to the Father was not the only issue that emerged as the theology of the Trinity was worked out. Because Paul's letters and the gospels referred frequently to a Spirit (*pneuma*) or a Holy Spirit (*hagion pneuma*), the word "Spirit" was embedded in Christian prayers, liturgy, and expressions of belief. But there was no single understanding of what the word "Spirit" meant. The abundant pre-fourth-century references to the Spirit generally centered not on who or what the Spirit might be but rather on what the Spirit did. The Spirit was described in such varying ways as the comforter, the giver of knowledge, the giver of charismatic gifts, the strengthener of the persecuted, the justifier of sinners, and the sanctifier who made believers holy. How the Spirit related to the Father and the Son was fluid and imprecise. For instance, some early writers thought the Spirit was an angel, perhaps the chief angel. Others thought that the Spirit was not a person but rather an attribute or power of the Son: It was Jesus' Spirit. In the heated fourth-century debate about the relation of the Son to the Father, the Spirit was at first more or less ignored. The Creed of Nicaea, for example, spelled out in some detail the relation of the Son to the Father, culminating in the controversial adjective *homoousios*, but the Spirit was treated in that creed with the brief statement that "And [we believe] in the Holy Spirit." The status of the Spirit was not then a pressing issue.

The fourth-century debates about the relation of the Father to the Son naturally raised questions about the relation of the Spirit to both. In the second half of the fourth century, the status of the Spirit emerged as a matter of serious disagreement. Anti-Nicenes leaned toward positions that denied full divinity to the Spirit, just as they denied full divinity to the Son. From their point of view, a fully divine Spirit was, like a fully divine Son, a threat to the oneness of God. Their opponents called some of those people "Battlers against the Spirit" (Pneumatomachoi). The pro-Nicene thinkers who argued for the full divinity of the Son came to defend the full divinity of the Spirit. The victory of the pro-Nicene views of the Son led to an insistence that the Spirit was distinct from but also co-equal and co-eternal with the Father and Son. The technical language was that the Spirit "proceeded from the Father." Unlike the Creed of Nicaea, which passed over the Spirit briefly, the bishops at the Council of Constantinople (381) declared that they believed "in the Holy Spirit, the Lord, the Giver-of-Life, who proceeds from the Father, who with the Father and the Son together is worshipped and glorified, who spoke by the prophets" (The Creed of Constantinople [381], in NPNF, second series, vol. 14, p. 163, altered). By the late fourth century, the pro-Nicene Christian churches affirmed the doctrine of the Trinity, that the Father, the Son, and the Spirit were three separate divine persons who shared fully and equally in the essence of God.

THE SURVIVAL OF ARIANISM

Although the Council of Constantinople (381) and the emperor Theodosius I strongly rejected the diverse anti-Nicene views often lumped together as "Arianism," history's unexpected twists enabled the anti-Nicene views to survive both inside and outside the Roman Empire. Fourth- and fifth-century developments north of the imperial border favored Arianism. In about 340, during the reign of the anti-Nicene Emperor Constantius, bishops who favored the Homoian ("the Son is like the Father") theology consecrated a man named "Ulfilas" (about 311–383) to be bishop of the Christians who lived among the Visigoths north of the Danube River. Ulfilas might have been descended from Christian captives who had been carried off by Gothic invad-

ers in the mid-third century. We do not know how he received his education, but he knew Greek, Latin, and the Gothic language. He invented an alphabet adapted to the Gothic language and translated much of the scriptures into Gothic. Extensive parts of his translation, the oldest document in any Germanic language, survive. After working among the Goths from 341 to 347/348, he fled with followers to Roman territory because of a persecution. So far as we know, he never returned to the Visigoths. He spent the last thirty-five years of his life inside the empire, where he participated in councils and defended his anti-Nicene views in written works, most of which do not survive. He has been called the "Apostle to the Goths," but, in fact, their conversion to Arian Christianity took place between 382 and 395, after the Visigoths had settled inside the empire. In circumstances difficult to grasp, Arian Christianity spread from the Goths to some other Germanic peoples. When those Germanic tribes invaded and settled in the Roman Empire between 378 and 476, many of them were Arian Christians, with their own clergy, their tents and wagons that served as churches, and the scriptures and the liturgy in their own language. Their theology and their own desire to remain distinct within Roman culture alienated them from their Roman subjects, who were by then overwhelmingly adherents of Nicaea. Eventually catholic nicene Christianity prevailed: The last Arian Germanic kingdom, that of the Visigoths in Spain, accepted nicene Christianity in 589, more than two centuries after the Emperor Theodosius I and the Council of Constantinople rejected Arianism.

Political circumstances within the empire favored temporary toleration of Arian Germans. The empire had a chronic shortage of soldiers and relied extensively on mercenaries, many of them recruited from Germanic tribes. In the later fourth and early fifth centuries, the emperors were particularly dependent on Gothic soldiers, who were mostly but not always Arian Christians. Gothic commanders had great influence at the imperial courts in Milan and Constantinople. Goths had their own clergy and their own churches in Constantinople and other cities. No emperor could afford to crack down hard on the Gothic adherents of outlawed Arianism while his position and his life depended on Arian Gothic soldiers. The eastern emperors gradually found replacements for the Gothic soldiers by recruiting troops from fierce peoples within the empire. For instance, the Emperor Leo I (457–474) recruited warriors who lived in Isauria, a region in Asia Minor. The Isaurians were Roman citizens and catholic Christians, but they were also tough soldiers. When the Goths were no longer needed in the army, the toleration of Arianism ended. Within the empire, the Arians became one of the small, disadvantaged heretical groups, sometimes persecuted and sometimes ignored and eventually extinct.

FURTHER READING

Ancient Sources

William G. Rusch ed., trans., *The Trinitarian Controversy*, in *Sources of Early Christian Thought* (Philadelphia, 1980). An introduction and translated sources about the Trinitarian Controversy.

James Stevenson, ed., *A New Eusebius: Documents Illustrating the History of the Church to AD 337*, revised with additional documents revised by W. H. C. Frend (London, 1987), pp. 321–365, has important documents on Arianism, the Council of Nicaea, and Athanasius.

Modern Works

A good way to approach the complexities of the Arian Controversy is through a biography, which puts human faces on abstract matters. I suggest Alvyn Pettersen, *Athanasius* (London, 1995), or Timothy D. Barnes, *Athanasius and Constantius: Theology and Politics in the Constantinian Empire* (Cambridge, MA, 1993), or Anthony Meredith, *The Cappadocians* (Crestwood, NY, 1995).

Lewis Ayres, *Nicaea and Its Legacy: An Approach to Fourth-Century Trinitarian Theology* (Oxford and New York, 2004).

R. P. C. Hanson, *The Search for the Christian Doctrine of God* (Edinburgh, 1988). A monumental, challenging treatment of the Trinitarian Controversy in more than nine hundred pages.

J. N. D. Kelly, *Early Christian Creeds*, third edition (New York, 1972), pp. 205–262, on the Creed of Nicaea.

J. N. D. Kelly, *Early Christian Doctrines*, revised edition (New York, 1978), especially pp. 223–279, on Arianism and Trinitarian doctrine.

Frances Young, *The Making of Creeds*, second edition (London, 2002), offers a brief readable account of the long process of working out official statements of belief.

CHAPTER 14

Jesus, the God/Man

Up to the fifth century, many orthodox Christians believed, without probing too deeply into the intellectual challenges that lay just below the surface, that Jesus, the being in whom the Word of God became flesh, was both God and man. Ordinary Christian speech and the liturgy made it natural to accept Jesus as somehow a man and God. Christians baptized in the name of Father, Son, and Spirit. They prayed to the Son, although some thinkers were reluctant to address prayers directly to anyone except the Father. Most Christians probably found such a view of Jesus satisfying. But when some Christian thinkers began to investigate these seemingly simple, straightforward elements of their faith, orthodox Christianity was torn apart for generations, for centuries, even to the present day.

The Trinitarian Controversy, which had been intense for about five decades of the fourth century, centered on the relationship between the Father and the Son (and the relationship of the Spirit to both). What emerged was the orthodox formulation of the doctrine of the Trinity, which held that God had revealed himself as a tri-unity, three distinct persons, called *hypostases* in Greek and *personae* in Latin, sharing one divine nature, called *ousia* in Greek and *substantia* in Latin. The Council at Constantinople (381) supported the views of the victorious pro-Nicene parties, but it did not end controversy. Although theological disagreements never ended, for about forty-five years there was *relative* theological quiet within the empire, although the British monk Pelagius' teachings about grace stirred responses from Augustine of Hippo and others. In 428, another significant theological disagreement broke out, which over the next two centuries led to divisions within Christianity that have never been repaired.

Like the fourth-century Trinitarian Controversy, the fifth- and sixth-century debates were also about the nature of the Son or Word of God, but from a different angle. The Trinitarian Controversy had been about the way that the Son/Word related to the Father. The struggles of the fifth and sixth centuries were about how a divine Son/Word and a human nature were related within the Palestinian man Jesus Christ. Godness, if I may use such a word, and humanness seemed so distant that many found it difficult to understand how they could in any real sense have been joined in a single human person. Then, as now, many people imagined God in concrete images, such as an elderly, fatherly figure with a flowing beard. But influential philosophical and theological traditions in the ancient world, particularly Platonic and Stoic, taught that God was beyond imagining in a physical way, beyond any category of analysis, and certainly beyond entanglement with matter. When philosophers and theologians wrote and talked about the mystery of God, they insisted that he (or it) was immortal, unchangeable, incapable of suffering or feeling emotion. Those same philosophical views often held that human beings were entirely different from God. Humans were limited in every way, tiny in the great scheme of things, changeable, emotional, open to suffering, and wallowing in ignorance and sin. Many educated people, including educated Christians, thought it seemed impossible and even inappropriate that the immaterial, untouchable, and unseen God could enter into matter or could truly unite with a human nature. Bishop Eusebius of Caesarea, who leaned toward a subordinationist view of the Word, expressed the reluctance to think that God himself appeared directly to humans. When Old Testament figures such as Abraham

(Gen 18) had theophanies ("appearances of God") and worshipped a visible being, Eusebius thought it was the Word, not God, "For if reason does not permit that the uncreated and immutable essence of God Almighty should be changed into the form of a man.... Who is seen in the form of a man except His only preexistent Word?" (EH 1). Yet, in their prayers, their hymns, their liturgy, their creeds, and their ordinary speech, orthodox Christians affirmed that somehow the divine and the human had co-existed in the Palestinian Jew, Jesus. The efforts to understand how there could be a God/Man unleashed bitter struggles that never reached a consensus that most Christians accepted.

Before the fourth century, several explanations were proposed for how the divine and the human related in Jesus Christ. For instance, Paul of Samosata, bishop of Antioch from about 260 to 268, was said to have argued for a view that is called "adoptionism" in the history of Christian theology. He believed that God "adopted" the good man Jesus at a moment when the power or spirit of God took over or descended upon him. Sometimes adoptionists argued that God adopted Jesus when John baptized him in the Jordan River (Mt 3:16–17): "And when Jesus had been baptized, just as he came up from the water, suddenly the heavens were opened to him and he saw the Spirit of God descending like a dove and alighting on him. And a voice from heaven said, 'This is my Son, the Beloved, with whom I am well pleased.'" Luke's gospel at 3:22 had an alternate text that was well known to ancient Christian writers but was not accepted in the modern Greek editions of that gospel. It said, "You are my Son, today I have begotten you," which could be interpreted to support an adoptionist view. Other adoptionists argued that God adopted Jesus after he had been crucified or raised from the dead. Such a view could find support in Peter's speech in Acts 2:14–36, which concluded that God "made" Jesus "Lord and Messiah." Orthodox Christians eventually rejected adoptionist explanations of how or even whether a divine and a human nature existed in Jesus. The problem of how there could be a God-Who-Is-a-Man or a Man-Who-Is-a-God remained difficult to understand. During the fifth century, that difficulty erupted into serious dissension

when conflicting theologies of the God/Man were openly proposed.

NESTORIANISM — Dyophysite

Simmering theological issues often need a real-life incident to provoke debate and mobilize opposing forces. The flashpoint in the prolonged debate over Jesus' nature came during a disagreement at Constantinople about a title commonly attributed to the Virgin Mary. By the fifth century, Mary had many admirers among Christians, and especially among consecrated virgins and nuns, who identified with her. Since the third century, many Christians, including such prominent figures as Origen, Eusebius of Caesarea, and Athanasius, referred to her in Greek as *Theotokos*, literally the "God-bearer" or "Mother of God." Nestorius, bishop of Constantinople from 428 to 431, objected to the title *Theotokos* on the grounds that Mary could not literally be the "Mother of God" because God had no beginning and consequently no mother. He conceded that Mary had given birth to the man Jesus but not to the pre-existing Word, who was the eternal second person of the Trinity. Nestorius preferred to call Mary the *Christotokos* ("Mother of Christ") or *Anthropotokos* ("Mother of the Man"). Nestorius' strong views stirred up a storm of theological criticism and popular unrest among clergy, monks, and laypeople, especially in Constantinople. More important from a theological point of view, Nestorius' rejection of Mary's traditional title put front and center the issue of Jesus' nature: What was the being to which Mary gave birth? Nestorius' opponents charged that he separated Jesus too sharply into two distinct beings: the human person, to whom Mary gave birth, and the Divine Word, who somehow dwelt in or with that person but was not really united with him as a complete human person.

Theological quarrels rarely occur in a vacuum. Bishop Nestorius was a hothead. For instance, in his first sermon after his consecration as bishop of Constantinople, he addressed the Emperor Theodosius II (408–450): "Give me, my prince, the earth purged of heretics, and I will give you heaven as a reward. Assist me in destroying heretics, and I will assist you in vanquishing the

Persians" (Socrates, *Ecclesiastical History*, VII.xxix, in NPNF, second series, vol. 2 , p. 169, altered). Nestorius made good on his intention to drive out heretics. He began a campaign against the many kinds of Christian dissenters who lived in Constantinople and in Asia Minor. Within five days of his consecration as bishop, he ordered the destruction of a chapel where Arians worshipped quietly, although illegally. When the Arians saw their place of worship being destroyed, they set fire to it, igniting surrounding buildings. Many orthodox Christians blamed Nestorius for the fire and especially for needlessly disturbing the peace. Nestorius' outspokenness also made powerful enemies. Pulcheria (399–453), granddaughter of the Emperor Theodosius I (379–395) and older sister of the Emperor Theodosius II, was a prominent figure in the court. As a teenager she had taken a vow to remain a virgin. She favored the title *Theotokos*, "Mother of God," for the Virgin Mary. Probably because of Pulcheria's piety and her exalted imperial status, she was granted unusual privileges during the Eucharistic liturgy. For instance, she took the Eucharist in the sanctuary of the church, which was ordinarily open only to the male clergy. Bishop Nestorius foolishly insulted her when he forbade her to do that. In addition, he ordered her to sit in the part of the church reserved for women. She was furious and powerful enough to do something about it. Nestorius' imprudence meant that theological disagreement about the divine and human nature(s) of Christ was reinforced by Pulcheria's personal dislike for him.

The theological dispute about the divine and human in Christ soon intersected with other issues in the fifth-century church. Nestorius' controversial view of the person to whom Mary gave birth was caught up in the ecclesiastical rivalry that pitted Alexandria against Constantinople for predominance among the eastern churches. Alexandria was a rich, populous city that had a long heritage of Christian martyrs and thinkers, including Clement, Origen, and Athanasius. It claimed apostolic foundation through Peter's disciple Mark, who was said to have been its founding missionary. The bishop of Alexandria was perhaps the single most important person in his city. In contrast to Alexandria (and also to Rome, Antioch,

and Jerusalem), the city of Constantinople owed its importance to the emperors. In an emperor-centered society, the presence of the emperor and his court was a powerful stimulus to the growth of Constantinople's population, wealth, and prestige. Fourth- and fifth-century emperors and bishops of Constantinople wanted to make its religious status more like its political status, to make it equal to the great bishoprics that claimed apostolic origins. Bishops of Alexandria and Rome objected because they thought that the church at Constantinople had a weak theological case for its claim to importance in the wider church. Constantinople had not been mentioned in the New Testament (it did not yet exist) and had no widely accepted association with the apostles. By the end of the seventh century, some claimed that Constantinople's first bishop had been appointed by Peter's brother, Andrew, but that argument played no role in the fifth century. Canon three of the Council of Constantinople (381) ordered that Constantinople be elevated to second in dignity among the churches because of its political position as the New Rome: The bishops of Rome, who had no representative at that council, refused to accept the third canon because they believed that the status of a bishopric should depend not on secular politics but rather on the apostolic succession and links to Peter. The bishops of Alexandria, who aspired to be the leading bishops of the east, were especially outraged that the bishop of Constantinople had been placed ahead of them in the order of eminence. Thus, Rome and Alexandria shared reasons for wishing to thwart the rising ecclesiastical status of the bishopric of Constantinople. They got their opportunity when Nestorius put forth his strong version of a two-nature christology. If the bishop of Constantinople was a heretic, then the reputation of his church would be tarnished. Throughout the theological quarrels of the fifth century, Alexandria and Rome were often allies, although the bishops of Alexandria were more aggressive in openly attacking the orthodoxy of several bishops of Constantinople.

Nestorius' main opponent was Cyril, bishop of Alexandria (412–444), a significant theological thinker, an effective politician with access to the great resources of the Alexandrian church, and a rather ruthless man. He had at his disposal hundreds of hospital attendants, called *parabolani*, who could be mobilized as a fighting force. He closed churches in Alexandria that followed the teachings of the third-century schismatic Novatian and confiscated their property. When an outbreak of Jewish violence led to the killing of Christians, Cyril expelled the Jews from Alexandria by force and seized their synagogues. He was not a man to anger. To settle the questions raised by denying to Mary the title "Mother of God," the Emperor Theodosius II summoned a council to meet at Ephesus in modern Turkey (431), in a church dedicated to Mary, whose ruins are still visible. At Ephesus, Cyril and his supporters, who favored the title of *Theotokos* and disliked the two-nature view that they attributed to Nestorius, were victorious. Nestorius was condemned and deposed. Cyril was also deposed but managed to regain his position in Alexandria. Nestorius returned to his monastery in Syria, but as the quarrel grew hotter he spent the last twenty years of his life in exile, part of the time at an oasis in the Egyptian desert.

Most modern scholars agree that Nestorius' enemies distorted his theological views in the heated atmosphere and that he did not hold that Jesus Christ was somehow two distinct beings cohabiting but not united in a single person. But he has forever been identified with such a view. Whatever Nestorius believed, some Christians did believe in a sharp distinction between the divine nature and the human nature in Jesus. They are sometimes called "dyophysites" ("believers in two distinct natures"). After such views were rejected, the theological schools at Edessa, inside the empire, became a center for training Nestorian clergy, especially those who spoke Syriac, Armenian, and Persian. When the Emperor Zeno (476–491) expelled the Nestorian scholars from Edessa in 489, they migrated across the imperial border into Persian territory and settled at Nisibis, where they reestablished their school. The Church of the East, as modern Nestorians prefer to call themselves, emerged as a distinct Christian community, which was self-governing by 410. They developed their own distinctive church discipline. They used Syriac, a Semitic language, in their scriptures, liturgy, and preaching; they organized under a senior bishop called the "Catholicos," who lived in

Persian territory at the city of Seleucis-Ctesiphon; they held their own church councils; they had their own canon law; they had married clergy, including married bishops; and they adopted a theology that emphasized the distinctiveness of the two natures of Christ. Between the sixth and tenth centuries, the Church of the East carried on missionary work to its east. There is evidence of its presence in India, central Asia, and China, where it had a flowering for a time. The Church of the East had no one like Constantine to grant it lasting favor. No state supported it, so it led a precarious existence, dependent on the tolerance of rulers, who included Zoroastrians and Muslims. After the fourteenth century, it declined in numbers and influence, although it has survived to the present in parts of the Middle East, India, and North America (due to emigration).

MONOPHYSITISM

Cyril of Alexandria's victory over Nestorius was not the end of controversy because when he expressed his own views of how the divine and human were linked in Christ, some bishops, monks, and laypeople were attracted to it, and others were repelled by it. Cyril was a skilled, subtle theologian whose views were carefully formulated. The core of what he taught was that before the Word became flesh in Mary's womb, there were certainly two natures, one divine and the other human, and that after the Word became flesh the divine and human natures remained, although united in one person. Some supporters of Cyril went much further. At Constantinople, Eutyches, an elderly abbot, stated a strong, extreme form of the one-nature christology, called "Monophysitism" from Greek words meaning "of one nature." Eutyches declared that there were two natures before but only one nature after the union of the Word and the human flesh. He concluded that the divine nature so completely absorbed the human nature that Christ's body was not consubstantial with the bodies of other human beings. Eutyches and those who agreed with him taught or strongly implied that when Jesus lived, worked, and preached in Palestine, he was simply God in his nature. Nestorius had been accused of keeping the divine and human natures so distinct that Jesus was two beings. Some of Cyril's more zealous followers were accused of so emphasizing the divine nature that Jesus was not a complete or real human being like other human beings.

THE COUNCIL OF CHALCEDON (451)

Cyril died in 444, but Dioscorus, his successor at Alexandria, supported both his predecessor's one-nature theology and his desire to make Alexandria the dominant bishopric in the east. The disagreement over the divine and human natures in Jesus continued to disturb the peace of the eastern churches. The participants in the debate wrote learned treatises on the subject but also denounced, excommunicated, and deposed one another, accompanied sometimes by riots and violence. The position of the emperor was always weighty in such matters. The Emperor Theodosius II was a determined foe of Nestorius and favorable to Cyril's views. But in 450 Theodosius was killed in a fall from his horse. He was succeeded by a general named "Marcian" (450–457), whose position was ratified by a chaste marriage to Theodosius' fifty-one-year-old sister and nun Pulcheria, who had played such a prominent role in the fall of Nestorius. The imperial couple summoned a council that met at Chalcedon (451), across the Bosporus from Constantinople, to take up the issue of how the divine and human natures were related in Jesus.

The Council of Chalcedon, held in the huge church of the martyr St. Euphemia, was the largest council in the ancient church, with between five hundred and six hundred bishops in attendance. All were easterners except for two bishops fleeing from persecution in Vandal-controlled North Africa and four representatives of Pope Leo I the Great (440–461). Until the 380s, the bishops of Rome had not been important participants in the theological debates in the east. That changed in the later fourth and fifth centuries with a succession of vigorous bishops of Rome, none more active than Leo I, who had an exceptionally long papacy of about twenty years. Although Leo was not at the Council of Chalcedon, he was a major influence. He composed a document (Letter 28),

called the *Tome of Leo*, which laid out the western view of the relation of the divine and human in Jesus. He asserted his right to teach the eastern churches because he was the successor of Peter and Paul. After some debate, his *Tome* was accepted as the basis for the theological statement, called a "Definition," which the bishops at Chalcedon adopted. The Chalcedonian Definition of Faith is long, but the crucial portion that dealt with the nature of the God/Man runs as follows: "Following the holy Fathers, we teach with one voice that the Son [of God] and our Lord Jesus Christ is to be confessed to be as one and the same [Person], that he is perfect in Godhead and perfect in manhood, truly God and truly man, consisting of a reasonable soul and [human] body, consubstantial with the Father as touching his Godhead, and consubstantial with us as touching his manhood; made in all things like us, sin only excepted; begotten of his Father before the ages according to his Godhead; but in these last days for us men and for our salvation born [into the world] of the Virgin Mary, the Mother of God [*Theotokos*] according to his manhood. This one and the same Jesus Christ, the only-begotten Son [of God], must be confessed to be in two natures, unconfusedly, immutably, indivisibly, distinctly, inseparably [united], and that without the distinction of natures being taken away by such union, but rather the special property of each nature being preserved and being united in one Person and subsistence, not separated or divided into two persons, but one and the same Son and only-begotten, God the Word, our Lord Jesus Christ, as the Prophets of old times have spoken concerning him, and as the Lord Jesus Christ taught us, and as the Creed of the Fathers has delivered to us" (The Definition of Faith of the Council of Chalcedon [451], in NPNF, second series, vol. 14, pp. 264–265, altered). The insistence that Jesus was one person was anti-Nestorian, and the insistence that he remained both divine and human after the incarnation was anti-Monophysite. Many believed that if Jesus was a true redeemer, he had to be fully divine and fully human. The Definition of Chalcedon was central to the history of later Christian theology because it defined the doctrine of the incarnation, literally the "enfleshing" of God's Word in a man.

The council also had other consequences for contemporaries and later generations. Some accepted its theology, and others rejected it as too much like Nestorianism with its talk of two natures in Christ. The continuing debate over Jesus' nature stirred up not only bishops but also many ordinary clergy, monks, and laypeople. Both sides were noisy, often uncompromising, and sometimes violent. Like their predecessors since Constantine, the emperors of the later fifth and sixth centuries wanted to unite the empire around a single theology. They believed that incorrect belief—heresy—angered God, who might withhold his favor. In fact, the empire was threatened on all sides by enemies, including Germanic peoples, Huns in the Balkans, Persians in the east, and, after 632, Arab Muslims in the east and south. The emperors could also see that theological disagreement divided the population of the empire.

The differing reactions to the Definition of Chalcedon also reflect the growing regionalism of the empire. The Latin west, led by the bishops of Rome, generally remained loyal to the christology of Chalcedon, so emperors could not simply reject the council if they hoped to keep the west from slipping into the control of Germanic kings. (That happened anyway.) But many Christians in the east were divided among Nestorians, pro-Chalcedonians, and anti-Chalcedonians. Particularly in the areas such as Egypt and eastern Syria, where Greek was not the ordinary people's language, many would not accept the Chalcedonian view of Christ's nature. Some favored the Nestorian view, but in Egypt and much of the Near East, the Monophysite view attracted a large, fiercely loyal following.

Changes within orthodox Christianity also made the controversy after Chalcedon more volatile and more violent than the theological debates had been during the fourth century. During the Trinitarian Controversy, monasticism was in its formative stage and had played a marginal role. Monks were minor participants. For instance, Bishop Athanasius wrote that the famous hermit Anthony left his desert retreat and came to Alexandria to lend his support to the pro-Nicene view. But by the fifth and sixth centuries, the thousands of monks had become a major force in the church and in society. The monks will be treated more fully in chapter 16. Some monks were pro-Chalcedon and others anti-Chalcedon. They were often spokesmen for the religious views of ordinary people and could mobilize their lay admirers to a degree not seen before. The partisan monks expressed their views loudly and sometimes by violence against those whom they regarded as heretics. The bishops at Chalcedon (canon 4) had tried to prevent monks from participating in the debates and to put them under their control. But the monks remained a source of disorder and violence when they thought serious theological matters were at stake.

For two centuries after the council of Chalcedon, emperors pursued the traditional methods for dealing with theological controversy. Some ordered their subjects to stop talking about the matter—that did not work; some summoned councils; some tried to find a compromise in a set of words that would satisfy all or most; and others deposed and exiled some bishops. Especially after 519, when an anti-Monophysite dynasty of emperors began to rule, imperial policy toward Monophysites became harsher. The Monophysite clergy, monks, and laity who had been inside the church for about seventy years grew embittered and alienated from empire and church. Especially in Egypt and eastern Syria, Monophysites resisted imperial repression and began to organize as a separate church. The most prominent Monophysite church organizer was Bishop Jacob, nicknamed "Baradai" ("the ragged") because he wore a ratty cloak to escape detection by imperial secret police. It is said that from the 520s until his death in 578, he ordained as many as twenty-seven bishops and 100,000 Monophysite clergy. He organized Monophysite churches in Syria, Palestine, and beyond the eastern imperial borders. The "Jacobite" churches, so named for Jacob, were close to the orthodox Chalcedonians in their organization, liturgy, and doctrine, but their serious theological differences over Christ's nature and their bitter political grievances over imperial repression prevented any permanent reconciliation.

When in the 630s and 640s the armies of Islam moved out of Arabia into the Roman territories of Egypt, Palestine, and Syria, the local resistance was modest, in part because the numerous Monophysites and Nestorians probably saw no reason to fight for the Chalcedonian imperial government, which they regarded as repressive and heretical. Islamic armies conquered the regions of the empire where Monophysitism and Nestorianism were strongest. Within what was left of the empire, which by 650 consisted primarily of Greece, Asia Minor, and parts of the west, the Chalcedonian theology of Christ's nature triumphed, just as it did in the Latin west, where Germanic kingdoms had replaced the western Roman Empire.

The Definition of the Council of Chalcedon about Christ's nature and the bitter disputes that followed it split the eastern Christian world permanently. Monophysite churches, often called "Oriental Orthodox churches," which survive to the present day as minorities in Muslim lands, include the Jacobite Churches in Syria, the Coptic Church in Egypt, the church in Ethiopia, and the Armenian Church, which rejected the Council of Chalcedon and its two-nature christology at its Council of Dvin (506). Those churches that accepted the christology of the Council of Chalcedon include the Greek Orthodox Church, the Russian Orthodox Church, Orthodox Churches in the Balkans and elsewhere, and the Roman Catholic Church.

One important historical lesson of the fourth, fifth, and sixth centuries is that even when the government and society were favorable to orthodox Christians, theological unity remained difficult to achieve. The freer conditions under the Christian empire unleashed existing internal tensions rooted in theology, politics, church rivalries, and regional differences. The Christians' tendency to split among themselves over discipline and belief intensified. That has remained true.

FURTHER READING

Ancient Sources

Richard A. Norris Jr., *The Christological Controversy*, ed., trans., in *Sources of Early Christian Thought* (Philadelphia, 1980). An introduction and translated documents about the background to the Council of Chalcedon.

James Stevenson, *Creeds, Councils and Controversies: Documents Illustrative of the History of the Church A.D. 337–461*, ed. revised with additional documents by W. H. C. Frend (London, 1989), especially pp. 287–368, has an excellent collection of documents tracing the God/Man controversy from Nestorius to the Council of Chalcedon.

Modern Works

For an accessible, detailed account of developments after the Council of Chalcedon, see John Meyendorff, *Imperial Unity and Christian Divisions: The Church from 450–680 A.D.* (Crestwood, NY, 1989).

Henry Chadwick, *The Church in Ancient Society: From Galilee to Gregory the Great* (Oxford, 2001), pp. 515–632, provides a richly detailed account of the christological controversies.

W. H. C. Frend, *The Rise of the Monophysite Movement: Chapters in the History of the Church in the Fifth and Sixth Centuries*, second edition (Cambridge, 1979).

J. N. D. Kelly, *Early Christian Doctrines*, revised edition (New York, 1978), especially pp. 310–343, on Nestorianism, Monophysitism, and the Council of Chalcedon.

PART IV

✠

Life in the Christian Empire

Timeline for Later Christianity

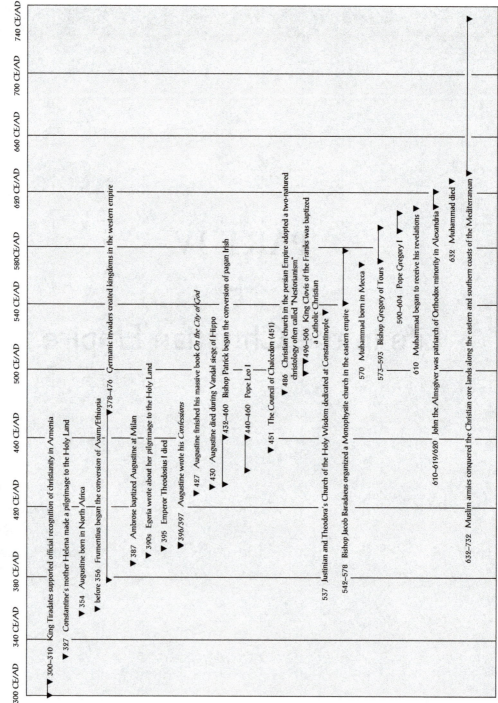

- 300–310 King Tiradates supported official recognition of christianity in Armenia
- ▼ 327 Constantine's mother Helena made a pilgrimage to the Holy Land
- ▼ 354 Augustine born in North Africa
- ▼ before 356 Frumentius began the conversion of Axum/Ethiopia
- ▼ 378–476 Germanic invaders created kingdoms in the western empire
- ▼ 387 Ambrose baptized Augustine at Milan
- ▼ 390s Egeria wrote about her pilgrimage to the Holy Land
- ▼ 395 Emperor Theodosius I died
- ▼ 396/397 Augustine wrote his *Confessions*
- ▼ 427 Augustine finished his massive book *On the City of God*
- ▼ 430 Augustine died during Vandal siege of Hippo
- ▼ 432–460 Bishop Patrick began the conversion of pagan Irish
- ▼ 440–460 Pope Leo I
- ▼ 451 The Council of Chalcedon (451)
- ▼ 486 Christian church in the persian Empire adopted a two-natured christology often called "Nestorianism"
- ▼▼ 496–506 King Clovis of the Franks was baptized a Catholic Christian
- 537 Justinian and Theodora's Church of the Holy Wisdom dedicated at Constantinople
- 542–578 Bishop Jacob Baradaeus organized a Monophysite church in the eastern empire
- ▼ 570 Muhammad born in Mecca
- ▼ 573–593 Bishop Gregory of Tours
- ▼ 590–604 Pope Gregory I
- ▼ 610 Muhammad began to receive his revelations
- ▼ 610–619/620 John the Almsgiver was patriarch of Orthodox minority in Alexandria
- ▼ 632 Muhammad died
- 632–732 Muslim armies conquered the Christian core lands along the eastern and southern coasts of the Mediterranean

| 300 CE/AD | 340 CE/AD | 380 CE/AD | 420 CE/AD | 460 CE/AD | 500 CE/AD | 540 CE/AD | 580CE/AD | 620 CE/AD | 660 CE/AD | 700 CE/AD | 740 CE/AD |

CHAPTER 15

Worship and Piety in the Christian Empire

Between about 300 and 600, the developments within Christian doctrine and practice were remarkably complex. In the bitter theological debates that split the orthodox Christians, passionate believers took sides about the Trinity and about the relation of the divine to the human in Jesus. Many Christians probably could not follow the subtle theological arguments, partly because most of them could not read. But they were moved by theological slogans or by loyalty to the theological views of their local bishop or influential ascetics. Many modern Christians cannot understand the arguments either. There must have been people who were only dimly aware of the theological controversies. Bishop Hilary of Poitiers (353–367) wrote that he had not heard about the Council of Nicaea until the Emperor Constantius exiled him to the east in 356, about thirty years after the event. The doctrinal disputes of those centuries, important as they were, can be overemphasized. If we look beyond the disputes, we can see that in the favorable conditions of the Christian empire, Christian life went on both in well-defined patterns and in new ways. Baptisms, Eucharists, sermons, processions, and the celebration of saints' anniversaries flourished in every corner of the empire. The flow of converts grew until in the late fifth century the orthodox Christians were probably a majority, although pagans, heretics, and Jews survived in significant numbers. Four areas in particular—liturgy, church buildings, the veneration of the holy dead, and pilgrimages—blossomed in the new age of freedom, prosperity, and political/social favor.

LITURGY

"Liturgy" is usually defined as public worship that is carried out in ways that are more or less fixed.

Eucharists, baptisms, ordinations, and religious meals that had developed before the fourth century continued to form the rich, recurring framework of local religious life. Although the main features of the Christian liturgy were similar everywhere, the ceremonies were carried out in small and large ways that differed from region to region. No bishop or emperor had the desire or the power to make the liturgy the same everywhere. But there were slow-working pressures to spread some forms of liturgy at the expense of others. Constantine's conversion opened an era of freer movement for Christians who went on pilgrimages and traveled for personal or church business. Clergy and laypeople who saw that another church did something well might introduce into their own churches such elements as new architectural forms, artistic motifs, and liturgical practices. Important regional churches became powerful forces in defining liturgical practices within their spheres of influence. Over time, the regional liturgies became more fixed and were often named for prestigious figures in the history of the dominant church, such as the liturgy of St. Peter at Rome, the liturgy of St. James at Jerusalem, and the liturgy of St. Mark at Alexandria.

As larger congregations gathered in larger churches, the atmosphere of the liturgy changed. The Eucharist illustrates the new situation. Sacred and secular ceremonies, then and now, are usually intended to evoke certain emotions in participants (of course, they are not always successful). A funeral has one effect on participants, a birthday party has a different effect, and a pep rally before a football game has yet another. From the fourth century, many clergy apparently wanted the participants in the Eucharist to feel awe and holy fear. They wanted them to be aware that they were in the presence of a holy, mysterious event. Such ideas had roots in the period before Constantine. Paul had told the Christians at Corinth that some of them were ill and others had died because they ate the bread and drank the cup of the Lord in an unworthy manner (1 Cor 11:27–30). In the early second century, the author of the *Didache* (c. 9) commanded that no unbaptized person be allowed to participate in the Eucharist because Jesus had commanded that holy things not be given to dogs (Mt 7:6). In the early third century, Hippolytus' *Apostolic Tradition* (c. 37) warned that because the Eucharistic bread was the body of Christ, it should be protected from unbelievers and that none of it should be dropped or lost. The stress on the holiness of the Eucharistic bread and wine became more intense. Jerome (letter 114) praised Bishop Theophilus of Alexandria (384–412) for instructing his clergy to treat with reverence the chalices and other objects used in the Eucharist because they were made holy through their association with the body and blood of Christ. From the later third century, the sexual activity of clergy and married laity was regulated because they "handled holy things," especially the Eucharist.

Liturgy is usually conservative. The pre-Constantinian features of participation by the congregation during the Eucharistic liturgy continued. For example, the congregation had a dialogue with the clergyman who was presiding. But by the second half of the fourth century, the atmosphere of drama and awe at the Eucharist (and all liturgical ceremonies) was intensifying. As a general practice, late Roman society used ceremonies to make the importance of people and events visible to onlookers. At the emperor's court, the social and political hierarchy was made visible by such things as titles, distinctive clothing, the position where a person was allowed to march in a procession, and even who could and could not speak to the emperor. Church authorities borrowed from the honors given to the emperor to enhance the worship of the creator of the universe. They and many ordinary believers thought that it was proper that the Eucharist also be honored by ceremony. At a Eucharist, stress was placed increasingly on solemnity and dignity, on art and gestures full of symbolism, on magnificent surroundings, and on elaborate prayers that the congregation saw and heard. Because traditional Eucharistic prayers were beginning to be written down, the clergy had less freedom to improvise prayers. Especially in the east the clergy began to wear special garments—vestments—during the Eucharistic liturgy. Portions of the scriptures were read in the language of the people during each Eucharist. Preachers taught the word of God during the liturgy in sermons, of which about four thousand survive from ancient Christianity. The liturgical ceremonies also educated participants by reenacting before their eyes events important to Christians, such as Jesus' Last Supper with his disciples.

CHURCH BUILDINGS

The elaboration of liturgy and the changing design of church buildings were almost inseparable. In many places, house churches continued in use or were renovated to fit a local congregation's needs. But Constantine's conversion allowed the Christians to construct publicly identifiable churches, which met the needs of larger congregations and impressed on viewers the new status of orthodox Christianity. Emperors provided funds to build and decorate churches on a large and sometimes magnificent scale. The Christians avoided the temple "style" for their own buildings because they hated the temples within which the statues of the gods stood and the animal sacrifices took place. Instead they adopted for their churches the architecture of a common Roman building, called a "basilica," which had few associations with paganism. A basilica was a long hall, usually divided into a central space and side aisles that were set off by rows of columns. At the end of the basilica, opposite the entrance doors, there was a raised platform, often within semicircular niche, called an "apse." In ordinary life, Romans used basilicas for markets, for magistrates to conduct official business, and for judges, plaintiffs, defendants, and lawyers to settle legal cases. The basilica was suited for Christian worship, with its open central space for the congregation and its special place at the front for the clergy to read, pray, preach, and perform the Eucharist at the altar. Perhaps Constantine set the policy of promoting basilicas

Figure 15.1 Basilica of Saint Peter at Rome. Constantine paid for a large basilica-style church to be built on the Vatican Hill over what was believed to be the tomb of Peter. The church had a spacious, highly decorated central space, side aisles, and, at the east end, the area for the altar and the clergy, which was above the cemetery where Peter was thought to be buried. "Old Saint Peter's," as this church is often called, was worn out by the sixteenth century, when it was replaced by the present Saint Peter's. This fresco painting gives a muted view of the Constantinian church. *(Scala / Art Resource, NY)*

as the architecture for the buildings of his new religion, but in any case the basilica became the ordinary form that a newly built church took. The Basilica of St. John Lateran at Rome, whose construction probably began soon after Constantine's victory at the Milvian Bridge (312), could hold as many as three thousand people. Because it housed the Roman bishop's chair—his *cathedra*— it was the city's cathedral. St. John Lateran was an impressive building, 312 feet long, 180 feet wide. and 98 feet high. But the largest church built by

Constantine was Old St. Peter's at Rome (which was replaced in the sixteenth century by the present St. Peter's). Constantine's basilica on the Vatican hill was a huge martyr-church built over the place where Peter's tomb was thought to be. Constantine and his mother Helena and then his sons paid out of public funds for other basilicas to be built at important Christian sites, including the Holy Sepulcher (Jesus' burial place) in Jerusalem, the Cave of the Nativity in Bethlehem, and the grave of Paul at Rome. The basilica-style church

Figure 15.2 Bishop Ambrose of Milan (374–397). In the Church of Saint Ambrose (San Ambroggio) in Milan there is a mosaic, probably made within a few decades of Ambrose's death. In the mosaic, he is dressed in his bishop's garb and stares out at church-goers and pilgrims. *(Scala / Art Resource, NY)*

did not quite have a monopoly on church architecture. At Jerusalem, the Martyrium, a church in the group of buildings that surrounded the Holy Sepulcher, was round in shape. Some pilgrims to Jerusalem, including bishops and rich lay men and women, imitated the round structure in some churches they built.

The setting of the Eucharistic liturgy was enhanced by the decoration of church interiors that reinforced the growing sense of awe that worshippers were expected to feel during the liturgy. The churches' exteriors were usually plain, but the interiors were as artistically magnificent as the patrons, church leaders, and members could afford to make them. In the churches that have survived to modern times without too much damage or remodeling, primarily at Rome and Ravenna, we can still see the marble and other expensive stone used for walls,

columns, and floors, and the frescoes, the mosaics, and the metalwork. What we usually can no longer see are the moveable items that were once there but have been looted, confiscated by hostile governments, or disintegrated through sheer age. A few of them, such as expensive candelabra, altar vessels made of gold, veils of valuable cloth, and wall hangings, can now be seen only in museums. The decoration reinforced the worshippers' sense that they were in the presence of something holy. The *Book of the Popes (Liber Pontificalis)*, a complex history of the popes from Peter to Pius II (1464), perhaps fictionalized in its early parts, listed an amazing inventory of precious goods supposedly given by Constantine to the Basilica of St. John Lateran at Rome. In the account of Pope Silvester (314–335), the *Book* reported that Constantine gave hundreds of pounds of gold, silver, and gems to make candelabra, lamps, altars, altar vessels, candlesticks, and representations of Christ and the apostles. The *Book* gives an insight into what its authors thought a church's interior decoration should look like. Whether or not Constantine actually gave the gifts, emperors, empresses, and aristocrats certainly did endow churches with fine objects.

Architecture also began to emphasize the importance of the clergy who carried out the Eucharist. The front portion of the churches—the apse or sanctuary where the altar and the seats of the presbyters and bishop were placed—began to be reserved for clergy. Laypeople were not allowed there. In some churches, low railings or curtains separated the sanctuary from the main portion of the church where the ordinary worshippers gathered. The tendency to instill holy awe by artistic and architectural choices culminated late in antiquity in the huge, important church of Hagia Sophia ("Holy Wisdom") built by the Emperor Justinian (528–565) in Constantinople. In front of Hagia Sophia's altar, there was a magnificent curtain on which there was a picture of Christ blessing the worshippers with his right hand and holding a gospel book in his left hand. Between the clergy's sanctuary and the ordinary worshipper's nave, there was also a wall, called an "iconostasis," decorated with icons (painted images) of angels and prophets, along with symbols of the builders,

Figure 15.3 The Baptistery of St. John Lateran in Rome (Fifth Century). Many churches had a separate building for baptisms. The baptistery of St. John Lateran is not a basilica but rather a six-sided building. The plain exterior is typical of ancient churches. The builders reserved for the interior the exuberance of marble and fine wood, liturgical vessels and altar fronts made of gold or silver, and the rich cloth hangings. To walk from the drab outside to the stunning inside was sometimes described as a foretaste of heaven's magnificence. (*Scala / Art Resource*)

the Emperor Justinian and his wife Theodora. There were three doors in the iconostasis that could be opened at some times but closed when the most sacred parts of the Eucharistic liturgy took place. The laity could not see the sacred mystery, although they could hear the prayers of the clergy recited in Greek. Hagia Sophia's iconostasis was imitated in churches throughout the Greek east and became a necessary part of every Byzantine church. The western churches were slower in elaborating the surroundings of

the Eucharistic liturgy, but they also followed the same general path.

Already at the third-century house church at Dura-Europas, a room was set aside for baptism, perhaps to provide privacy for the adults, who were baptized naked. The tendency to build a separate baptistery, as such a building is called, in or near the church grew. There is evidence of about four hundred baptisteries built between the fourth and seventh centuries in all sorts of shapes, although round and octagonal buildings were common.

The words "church building" might suggest to us a single, free-standing structure. But important churches from the fourth century onward were often church compounds, with a church, residences for some clergy and the bishop, a separate building for baptisms, a building to store food and clothing for distribution to the poor, and a resting place for travelers and the ill. As the Christian church became more central to Greco-Roman society, its important buildings became more prominent.

CHRISTIAN TIME: THE LITURGICAL CALENDAR

When religious celebrations occur in a regular cycle they are often imagined as a liturgical or religious calendar. In the pre-Christian Roman Empire, much of social life had been shaped by recurring religious festivals that honored such things as local gods and the emperor's birthday. Depending on the occasion, there might be the sacrificing of animals and the making of vows, but also feasting, dancing, and gladiatorial games. The Jews also had festivals that recurred every year and could be boisterous public events in the Greco-Roman cities where they lived. Some Christians participated in the religious celebrations of their pagan and Jewish neighbors. About 400, John Chrysostom noted that the Jews of Antioch took over the city's public square for their celebrations, which included dancing. He and other strict bishops were troubled that Christians joined in the religious fun of the Jews and of their pagan neighbors but apparently could not stop it.

Christian leaders gradually developed their own liturgical calendar, which varied from place to place but had a recognizable structure. They "Christianized" time, so that their religious universe had its own special days, seasons, fasts, and festivals. The creation of a Christian liturgical calendar was slow. But from early times its structure was visible. It had a weekly aspect. Christians gathered every Sunday for scripture reading, preaching, and Eucharist. They fasted on certain days of the week and at certain seasons. The Christian calendar also had an annual aspect. In the second cen-

tury, churches began to record the day on which martyrs died and to observe that day each year, sometimes with boisterous celebrations in church and out of doors that involved music, dancing, wine, and food that rivaled those of the religious celebrations of pagans and Jews. Some bishops did not approve of the fun but usually could not stop people from celebrating the local Christian heroes. The devotees of a saint visited his or her burial place, over which they built shrines and churches. Sometimes only the name of a martyr and the date of his or her death survived, but at other times there were written accounts, some reliable and others fictionalized, that were read in private and in public, even in church on the anniversary day of the martyr's heavenly rebirth. The saints' festivals may have substituted for the public celebrations in the pagan and Jewish religious calendars that still had appeal for many late ancient Christians.

Easter was the most important annual festival in the Christian liturgical calendar. By the second century, some were commemorating the anniversary of Christ's resurrection on a Sunday, which they called in Greek "Pascha," and others were celebrating it on the fourteenth of the Jewish month Nisan, whatever day of the week it was. The Council of Nicaea (325) established a uniform way of calculating the date of Easter. It was to be celebrated on the Sunday that followed the first full moon that fell on or after the vernal equinox, which was fixed for calculation purposes at March 21 (Eusebius, *Life of Constantine*, 3.18). By the fourth century, Christians observed a period of fasting in preparation for Easter. In the east, the fast lasted seven days and in the west, forty days. During one of his exiles to the west, Athanasius was impressed by the forty-day fast and introduced it when he was restored as bishop of Alexandria. By the second quarter of the fourth century, Christians were marking Christ's birth, on 25 December in the west and on 6 January in the east. Christ's ascension (forty days after Easter) and the sending of the Spirit at Pentecost (fifty days after Easter) were also incorporated into the calendar.

The liturgical and architectural practices at Jerusalem had a major influence across the church.

A woman from western Spain or Gaul, whose name was probably "Egeria," participated in the well-developed Easter observances at Jerusalem between 381 and 383. She loved liturgy and recorded what she saw and heard. Jerusalem was a special place for reenacting the events of Jesus' life. Pilgrims and local inhabitants thought they were looking at or standing in the actual places where the events had originally occurred. At Jerusalem, Egeria participated in the eight-week period of fasting and preparation for Easter. The most religiously and liturgically intense week was the eighth, called the "Great Week," which culminated on Easter Sunday. The Jerusalem clergy were kept busy by the liturgy of the Great Week. Many of the local faithful and the pilgrims must have devoted the entire week to the frequent, long, and exhausting but, according to Egeria, exhilarating services. She recorded enthusiastic crowds that joined in all-night vigils, heard extensive reading from the gospel accounts of Jesus' last days, and joined processions to the places where the faithful believed the final events in Jesus' life had occurred. She noted that the crowds were vocal, at one point moaning and groaning as a priest read Matthew's account of Jesus' sufferings and death. She mentioned in some detail the preaching to and exorcisms of the catechumens who were to be baptized at dawn on Easter. Jerusalem's resident Christians were multilingual (Greek and Aramaic). In addition, Latin-speaking pilgrims from the west were common. Egeria noted in passing that the liturgical services, including scripture reading and preaching, were in Greek, but there were translators to help the local Aramaic speakers and the Latin-speaking visitors.

The liturgy of fourth- and fifth-century Jerusalem is well documented, but in all churches, the period before Easter was the high point of the Christian liturgical calendar. The oldest surviving Christian calendar, *The Calendar of 354*, reflected the situation at Rome, where Christian and pagan arrangements of time still co-existed in the fourth century. The *Calendar* recorded the dates on which the Roman bishops and martyrs had been buried. It listed the Roman bishops from Peter to Liberius (352–366). It included a document for determining the date of Easter. But there were also lists of Roman consuls, the dates of pagan festivals, brief histories of Rome, and other information that was not specifically Christian.

There were recurring liturgical events that were more restrained than the public celebrations of the saints. Some churches had daily prayers in the morning and in the evening, attended by the clergy, some ordinary Christians, and especially by the growing number of ascetic men and women. Some public religious activities were firmly under the control of the clergy, such as the Sunday Eucharist. Other liturgical activities had a more popular tone, such as public processions and the celebrations of the saints' anniversaries. But everywhere believers' lives were shaped more and more by Christianized time recorded in a liturgical calendar that marked out times for fasting, mourning, rejoicing, processions, Eucharists, baptisms, and much more.

THE HOLY DEAD

Christianity was about people as well as about liturgy, buildings, beautiful objects, and the Christianizing of time. The apostles, martyrs, and ascetics had their place within the Christian "geography" of the universe. Christians generally did not doubt that the apostles and martyrs were still alive: They had been reborn on the day they died, which was called their "birthday" (*dies natalis*). Few doubted that the apostles and martyrs were God's friends and were in the upper realm of the universe, heaven, with God. Even in heaven they continued to be interested in their fellow Christians on Earth. The image that predominated was that of a royal court—the emperor's court perhaps—in which God's friends asked him to grant favors to the people for whom they interceded.

When the holy men and women died, their spiritual part, the soul, ascended to heaven. Their physical bodies remained behind, which is what the word "relic" means, "that which is left behind." The spiritual and the physical aspects of people would be united again at the resurrection of the dead. To many modern Western people, corpses and disconnected human bones are frightening or repellent or creepy. Some fourth- and fifth-century people felt the same way. Pagans and Jews avoided dead bodies because they were thought to pollute people and things near them. To avoid pollution, pagan legislation forbade the burial of the dead within a city's sacred boundary, called the *pomerium*. Roman law forbade the disturbance of graves and the moving of corpses. Christians had a different, positive view of the holy dead that changed the traditional geography that separated the living and the dead. Christians brought the bodies of the holy dead within the cities, often accompanied by crowds moved by the spectacle. They placed them in churches in which or near which other Christians sought to be buried. The physical remains of the holy men and women, their relics, were no longer feared but rather were respected, held in awe, and sought out as a strong focal point where the holy person could be asked to intercede with God. Christians believed that the remains of the holy dead did not pollute; they sanctified. In ancient Christianity, there was no official procedure for what was later called "canonization." A dead person was holy—which is what "saint" means—if enough people believed that he or she was holy and especially if the local bishop agreed to have the holy person's name read out during the liturgy. The eagerness for relics was satisfied in part by discoveries, called "inventions" (from a Latin word meaning to "find"). Of course, the word did not mean to "make up" or "create." When the remains of a saint were found, they were often "translated," that is, moved, to a place more suitable for veneration, such as a shrine or church. The discovery and translation of a saint were an occasion for great rejoicing, especially when accompanied by events that the participants interpreted as miracles. The demand for relics was so great that saints' bodies were dismembered and pieces sent sometimes as a sort of religious diplomacy or a generous gift to other churches and individuals.

There were critics of the veneration of the saints. When Bishop Augustine of Hippo was asked if there was any reason to be buried near a holy man or woman, he replied that it comforted the survivors but gave no advantage to the dead person. At least one Christian writer objected to the forms that the cult of the saints was taking in the fourth century. His criticisms and the response of his critic, Jerome, tell us what the

activities at a martyr's shrine looked like in about 400. Vigilantius, a priest from southwestern Gaul, had visited Jerome in Bethlehem in 395, but they did not like one another. In about 404, Vigilantius wrote a pamphlet criticizing developments in piety that were taking root in southern Gaul. Jerome responded in *Against Vigilantius*, which he boasted that he had written in one night. According to Jerome's counterattack, Vigilantius criticized the veneration of martyrs' relics, which he called "dust covered in costly veils." He disapproved of lighting candles at the shrines during daylight hours. He thought that some miracles claimed at martyrs' shrines were fraudulent. He approved of the traditional all-night vigil that proceeded Easter dawn, but he did not like the multiplication of new vigils that were being held at martyrs' shrines. He did not believe that the dead martyrs and apostles could intervene for living people. They were, he wrote, held in a kind of honorable confinement until Judgment Day. Jerome rejected Vigilantius' criticism and sketched out what was to become the standard defense of venerating the relics of the holy dead. He responded that the honor given to relics was not intended for them but rather for God, for whom the martyrs had shed their blood. God chose to work miracles through the martyrs' remains, but they were God's miracles. Jerome granted that candles in the daytime and all-night vigils could be abused, but if they were used in an appropriate spirit, they did no harm. Vigilantius, who had some supporters in Gaul, could not impede the rising prominence of the martyrs' cult in the Christian empire.

Probably the most important discovery of a relic in late antiquity was that of the True Cross, which took place in the fourth century. It is difficult to sort out legend from fact. The discovery is linked to Helena, Constantine's mother, but the earliest references to that link were written more than sixty years after her death. But from the 350s, Christians believed that she had found and they still had the wood of the cross, the nails that held Jesus to the cross, and the piece of wood on which was written the inscription that had been placed over his head. In the early 380s, the pilgrim Egeria saw how the wood of the cross was venerated at Jerusalem. On Friday of the Great Week, the bishop of Jerusalem sat on his chair at Golgotha, the site of the crucifixion, with a table covered with white linen in front of him. A gilded box containing the wood of the cross and the inscription was brought out and opened. The piece of wood and the inscription were placed on the table. The baptized and the catechumens came forward to venerate them. They observed a ritual of touching the objects with their foreheads and then kissing them. No one was allowed to touch the objects with their hands. The bishop held the wood firmly with both hands, and deacons vigilantly watched the table because someone once tried to bite off a piece of the cross when he kissed it.

By the fifth century, the martyrs were still venerated, but they were figures of a distant age, just as medieval knights are in our time. The contemporary ascetics (hermits, monks, and nuns), growing in numbers and in religious importance, provided a new pool of living (and eventually dead) holy men and women. Not all ascetics attracted disciples or admirers, but some did. People of all social classes sought ascetics' help to deal with or escape from the woes of human life. Visitors to the ascetics sought cures for themselves and their children. But they also consulted the ascetics for advice on all sorts of matters, including protection from tax collectors, marriage counseling, and exorcisms to expel the ever-present demons. There was a widespread view that when such revered holy men and women died, they joined the apostles and martyrs in heaven, where they could also intercede for those who sought their help. Their physical remains were honored as those of the martyrs were. One example of out many will be useful. Daniel (409–493) joined a monastery at age twelve and stayed for twenty-five years. Then for five years he traveled to the "fathers," that is, revered ascetics. When he was forty-two he came to Constantinople, where he lived in a church for nine years, standing on a column indoors. Then he became a true stylite ("pillar dweller"), living on three outdoor columns where he stood and sat for thirty-three years and three months. He gave advice to visitors; emperors climbed a ladder to speak to him about foreign policy; and he exorcised demons. In short, he was a powerful charismatic figure in the life of the empire's capital. When he died on

11 December 493, at age eighty-four, his burial was a major event, a concern for all classes from the Emperor Anastasius (491–518) to the urban poor of Constantinople. A rich female admirer, Herais, who believed that Daniel's intercession had enabled her to give birth to a child, provided for his funeral. She also contributed gold to be distributed to the poor. His biographer wrote that the scaffolding to bring him down from the pillar was adorned with thousands of candles. A large crowd gathered to witness the descent of Daniel's body. When the crowd demanded to see the body, he was attached to a wooden plank and lifted so as to be seen for several hours. To prevent the crowd from grabbing for relics, Daniel was brought down in a lead coffin, provided by Herais. The crowd rushed forward, and the coffin-bearers dropped their load. But Daniel was successfully brought into an oratory and buried beneath relics of other saints. Contemporaries thought that he continued to exercise power even from his grave.

As more holy people populated heaven, their veneration on Earth grew. In a complex system or non-system, saints ranged from a holy person honored in just one place to universally honored saints such as apostles, prominent martyrs, and the Virgin Mary. Bishops and theologians tried to regulate some aspects of the veneration of the saints, but they and less-educated people believed in the reality and the power of the holy dead, God's friends.

Pilgrimage

Many religions encourage travel to places regarded as especially holy. That practice continues in the modern world, where, for instance, an estimated two million Muslims make a pilgrimage to Mecca each year. Tourists and pilgrims might seem to be the same, but they can be distinguished. A tourist is a person who goes to a traditionally holy site, such as Jerusalem or the Temple of Athena at Athens, to satisfy curiosity but not to seek the holiness that believers find there. A pilgrim is a person who goes to a traditionally holy site for a religious purpose, such as to fulfill a vow, seek a favor, obey a divine command, or pray. Through their reading of the Old Testament and their experience of contemporary Jews, Christians knew that the

Jews had a tradition of pilgrimage to Jerusalem. In Deuteronomy 16:16, God commanded all Jewish men to appear before him three times each year: on the festival of the unleavened bread, the festival of weeks, and the festival of tabernacles. Many Jews who lived outside Palestine in the Diaspora came to Jerusalem on an important feast day, perhaps once in a lifetime. After the rebellion led by Simon bar Kochba (132–135), the Jewish pilgrimage was impossible for centuries because Jews were prohibited from living in Jerusalem. But the yearning for pilgrimage remained strong.

The Christian pilgrimage to Jerusalem and the surrounding Holy Land had a special history. The Old and New Testaments were full of references to concrete places in the landscape such as rivers, mountains, tombs, battle sites, and towns. The people of the Old Testament—lawgivers, kings, prophets, saints, and sinners—whom the Christians regarded as their predecessors lived, died, and were buried in that landscape. Jesus and his followers had lived in places that had names and could in many cases still be pointed out in the fourth century. You might think that Christians had always wanted to go to see the places where Jesus had lived and died. But that was not true until the fourth century. Christians had no religious command to go on pilgrimage. Before the fourth century, Christians apparently had no sense that certain places were holier than other places. Only a few Christian pilgrims went to Palestine, either for scholarly or religious purposes. As a practical matter the "holy land" had almost no importance in Christian thinking before the fourth century. The place was not inviting. The pagan Roman authorities in Palestine made no provision for the religious yearnings of Jews or Christians. In fact, Roman policy was to blot out the associations of Jerusalem with Judaism in order to discourage further rebellions. In Jewish eyes, the site of the Temple had been polluted by statues and altars dedicated to the Emperor Hadrian and the God Jupiter. There were probably local Christians who knew oral traditions about their holy sites, but in 300 the sites were not marked by any significant Christian buildings. For instance, a temple to Venus stood on the spot where Christians believed that Jesus had been crucified.

Constantine's conversion changed the situation for Christians, although it did not open the way for Jews to make their pilgrimages to Jerusalem. As a consequence of the generous building program of Constantine and his mother Helena, the scattered and often unmarked places were reshaped into a coherent "holy land," roughly modern Israel, the Egyptian Sinai, and the Palestinian West Bank. Constantine and his successors identified as best they could and adorned the sites of the great events in the life of Jesus. They sponsored or approved digging at places where oral accounts said the sacred sites were. The imperial family built fine churches and extensive church compounds at the sites identified correctly or incorrectly with biblical events and people. In about 327, Constantine's mother Helena made a long pilgrimage to Palestine. As was fitting for an empress she performed traditional acts of charity such as giving lavishly to the poor and freeing prisoners. In Palestine, she endowed churches at Bethlehem and on the Mount of Olives. The pilgrimage of such an important person must have publicized for the rest of the empire the significance of the emerging "holy land." Between about 330 and 360, the holy sites of the Old Testament and the New Testament merged into a "holy land" marked out by impressive buildings, rich liturgical activities, and settlements of clergy, nuns, monks, and hermits. The growing number of pilgrims could follow an itinerary from one church or grave to another. Industries developed to feed, house, protect, and guide the pilgrims—and get their money. Holy places in the Holy Land became magnets for pilgrims who wanted to see, touch, and pray in them. What made the Holy Land special was that when the local liturgy commemorated something in the Christian calendar, for example, Jesus' birth, the participants could stand in the church built over the very cave where they believed Jesus had been born.

When an anonymous pilgrim from Bordeaux in modern France wrote an account of a pilgrimage in about 333, the long tradition of pilgrims telling about their journey to the Holy Land began (think of the modern slide shows given by pilgrims in living rooms and church basements!). About sixty years later, Egeria, who told us so much about the Great

Week at Jerusalem, also provided an account of the well-developed pilgrim routes in the east. She was on pilgrimage for about three years, which must have been expensive. In dangerous places she had escorts of Roman soldiers, which perhaps indicates that she was of high birth. The center of her interest was the "holy land," but she visited living ascetics and saints' shrines in Egypt, modern Turkey, and Jordan. She met many bishops, clergy, and monks. If you read only her account, you might think that no one but clergy and ascetics populated the Near East—but that was what interested Egeria. Not only was there a well-developed path for pilgrims to follow in the Holy Land, but also there were special ways for pilgrims to act. When Egeria and her companions reached any holy site, they read aloud the passages from the Old or New Testaments that related to that place. They then prayed and often had a priest celebrate the Eucharist there. The biblical readings and the Eucharist reminded the pilgrims of why they were there.

Some strict moralists were critical of pilgrimages and of the motives and behavior of some pilgrims. Bishop Gregory of Nyssa (died in 395) had made a pilgrimage to the Holy Land in 381 and wrote that he was spiritually moved. But he also wrote a letter in which he stated the theological arguments against pilgrimages. He wrote that because God is everywhere there is no need to go to Jerusalem or anywhere else for a special encounter with him. But such criticism made no serious dent in the desire of many Christians to see and to pray at the places where Moses, the Hebrew prophets, Jesus, Mary, and the apostles had lived and carried out their role in God's plan. A long pilgrimage was not a light undertaking. It was a temporary break with ordinary life and was viewed as an opportunity for ascetic withdrawal and self-denial. Some pilgrims died on the long journeys.

The pilgrimage to the Holy Land was the deluxe model, expensive in the pilgrim's money and in time. Pilgrims went in growing numbers not only to the Holy Land but also to all sorts of places they regarded as particularly holy. Many Christians thought that to gain a saint's intercession, they ought to go to a place where his or her relics were. Many pilgrims undertook the less demanding journey to the shrines of local saints or to the major feasts at important churches, especially the annual commemoration of the day on which a church had been dedicated. For instance, the feast of Peter and Paul in Rome on 29 June drew large crowds each year. Between the fourth and sixth centuries, places that Christians regarded as holy, especially the tombs of apostles, martyrs, and some ascetics, stood out prominently in the mental and physical landscape of Christian society. From a wider point of view, Christians had more or less successfully seized from paganism and Judaism sacred time and sacred space.

FURTHER READING

Ancient Sources

Raymond Davis, trans., *The Book of the Pontiffs (Liber Pontificalis)*, an introduction by the translator, Translated Texts for Historians, Latin Series V (Liverpool, 1989). Biographies of the first ninety Roman bishops to 715.

Elizabeth Dawes and Norman H. Baynes trans., *The Life and Works of Our Holy Father, St. Daniel the Stylite*, in *Three Byzantine Saints* (Oxford, 1948), pp. 7–84. A vivid portrayal of the physical sufferings, theological views, and day-to-day influence of a stylite.

George E. Gingras, trans., On the "Great Week" at Jerusalem, see *Egeria, Diary of a Pilgrimage*, the trans., annotated by ACW 38 (New York and Ramsey, NJ, 1970), chapters 24–39, pp. 89–116, and the notes on pp. 215–243. Egeria's entire account is worth reading for the vivid light it throws on fourth- and fifth-century pilgrimage, worship, and piety.

Modern Works

On pilgrimage to the Holy Land, see E. D. Hunt, *Holy Land Pilgrimage in the Later Roman Empire A.D. 312–460* (Oxford, 1982). John Wilkinson, *Jerusalem Pilgrims before the Crusades* (Warminster, England, 2002), has a fine collection of translated pilgrims' accounts and guidebooks to the Holy Land. On church architecture, see L. Michael White, *The Social Origins of Christian Architecture*, vol. 1 (Valley Forge, PA, 1990), especially pp. 102–139.

Gregory T. Armstrong, "Basilica," in *Encyclopedia of Early Christianity*, second edition 1997), pp. 172–176, on the preferred form of church architecture after the fourth century.

Peter Brown, *The Cult of the Saints: Its Rise and Function in Latin Christianity* (Chicago, 1981). An illuminating inquiry into the social realities that supported the cult of the saints.

Hippolyte Delehaye, *The Legends of the Saints*, translated by Donald Attwater (New York, 1962). Although written a century ago, this remains a useful introduction to the details of the cult of saints. Be sure to use the Attwater translation.

Robert Wilkins, *The Land Called Holy: Palestine in Christian History and Thought* (New Haven, 1992), on the emergence of the Holy Land as a focus of Christian attention.

CHAPTER 16

The Ascetic Movement

As if the unfolding Christian empire, the growing institutionalization of the church, and the simultaneous internal theological quarrels were not enough, there was another important development between the third and sixth centuries: the emergence of asceticism as a religious ideal and of ascetics as people of influence. Sometimes societies are transformed by long-lasting movements that cross lines of religion and social status. For instance, in the modern world, one such transformation (still going on) has been the rise of "fundamentalism," which is an attitude that can be adopted in many religions. Religious fundamentalists often reject what they regard as contemporary religious compromises and lukewarmness. They want to return to a pure, uncompromised past, whether that past is real or imagined. In America, the term "Christian fundamentalist" is familiar, but on a global scale there has also been a growth of fundamentalism among such diverse religious groups as Jews, Muslims, and Hindus. If such a movement lasts long enough and penetrates deep enough into society, it can undermine or transform old ways.

The ancient world experienced a profound religious transformation that I am going to call the "ascetic movement." The Roman Empire was a complex place in which the search for pleasure and a zest for life were strong. Modern novelists and filmmakers have made fortunes depicting those aspects of Greco-Roman life—think of those films with orgies! But between the first and the sixth centuries, many in the Roman Empire embraced a different attitude when they turned away from the flesh and toward the spirit. Some people experienced a growing distaste for the material world of ambition, money, property, family, violence, and sexuality. The ascetic movement was broader

than any particular religion, although it influenced Jews, pagans, and Christians in varying degrees. The Greeks, who loved athletic competition, used the word *askesis* to refer to the demanding training that an athlete had to endure in order to gain the sign of victory, often a crown of leaves, comparable with the modern Olympic gold medal. The image of the athlete in intense training appealed to many who struggled to escape the world, to embrace the spiritual, to abandon life's pleasures, and to reject ordinary values such as wealth and success. The person who embraced a life of self-denial was also an "ascetic," an athlete in a spiritual struggle.

Jews observed ascetic practices in such things as sexual behavior and diet, especially fasting. Some Jews adopted an asceticism that was stricter than that of ordinary co-believers. For instance, the Nazirites (Num 6:1–21) took a vow that they would temporarily or permanently abstain from wine and grape products, would avoid pollution from contact with the dead, and would not cut their hair during the period of their vow. Luke reported that Paul took a temporary Nazirite vow (Acts 21:23–24). Within Judaism, world-denying asceticism that included permanent celibacy was rare and survived only for a while. For instance, the Jewish sect of the Essenes had a community near the Dead Sea at Qumran, where men pooled their property and sought strict separation from outsiders through celibacy, fasting, prayer, and scriptural study. The Romans destroyed that community in 70. The Jewish scholar Philo of Alexandria (20 BCE–50 CE) reported that in Egypt there were Jewish ascetics, the Therapeutae, who were celibate men and women living in a community, fasting severely, and studying the scriptures. In general, however, the ascetic movement of the Greco-Roman

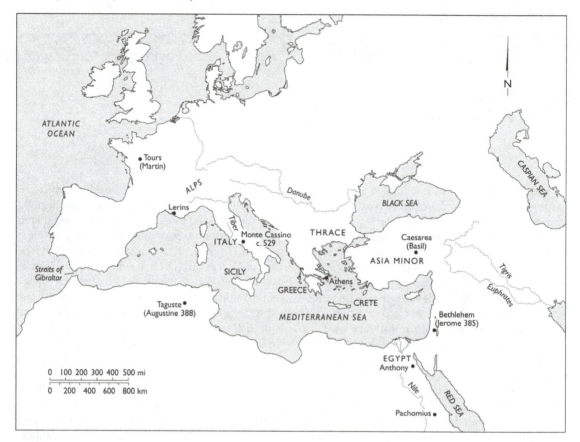

Figure 16.1 Major Centers of Monastic Influence to about 540. Hermits and communities of monks and nuns proliferated between the fourth and sixth centuries. A detailed map of all known monastic sites in 500 would be very crowded. However, some monasteries stood out because they influenced wide circles of ascetics and led to monastic foundations that imitated them.

world did not influence Judaism much, especially the demand for celibacy, which seemed to be discouraged by God's first direct command in Genesis, "Be fruitful and multiply" (Gen 1:28). As a practical matter, when Roman law restricted Judaism's opportunities to make converts, the need to perpetuate the religion through the begetting of children discouraged celibacy as an ascetic practice, although fasting remained important.

Asceticism found favorable ground in some types of Greco-Roman philosophy. Some philosophers recommended that their followers minimize the physical aspects of their lives and seek their "true" selves, which they thought were spiritual rather than material. To achieve a more spiri-

tual life, some pagan philosophers recommended ascetic attitudes and practices. The followers of Plato were often suspicious of the body and its desires. They recommended ways to minimize or escape the body's pull toward pleasure. The neo-Platonist Porphyry (234–about 305), who was a distinguished philosopher and an outspoken critic of Christianity, wrote a biography of his teacher Plotinus (205–270), an important neo-Platonic philosopher. The opening line of Porphyry's biography of Plotinus set the ascetic tone: "Plotinus, the philosopher of our times, seemed ashamed of being in the body" (Porphyry, *On the Life of Plotinus and the Order of His Books*, c.1, in *Plotinus*, with an English translation by A. H. Armstrong, LCL 440

[Cambridge, MA, and London, 1966], p. 3). Porphyry described his teacher Plotinus as an ideal philosopher, always contemplating high philosophical matters and detached from worldly cares. His unhappiness with bodily existence expressed itself in many ways. Upper-class Romans and Greeks in the second and third centuries loved to commission paintings and sculpted busts of themselves, but Plotinus refused to sit for a painter or sculptor because he saw no point in making a copy of his body, which was a mere container for his true self. Plotinus refused to talk about such worldly things as his country of origin, his parents, or the date and year of his birth. He was a vegetarian who minimized his sleep and his intake of food. He avoided that Greco-Roman pleasure, the baths. In line with his view that material life was distracting to the true philosopher, he encouraged his disciples to withdraw from the cares of public service and public office. One disciple, a senator named "Rogatianus," "advanced so far in renunciation of public life that he gave up all his property, dismissed all his servants, and resigned his rank" (Porphyry, *On the Life of Plotinus*, c. 7, in *Plotinus*, p. 27). To put things in perspective, Plotinus' asceticism was moderate in its physical demands. He lived among the highest circles of cultivated pagan intellectuals. He had wealthy upper-class disciples, some of whom studied with him for decades. He taught in their fine urban houses and country villas. He did not practice the rough, harsh ascetic life of later Christian hermits who lived in a hut in the desert, wore one filthy garment, ate crude bread, and drank only water. But even though Plotinus and the Christian monk would probably have disapproved of one another, each in his way participated in the broad ascetic movement of the later Roman Empire.

Christians did not invent asceticism and were not the only group that practiced it, but many of them eagerly embraced and intensified the ascetic tendencies of the world around them. They liked the athletic image of *askesis*, of actively shaping one's life and mind for spiritual perfection. But they transformed the athletic image from that of an actual athlete lifting weights or running to that of a believer striving for salvation. Paul used the image of the athlete striving for a crown to describe the effort required of believers, including himself

(1 Cor 9:24–27). Christians regarded martyrs as the perfect ascetics because they had literally died to the world and had received not a perishable but rather an imperishable crown in return for their sacrifice. The urge to reject wealth, family, and sexuality was one strand of Christian opinion that went back to the early days. In Paul's letters, in the gospels, and in other early Christian writings, there were numerous strong statements, sometimes called "hard sayings," that encouraged Jesus' followers to abandon the conventional values of the world. A few of the more striking texts are worth quoting because they were immensely influential in the spread of the ascetic movement among Christians.

> A man asked Jesus "what good deed must I do to have eternal life?" Jesus told him to keep the commandments. The young man said he did that and asked, "What do I still lack?" Jesus said to him, "If you wish to be perfect, go, sell your possessions and give the money to the poor and you will have treasure in heaven; and then, come follow me." When the young man heard this word, he went away grieving, for he had many possessions. Then Jesus said to his disciples, "Truly, it will be hard for a rich person to enter the kingdom of heaven." (Mt 19:16–26; see also the versions of this in Mk 10:17–27 and Lk 18:18–26)
>
> But he [Jesus] said to them [his disciples], "Not everyone can accept this teaching, but only those to whom it is given. For there are eunuchs who have been so from birth, and there are eunuchs who have been made eunuchs by others, and there are eunuchs who have made themselves eunuchs for the sake of the kingdom of heaven. Let anyone accept this who can." (Mt 19:10–12)
>
> "And everyone who has left houses or brothers or sisters or father or mother or children or fields, for my name's sake, will receive a hundredfold and will inherit eternal life." (Mt 19:29; see also Mk 10:28–30)

Paul also recommended forms of asceticism in regard to sexual activity. Someone informed him about a view that was circulating among his converts at Corinth (1 Cor 7:1: "It is well for a man not to touch a woman"). He was not willing to endorse such a radical form of asceticism because he approved of marriage, although not with a ringing endorsement. He thought that marriage kept people from seeking sexual satisfaction in ways that he did not approve. But he did express an opinion that favored the unmarried state over the married: "I wish that all were as I myself am [i.e., unmarried]. But each has a particular gift from God, one having one kind and another a different kind. To the unmarried and the widowed I say that it is well for them to remain unmarried as I am. But if they are not practicing self-control, they should marry. For it is better to marry than to be aflame with passion" (1 Cor 7:1–9).

Some modern biblical scholars interpret the "hard sayings" of Jesus, Paul, and others as an outgrowth of the early Christian belief that Jesus would return soon. If the world was about to end, so the reasoning goes, it made no sense to worry about a good job, tasty meals, worldly prestige, or getting married. Paul explicitly drew ascetic conclusions from his own strong belief that the end of time was near. Because the time was short and the present arrangement of the world was passing away, he told those with wives or possessions to act as if they had neither. He told mourners and rejoicers to act as if they did neither (1 Cor 7:29–31). Whatever Jesus and Paul meant in their historical time and place, many Christians in the ancient world (and later) thought the "hard sayings" were directed to them in some more or less literal way. The hard sayings provided a biblical reinforcement for the growing influence of the broad ascetic movement within Christianity.

Between the second and the fourth centuries, rival Christian groups reacted to the broad-based ascetic movement in different ways. Gnostic Christians, who often hated the created world and their own bodies, were sometimes strict ascetics who fasted, became vegetarians, and avoided reproduction. The Montanist Christians, who expected the return of Christ very soon, rejected second marriages and fasted severely to prepare themselves for Christ's appearance. Even proto-orthodox Christians, who defended the goodness of the Creator and his created world, adopted mild (but still demanding) forms of asceticism. From the second century onward, they fasted on Wednesdays and Fridays and for a day or two before baptisms and ordinations of clergy. Many held a strong opinion that Christians should avoid such worldly pleasures as the public games and the theater because in those places the pagan gods were honored, immoral acts were performed, and human beings were maimed or killed. Stern moralists, including Tertullian, discouraged women from dyeing their hair and from wearing lipstick, rouge, and jewelry. As a sign of their sincerity and remorse, Christian penitents had to adopt severe asceticism, particularly fasting, or they would not be readmitted to the church.

Some Christians went beyond the ordinary level of asceticism that everyone was expected to observe and tried to live more or less literally by the "hard sayings" of Jesus. They were the much-admired virgins, widows, and celibate men. Such pious women and men prayed frequently, read the scriptures or heard them read, observed a strict diet with extra fasting, wore simple clothing, and engaged in charitable activity. The influential Christian theologian and biblical scholar Origen of Alexandria (about 185–254) lived an ascetic life. (Note that when the quotation that follows says "philosopher" and "philosophic," it means ascetic): "For a great number of years he [Origen] continued to live like a philosopher, putting aside everything that might lead to youthful lusts; all day long his discipline was to perform labors of no light character, and the greater part of the night he devoted himself to studying the divine scriptures; and he persevered, as far as possible, in the most philosophic manner of life, at one time disciplining himself by fasting, at another measuring out the time for sleep, which he was careful to take, never on a couch, but on the floor. And above all he considered that those sayings of the Saviour in the Gospel ought to be kept which exhort us not [to provide] two coats nor to use shoes (Matthew 10:10), nor to be worn out with thoughts about the future (Matthew 6:34). He had a zeal beyond his years, and by persevering in cold and nakedness and going to the extremest limit of poverty, he greatly astounded his followers who asked him to share their goods, when they saw the labor he bestowed on teaching divine things. But he was not one to slacken endurance. He is said, for example, to have walked for many years without using a shoe of any description, and to have refrained for a great many years from the use of wine and all except necessary food..." (EH 6.5, altered).

Not every Christian could or would live as Origen did. Distinctions were made about what Christians *must* do and what they *should* do. Christian teachers said that all Christians should obey God's direct commands, called "precepts." The Ten Commandments are a good example of precepts that bound every believer to avoid such things as the worship of idols, killing, stealing, and sexual sins. The teachers began to interpret Jesus' hard sayings as advice or "counsels" that did not bind every Christian. For instance, the second-century *Didache* (6.2) told its readers that they would be perfect if they could bear the full yoke of the Lord, but if a person could not do everything, he should do as much as he could. Clement of Alexandria (about 160–215) wrote a pamphlet with the title *Who Is the Rich Man That Shall Be Saved?* in which he argued that wealth was acceptable for a Christian if it was used in proper ways, such as almsgiving. Ascetic Christians voluntarily chose to go beyond the precepts and to live the ascetic life according to Christ's or Paul's advice. The emergence of a visible ascetic minority within the Christian community introduced a division that was to have a long history. The ascetics were set apart from the majority of Christian laity and clergy, who might be married, have children, have a job, and be harried by worldly cares. The ordinary believers and even clergy who did not adopt an ascetic way of life were increasingly regarded (and regarded themselves) as real but second-class Christians. The ascetics gradually became the Christian elite, who did what Jesus had recommended to those who wanted to be "perfect." The ascetic men and women, whose numbers were modest, lived what was regarded as a higher, purer, and more perfect way of life. Some said that they experienced "the life of angels" in so far as that was possible for living people. The influence of ascetics grew because many Christians thought that through self-denial and holy living the ascetics gained access to the Holy Spirit, from whom they received spiritual gifts and powers. Increasingly, the ill and the troubled went to ascetic men and

women to ask them to obtain from God visions, healings, and other miracles. Ascetics were thought to be able to read human hearts and to give inspired spiritual advice. For a long time, ascetics were ordinarily laypeople, not clergy. A bishop, presbyter, or deacon could choose to be an ascetic, but before the later fourth century the clergy as a group were not required to be ascetics. In fact, it was difficult for a clergyman to be too ascetic because his duties of ministering to his congregation were probably incompatible with his being exhausted from sleeplessness and weak from hunger, which must often have been the real-life situation of strict ascetics. Many pre-Constantinian clergy were married, had children, and had ordinary jobs to supplement their clerical income. But from the fourth century, Christian communities sometimes preferred ascetics as their bishops or presbyters. Some churches also pressured their clergy to become more ascetic.

By the third century, admiration for asceticism and for individual ascetics was well established in proto-orthodox Christianity. After the outburst of persecutions between 250 and 260, the Christian churches enjoyed peace and experienced growth that intensified in the fourth and fifth centuries when the Roman Empire actively promoted orthodox Christianity. In almost every historical period, Christian moralists have criticized their contemporaries for laxity. In the ancient world, such criticism, often but not always from ascetics, became more intense as the churches grew in size and prosperity. Bishop Cyprian of Carthage, executed in 258, was a relatively recent convert who may have had high expectations of his fellow Christians. He attributed the persecutions of his day to the lukewarm faith and sinful behavior of his fellow clergy and laypeople. He described or perhaps exaggerated the situation in the church at Carthage in his day: "Each one was desirous of increasing his estate; and forgetful of what believers had done in the times of the apostles, or always ought to do, they, with the insatiable ardor of covetousness, devoted themselves to the increase of their property. Among the bishops there was no devotedness to religion; among the clergy there was no sound faith: in their work there was no mercy; in their behavior there was no discipline." Cyprian disapproved that Christian men plucked their beards and women used cosmetics and dyed their hair. "They contracted marriages with unbelievers, they prostituted members of Christ to pagans. They would swear not only rashly, but even more, would swear falsely; with swollen pride they would despise those set over them; they would speak evil of one another with poisonous tongues; and they would quarrel with one another with obstinate hatred. Too many bishops, instead of giving encouragement and example to others, despised their divine duty, and became agents in secular business; they left their sees, abandoned their people, and wandered in foreign provinces to hunt for markets for profitable merchandise, while brethren were starving in the Church" (Cyprian, *On the Lapsed*, c. 6, in ANF, vol. 5, p. 438, altered).

Ascetics' criticism of fellow Christians became more intense in the fourth century, when the social and legal acceptance of Christianity led to a flood of converts who had varying degrees of commitment to their new religion. The small, strict proto-orthodox Christian communities of the second century were transformed into the larger, more diverse communities of the fourth and fifth centuries. In particular, the clergy's status changed considerably in the favorable conditions after Constantine's conversion. Imperial legislation gave the Christian clergy special legal rights, financial advantages, and social dignity. To be a clergyman became a career that was worth seeking for practical as well as religious reasons. Some fourth- and fifth-century critics reemphasized Cyprian's theme, quoted earlier, that some bishops and presbyters were unworthy of their sacred calling. To be bishop of one of the great cities was a prize for which even violence seemed justified. For instance, Pope Damasus (366–384) was chosen bishop of Rome in a disputed election. When his supporters clashed violently with those of his rival Ursinus, 137 of Ursinus' supporters were killed in a church. A pagan Roman senator once joked with Damasus, "Make me bishop of Rome, and I will at once be a Christian" (Jerome, *To Pammachius against John of Jerusalem*, c. 8, in NPNF, second series, vol. 6, p. 428).

The changes in Christianity's status displeased some ascetic-minded Christians, who regarded peace and favor from the empire as a mixed blessing. In reaction against the growing accommodation of many clergy and laity with ordinary life, some ascetics not only criticized what they regarded as the lukewarmness of church life but also sought to one degree or another an even more demanding asceticism. In late third- and fourth-century Egypt, Syria, and Palestine, the Christian form of the ascetic movement found new and long-lasting forms in what is called "monasticism." The words "monasticism" and "monk" are derived from the Greek word *monos*, meaning "alone." The Christian ascetics of the first, second, and third centuries had almost always practiced their distinctive way of life *within* the Christian communities. Sometimes they lived outside but near the community. For example, in Egypt some ascetics lived on the outskirts of villages, separate from the villagers but available to them for prayers, advice, and healing. Such "community" ascetics continued to exist in the ancient (and medieval) congregations. But after about 280, a few ascetics took their quest for spiritual perfection a major step further when they withdrew from the surroundings of ordinary life into isolated places, especially into the deserts of Egypt and the Near East. During the fourth and fifth centuries, the trickle of ascetics moving to deserted places grew into a significant stream. The first monks were mostly anonymous lay Christians of modest social standing who adopted a stern version of the ascetic life. They needed no one's permission because monasticism was a spontaneous, from-the-bottom movement. There was no single blueprint for how to live an ascetic life in the desert, so ascetic men and women improvised structures and practices based on their interpretations of the New Testament's "hard sayings" and on the accumulated experience of their predecessors in the ascetic life. When Athanasius, the bishop of Alexandria (328–373), wrote *Life of Anthony* about a man who is sometimes, although incorrectly, called the "first hermit," he created a vivid picture of the severe ascetic who lived alone in the desert. At this distance in time, we have difficulty figuring out how much in the *Life of Anthony* really did happen and how much Athanasius created. But the *Life* created a powerful literary model of the perfect hermit.

ANTHONY (ABOUT 251–356)

Anthony was a Coptic Christian, that is, one of the native Egyptians who had been dominated by Greek-speakers since Alexander the Great conquered Egypt more than five hundred years earlier. Athanasius' *Life* is our main guide to Anthony's long ascetic career. As a young man, Anthony experienced a call to asceticism when he heard in church the gospel passage, "If you wish to be perfect, go, sell your possessions, give the money to the poor, and you will have treasure in heaven; then come, follow me" (Mt 19:21). After he had provided financially for his sister to live among faithful virgins, he gave away all that he had. Under the guidance of an experienced ascetic, he learned how to live the ascetic life. He was not a clergyman. In fact, his life of growing isolation meant that he was not even a member of an ordinary church. It was possible that he went years or decades without tasting the Eucharistic bread and wine. He became a hermit (*eremita*), from the Greek word *eremos*, which meant "desert"—he was literally a "desert dweller." He earned his meager necessities by the work of his own hands, weaving reeds into baskets, rope, or mats. He prayed, fasted, and kept exhausting nightly vigils while he repeated from memory biblical passages in the Coptic language. When he ate his one meal a day, he consumed only bread, salt, and water. Bishop Athanasius described vividly Anthony's harsh solitary life as a never-ending struggle against the urgings of his own flesh, the world's enticements, and the devil himself who took visible shapes. Anthony was depicted as fighting lonely battles at night against demonic foes and erotic visions. Over the course of his long life, he moved to ever-more-remote places in the Egyptian desert. Disciples followed him to learn the ascetic life at his feet. Ordinary people and other ascetics visited Anthony for wise advice, for prophecies about their futures, and for healings. Athanasius wrote that Anthony left his solitude only twice for emergencies. During Diocletian's early fourth-century persecution Anthony came to Alexandria, risking or maybe seeking martyrdom, to comfort imprisoned Christians. He came to Alexandria again during Athanasius' struggles against Arianism to lend his great prestige to the pro-Nicene cause.

Athanasius' *Life of Anthony* was a thousand-year best-seller, translated from Greek into Syriac, Coptic, Armenian, Arabic, and Latin. It inspired generations of monks, nuns, and pious laypeople. In Augustine's *Confessions* (VIII, c. 14–15), written in the late 390s, he attested to the power of Anthony's example. While living in Milan, Augustine met Ponticianus, who was a fellow North African, a high imperial official, and a baptized Christian. Ponticianus told Augustine about Anthony, of whom Augustine had never heard, although the hermit had died only about thirty or forty years earlier. Ponticianus told Augustine about the power of Anthony's story to change lives. He said that while the emperor was at the circus at Trier in the modern German Rhineland, some Christian officials went for a stroll. Two of them met a group of ascetics who had a Latin translation of Athanasius' *Life of Anthony*. When the officials began to read the *Life*, they were moved to a crisis about their lives as married imperial bureaucrats. They debated what to do. Ponticianus told Augustine that they experienced an inward conversion and felt that they had been born to a new life. They decided to leave ambition, property, high office—and their wives. Ponticianus told Augustine that when he and his walking companion joined up again with the two new ascetics and heard their decision, they did not themselves abandon ordinary life, but they wept for their weakness. Many Christians in the fourth century and beyond were faced with similar moral crises about how best to live. Some adopted an ascetic life, and others adopted some ascetic practices.

Hermits in the strict sense dwelt alone, although some lived with a brother or a servant, perhaps a person learning the ascetic life through the hermit's example. They pushed themselves to their physical and mental limits (and sometimes beyond their limits) to live according to Jesus' hard sayings. But loosely organized settlements of hermits also developed in Egypt and the Near East, in which each ascetic lived in his own hut, pursued his own ascetic way of life, and earned his own meager livelihood by manual labor but gathered with other hermits on Sundays for worship. If a hermit was famous enough, disciples gathered around him to practice the ascetic life, which was not learned in a school or from books but rather in an apprentice-ship with an experienced ascetic. Because hermits were widely regarded as the pinnacle of the ascetic life, and in the most spiritual state that a human being could achieve in the flesh, by the fourth century Christian pilgrims and tourists were travel-ing into the desert to see and seek advice from a grizzled *abba* ("father") and occasionally an *amma* ("mother"), as the leading ascetics were called. There was much room for individualism and exper-imentation, as many men and some women tried to find their personal way to live out Jesus' hard sayings. From the fourth century onward, growing numbers of ascetics fasted, prayed, treated their bodies harshly, saw visions, gave advice, and made prophecies. But there were also disorder and what we might interpret as mental and physical break-downs from the sheer difficulty of such a demand-ing life. Experience showed that for some ascetics the lonely hermit's life was too demanding for bod-ies and minds.

PACHOMIUS (290–345)

Pachomius, another Coptic Christian, put a lasting stamp on the ascetic life by organizing ascetics into groups, although he did not invent the community form of asceticism. Some evidence indicates that monks and nuns had lived in groups since the later third century. Ascetics who lived in groups were called "cenobites" because they lived a "common life" (*koinos bios* in Greek). By the time Pachomius died in 345, he was directing nine communities of men and two communities of women. The dis-orderly spontaneity of the hermits still existed, but Pachomius' communities were structured. Pachomius composed the first written monastic rule, which regulated the basic features of ascetic life carried on inside a community. His monaster-ies, which sometimes had hundreds of members, had architectural features that made it possible to live in a structured group. There were houses where groups of men or women lived, workshops, a dining hall, a church, all surrounded by a wall. Put out of your mind the image of grand stone monasteries that existed in the Middle Ages. Pachomius' build-ings were rough, humble structures of mud, straw, and wood. His written rule prescribed a stern and

difficult life. The monks and nuns memorized scrip-ture but also worked in agriculture or at a trade or craft, wore simple uniforms, and were under the strict discipline of senior ascetics. They did not live in the inhospitable desert as Anthony did but rather in abandoned villages where they planted orchards, farmed the fields, produced necessities for their communities, and sold the surplus. During the harvest season, they might be hired to work in other peoples' fields and earned enough to support them-selves and to provide charity to the poor. Make no mistake, their life was difficult, but it provided for some social interaction—daily worship, communal meals, and group labor—while discouraging the extreme forms of individual asceticism that some-times cropped up among hermits. Monastic life in a community did not replace the hermit's life. They co-existed for centuries, although there were soon many more cenobites than hermits.

BASIL OF CAESAREA (ABOUT 330–379)

The dominant cultures in the later Roman Empire were expressed in Greek and Latin, not Coptic or Syriac. It was not inevitable that a monastic move-ment that began among cultural outsiders would be embraced by the Christian religious elite or the Christian masses in other places. As you recall, Bishop Basil of Caesarea in modern Turkey played an important role in the victory of pro-Nicene Trinitarian views. He was also a crucial figure in the acceptance of monasticism in the Greek-speak-ing world. He was a highly educated, upper-class man. Like many of his contemporaries, he trav-eled to Egypt to see the ascetics and even lived for a while as a hermit. But he decided that life in a community was better suited for most people. He remarked that some gospel commandments about love of and service to others could not be observed in solitude. In Asia Minor, he created a form of cenobitic monasticism that spread widely in the Greek-speaking eastern Mediterranean, influenced western monasticism, and has retained its impor-tance even today in Greek Orthodox Christianity. He was impressed by Egyptian and Palestinian monastic life, but he discouraged excessive bodily asceticism. He wanted something less harsh, more balanced, and more favorable to the spiritual growth of individual monks. He proposed an image of monastic life as climbing a ladder of increasing perfection. The individual monk tried to progress to ever higher degrees of spiritual attainment through self-denial, prayer, and charitable works. Within his monastic community, he organized an orderly life that was divided into six gatherings for prayer in the daylight hours and two at night. Every monk worked according to his talents: There was a place in Basil's monastery for scholars as well as for craftsmen and farmers. Basil also wanted his monasteries to do practical good. Basil's monks, who lived not in a desert but within the city of Caesarea, supported orphanages, distributed food to the needy, and maintained hostels for travelers and hospices for the sick. He wrote two influential documents, which are called the *Longer Rule* and the *Shorter Rule*. Unlike most documents called "rules," they do not lay down a blueprint for monastic life. Instead, they are discussions and solutions to problems, generally in a question/answer form.

MONASTICISM IN THE WEST

In the west, ascetics of the traditional sort, especially widows and virgins who lived in their own homes, were common. Even before there were actual cenobites or hermits in the Latin-speaking west, their amazing stories reached the region by many channels. Western pilgrims to the holy places in Palestine often made a side trip to Egypt and brought back glowing reports about the monks. Some people who had lived in Egypt moved west, including Athanasius, the author of the *Life of Anthony*, who was exiled to Gaul in 335–337 and to Rome in 339–346, where he spread the news of monasticism. Jerome (347–419/420), the biblical translator, was a vigorous promoter of asceticism and monasticism in the west, especially among women. He tried but failed to become a desert ascetic. He settled at Bethlehem with two aristocratic converts to the ascetic life, Paula and her daughter Eustochium. Paula's fortune allowed him to spend the last thirty years of his life in Bethlehem as head of a monastery for men, a monastery for women, and a hospice for pilgrims. His enthusiastic promotion of the ascetic life continued in letters

and treatises. The eastern monastic movement also generated a surprisingly large amount of literature, which reached the west in Latin translations. John Cassian (about 365–about 433) was important in the transmission of monastic ideas and practices to the west. He had lived as a monk in Bethlehem and had visited the Egyptian ascetics. He settled in southern Gaul at Marseilles about 415, where he founded one monastery for men and another for women. His writings were influential in the spread and structure of monasticism in the west. His *Institutes* laid out the way a monastery should be organized—food, clothing, officers, and the like. His *Conferences*, which purported to re-create the teachings of 120 prominent eastern ascetics, 117 of whom were *abbas* (men) and 3 were *ammas* (women), gave western ascetics access in their own Latin language to the complex spiritual teachings that had developed in Egypt.

But Christians in the western, Latin-speaking parts of the empire were slower than the easterners to accept monasticism. When the westerners did accept it, they put their own cultural stamp on it. During the later fourth and fifth centuries, monasticism in all its luxuriant, unregulated, and occasionally frightening forms began to spread into Latin-speaking North Africa, Italy, southern Gaul, and Spain. But the west was not the east, and monasticism adapted to new surroundings. The climate in much of the west, especially the cold winters, prevented some kinds of eastern monasticism from taking root there. For instance, Simeon (about 389–459) was a Syrian ascetic who lived for forty-seven years on a high pillar, called a *stylos* in Greek—from which he got his nickname "the Stylite." His pillar, surrounded by a ruined church, still stands in the desert near Antioch. In northern Gaul in the late sixth century, Bishop Gregory of Tours wrote about a monk named "Vulfoliac," who told the long story of his conversion to monastic life. At one point he decided to be a stylite. He set up a column on which he stood without shoes in great discomfort. The winter was horrible, but he drew some local peasants to hear his denunciations of a goddess he called "Diana," whom they worshipped. Some local bishops came to Vulfoliac and said, "Your way is not right! Such an obscure person as you can not be compared to Simeon of

Antioch who dwelt on a column. The location of this place does not permit you to suffer in this way. Come down and live with the brethren whom you have gathered around you." Vulfoliac told Bishop Gregory, "Because it is a sin not to obey bishops, so, I [Vulfoliac] came down and I walked with them and I also took a meal with them" (Gregory of Tours, *History*, VIII.15).

Vulfoliac's reference to his obedience to bishops points to deeper reasons than climate that pushed monasticism in new directions in the west. In the fourth and fifth centuries, many western bishops were members of aristocratic families and expected to govern and to be obeyed. They were sometimes less tolerant than eastern bishops of the unregulated independence of hermits and monks. As part of the bishops' duty to supervise religious life in their dioceses, they tried—not always successfully—to gain some control over ascetics. Western bishops favored cenobitic communities, which they might endow with property, protect, and also control. Some bishops even tried to organize their priests into monastic communities, with a stress on personal poverty, but they had only modest success.

BENEDICT OF NURSIA (ABOUT 480–ABOUT 545)

Just as Basil created a long-lasting form of monastic life in the east, Benedict of Nursia did the same in the west. In later centuries, monks revered Benedict as the "Father of Western Monasticism" but in his own day he was one Italian abbot among many. Benedict's future fame was assured because in book 2 of Pope Gregory the Great's popular *Dialogues*, there was an admiring "biography" of the abbot, who had died about fifty years earlier. According to Pope Gregory, Benedict was born to a good family in central Italy, attended the schools at Rome, but was repelled by the immorality of the students. He abandoned secular life and lived as a hermit for three years in a cave at a place called "Subiaco." He was asked to be the abbot of a monastery, but his strictness alienated the monks, who tried to poison him. He returned to his solitude, but disciples followed him, whom he organized in groups of twelve, each under an abbot. In about 529, he converted pagans living on Monte Cassino,

a hilltop that overlooks the Roman road between Naples and Rome, burned the groves of trees sacred to the gods, and founded a monastery that still sits atop the mount. Pope Gregory warmly endorsed the *Rule* that Benedict had composed for his monastery: "He wrote a Rule for monks that is remarkable for its discretion and its clarity of language. Anyone who wishes to know more about his life and character can discover in his Rule exactly what he was like as an abbot, for his life could not have differed from his teaching" (Gregory I the Great, *Dialogues*, book 2, c. 36, in *Saint Gregory the Great: Dialogues*, translated by Odo John Zimmerman, FOC, vol. 39 [New York, 1959], p. 107).

In Benedict's lifetime (about 480–about 545), the monastic movement was about two hundred years old and had produced a rich body of literature that distilled the wisdom, successes, and failures of generations of hermits and cenobites. Benedict also had decades of personal experience as a hermit and an abbot. He drew on his own experience and on monastic literature when he composed his influential *Rule for Monks*, which consists of a prologue and seventy-three brief chapters. Benedict knew what he did *not* want in his monastery. He disapproved of what were perhaps common features in the complex world of monasticism: wandering monks whom he thought exploited the generosity of others; monks who obeyed no one and did as they pleased; and inexperienced monks who rushed to become hermits before they were tested by years of ascetic practice in a cenobitic community. In reaction against what he saw as flaws in other forms of monasticism, he demanded that entrants to his community promise to stay for life (a vow of stability), to give up all personal possessions (a vow of poverty), and to give up their selfish will and adapt to the way of life in the little community (the vow of conversion of behavior). He coined the phrase "idleness is the enemy of the soul" (*Rule*, c. 48), and his monks were never to be idle. The essential framework of Benedict's monastic life was the worship of God, called the *opus Dei* ("the work of God"). The monks gathered in church eight times a day to hear readings from the scriptures, to sing hymns, and above all to sing the 150 psalms of David over the course of each week. Everything else was fitted around the liturgical "work of God."

Some hours of the day were set aside for reading scripture and other spiritual literature. When they were not praying, reading, eating, or sleeping, the monks worked at the tasks needed to manage a farm and provide for the needs of a community that Benedict organized as a family.

Most modern Western people would find Benedict's asceticism quite demanding for their bodies and their egos. But in the spectrum of ancient Christian ascetic practices, it was moderate. He wrote that he hoped to impose nothing harsh and nothing burdensome (*Rule*, prologue). In his monastery, a moderate physical asceticism was practiced, including such things as celibacy; a vegetarian diet that allowed meat only to sick monks and child monks; adequate but not excessive sleep; and physical labor alternating with worship, prayer, and reading. Benedict did not allow his monks to practice the harsh and dramatic feats of asceticism that were associated with the eastern desert monks. He wanted his monks to seek a more "interior" and spiritual asceticism, which stressed humility and the abandonment of self-will, of selfishness, and of egotism. Benedict emphasized the importance of offering a willing obedience to the abbot, who was portrayed in the *Rule* both as standing in the place of Christ and as a strong Roman father who could be quite stern if necessary. Benedict's community, which was probably small, was cut off physically and psychologically from the surrounding world. He wanted no unnecessary contact with outsiders. The monks were in a "school of the Lord's service" (*Rule*, prologue) and were striving for their own salvation. Their gaze was inward. Benedict's monks provided virtually no services to outsiders. The exception was that Benedict's monks welcomed travelers and guests "as if they were Christ" (*Rule*, c. 53), but the guests ate and slept in an area separate from the monks, who would ordinarily never meet or speak to them. Benedict wanted his community to govern itself. The monks elected the abbot on whose character, judgment, and diligence the entire monastery depended. Although Benedict wanted no interference from outside, he knew from experience that monasteries could lose sight of their purposes. If the monastic community became disorderly and especially if it elected an unsuitable abbot, Benedict allowed the

local bishop and other leading Christians to intervene (*Rule*, c. 64). Benedict's insistence on separation from the world is important to stress because centuries later, in the Middle Ages, Benedictine monks reached out to the world in such things as doing missionary work, managing their estates, teaching youngsters, copying manuscripts, distributing food to the poor, and serving as scribes, advisers, and officials for secular rulers. Benedict did not mention such activities, and he would probably have been surprised or perhaps even displeased at those developments. Benedictine monasticism predominated in the medieval west between the ninth and twelfth centuries, but in the late ancient church it was just one monastic experiment among many—although in the long run the most enduring and influential in the west.

CRITICISM OF ASCETICS

In the fourth and fifth centuries, no one regulated the many kinds of ascetics. The freedom, spontaneity, successes, and failures of the ascetic movement opened it to criticism because no powerful movement is without opponents. Different people had different criticisms. As might be expected, some Greco-Roman pagans thought monks were just what was wrong with Christianity. They regarded them as filthy, ignorant, and unwilling to bear the responsibilities of civilized life, such as tax-paying and child-rearing. Some Christians criticized the stricter forms of asceticism. Even though the Christian churches had embraced the spiritual value of asceticism in general, many specific forms of asceticism, including monasticism, had developed on their own. As the ascetic tide was rising in the west in the last decades of the fourth century, some Christians objected to a central belief of ascetics, that celibacy and virginity were spiritually superior to marriage, which was regarded as merely good. In the city of Rome itself, some Christians expressed doubts about ascetic claims to special status. Helvidius, a layman at Rome who was active in the 380s, wrote against a monk named "Carterius," who had declared that sexual continence was superior to marriage. Carterius had held up the Virgin Mary as his prime example of lifelong virginity. Helvidius defended the view that marriage and celibacy were equally good and spiritual. He argued that Mary had been a virgin when she conceived Christ but had subsequently lived with Joseph in ordinary marriage. Jovinian (died about 406), a monk who at first embraced strict asceticism—he was said to have been pale from fasting, barefooted, dressed in a dirty black robe, and unwashed—later adopted a more moderate form of life, even though he remained a monk. He also wrote at Rome to defend the spiritual equality of marriage and celibacy. He thought that the reward after death would be the same for all Christians who preserved the purity of their baptism and repented for their sins. Vigilantius (late fourth–early fifth century), a priest from Gaul, wrote against the growing cult of martyrs' relics and the high value placed on asceticism in general and on celibacy and virginity in particular. Such written and verbal attacks on the spiritual superiority of the ascetic life provoked a storm of opposing responses. Prominent figures, including Ambrose of Milan, Augustine of Hippo, Pope Siricius, and, above all, Jerome, wrote vigorously against the criticism that virginity and continence were not better than marriage. Many writers, especially Ambrose and Jerome, argued that virginity or sexual continence were the ideals toward which all Christians should aspire. Even the emperor took notice: In 398, Theodosius I exiled Jovinian to an island in the Adriatic Sea. When the controversy died down, the growing admiration for asceticism was not impeded at all.

Milder forms of criticism directed at the behavior of ascetics did not stop. Some fourth- and fifth-century bishops criticized ascetics because they lived outside ordinary church life and discipline. Some Christians regarded the ascetics as rivals to the official clergy. Due to their prestige, numbers, and activism, monks also became an important constituency in the church at large. Many people who admired them for their charismatic access to God's power were willing to follow their lead. In the theological quarrels about Christ's nature that shook the churches in the fifth and sixth centuries, fiercely partisan monks, often quite uneducated in the subtleties of theology, used violence to support their views. Monks were often the leaders or the ground troops in attacks on pagan temples and Jewish synagogues. The imperial authorities saw in the monks' unruliness and violence a threat to public order.

For several generations, no one had effective control over the many ascetics. Monasticism could have become so extreme that it discredited itself or so independent that it moved into schism or heresy. But the church of the bishops and the world of the monks found ways to cooperate. At the Council of Chalcedon (451), the bishops asserted the principle that monks were, like all Christians, members of the church and subject to the bishops' direction. Canon 4 declared: "Let those who truly and sincerely lead the monastic life be counted worthy of appropriate honor; but because certain persons use the pretext of monasticism to bring confusion both upon the churches and into political affairs by going about freely in the cities and at the same time seeking to establish monasteries for themselves; it is decreed that no one anywhere build or found a monastery or oratory contrary to the will of the bishop of the city; and that the monks in every city and district shall be subject to the bishop, and embrace a quiet course of life, and give themselves only to fasting and prayer, remaining permanently in the places in which they were set apart; and they shall meddle neither in ecclesiastical nor in secular affairs, nor leave their own monasteries to take part in such.... But the bishop of the city must make the needful provision for the monasteries" (Council of Chalcedon [451], canon 4 in NPNF, second series, vol. 14, p. 270, altered). The bishops at Chalcedon expressed a utopian view of pious, peaceful, obedient monks, but in reality they could not immediately bring monasticism under their control. Over time and with the imperial government's support, the monks were integrated into the church and, in a sense, "tamed," although their influence remained large and sometimes uncontrollable.

THE IMPACT OF ASCETICISM WITHIN CHRISTIANITY

The ascetic movement had a profound, long-lasting impact on Christianity. In the second and third centuries, proto-orthodox Christians admired the martyrs who imitated Christ in their innocence, steadfast suffering, and blameless deaths. Individual Christians had adopted ascetic practices such as fasting and sexual continence. When Christian emperors ended persecution, martyrdom vanished or at least became rare. The pre-Constantinian martyrs continued to be revered as heroes, the accounts of their suffering were popular Christian reading, and their burial places were marked with shrines and churches to which pilgrims came. But they were figures of an increasingly remote past. Asceticism could in a sense replace martyrdom. Living and recently deceased ascetics became the new Christian heroes. Christians read or listened to an extensive popular literature about the ascetic men and women of recent times. Monks represented an alternative to the imperial church. During the later fourth and fifth centuries, the Christian empire, the bureaucratic bishops, the magnificent churches, and the solemn liturgies developed alongside scruffy, unregulated monks who promoted an ideal based on Jesus' hard sayings. In the class-conscious and hierarchical world of the late Roman Empire, the ascetic life was open to ordinary men and women because it required no formal education, no wealth, not even literacy. Monasticism had developed at least in part as a reaction against the complacency of ordinary Christian life. The living ascetics and the stories that circulated about them after they died were a reminder to many believers that Christianity was not or at least should not be a comfortable religion. In place of the martyrs who shed their blood, the ascetics were said to "die daily" through their fasting, prayers, poverty, sleeplessness, and exposure to cold and heat. They were living martyrs, sometimes called "white martyrs" because they did not shed their red blood. Christians could see, talk to, and seek advice from living ascetics. After a prominent ascetic died, pilgrims might visit his tomb, where they sought miracles.

Some ascetics saw themselves as successors to the Old Testament prophets and the New Testament apostles, through whom God had worked wonders. John the Baptist, who lived in the Judean desert dressed in camel hair and eating locusts and honey, was a particular inspiration for ascetics. The ascetics' widely accepted access to divine power was a reminder that God still worked miracles in the here-and-now through his heroic followers. Monks and hermits were often close to ordinary people as

advisers, charity-givers, and intercessors for them with God. Monks gained a strong position in the religious life of all classes. They were increasingly chosen as bishops because of their holiness. Many Christians chose monks and hermits as spiritual guides to whom they confessed their sins and from whom they sought advice. Poor peasant Christians and urban lower-class Christians sought them as protectors from demons and from the oppressions of powerful men. The monks were regarded as ideal arbitrators and defenders of the oppressed because they were regarded as without personal ambition, dead to the temptations of the world. Powerful people often respected the monks' commitment and feared their access to spiritual power.

Except for the deaconesses who had a special role in the care for sick women, in the religious instruction of women, and at the baptism of women, women did not hold official, public roles in orthodox Christianity. There was debate about whether the deaconesses were clergy or laypeople. By the fifth century, the prevailing view was that the deaconesses were not members of the clergy. But there were two public roles where women could have equality with or even superiority to men: as martyrs and as ascetics. During the persecutions of the second, third, and early fourth centuries, women witnessed with their blood as did men. Their sufferings were recorded with dignity and admiration. The account of the persecution at Lyons in 177 compared the Christian slave girl Blandina with Christ as she hung on a post: "Even to look on her, as she hung cross-wise in earnest prayers, wrought great eagerness in those [other Christians] who were contending, for in their conflict they beheld with their outward eyes in the form of their sister Him who was crucified for them...." (EH 5.1.41). The female martyr was as honored as the male martyr.

The ascetic life was open to women as well as men. When persecution ended, asceticism became an avenue for women to gain admiration, status, and religious equality with ascetic men and even religious superiority to non-ascetic men. By the fourth century, some prominent women, and many humbler women, saw the ascetic life as both religiously and socially appealing. The sources tell most about upper-class widows and virgins who adopted the ascetic way of life and used their often considerable fortunes to support other ascetic women. We know the most about the upper-class ascetic women of the city of Rome because Jerome wrote to them and about them. In the 380s, he became the spiritual adviser to a group of wealthy Roman women, some young and some mature, who were interested in or had actually adopted a demanding form of the ascetic life. Paula (347–404) was a wealthy woman from the Roman aristocracy who became a widow at about age thirty-five with five children. After her husband's death, she had withdrawn from the whirl of Roman aristocratic social life, lived in ascetic seclusion in her mansion, studied the Bible, wore coarse clothing, ate simple food, and spent large sums on charity. Jerome, a fervent advocate of the ascetic life, was her adviser in spiritual matters. When Jerome left Rome to settle in Bethlehem, Paula and her daughter Eustochium went with him. She used her fortune to found a monastery for men, headed by Jerome, and a monastery for women, as well as accommodations for pilgrims to the Holy Land. In another instance, a Roman aristocratic grandmother and her granddaughter, both named "Melania," also embraced the ascetic life. Melania the Elder (about 342–about 410) became an ascetic when her husband died. She went to Palestine, where she paid for a monastery inhabited by both men and women on the Mount of Olives. In the next generation, the ascetic urge became stronger. Some women did not have to wait for widowhood. Her granddaughter, Melania the Younger (about 383–439), convinced her husband to live in a chaste, that is, sexless, marriage. When the Germanic Visigoths captured Rome in 410, she and her husband escaped to North Africa, where they met Bishop Augustine of Hippo. Like her grandmother, she eventually settled in Palestine in a monastery on the Mount of Olives.

Asceticism had serious practical consequences for upper-class women, whose families usually arranged marriages for them when they were young. A teenaged wife had little room for personal choices because her husband and mother-in-law controlled her. A woman who vowed to remain a virgin or to remain celibate after her husband died could escape those restrictions and find a socially acceptable zone of freedom for herself. Aristocratic families often opposed the ascetic choices of their female members because they led to dispersal of a part of the family fortune, to the loss of an asset in the marriage market, and to a lack of heirs. Bishops and male ascetics defended the woman's right to choose to be an ascetic, and often they won by arguing, as Paul did in 1 Corinthians 7:32–35, that unmarried women (and unmarried men) were freer to serve the Lord. By choosing to be an ascetic, a woman gave up certain of life's pleasures, but she gained things as well, such as the right to direct her own life, to read and study, to travel as a pilgrim, to be a leader to other women, to be an admired figure in the wider world, and to devote herself fully to God.

The spread of the ascetic ideal also had a considerable influence on the clergy. Some ascetic teachers discouraged monks and hermits, who were mostly laymen, from seeking to become bishops or presbyters because ordination might immerse them in worldly cares and might tempt them to take pride in their new status. The ascetic opponents of ordination sometimes expressed their warnings in colorful, pithy sayings. For instance, John Cassian, who had lived among the desert hermits in Egypt, quoted Abba Moses on the varied temptations sent by the devil to ascetics. Abba Moses warned that impossible fasts, excessive sleep deprivation, and too much praying could be demonic temptations to discourage the ascetic and break his will to endure. He warned ascetics to reject the seemingly worthy desire to advise nuns or poor women. That might entangle them in worldly responsibilities that could destroy their spiritual calm. He saw ordination to the clergy in a similar way. "Or else when he [Satan] incites a man to desire holy office under the pretext of inspiring many people…by which he draws us away from the humility and strictness of our life. All of these activities, although they are opposed to our salvation and to our profession, yet when covered with a sort of veil of compassion and religion, easily deceive those who are lacking in skill and care" (John Cassian, *Conferences*, "First Conference with Abbot Moses," 1.20, NPNF, second series, vol. 11, p. 305, altered). In another place, John Cassian put the matter simply: "a monk ought by all means to fly from women [who might tempt him] and bishops [who might try to ordain him]" (John Cassian, *Institutes*, 11.18, in NPNF, second series, vol. 11, p. 279). Because laypeople were often impressed by the ascetic life, they sometimes sought monks as good candidates to be holy and Spirit-filled bishops or priests. Monks were sometimes literally kidnapped and forced to accept ordination. Augustine, a learned and ascetic layman but not a monk, was in church while passing through Hippo, when he was grabbed by churchgoers, brought before the elderly Greek bishop Valerius, who ordained him a presbyter. Martin of Tours, a middle-aged hermit, was tricked into entering the city of Tours, where crowds pressed the reluctant ascetic to accept consecration as bishop. Bishops who had been monks then used their influence and access to the diocese's wealth to favor monasticism and to "monasticize" the churches—or at least the clergy.

A CASE STUDY: CLERGY, LAITY, AND SEXUAL ACTIVITY

Students often ask about the origins of clerical celibacy, which Roman Catholic priests and bishops and Orthodox bishops still observe. That practice arose during the fourth century but had roots in the earlier ascetic movement. Before there can be intelligent discussion of the origins of clerical celibacy, some ideas of ancient Christianity need to be clarified. Celibacy, from the Latin word *caelebs*, was the state of being unmarried. A man or woman could be *caelebs* because he or she was never married or was widowed or was divorced. I am going to put the word "celibacy" aside because that is not how the ancient Christians discussed the matter. I shall use a different word that more clearly reflects the thought of ancient Christians. That word is *continence*, which means "sexual self-restraint" and especially the choice not to have sexual intercourse. Anyone could choose to be continent. A female or male virgin was by definition continent. Any man or woman, including widows and widowers, who had previous sexual experience could decide to give up sexual activity and so become continent. Married couples could become continent if they chose to live together (or apart) without sexual activity. Some married people chose to be temporarily continent, but others

chose to be permanently continent. Keep the word "continent" in mind as this case study proceeds.

In spite of the criticisms from Jovinian and Helvidius, Christians generally did not regard virginity, continence, and marriage as equally spiritual. They generally accepted a gradation from higher (virginity) to lower (marriage). Epiphanius (315–403) expressed widespread views. He had been born near Jerusalem, converted from Judaism, spent about thirty years as an abbot. In about 376, he was chosen bishop of Salamis on the island of Cyprus. He wrote a great deal, especially against heresy. In one work, he expressed the view that there was a ladder of moral perfection based on degrees of distance from sexual activity. He asserted that the foundation of the church was virginity that was observed by many and honored by others. Second to virginity was the monastic life, whose practitioners gave up sexual activity. Then came continence, then chaste widowhood. Finally there was faithful marriage, which, he said, deserved great respect, especially if it was a first and only marriage. He linked the recruitment of clergy to this hierarchy of sexual statuses. He declared that most higher clergymen (he may have been referring only to bishops) were recruited from among virgins, but if there were not enough male virgins, then from among the monks. If no suitable monk could be found for ordination, then clergy could be chosen from continent widowers or from among those who agreed to abstain from sexual relations with their wives (Epiphanius, *De fide*, 21.3–21.9).

Sometimes the loud praise for virginity and for sexual continence led to scorn, disapproval, or attempts to prohibit marriage itself. Epiphanius, like other orthodox defenders of the superiority of continence, asserted that marriage, although lower in spiritual value than virginity or sexual continence, was sanctioned by God and therefore good. Marriage deserved respect, even if it was at the bottom of the list. But the exaltation of virginity and continence occasionally led to a negative view of marriage. A council of bishops at Gangra in Asia Minor at an uncertain date in the fourth century repudiated Christians who condemned marriage as wrong in itself. The bishops rejected the claim that a Christian woman who had sexual relations with her husband could not enter the kingdom of heaven. The bishops also condemned the group's view that no one should consume the bread or wine offered by a married presbyter. The dissenters in Asia Minor were drawing on a persistent, powerful view that intercourse, even in marriage, was polluting or, to use a clear modern expression, dirty.

When many early Christians read the Old and New Testaments, they thought that the sacred books were positive about sexual activity in marriage but not entirely positive. Three biblical texts were cited frequently to support the view that any sexual activity, even by married laypeople or married clergy, was incompatible with being in the presence of God or with touching things that were regarded as holy because they were connected to God. First, when the Israelites prepared themselves to meet God on Mount Sinai, Moses ordered the men to abstain sexually—to be continent—for three days, although they could then return to their wives: "prepare for the third day: do not go near a woman" (Exodus 19:15). Second, in 1 Samuel 21:4–5, David asked the High Priest Ahimelech for five loaves of bread. Ahimelech had only holy bread, which he gave on condition that "the young men have kept themselves from women." When David assured him that the young men were "holy," that is, sexually continent, Ahimelech allowed them to eat the holy bread. Third, the key New Testament text that was generally interpreted as discouraging the intermingling of the sexual and the holy was 1 Corinthians 7:5, where Paul recommended that when husbands or wives wanted to pray, they should agree to separate sexually "for a while," and then come together again. Many later Christian thinkers interpreted these biblical texts to mean that all Christians (not just clergy or ascetics) should separate holy activity and sexual activity from one another by some period of time. Sexual continence at holy times and during holy activities was thought to be right, even required for every lay and clerical Christian.

The view that sexual activity is so unclean, unworthy, and animal-like that it makes a person unfit to approach God is so out of favor in the twenty-first-century West that you have to make an effort to understand that it was the prevailing view of most pre-modern Christians (and other people, too). They—or at least the writers whose works we

can still read—said in various ways that there was something wrong with sexual desire and sexual acts, which needed to be controlled strictly or avoided entirely. There was agreement that all orthodox Christians should avoid a whole series of sexual acts—adultery, fornication, bestiality, homosexuality, and so on. Such behavior was serious enough to lead to expulsion from the community. But from at least the third century, some Christian clergy and theologians also urged married men and women to regulate their marital intercourse so that it could be kept separate in time from their religious activities. The idea that the sexual and the holy should be kept separate is sometimes called "ritual purity," whose central notion is that sexual activity disrespected and even polluted holy things. It is important to note that laypeople as well as clergy were encouraged to maintain that separation.

How were they to do that? Virgins and continent people were always separated from sexual activity. Christian married couples presented a dilemma. By the third century in some Greek-speaking churches, there was concern about sex and the Eucharist. A bishop named "Basileides" sent four questions to Bishop Dionysius of Alexandria (about 247–about 265). In question 3, Basileides asked about the conditions under which married people could take the Eucharist. Dionysius recommended that they listen to Paul's advice about separating sexually for a time in order to pray, but he left them to judge their own behavior. Over time, such recommendations became customs or even rules. The Canons of Timothy of Alexandria (died about 385) were a brief set of questions and answers about religious topics. Question 5 asked, "If a woman has relations with her husband during the night, or a man has relations with his wife, and there is a liturgical assembly, can they take communion?" The response was, "They can not do it right away...." Question 13 of Timothy's consultations was even clearer about the need for married people to separate their times of sex from their participation in the Eucharist. "For those who are united by the bonds of marriage, on which days of the week must they abstain from sexual relations and on which days are they free to do as they wish? I repeat what I have already said above [the canon then quotes 1 Cor 7:5 on married couples separating for prayer]. It is necessary to abstain [from sexual activity] on Saturday and Sunday, because on those days, the spiritual sacrifice [Eucharist] is offered to God" (Canons of Timothy of Alexandria, canons 5 and 13, cited in Roger Gryson, *Les Origines du célibat ecclésiastique du premier au septième siècle* [Gembloux, Belgium, 1970], p. 123, author's translation). An anonymous but influential western theologian, whom scholars since Erasmus (died 1536) have called "Ambrosiaster," writing in the mid-fourth century at Rome, argued that married couples needed to be temporarily continent before they consumed the Eucharist: "Who does not know that everyone, in accordance with his role and dignity, also has a law. For there is that which is entirely forbidden to everyone [Ambrosiaster cited fornication as something forbidden to everyone]. And again there are things that are permitted to some people but not to other people [He noted that a layman could make a living as a trader, but a clergyman could not]. And there is that which is permitted sometimes and is not permitted other times. Sometimes a Christian is permitted to unite with his wife, and sometimes that is not permitted. Because of days on which there is a liturgical gathering (*processio*), it is not permissible for them to unite. It is necessary to abstain even from permitted things to obtain more easily that which one seeks. Whence the Apostle [Paul] says [1 Cor 7:5] that it is necessary to abstain 'with a common accord, temporarily, in order to give oneself over to prayer'" (Ambrosiaster, *Quaestiones veteris et novi testamenti*, question 127, c. 35, edited by A. Souter in *Corpus Scriptorum Ecclesiasticorum Latinorum*, vol. 50 [Vienna, 1908], pp. 414–415, author's translation).

In some places, a custom took root that married people observe a day or two of sexual continence before they participated in the Eucharist, which was the holy activity in which laypeople were most commonly involved. There was no fourth-century Gallup poll about sexual behavior, so we do not know what portion of Christian married couples observed the recommended periodic abstinence from sex. But clergy declared with increasing emphasis that they should. Pious couples were depicted in written sources as observing the practice. After the fourth century, the sexual continence required for the higher clergy began to emerge out of the more general view that sexual intercourse and the Eucharist should be separated from one another in time. When all married fourth-century Christians were advised to separate their sexual activity from their religious activities, the married clergy received the same advice. But because the bishops, presbyters, and deacons so frequently touched holy objects and performed holy acts, their married life drew a lot of attention.

Marriage of the Clergy before the Fourth Century

Remarkably little is known about the marital status of pre-fourth-century clergy. Christians classified the clergy into the "higher clergy" who were mentioned in the New Testament (bishops, priests, and deacons) and the "lower clergy" such as sub-deacons (who were sometimes classified with the "higher" clergy), readers, acolytes, doorkeepers, exorcists, and gravediggers. The lower clergy were never expected to be permanently continent as a condition of their job. As the ascetic ideal grew more prominent, some important Christian thinkers, including Tertullian and Origen, tried to persuade every Christian to be more ascetic, but they singled out the higher clergy. There is, however, an important distinction between an ideal and a rule. The opinions of second- and third-century leaders were influential expressions of the ascetic ideal, but they were just opinions. Local communities and individual clergy chose to follow them or not. The sparse evidence from the first three centuries of Christianity indicates that for most clergy there was no explicit evidence on their marital status. Some of the higher clergy were unmarried, but some were married men—one study found evidence for only thirteen married bishops, priests, and deacons before the fourth century. Those clergy who were continent were admired, but until the fourth century church custom and canon law did not require the higher clergy to be sexually continent.

Marriage of the Clergy after the Fourth Century

Even though the Latin-speaking and Greek-speaking churches shared the view that sexual activity, even within marriage, was incompatible with holy acts and the touching of holy objects, they diverged on how to implement that view in the real world of bishops, priests, deacons, and sometimes subdeacons. The eastern and western churches differed on the practical details of clerical continence. Greek-speaking bishops, theologians, monks, and others certainly praised virginity as the highest state of purity that a living man or woman could achieve. Epiphanius, quoted earlier, thought that the best clergy were those recruited from among virgin men, although continent men were acceptable to him as well. The logical outcome of that view might have been to ordain only unmarried men, but that was apparently not feasible. Contemporary writers sometimes commented on the shortage of clergy needed to minister to the growing number of Christians under the favorable conditions of the Christian empire. The ordination of married men was necessary and common. Like the Apostle Paul, who saw marriage as a concession to human weakness (1 Cor 7:9), the Byzantine bishops sometimes expressed the view that most clergymen needed a wife. But that need had to be reconciled with the view that holy things, especially the Eucharist, must be separated from sexual activity.

The discipline of the Byzantine church regarding married clergy took shape between the fourth and seventh centuries. The Byzantine church law on marriage, elaborated by councils and emperors, treated bishops differently than priests and deacons. Bishops, who presided frequently at the holiest activities, had to be completely continent while they were bishops, although at the time of their consecration they might have been single, widowed, or married men. The requirement of permanent continence meant that Byzantine bishops were ordinarily, but not always, chosen from among the monks, who were already continent and usually childless. I write "usually" because a monk could have children from a marriage before he became a monk. But after their consecration, Byzantine bishops had to be permanently continent. Byzantine priests, deacons, and subdeacons lived under a different church discipline. They could be married, although the canon law laid down conditions. If a man was married before he was ordained a priest, deacon, or subdeacon, he could continue to have sexual rela-

tions with his wife. If a man was unmarried before accepting ordination, he could not afterward decide to marry. Thus, in the Byzantine church, all bishops were continent, as were some priests, deacons, and subdeacons. But most Byzantine priests, deacons, and subdeacons were married. The important point is that like all married Christians, the married Byzantine clergy were expected to manage their sexual activity so as to be temporarily continent when they performed their sacred duties and handled holy things, especially the Eucharist.

The Byzantine church's canon law on the marriage and sexual behavior of its clergy reached a synthesis in 692 at the Council in Trullo, a domed hall in the imperial palace at Constantinople. In canon 13, the bishops laid out the discipline that had developed to govern the marriages of presbyters, deacons, and subdeacons. "We...will that the lawful marriages of men who are in holy orders be from this time forward firm, by no means dissolving their union with their wives nor depriving them of their mutual intercourse *at a convenient time* [my italics]. Wherefore, if anyone shall have been found worthy to be ordained subdeacon, or deacon, or presbyter, he is by no means to be prohibited from admittance to such a rank, even if he shall live with a lawful wife. Nor shall it be demanded of him at the time of his ordination that he promise to abstain from lawful intercourse with his wife.... *But we know ... that subdeacons, who handle the Holy Mysteries, and deacons, and presbyters should abstain from their consorts when it is their turn to minister* [my italics]. So that what has been handed down through the Apostles and preserved by ancient custom, we too likewise maintain, knowing that *there is a time for all things and especially for fasting and prayer. For it is appropriate that they who assist at the divine altar should be absolutely continent when they are handling holy things, in order that they may be able to obtain from God what they ask in sincerity* (Quinisext Council [692], canon XIII in NPNF, second series, vol. 14, p. 371, altered)." The Byzantine clergy thus reconciled the competing desires for marriage and for sexual continence in the presence of the Eucharist.

The western, Latin-speaking churches shared with the Greek-speaking churches the basic ideas surrounding sexuality and holy things but went in a different direction to separate the higher clergy's religious ministrations from sexual activity. The first evidence of an effort (probably not successful at that time but an indication of things to come) to make permanent sexual continence a requirement for the higher clergy comes from a council of nineteen bishops, which met at Elvira in Spain in about 300. Canon 33 ordered all bishops, priests, and deacons to abstain from their wives under penalty of being expelled from the dignity of the clergy. A succession of vigorous bishops of Rome between about 366 and 460 launched the sustained effort to require complete continence for the higher clergy in the Latin church. The issues were complicated, the solutions were complicated, but this is the essence of the matter in the places where the bishops of Rome had authority. Every man ordained to the higher clergy, whether married or continent at ordination, had to be permanently continent after his ordination. A man who was not married before his ordination to the higher clergy could never marry. A man who was married before his ordination remained married but had to cease to have sexual relations with his wife, that is, he had to become continent (and so did his wife, who might not be willing).

Some scholars have argued that in the west developments in the practice of the Eucharistic liturgy—the most holy of "holy things"—prompted the spread of complete continence for the higher clergy. In earlier times, the Eucharist may have been performed only once a week, so the separation of sexual behavior and holy things could be managed. In the fourth-century west, the Eucharist became more frequent—in some places daily. If the clergy participated in the Eucharist often, it became difficult, if not impossible, for them to observe a day or two of continence before they carried out their clerical duties. Jerome (about 347–419/420), an ardent advocate of virginity or continence for every Christian, stated the case for clerical continence succinctly: "A layman, or any believer, cannot pray unless he abstains from sexual intercourse [this is a reference to 1 Cor 7:5]. Now a priest must always offer sacrifices for the people: he must therefore always pray. And if he must always pray, he must always be released from the duties of marriage" (Jerome, *Against Jovinian [Contra Jovinianum]*, 1.34 in NPNF, second series, vol. 6, pp. 371–372).

Whether or not an increased frequency in the offering of the Eucharist was a contributing reason, the popes of the later fourth and fifth centuries wrote to the bishops of their large patriarchate, which included Gaul, Spain, North Africa, and Italy, demanding vigorously that the permanent continence of the higher clergy be observed (or imposed because it was a new requirement). Pope Leo I (440–461) extended the requirement of permanent continence to subdeacons as well, probably because with the growing complexity of the liturgy, subdeacons had frequent contact with holy things. Wherever the popes were successful, whether men were single, widowed, or married before they received ordination, they were expected to accept continence after they were ordained. Ordination was not a divorce because a wife was still a wife, who was supported by her clergyman husband. She might live in the same house in a chaste marriage (but that aroused suspicions), she might live elsewhere, or she might become a nun (that was the ideal solution from the ordaining bishops' point of view). Married but continent bishops, priests, deacons, and subdeacons might have children born from their marriage before their ordination, but they had better not have a child after ordination because that was proof that they were not continent. The growing practice of choosing monks as bishops increased the number of continent men in the western episcopate, just as it did in the eastern church.

Sexual continence was (and is) difficult, so it is not surprising that the sources record many lapses among the clergy. Furthermore, some clergy resisted the efforts to impose the discipline of continence on them. In North Africa, a highly educated man named "Synesius" (about 370–about 414) was chosen bishop of Ptolemais in modern Libya. In a letter to the bishop of Alexandria, he conceded that most Egyptian bishops were unmarried, but he declared that he would not accept consecration if he was required to give up his wife and his hope for children. He was made bishop anyway. In spite of resistance to and lapses from continence, over time the ascetic movement left a deep mark on the way the clergy in the East and West lived their lives.

Temporary or permanent sexual continence was important but should not overshadow the other aspects of asceticism that the higher clergy were expected to observe. Their asceticism was not so severe as that of monks, but they were expected to fast, to pray, and to cultivate such inner virtues as humility and avoidance of greed. For their congregations they were expected to be models of the ideal of withdrawal from worldly concerns and pleasures, even as they performed their tasks in the world.

The "triumph" of asceticism is a major feature of the ancient church. Arising out of world-denying tendencies in the Greco-Roman world and supported by biblical texts, the ascetic movement affected many, even those who did not like it. Christians incorporated it into their lives in various ways. Christian laypeople and clergy observed some ascetic practices in their daily lives, such as fasting and temporary sexual continence. When strict asceticism found institutional forms in monasticism, it gained a permanent place within Christianity. Hermits, monks, and nuns sought to live as fully as they could according to Jesus' hard sayings. In many varieties, monasticism swept across the Christian world between the fourth and sixth centuries, from Egypt, Syria, and Palestine into the eastern parts of the Roman Empire and into the entire empire. Asceticism was flexible enough to adapt successfully to cultures beyond the imperial borders in such diverse places as Ethiopia, Persia, Ireland, and Anglo-Saxon England.

Although monasticism was integrated into the larger church, it never lost an element of freedom and spontaneity that made it a recurring source of religious reform, experimentation, agitation, and, occasionally, disorder. The monks had their own ideas and ways of life. For instance, they preserved Christian apocalyptic ideas, that is, the vivid sense that this world was passing away and that one should prepare now for the end.

Monks and hermits were also important in the spread of Christianity into the countryside of the Roman Empire and beyond the empire's borders. The conversion of an emperor or of a tribal ruler was only the beginning of the process by which Christianity penetrated the living experience of ordinary people. Someone had to perform the down-to-earth task of bringing Christian teachings, moral values, and customs to every rural village.

Some bishops and thousands of anonymous priests did much of the work in the face of great difficulties. But monks and hermits who purposely sought rural isolation in order to find separation from the world contributed to the practical steps needed to convert the countrypeople among whom they lived. They provided their personal example, they gave assistance to their neighbors in hard times, they sometimes preached, and they sometimes opened their churches so that non-monks could worship. In the seventh, eighth, and ninth centuries, monks were the missionaries who brought Latin Christianity to the pagan peoples in England and Germany. Between the ninth and eleventh centuries, Byzantine monks brought Christianity to the Slavic peoples north of the Danube and the Black Sea. Nestorian monks made converts in central Asia and China.

FURTHER READING

Ancient Sources

A. H. Armstrong ed., Porphyry, *On the Life of Plotinus*, in *Plotinus*, LCL, vol. 1 (Cambridge, MA, and London, 1966), pp. 1–85. A depiction of a highly educated pagan philosopher who was an ascetic.

Owen Chadwick, ed., *Western Asceticism*, Library of the Christian Classics, 12 (Philadelphia, 1958). Translated selections from "The Sayings of the Desert Fathers," John Cassian's "Conferences," and the entire *Rule of St. Benedict*.

Owen Chadwick, ed., John Cassian, *Conferences in Western Asceticism*, Library of Christian Classics 12 (Philadelphia, 1958), pp. 190–289. Six desert fathers speak in long discourses that are shaped to a degree by John Cassian's memory and his theological preferences.

Elizabeth Dawes and Norman H. Baynes, trans., *Three Byzantine Saints: Contemporary Biographies*, (Oxford, 1948). Insight into the attraction that ascetics had in ancient society.

Timothy Fry, ed., Benedict, *The Rule of St. Benedict in English*, (Collegeville, MN, 1982). The brief but influential monastic rule that eventually became a standard in the West.

Robert C. Gregg, ed., trans., Athanasius, *The Life of Anthony and the Letter to Marcellinus*, Classics of Western Spirituality (New York, 1980). The influential and vivid account of an ideal hermit's way of life.

David G. Hunter, ed., trans., *Marriage in the Early Church*, by in *Sources of Early Christian Thought* (Minneapolis, MN, 1992). A brief selection of important documents from the second to the fifth centuries on sexuality, marriage, and related topics.

Armand Veilleux, ed., *Instructions, Letters and Other Writings of Saint Pachomius and His Disciples*, the translator with an introduction by (Kalamazoo, MI, 1982).

Benedicta Ward, trans., *The Desert Christian: Sayings of the Desert Fathers: The Alphabetical Collection*, (New York, 1980). The sayings of the desert fathers (*Apothegmata Patrum*) offer stimulating and sometimes paradoxical insights into the spiritual and psychological richness of the teaching of the *abbas* and *ammas*.

Vincent L. Wimbush ed., *Ascetic Behavior in Greco-Roman Antiquity: A Sourcebook*, by (Minneapolis, MN, 1990). Sources on Jewish, pagan, and Christian asceticism.

F. A. Wright, trans. Jerome, *Letter 22 to Eustochium*, in *Select Letters of St. Jerome*, English translation LCL (London and New York, 1933), pp. 53–159. Jerome's advice to a young aristocratic Roman virgin on how to live her ascetic life. The letter reveals much about Jerome, about the ascetic life, and about the remarkable circle of Roman aristocratic ascetic women in the later fourth century.

Odo John Zimmerman, *Saint Gregory the Great: Dialogues*, trans. FOC, vol. 39 (New York, 1959). Book 2 is an account of Benedict's life.

Modern Works

Peter Brown wrote an influential article on the roles of ascetics in later Greco-Roman society. Peter Brown, "The Rise and Function of the Holy Man," *Journal of Roman Studies* 61 (1971), pp. 80–101, and reprinted in *Society and the Holy in Late Antiquity* (Berkeley, CA, 1982), pp. 103–152. Brown updated and revised his views twenty-five years later in "The Rise and Function of the Holy Man in Antiquity: 1971–1997," *Journal of Early Christian Studies* 6 (1998), pp. 353–376.

Peter Brown, *The Body and Society: Men, Women, and Sexual Renunciation in Early Christianity* (New York, 1988). A challenging interpretation of sexual attitudes among ancient Christians.

Gillian Clark, *Women in Late Antiquity* (Oxford, 1993). A treatment of ascetic women along with other interesting topics on the lives of pagan and Christian women.

Roger Gryson, *Les origines du célibat ecclésiastique du premier au septième siècle* (Gembloux, Belgium, 1970). A sensible, useful treatment of the origins of clerical celibacy and clerical sexual continence. It should be translated.

William Harmless, *Desert Christians: An Introduction to the Literature of Early Monasticism* (Oxford and New York, 2004). A clear, systematic introduction to early monasticism through an analysis of the abundant monastic literature of the fourth and fifth centuries. If you can read only one book on early monasticism, read this one.

CHAPTER 17

Fourth- and Fifth-Century Christian Thinkers

The conversion of Constantine caused (or perhaps coincided with) a rise in the social status and intellectual firepower of orthodox Christianity. There had been influential Christian thinkers and leaders in the second and third centuries, but not much is known about their social origins, personal lives, and education. Tertullian and Cyprian were lawyers; Justin was a philosopher; Origen was a teacher and scholar who had received an education in philosophy; and I do not know about Irenaeus' education or social standing. In one generation, from about 330 to about 360, a number of men were born who later would be honored in that somewhat elastic category of "church fathers." In the west, the main church fathers were Ambrose, Jerome, Augustine, and the much later figure Gregory the Great, who will be treated in chapter 19. In the east, Basil of Caesarea, John Chrysostom, and Gregory of Nazianzus were referred to as "fathers," although others were as well. The fourth-century figures enhanced the respectability of Christianity by their educations, social standing, and prolific writings. They generally came from prosperous, even wealthy families who had been Christian for one or two generations. They were the sorts of people who felt free to advise or criticize emperors. They were influenced in varying degrees by the ascetic movement that was gaining ground in the later fourth and fifth centuries. For instance, they not only adopted ascetic practices, but they also had brothers, sisters, and parents who adopted an ascetic way of life. A few brief sketches may illustrate the influence of that generation.

AMBROSE (339–397)

Ambrose was born into a prominent family which had been Christian for one or two generations. His father had been praetorian prefect in charge of Gaul. Ambrose also held offices in the Roman imperial administration in Italy and seemed to be moving toward a career in the service of the empire. In 373, serious tensions at Milan between Catholics and Arians about who would choose the next bishop threatened to lead to riots, which were not uncommon in later Greco-Roman cities, incited by economic, political, and religious issues. As governor of the important province that included Milan, Ambrose intervened to keep order. Quite unexpectedly he was elected bishop by acclamation of the crowd. Like many fourth-century upper-class men, he was a catechumen and therefore unbaptized. In spite of the Council of Nicaea's ban (canon 2) on the rapid promotion of catechumens, he was quickly baptized and within a week consecrated the Catholic bishop of Milan. There were no seminaries, so Ambrose threw himself into the study of scripture with the guidance of an elderly priest. He knew Greek in a period when such knowledge was waning in the west. He drew upon Greek thinkers such as Origen, Basil of Caesarea, and Athanasius to enrich the theology of the west. He turned his training in rhetoric to the needs of preaching and gained a reputation as a learned, effective preacher. He redirected his skills as a Roman magistrate to the service of his church.

Ambrose performed the time-consuming duties that fell to every bishop. Even with all those demands on his time and energy, he was a copious writer. He wrote commentaries on much of the Old Testament. He wrote works of guidance and pastoral care for clergy, virgins, and others. He and his family were touched deeply by the mounting attraction of asceticism. His sisters became vowed virgins in a ceremony in St. Peter's Basilica at Rome in 353/354. He and his brother remained unmarried. As bishop, Ambrose promoted the superiority of virginity in his writings. He wrote hymns for religious services, something not common before his efforts. Hymns were a way to instruct believers in a pleasant and easily remembered way. Fifty years earlier, Arius had composed the long poem called the *Thalia* to promote his views of the relation of Son and Father to dock workers and others. Ambrose preached notable funeral sermons for his brother and three emperors. He preached every Sunday, feast day, and every day when catechumens were being prepared for baptism. His sermons, taken down by stenographers, were often the basis on which other works were built. His most famous convert was Augustine, whom he baptized in 387.

The court of the western emperors was located in Milan. As a consequence, Ambrose participated in the theological disagreements and politics of the later fourth century. Ambrose threw himself into the theological turmoil of his day. He defended vigorously what he saw as the rights of the orthodox church. For instance, he resisted attempts to grant favors to non-orthodox Christians, particularly anti-Nicene Christians. At Milan, the emperor Valentinian's mother Justina tried to gain control of the Basilica Portiana, a church outside the city walls, for use by Arians, more precisely anti-Nicene Homoians, whom she supported. Ambrose resisted. When a basilica was seized for the Homoians, he held a sit-in with fellow Catholics in a church surrounded by soldiers until the emperor and his mother gave in. Ambrose prevented the assignment of any Milanese church to the Arians. By persuasion and threats of religious sanctions, he induced the Emperor Theodosius I (379–395) not to rebuild a synagogue and a Valentinian church that had been illegally destroyed by orthodox Christians. On another occasion, the Emperor Theodosius had ordered a mass execution at Thessalonika in Greece. He soon regretted it, but his message rescinding the order did not arrive in time. Seven thousand people are said to have died. Ambrose refused communion to Theodosius until he did public penance. Ambrose's writings and actions pointed toward a theory of the relation of church and state in which they cooperated, but the church stood above the state because it was a judge of behavior. Ambrose is representative of men who in earlier periods might have been secular judges, magistrates, governors, and generals but were increasingly seeking the ascetic life or the life of a bishop.

JEROME (ABOUT 347–419)

Some talented, educated men became ascetics rather than secular officials or bishops. Jerome was one of them. He had an excellent literary education, paid for by his prosperous Christian family. He was about nineteen when he was baptized in 366. He was later ordained a presbyter but probably never functioned as one with any regularity. He was primarily a scholar but with a pugnacious, sarcastic personality. What set him apart from so many contemporaries was that over the course of his life he mastered Greek and Hebrew in addition to his native Latin—he was a trilingual scholar. He is best known as the translator and reviser of the Latin version of the Bible called the "Vulgate," which predominated in the west after about 600. Before Jerome, the scriptures had been translated into Latin bit by bit by missionaries and others who often did not have the language skills to do it right. The Old Latin Bible (*Vetus Latina*), as such translations are called, needed to be corrected. In his revision of the Old and New Testaments, Jerome paid close attention to the Greek and Hebrew texts. His revision of the Latin Bible was met with some resistance: People often disapprove the change of wording in well-known sacred texts. Latin-speaking scholars were indebted to him for tools to understand the scriptures. For instance, he revised Eusebius' guide to places mentioned in the Bible (*Onomasticon*). He also composed a companion volume of personal names in the Bible. Drawing on the work of Greek Christian scholars, he wrote learned commentaries on biblical books.

He translated some sermons of Origen, Origen's controversial *On First Principles*, the *Rule* of the Egyptian monk Pachomius, the historical *Chronicle* of Eusebius of Caesarea, and other Greek documents. At a time when the number of westerners fluent in Greek was declining, he made available to Latin speakers some important religious texts of the Greek east.

Jerome was at Rome from 382 to 385 as secretary to Pope Damasus, who had asked him to revise the Latin Bible. Jerome gathered around him a circle of wealthy women and their virgin daughters to whom he gave advice and wrote letters in which he argued for the adoption of an ascetic life. He was a vigorous, even a radical proponent of the ascetic life. Because the ascetic life had been introduced relatively recently into Rome, some Christians and pagans resisted it. Jerome drew criticism when his hot prose and strong ascetic views seemed to disapprove of marriage itself, which was not an orthodox view. One disciple, Blesilla, died young, and some critics attributed the death to too much fasting under Jerome's influence. After Pope Damasus died, Jerome was out of favor at Rome and left, eventually settling at Bethlehem.

He tried living as a hermit in the Syrian desert but could not endure it. He lived in some short-lived ascetic communities, but that, too, ended. He eventually moved to Palestine, where a wealthy disciple named "Paula" founded a monastery for men and women at Bethlehem. Jerome spent the rest of his life there producing his huge literary output. Even in a monastery, Jerome was connected to the wider world through letters, visitors, and pilgrims to the holy places. He wrote many letters and pamphlets in response to contemporary events. He knew how to use his pen. He was harsh in his arguments. Often his criticisms were bitter, mocking, and even unfair to opponents, especially those who disagreed with him about the importance of virginity and asceticism. He exalted virginity and defended that view that Mary had always remained a virgin, which was disputed by some in the later fourth century. Without the responsibilities of a bishop or presbyter, Jerome could work from his monastic ivory tower. For Latin speakers, Jerome's handbooks and biblical commentaries were essential for the study of scripture.

GREGORY OF NYSSA (BETWEEN 331 AND 340–ABOUT 395)

Gregory was born into a wealthy Christian family. One brother was the important Bishop Basil of Caesarea, and another brother was Bishop Peter of Sebaste. He studied rhetoric and philosophy, as virtually all upper-class men did. He was married and did not become an ascetic. In 372, Basil of Caesarea consecrated him bishop of Nyssa, a new bishopric created in a relatively unimportant place. This may have been part of Basil's efforts to fill as many bishoprics as possible with pro-Nicene bishops. He was deposed for two years on Homoian (Arian) charges of mismanagement (he was not an effective administrator) but restored to Nyssa in 378. He was influential at the Council of Constantinople (381), which ratified a modified form of the Nicene Creed. For instance, the emperor named Gregory as one of the bishops with whom a person had to be in communion in order to be recognized as orthodox.

Like so many bishops with a traditional rhetorical education, Gregory wrote a great deal, including letters, refutations of some views of Christ's nature, sermons, and pastoral treatments of the Lord's Prayer, the beatitudes, and the psalms. He preached against greed and in favor of just treatment of beggars, lepers, and the homeless. Gregory had a mystical aspect to his thought. He described Christianity as a lifelong progress, a striving, toward God. His emphasis on the unending ascent to God and on God's existence beyond the grasp of the human mind because of his infinity had influence on later writers.

AUGUSTINE OF HIPPO (354–430)

Augustine was born in Roman North Africa in what is modern Algeria. When he was about forty-five, he wrote his *Confessions*, which told of his life up to the 390s. At one level, the *Confessions* is about the complicated paths by which he believed God had led him to orthodox Christianity. At another level, it is the story of every human being who is unaware that divine providence is guiding his or her steps. In his many sermons, letters, treatises, and biblical commentaries he referred occasionally to his life and his personal views. In his old age, he reread ninety-three of his works (he did not examine his numerous letters and sermons) and commented on them in a book called *Retractationes* ("Reconsiderations"), defending some, correcting others, and admitting that he no longer agreed with what he had written in some cases. Possidius, bishop of Calama, wrote a valuable *Life of Augustine* within about eight years of the bishop of Hippo's death in 430. We know more about his life, his inner thoughts, and his intellectual development than about those of any other figure in the ancient world.

Augustine's family was lower in the social scale than that of many of the Christian leaders born between 330 and 360. His father belonged to the class of local landowners that was required by the imperial government to govern and support financially the towns of the empire. They were relatively poor but still well above the vast majority of Romans and Greeks. His mother Monica was a Christian. His father Patrick was a pagan who became a catechumen and was baptized on his deathbed. Augustine's intellectual promise was recognized early. His family tried to provide him with an education that would open a path for him to a prosperous career as a teacher of rhetoric or as an imperial bureaucrat. After Patrick died, Romanianus, a wealthy noble, became the youngster's generous patron and paid for his expensive education. To continue his education Augustine eventually moved from his hometown of Thagaste to Carthage, the chief city in Roman North Africa. He later went to Italy, where he eventually received a prestigious public post as a teacher of rhetoric in Milan. He expressed hopes that his education and patrons might someday get him a provincial governorship. At Carthage, he took a concubine, whose name he never mentioned and with whom he lived apparently happily for thirteen years. They had a much-loved son named "Adeodatus" ("Given by God"), who died as a teenager. At Milan, Augustine sent his unnamed concubine back to North Africa. He was engaged to an heiress, who was two years below the legal age for marriage. While he waited for the heiress to reach marriageable age, he took another concubine.

Augustine recounted in the *Confessions* the religious odyssey that led him to baptism. When Augustine was young, his mother delayed his baptism. Contemporaries expected that boys and men would sin sexually. If they had been baptized too young, they would be subject to the severe penances of the church. In some fourth-century Christian families, men often put off baptism until they were settled down in a legal marriage, perhaps in their thirties. When Augustine was about eleven, he was so ill that his mother feared he would die. She allowed him to become a catechumen and probably would have arranged his baptism if he had not recovered. After he recovered, his baptism was put off indefinitely. Augustine's mother, who often traveled with him, never let him forget Christianity, but he rejected it for decades. He thought the religion was simple-minded and unintellectual. The Latin language into which poorly educated second- and third-century missionaries had translated the scriptures repulsed him. It was inferior to the language of Cicero and Virgil. He was also troubled by the content of the scriptures, including such things as the dubious morality of the patriarchs and the conflicting genealogies of Jesus in the gospels of Luke and Matthew.

While Augustine was teaching rhetoric in Milan, Ambrose was the bishop. Augustine went to hear his rival's techniques as a rhetorician. He soon became interested in the Christian message of Ambrose as well, which seemed more sophisticated than what he was used to in North Africa. Ambrose used allegory to explain seeming barbarities or contradictions in the scriptures. Augustine experienced a conversion that centered on his willingness to abandon sexual activity and to become continent. Ambrose baptized him and his son Adeodatus on Easter of 387.

After his conversion and baptism, Augustine renounced his secular ambitions, called off his marriage to the heiress, and tried to determine what he should do next. He lived temporarily in quasi-monastic groups with his intellectual friends. When he had returned to North Africa, he went to religious services in the church at Hippo Regius in 391. The Christian congregation virtually kidnapped him because there was a shortage of clergy, especially of educated clergy. Valerius of Hippo, an elderly Greek-speaking bishop, laid hands on Augustine in order to have a learned priest to assist him. In 395, contrary to the Council of Nicaea (canon 8), Augustine was consecrated Valerius' co-bishop and became sole bishop the next year when Valerius died. He served as bishop until he died on 28 August 430, while Arian Germanic Vandals besieged Hippo.

Augustine's remarkable literary output might mislead us to think that he lived in a monastery or worked for a university or in a think tank where writing was his job. But he was no ivory tower intellectual. Like all conscientious bishops, he was busy with his duties as teacher, pastor, and disciplinarian of his flock. He preached regularly, and many sermons survive. He held a court two days a week to adjudicate cases that imperial law delegated to bishops. He wrote hundreds of letters to all sorts of people. He counseled individuals about their behavior and their consciences. He debated personally or in writing with contemporary religious opponents, including Manichaeans, Donatists, Pelagians, and pagans. He attended numerous church councils, where his learning and eloquence made him stand out. There must have been other bishops more or less like him whose entire careers were filled with the activity within their churches. They are just names or even unknown to us. Amid all his activity, Augustine wrote an impressive number of treatises and biblical commentaries. Because he had a long career and wrote so much, we can sometimes discern changes in his thought and theology. He generally wrote in response to contemporary debates. Because he had so many ideas and interests, I am going to organize the remainder of this chapter around the controversies in his life. The treatment will be more or less chronological, but he often returned to earlier controversies. Although Christian emperors had issued stern laws against religious dissidents, Augustine's career reveals vividly that religious diversity still flourished in his North African world, where there were pagans, Manichaeans, Donatists, Pelagians, Jews, orthodox Christians, and gnostic Christians.

Manichaeans

Put off by the unsophisticated Christianity of his mother and of his North African homeland, Augustine became a Manichaean for about nine years. He followed the teachings of a Persian religious prophet and teacher, Mani (216–276), who described himself as an apostle of Jesus Christ. The Manichaean religion fit within the broad, loose category of gnostic beliefs. The core of Manichaean belief was a revulsion against the material world and a call to a very strict asceticism to escape it. The Manichaeans were vigorous missionaries who spread the religion east to central Asia, China, and India and west to the Roman Empire. In Augustine's day, Manichaeism was organized within the empire as a counterchurch, with bishops and other traits of orthodox Christianity. But it was also illegal, and its followers, some of whom were prominent people, often kept a low profile.

Augustine was especially attracted to the Manichaean explanation of why there was evil in the world. Mani taught that in a cosmic struggle between a god of light and a god of darkness, light and darkness, or conceived another way, the good and the evil had become intermingled. The two powers continued to struggle, but neither was able to overcome the other. Evil was an eternal, powerful presence, a thing, in the world. Without vigorous exertion, people could not escape the grip of evil: They sinned because they had to. The Manichaeans taught their followers how to disentangle the good and the evil in their own lives and to return the good to its rightful place. Manichaeans recommended strict ascetic behavior (no sex, no wine, and no meat) and a vegetarian diet of a particular kind. For instance, they believed it was good to eat melons and cucumbers because these foods were especially endowed with light. The Manichaeans said that their views were reflected in the skies. They interpreted the waxing and waning of the moon as the filling and emptying of the liberated light that moved from Earth to the moon and then to the Milky Way, where it ascended to the place from which it had fallen. Mani interpreted Jesus in his own way as a non-physical, almost symbolic redeemer. The Manichaean religion had two classes of members. The Manichaean "elect" adopted the full rigors of the behavior required to liberate the light, including celibacy and vegetarianism. The Manichaean "hearers" supported the elect, protected them from discovery by the authorities, listened to their teaching, and attended their services, which even critics said were accompanied by beautiful singing. The hearers were not held to the strict life of the elect. For instance, hearers could have sexual intercourse but were encouraged to prevent conception. Some hearers went on to become elect, but many hoped that they would be reincarnated as elects. Augustine became a Manichaean hearer. He got his post at Milan in part through the intervention of high-status Manichaeans. But he grew increasingly disillusioned with Manichaeism, a disillusionment that intensified when he met the Manichaean Bishop Faustus, who could not answer questions to Augustine's satisfaction. Augustine abandoned Manichaeism. He attacked it in his works, especially his *Confessions,* which he wrote within a decade of leaving the group. Against them, he emphasized things that they denied. He asserted the harmony of the Old and New Testaments; he argued along neo-Platonic lines that evil was not a thing but rather a lack of goodness; and he criticized Manichaean behavior and praised Catholic belief and living as superior to their Manichaean counterparts. Ancient and modern critics of Augustine's views, especially his negative views on sexuality, accused him of bringing some remnants of Manichaeism with him into the church.

Donatists

When Augustine became bishop of Hippo in 395, the Christians in North Africa had been divided for about eighty-five years. The Donatist Schism broke out after Diocletian's persecution ended in 305. During the persecution, many North African clergy experienced moments of bravery or of cowardice when Roman officials demanded that they hand over the scriptures for burning. Some thought they could solve the moral dilemma by handing over other written documents, in one case medical books. Some clergy defied the authorities and were imprisoned, tortured, or even killed. But some bishops and priests handed over the scriptures. When persecution ended, those who had refused to hand over the scriptures contemptuously called those who had given up the scriptures *traditores* ("those who hand over"), which is related to our modern word "traitor." The tension between the resisters and the *traditores* boiled over

when the church at Carthage, the greatest city in North Africa, regrouped after the persecution and selected a new bishop named "Caecilian." Like any bishop, he had to be consecrated, which meant that other bishops laid hands on him to confer the Holy Spirit. His opponents charged that one of his consecrators, Bishop Felix of Aptunga, had surrendered the scriptures to the persecutors. (In 315, a Roman court found that evidence against Felix was forged and declared the bishop not guilty. Some of his attackers were plausibly charged with being *traditores* themselves.) Opponents of Caecilian argued that because of Felix's betrayal, he did not possess the Holy Spirit and so could not give the Holy Spirit to Caecilian. They regarded Caecilian's consecration as invalid because it had been contaminated by the *traditor* Felix. They elected a rival bishop of Carthage, who soon died and was succeeded by Donatus, called "the Great" by his followers (bishop 313–355), who gave his name to the rigorist schism that divided the North African church for at least three hundred years.

After the Great Persecution ended, Constantine granted financial subsidies, legal privileges, and the possession of church buildings *only* to Catholic Christians. For that reason, it mattered not only theologically but also in practical ways which group was recognized as the "Catholic" church in North Africa. Both groups claimed to be the real "Catholic" church. To an observer at the time, they must have looked almost the same, sharing such things as organization, a vigorous tradition of holding councils, liturgy, architectural styles, and most theological ideas. But who was to decide which group was Catholic and which was schismatic? The Donatists appealed to the Emperor Constantine to take part in the decision. Donatus, who died in exile in Gaul, lived to regret that he asked the emperor to intervene. In 347, he met with two representatives of the Emperor Constans. Optatus of Milevis wrote that Donatus raged at the emissaries and uttered famous words: "What has the Emperor to do with the Church?" (Optatus of Milevis, *On the Schism of the Donatists,* III.3, in *The Work of St. Optatus Bishop of Milevis against the Donatists,* translated by O. R. Vassal-Phillips [London, 1917], p. 131).

At first, Constantine turned to the traditional way that orthodox Christians settled their disputes.

He referred the matter to a council of bishops at Rome, over which the Roman bishop Miltiades presided (313). The decision went against the Donatists, who appealed to the emperor again. Constantine ordered a second council in southern Gaul at Arles (314), attended by about thirty bishops. When arranging for the council at Arles, Constantine issued a letter in the tone of a Christian emperor who thought he was responsible for pleasing God, especially by fostering unity: "...I consider it by no means right that contentions and altercations of this kind [the Donatist Schism] should be hidden from me, by which it may happen that God may be moved not only against the human race, but also against me, to whose care by His heavenly decree, He has entrusted the direction of all human affairs, and may in His wrath provide otherwise than heretofore" (Constantine to Aelafius, appendix 3, *On the Schism of the Donatists in Optatus: Against the Donatists*, p. 387, altered). When the council at Arles also recognized Caecilian as the legitimate Catholic bishop of Carthage and rejected Donatus, Constantine ratified that decision in November 316. The Donatists also sought to be recognized as "Catholic" by the other important apostolic churches of the empire. But those churches, including Rome, maintained communion with the churches loyal to Caecilian and refused communion with the churches loyal to Donatus.

The Donatists, who were convinced of the rightness of their cause, did not accept the decisions of councils, of the churches outside North Africa, or of the emperor. When the authorities of church and state rejected the Donatist claim to be the true, pure church, they were only strengthened in their alienation from what they regarded as the impure church of the *traditores* and the empire that supported it. During the fourth century, the emperors and the North African Catholic bishops hoped for reconciliation with the Donatists because they thought that the differences that fueled the schism could be overcome. For that reason, they were reluctant to stamp the Donatists with the label "heretics" because of the serious legal consequences that would follow. Emperors used various strategies, some gentle and some harsh, to end the schism. They sent high-ranking representatives to mediate; they arranged public debates between Catholics and Donatists; they issued decrees against the Donatists; they conducted trials; and sporadically they applied force. But the schism hardened into two rival churches, with the Donatists in the majority for much of the time.

Although emperors, individual bishops, and Catholic councils denounced the Donatist Schism, it took deep root in North Africa. The Donatists appointed their own bishops and took control of existing churches in the many small towns and villages. Some places had two bishops, a Donatist and a Catholic, although as the Donatists became more militant they expelled the rival bishops when they could. The outspoken Donatist defiance toward the imperial government and the rest of the Christian world pleased many Christians in North Africa, especially but not only rural and poor people. Between about 340 and 400, the Donatists gathered in councils that reflected their strength on the ground. For instance, in about 336, Bishop Donatus of Carthage presided over a council of about 270 bishops. In 394, 310 Donatist bishops gathered to try to heal a schism that had broken out within their own ranks. In 410, at a great "conference" at Carthage summoned by the emperor to debate the issues in public before a judge, 286 Catholic bishops confronted 284 Donatist bishops. In these cases, there were more bishops in attendance than there were at the "ecumenical" councils of Nicaea (325) and Constantinople (381). North Africa was full of bishops!

The Donatist revulsion at the *traditores* was rooted in their distinctive ecclesiology, that is, their view of the church, which they wanted to be "without spot or wrinkle" (Eph 5:27). The Donatist theology of baptism was a particular focus of argument. Even before the Donatist Schism, Christianity in North Africa had its own regional "atmosphere" and characteristics. It was morally strict, wary of the world, full of enthusiasm for the martyrs who defied the world, and reluctant to admit or readmit sinners to its ranks. Bishop Cyprian of Carthage (about 248–258), who died almost fifty years before the schism, spoke for many North African Christians when he declared that there was no legitimate baptism outside the Catholic church. He argued that when sin put Christian clergy or laity outside the church, they could go through the motions of a baptism, but they polluted rather than cleansed the person baptized. The Donatists looked back to Cyprian's declaration that baptism outside the church gave birth not to sons of God but to sons of the devil (Cyprian, *On the Unity of the Catholic Church*, c. 11). The Donatists, who had some able theologians, argued that the effectiveness of baptism depended on the holiness of the clergyman who administered it. A sinner could not transmit the Holy Spirit because he did not have it. Only a holy priest or bishop could carry out effectively a baptism because only such a person had the Holy Spirit of God to pass on to the recipient of the sacrament. The Donatists were convinced that their opponents had lost that Holy Spirit when they accepted the ministrations of the *traditores*. Because the Donatists dismissed as empty and ineffective the baptism given in the churches of their opponents, they rebaptized those who moved from the Catholic to the Donatist church. They fed the Eucharist of their opponents to dogs because it was unclean. When they were victorious in seizing a church building, they scraped it from top to bottom to wash away the filth they thought their opponents left.

The Donatists had a distinctive view of the church as well. They saw themselves as a suffering church, a persecuted church, a martyr church, above all the only true and pure church in a world full of sinful, erroneous churches. Their admiration for martyrs grew. Some Donatists are said to have provoked the authorities in order to create martyrs. Their opponents said that some fanatical Donatists even paid or forced people to kill them so that they could attain the high status of martyrs. Donatist towns and villages were dotted with the shrines of their martyrs, symbols of their fierce resistance to the sinful world and the sinners who threatened them. Donatism was the most successful of the rigorist schisms in ancient Christianity, probably because it tapped into economic and social discontent that was already widespread in Roman North Africa. The owners of great estates in North Africa tended to be drawn from an elite of emigrants from Italy, who had Mediterranean-wide interests and were Catholics. The majority of the population were poor peasants or townsmen, some of whom spoke Latin, but others spoke the Berber language or even the Semitic language of the Carthaginians, who had been conquered by the Romans almost five hundred years earlier. Donatism appealed to poor and marginal people, who could now regard their economic and political masters not only as oppressors but also as the religiously polluted successors of the *traditores*. Donatism began as a schism that became a theological movement and a well-organized church. It was the only ancient schism with the desire and the potential to overturn traditional religious, social, political, and economic institutions.

The Donatists did not restrict themselves to theological debate. They hated the Catholics as puppets of the empire. The Circumcellions, a radical group of Donatists, carried on a campaign of intimidation and violence against rich people, against the Catholic clergy, against those Donatists who converted to Catholicism, and against the still-vital paganism of North Africa. The Circumcellions, who got their name from the shrines of the martyrs where they gathered (*circum cellas*), used as their war cry "Praises be to God" (*Deo Laudes*), and carried clubs with such colorful names as "Israels," with which they beat their opponents. They disrupted Catholic services and pillaged opponents' churches. They kidnapped Catholic landowners or ambushed them on the road. They forced rich men to pull their own carriages while their servants or slaves sat in them. They intimidated people who lent money to the poor so that they would not collect the debts. The Circumcellions also hated paganism, which still had many adherents in fourth-century North Africa. They occasionally turned their wrath on pagan temples and statues, smashing them even at the risk of their own lives. The Circumcellions who died in such enterprises added to the stock of Donatist martyrs. The Circumcellions especially hated Catholic clergy, whom they blinded, whose tongues they cut out, or whom they beat mercilessly. They sometimes battled Catholics to gain physical possession of church buildings. An episode in about 330 illustrates the weakness of the imperial government, which used harsh rhetoric but rarely placed its force against Donatist force. At Cirta, the Donatists seized a basilica that Constantine himself had ordered to be built for the Catholics. Local Roman authorities and the emperor warned, cajoled, and ordered the Donatists to give it back. They did not. The Catholic bishops gave up and asked for another site for the church and another imperial subsidy to build it, which Constantine granted. He praised the bishops' "patience," a sure sign that the imperial authorities feared the consequences if they took back the basilica by force. The more responsible Donatist bishops did not approve of the extreme forms of Circumcellion militancy but could not stop it.

The tide began to shift against Donatism when the minority Catholics found an able champion in Augustine of Hippo, who once barely escaped an encounter with the Circumcellions. Augustine made the case against the Donatists on historical grounds when he argued that their account of the origins of the split was inaccurate. He countered the Donatist theological arguments about baptism by arguing that it was Christ who baptized through the ministration of human beings. He conceded that during the persecutions, some bishops had acted shamefully, but an individual bishop's sin could not disrupt the apostolic succession of bishops. No matter how sinful or unworthy a clergyman might be, he could not pollute Christ's sacraments. He argued against the Donatist view of a pure church to which no sinner (if he was detected) could belong. Augustine argued that the church on earth was not a pure church but rather contained all kinds of people who would be sorted out at the final judgment. He knew from his own experience as a pastor that many Christians were weak, negligent, and tempted to sin. But the church itself was purer than any of its members. Over a period of about twenty-five years, Augustine made the theological and historical case against the Donatists in a steady stream of books, pamphlets, letters, sermons, and public debates.

But even Augustine's theological and debater's gifts could not sway the core of the Donatist movement. A change in the policy of the emperors strengthened the new intellectual vigor of the Catholic side. During the fourth century, the emperors were reluctant to intervene too strongly in a theological debate that had mobilized such popular support. The imperial government's growing impatience with the disorder and violence in North Africa aided the Catholic cause. Rebellion against the empire was sure to get any emperor's attention. In 397, some Donatists made a major mistake when they supported the unsuccessful rebellion of Count Gildo against the Emperor Honorius (395–423). In 405, Honorius issued strong anti-Donatist legislation, which gave up hopes for reconciliation of the century-old schism between Catholics and Donatists. Ominously for the Donatists, Honorius equated Donatism with heresy, which opened them to the disadvantages and penalties that followed heresy, including a ban on the Donatist church's existence and confiscation of its property. Augustine did not approve of force in religious matters. But in his experience it seemed to work. Many Donatists who became Catholics seemed sincere. At Hippo, his congregation went from being the minority to the majority of Christians. Somewhat reluctantly Augustine accepted the intervention of the state to move against error and to force Donatists to yield, although he did not favor bloodshed or harsh physical penalties.

Donatism held on. The situation changed again after the 430s, when the Vandals, a Germanic tribe, conquered Roman North Africa. The Vandals were Arian Christians, who oppressed Catholics and Donatists because both accepted the Council of Nicaea's teaching that the Son was of the same substance as the Father. Donatism and Catholicism survived until the Muslim Arabs swept across North Africa and captured Carthage in 697. Unlike the situation in many places farther east, where Christian minorities survived until modern times under Muslim rule, North African Christianity in its Catholic and Donatist forms became extinct by the eleventh century, perhaps undermined by its own internal divisions.

Pelagius (about 350–about 425)

Augustine also confronted views about the nature of salvation with which he vehemently disagreed. Pelagius was a layman and an ascetic from the island of Britain who led an ascetic-minded circle of disciples in the city of Rome, just as Jerome had done a decade or so earlier. When the Visigoths sacked the city in 410, Pelagius and his disciple

Caelestius fled to North Africa and eventually to Palestine. Augustine's encounter with Caelestius sharpened Augustine's views on grace and predestination. Pelagius taught that human beings could by their natural attributes and choices become good, in exceptional cases even sinless. He believed that people were innately good. God gave grace to make it *easier* to be good. Pelagius did not believe that people inherited a corrupted nature from Adam. He taught that humans could choose to keep the religious commandments, although sinful social structures and Adam's bad example made that difficult.

Augustine had a very different view of human nature. During the literary exchanges with Pelagians, he sharpened his dark view of humanity, based in part on his understanding of Paul's letters. He championed the notion of the original sin (*peccatum originale*) that Adam committed and passed on by heredity, perhaps by sexual intercourse, to his descendants. Human beings were corrupt in their nature, unable to do anything good on their own. They absolutely needed God's grace, which they could not earn and did not deserve. The original sin doomed all humans to damnation. For reasons known only to God, he lifted some people out of the "lump of sin" (*massa peccati*) and did not lift others. The saved should be grateful for a mercy they did not deserve in any way; the damned should not complain because they received a just punishment for their personal sins and Adam's original sin.

Augustine did not think that the members of the church were identical with the saved, who were not identifiable in this life—a terrible sinner could in the end be plucked from the lump of sin, and a pious nun could be left in it. His views pointed to a predestination of some to salvation and others to damnation (although he never actually said that there was a predestination to damnation). Pelagius' followers disagreed, but Augustine had other critics, who thought that the view that grace was absolutely essential but that for reasons known to God only some got it could lead to moral laxity. Why bother with ascetic practices? Why bother to strive to be good if you could not tell whether you had been given God's grace? Some monks, whose lives were devoted to striving for perfection, especially disliked Augustine's implication that their prayers and fasting were not or at least might not

be pleasing to God. Augustine's view that Adam's sin utterly corrupted human nature, which needed undeserved grace to be healed, had a profound influence on western, Latin-speaking theology.

Pagans

The Visigothic King Alaric's capture of the city of Rome on 24 August 410, raised serious questions. During the siege, pagan priests had openly sacrificed to the gods, and Christian clergy had asked their God and patron saints Peter, Paul, and others to save the city. Alaric, who was an Arian Christian, respected the important basilicas, but much of the city was looted. After the shock subsided, intellectuals sought to explain the event. Pagan intellectuals said that such a thing had never happened in the past when the traditional gods were honored. They blamed the pillage of the city on the spread of Christianity. Some Christians were shaken by that accusation. Augustine set out to refute it in a work called *On the City of God* (*De civitate dei*). In the first five books, he tried to answer the pagan charge that the world was worse in "Christian times." He drew on historical documents to show that even before Christianity, the empire experienced invasions, military defeats, famines, and plagues. But he did not stop there. Over the course of thirteen years, from age fifty-nine to seventy-two, he expanded the work to twenty-two books (1,091 pages in one paperback translation). Books 6 to 10 were directed to the prevailing philosophies of the fourth century, especially neo-Platonism, which Augustine admired but argued was inadequate to bring true happiness and salvation. In books 11 to 22, Augustine discussed the origin and final destination of two intertwined but invisible communities—a City of God and a City of the World. Each city had its own destiny. The City of God aimed for salvation, and the City of the World was motivated by the search for power, wealth, and worldly pleasure. The City of God consisted of those predestined by God. It was certainly not simply identified with the church, some of whose adherents belonged to the City of the World. The City of the World consisted of sinners, although even in it, some predestined for salvation might temporarily reside. Empires and kingdoms came and went, but the two cities were more enduring and important than any political or social arrangements. Governments could provide order, justice of a sort, and peace that both cities enjoyed, but the members of the City of God would eventually have eternal peace, whereas the citizens of the City of the World were destined for damnation. Augustine had only modest influence in the Greek-speaking east, which had its own theological views, some more optimistic about human nature and salvation. But in the Latin-speaking west, his views on many topics became authoritative, although his strong views on predestination were always a problem.

Ambrose, Jerome, Gregory of Nyssa, Augustine, and others lived during a major transition of ancient Christianity. They showed us what was happening. They were well-born, wealthy, well connected, and well educated in the contemporary context. They enriched the theology of their time, and they defended orthodoxy vigorously. There were contemporary pagan intellectuals such as the rhetorician Libanius and the historian Ammianus Marcellinus. But with hindsight, we can see them as the end of traditions going back to Athens. It is not too much to say that in the Christian thinkers of the fourth and fifth centuries we see the shift of intellectual weight from pagans to Christians.

FURTHER READING

Ancient Sources

Henry Bettenson trans., Augustine, *Concerning the City of God against the Pagans*, with a new introduction by G. R. Evans (London and New York, 2003). Books XVIII and XIX treat Augustine's influential view of the City of God and the City of the World.

Henry Chadwick ed., Augustine, *Confessions*, translated with an introduction and notes by (Oxford, 1991).

James Stevenson, *Creeds, Councils and Controversies: Documents Illustrating the History of the Church AD 337–461*, ed., revised with additional documents by W. H. C. Frend (London, 1989).

Maureen A. Tilley, trans., *Donatist Martyr Stories: The Church in Conflict in Roman North Africa*, the translator, notes and introduction by (Liverpool, 1996). Donatist writers tell their side of the story.

Modern Works

Gerald Bonner, *St. Augustine of Hippo: Life and Controversies*, second edition (Norwich, 1986). A clear, careful presentation of Augustine's controversies and theological views.

Peter Brown, *Augustine of Hippo: A Biography*, a new edition with an epilogue (Berkeley, CA, 2000). A finely written biography.

Henry Chadwick, *Augustine* (Oxford and New York, 1986). A brief, masterly treatment of Augustine's theological views.

W. H. C. Frend, *The Donatist Church: A Movement of Protest in Roman North Africa*, third edition (Oxford, 1985).

J. N. D. Kelly, *Jerome: His Life, Writings, and Controversies* (San Francisco, 1975; reprinted 2000).

Neil B. McLynn, *Ambrose of Milan: Church and Court in a Christian Capital* (Berkeley, CA, 1994).

F. Van der Meer, *Augustine the Bishop*, translated by Brian Battershaw and G. R. Lamb (London and New York, 1961). If you read this book, you will learn a great deal about Augustine and about church life in his era.

CHAPTER 18

Conversion and Christianization

In about 250 years (50–300 CE), Christianity grew from a few hundred followers to a few million. During the two centuries after the Roman state began to favor Christianity, roughly 300 to 500 CE, the religion grew from a few million to tens of millions. The history of Christian growth is complex. Before I treat growth, I need to distinguish two terms from one another: "conversion" and "Christianization." A person or a group of people could decide for a variety of reasons to become Christian, that is, convert. New converts might not know much about the beliefs and standards of behavior that they were presumably embracing. Ancient Christians were generally reluctant to expose to outsiders a detailed knowledge of their "mysteries." Itinerant missionaries and local leaders tried to convert those who listened to them. But the missionary activity is not well documented. It may be significant that so far as we know Paul, who preached to Jews and pagans, never sent a letter to the unconverted. He sent letters to people who were *already* Christian converts. He advised and encouraged them, but he also vigorously criticized them when he thought they believed or behaved badly. Beginning in the later second century, many Christian congregations treated fresh-off-the-street converts as catechumens, who were instructed and observed for months or years before they were admitted to baptism and to the inner beliefs of the group. A decision to convert to Christianity and then to be baptized was often only the beginning of a process of change that might last a lifetime.

I shall use the word "Christianization" to describe the long-term changes in society that followed widespread conversion. In brief, Christianization was the complex process by which traditional religious practices and beliefs were replaced with Christian practices and beliefs both at the individual level and in the wider society. Christianization was usually only partly successful because there were significant obstacles. Somebody had to provide resources to pay for clergy, church buildings, monasteries, books, and liturgical ceremonies. Traditional celebrations associated with the earlier religion(s) had to be eliminated or at least co-opted in favor of Christian celebrations. Preachers had to condemn such things as traditional fertility magic and efforts to read the future. But they also had to suggest Christian ways to accomplish their flocks' desires to deal with such threats as illness, infertility, and fear. The physical landscape had to be slowly Christianized by churches, cemeteries, saints' shrines, and Christian religious symbols. When people no longer reported visions and dreams of the old gods but instead dreams of the saints and Christ, a Christianized mental landscape had emerged to match the Christianized physical landscape.

CONVERSION BEFORE THE FOURTH CENTURY

Before the fourth century, the rival Christian groups were on their own in the search for converts. Luke reported that the number of believers continued to grow—he even gave round numbers (Acts 1:15 [120 people]; Acts 4:4 [five thousand people]). But the widely held view that Christianity spread like a wildfire in dry brush is exaggerated. It took 250 years for Christians to become a significant minority of the Roman Empire's population. No precise figures can be determined, but if as seems likely the empire's population in about 300 was 60–70 million, and if Christians made up 5–10 percent of that group, then there were 3.5–6 million Christians, not an insignificant number but not amazing either. How did proto-orthodox Christianity grow in the many decades before the Roman Empire favored it? The question is difficult to answer from the surviving sources. We know some things that did *not* contribute to growth. Because of his prominence in the New Testament, Paul is often taken as the model of how early Christianity spread. In Acts, Luke depicted him as a full-time missionary, a public preacher, and a feisty opponent of his Jewish critics and of competing kinds of Christians. That may or may not be an accurate portrayal, but Paul had almost no successors who followed the missionary techniques of preaching and debating in public. Banish from your mind the image of a second-century preacher on a street corner. Public preaching to pagans and Jews died out quickly, perhaps because it was too dangerous for an illegal group. The missionary strategies of some modern Christian denominations are also misleading for the early period. Many modern denominations sponsor missionaries, whom they train and support financially. In the pre-Constantinian churches, there is no sign of such *organized* missionary work. Modern denominations also seek converts through written and visual media directed to outsiders, but second- and third-century Christians generally did not. The overwhelming majority of early Christian writings were for other Christians—to instruct them, to argue with them, to correct them, to inform them, and to attack them. Christians wrote very little for outsiders. The apologists wrote explicitly for outsiders, but it is difficult to say whether they had any success or even many non-Christian readers. Modern churches are also eager for walk-ins, that is, for non-members who come to church to see and hear what goes on. Pre-Constantinian Christians were secretive about their "mysteries" and specifically ordered non-baptized people to leave before the Eucharist began. No unbaptized person was allowed to see a baptism or participate in the community's meals.

So how did second- and third-century Christians gain converts? Some intellectuals such as Tertullian or Justin converted after they talked with educated Christians or read the scriptures, often the Old Testament, which their teachers interpreted from a proto-orthodox Christian viewpoint. Although educated people were important to the intellectual growth of the movement, they were a tiny percentage of those who converted. Face-to-face contact with believers was probably crucial for many conversions in the pre-Constantinian church. Christians found converts within their existing networks of relatives, friends, neighbors, co-workers, and dependents. Think of the process as "retail" conversion, where one individual, one family, or one household consisting of family, servants, and slaves converted. Merchants and traders carried their Christianity along with their products to sell. The head of a household who converted often brought his spouse, children, and slaves with him. Women who converted influenced their husbands, children, relatives, and friends. Conversion could also split households if one spouse converted but the other did not or if some household slaves converted but the master and mistress did not. But the one-on-one approach led to many conversions before the fourth century.

What did Christians say to their neighbors, co-workers, or kinsmen who were illiterate or at least uneducated, as were so many people in the Greco-Roman world? The aspects of Jesus' career that the proto-orthodox Christians stressed may give a hint. In the Synoptic Gospels, Jesus was portrayed in several ways. Apparently second- and third-century Christians told potential converts about his power as a healer, an exorcist who drove out demons, and a wonder-worker who could command the wind and the waves. Christians convinced some people that their God had power greater than that of other gods. Belief that Christians healed and exorcised led many to ally themselves with the Christian God of power and his followers, although at first they may not have understood Christian beliefs or moral demands. Only after pagans or Jews had already decided to convert did a local church introduce them to its beliefs and inner life. The converts could not fully belong to the community until a church had taught, exorcised, and judged them suitable for baptism. At first they were not told everything. After converts had been baptized, they were drawn deeper into the group's beliefs and values through such things as regular meetings, sermons, the reading or—more likely—hearing of scripture, the sharing of meals, the giving of mutual help, and the exhilarating sense of being one of the saved in a world where most were doomed.

Proto-orthodox Christianity emphasized the importance of giving practical help to needy people. Almsgiving, as it was called, was directed primarily but not always to their own orphans, widows, elderly, ill, imprisoned, and travelers. In Greco-Roman society, such care for the unfortunate was known but uncommon. Christian congregations that provided support for the needy created an unofficial social welfare system that had no significant rival in the world around them. In an epidemic in Alexandria in about 263, Bishop Dionysius described a situation in which pagans abandoned anyone with signs of disease, whereas Christians tended other Christians in their illness and gave the dead a proper burial. The caretakers, whom Dionysius compared with martyrs, died in large numbers (EH 7.22). Such mutual acts of kindness and practical help to the poor and the ill must have attracted converts and cemented many converts' ties within the group.

The widespread Christian strategy of secrecy about the most important beliefs, of caution in accepting new members, of the gradual separation of newly baptized members from their former background, and of their integration into the new community was often successful. Over time, many converts were changed intellectually and morally— they were Christianized in a personal way, although there was not yet any sense that the entire society was being Christianized. But the strategy of retail conversion sometimes failed. Many pagans did not find the power of the Christian God convincing. Some converts left. But enough stayed to contribute to growth in each generation between 50 and 300. But if after 250 years, only 5–10 percent of the population was Christian, the retail method of conversion was probably never going to convert the majority of the Greco-Roman population.

CONVERSION AFTER CONSTANTINE

During the fourth century, favorable circumstances broadened the opportunities to make converts.

The pre-Constantinian methods often continued. Retail conversions remained common, as Christian patrons, spouses, teachers, clergy, merchants, slaves, ascetics, and artisans encouraged their relatives, dependents, acquaintances, and fellow workers to convert. But Constantine's conversion made possible "wholesale" conversions. Over time, entire villages, cities, tribes, kingdoms, and the Roman Empire itself accepted the new religion. We can think of the new ways to bring about conversion as the interaction of the "soft" push and the "hard" push. The soft push was based on persuasion or example. The hard push took advantage of Christianity's growing prestige and imperial support to bring pressure on non-Christians to convert. Christians no longer needed to keep their profile low. They were free to promote their views vigorously. Christians were confident that their success was the working out of a plan that God had intended before the creation of the world. They could say with pride that they lived in "Christian times," the future belonged to them, and paganism in particular was outmoded and destined to vanish. Fourth-century Christians could expand many of the things they had done earlier on a smaller scale. For instance, their social services grew in scale. Individuals and congregations continued to give alms to the aged, the orphaned, the widowed, the disabled, and travelers. But charity became more institutionalized. Emperors, empresses, bishops, wealthy lay Christians, and monasteries supported hospices and orphanages where the poor, the old, and the ill could stay without cost. In a world where so many people were poor or ill, the charitable works of Christians encouraged conversion. The urban poor, who received material as well as spiritual help from the local church, were often reliable supporters of their bishops against outside interference.

But there was also a "hard" push for conversion. Before Constantine, Christians could not force anyone to convert. But after his conversion, a growing body of imperial laws made life hard for pagans and heretics, stripping them of legal protections and threatening serious punishments. For instance, their places of worship were closed down. The sacrifices of animals that were at the heart of pagan worship were banned. Made bold by favorable laws and cooperative imperial bureaucrats, bishops and monks now and then conducted campaigns to destroy pagan temples and statues of the gods. Although the laws against pagans were stated in harsh terms and sometimes enforced, pagans were generally not directly forced to convert. But there was social and legal pressure to do so.

As a consequence of the soft push and the hard push, converts flooded into the churches during the fourth and fifth centuries. Contemporary bishops were aware that the motives of some, perhaps many, converts were mixed. Some pagans calculated that their opportunities for careers in the bureaucracy and army would be improved if they converted to the emperor's religion. Bishop Augustine of Hippo (354–430) told of a non-Christian man who wanted to marry a Christian woman, but her family would not put her in a pagan household. He came to Augustine to arrange to become a catechumen. Augustine reluctantly agreed. Many fourth- and fifth-century bishops were not too choosy about such people, whom they admitted not directly to baptism but to an open-ended catechumenate that might last years. The bishops apparently believed that it was better that the person be in the church, whatever his or her motives. They hoped that over time the minimally converted person would be drawn in deeper through sermons, scripture readings, good example, almsgiving, and other aspects of church life.

The catechumenate had been quite rigorous in the third century. Fourth- and fifth-century bishops may have allowed converts to become catechumens rather easily, but many tried to guard access to baptism itself. When catechumens finally asked for baptism, they were enrolled as "seekers of baptism" (*competentes*) for a period that filled the weeks before Easter. Frequent preaching, scripture reading, and exorcisms were intended to impress on the *competentes* the importance of the transition they were undergoing as they moved from Christians-at-the-margin to baptized members.

Because Roman society was deeply hierarchical, upper-class people rarely experienced the "hard push." They often had wealth, so that they were not swayed by the material gains or improved careers that moved others to convert. For such upper-class people, adherence to paganism was not necessar-

ily a career killer. Whatever their religious views, some had the education, skills, and prestige that late Roman society admired. Well into the fifth century, some senators, intellectuals, and teachers kept to the old religion(s). Emperors continued to appoint pagan senators and scholars to high posts in the bureaucracy and in the army. High-born women were often the first in their families to convert. The situation was different for lower-class people, especially the peasant farmers on whose labors the imperial structure depended. Life in the countryside is not well documented, but when the sources permit a glance into it, the persistence of the pre-Christian religions and of heretical Christian groups is sometimes surprising. By the time of the Emperor Justinian (527–565), Christianity was five hundred years old, and the empire had actively favored orthodox Christianity for more than two hundred years. Yet, many (although we shall never know how many) inhabitants of the empire were not orthodox Christians. Asia Minor in particular bubbled with dissenters. For instance, Justinian commissioned the Monophysite Bishop John of Ephesus (died about 588) to evangelize in Asia Minor, where Paul had preached about five centuries earlier. John claimed to have converted eighty thousand heretics and pagans and to have established ninety-nine churches and twelve monasteries during his thirty-five-year career. The progress of Christianization can be measured, at least roughly, by the significant increase in the number of towns with bishops. They provided institutional continuity and were the key figures in the processes that turned conversion into Christianization.

Bishop Martin of Tours (about 316–397) embodied both the soft push and the hard push. Martin's disciple Sulpicius Severus (about 360–about 420) wrote his *Life*, a document that was read widely for centuries. According to Sulpicius, Martin was born to a pagan family, became a catechumen when he was about ten, was a reluctant Roman soldier, was baptized in his early twenties, and became a monk when monks were rare in the west. He settled near the city of Tours in modern France, where he founded what may have been the first monastery north of the Alps. In 372, when he was in his middle fifties, he was chosen bishop of Tours. Some fellow bishops in Gaul disapproved of Martin, who, they thought, lowered the dignity of the episcopate because he was a former soldier of humble birth and spotty education. Even after his election as bishop, he continued to live like a monk, wearing raggedy clothes and unruly hair. Martin criticized his fellow bishops for their moral weakness, especially their readiness to do what the usurper Emperor Maximus (ruled Gaul 383–388) wanted. Martin refused invitations to dine with Maximus because he had killed the Emperor Gratian and had seized the imperial title. Martin's humble origins and experience as a soldier, which irritated some bishops, may have been an advantage in his vigorous efforts to convert the numerous rural pagans in Gaul. Many countrypeople (and city people, too) regarded the monks as especially holy and possessors of charismatic power. Their rugged, self-denying way of life may have appealed to the poor countrypeople. The holy men like Martin were regarded as healers and wonder-workers whose visible expressions of power made an impression on people who were unlikely to be moved by complex theological arguments. Martin's "soft push," that is, his preaching to illiterate, poor, and alienated rural people, had limited success. His biographer wrote that he also worked wonders, cast out demons, and showed spiritual power that many ordinary people did understand. Martin impressed his listeners with the power of the Christian God and the weakness of their gods. He showed dramatically that the traditional gods could not defend themselves or their worshippers. The empire's anti-pagan laws supported Martin's "hard push," his direct attacks on paganism. But the laws could not prevent enraged pagans from killing people who burned or demolished their temples and holy objects. Martin was occasionally in danger, but he survived. For instance, Martin particularly angered some local people when he cut down a sacred pine tree. The shrine's pagan priest challenged him to test the power of the Christian God by standing where the tree would fall. The falling tree veered away from Martin, who was unharmed. Bystanders regarded that as a miracle. Sulpicius Severus concluded the story by observing that "…before Martin very few, rather almost no one in those regions received the Name of Christ. But now that Name, thanks to Martin's miracles and example, has gained such a hold that there is

no place which is not filled with crowded churches or with monasteries. For when he destroyed pagan sanctuaries, he immediately built churches or monasteries there" (Sulpicius Severus, *Life of Saint Martin of Tours*, c. 13, author's translation). Martin was just one of many who converted the inhabitants of the empire's countryside.

In the later fourth and fifth centuries, many pagans were discouraged by the religious changes going on before their eyes. The inability of the gods to defend themselves against the Christian god was especially disheartening. As the pagan temples were impoverished, abandoned, demolished, or converted to Christian uses, bishops, aided by thousands of mostly anonymous priests, monks, nuns, and the occasional hermit, created a new landscape of churches, cemeteries, martyrs' shrines, hospices, and monasteries. Roman emperors, nobles, bishops, and Germanic kings provided crucial support in the form of land, money, and pressure to convert. The visible later Roman world, like its society, was being converted. The processes of Christianization were under way.

CHRISTIANIZATION AFTER CONSTANTINE

Conversion could be rapid, but Christianization was slow because it touched on minds, feelings, social behavior, and even property. Each bishop had the main responsibility to carry out missionary work in his diocese, including the rural areas. But the bishops faced serious obstacles, such as the grinding poverty and illiteracy of the countrypeople, and their entrenched loyalty to traditional religious ways. Many bishops lacked the economic resources to build and staff the churches that would over time have planted the new religion. Bishops and the urban clergy had full-time jobs ministering to their own flocks and carrying out their multitude of duties. Furthermore, some clergy were unsuited for rural missionary work because their education and "city ways" placed a gulf between them and the peasants.

Some bishops encouraged Christian landlords to apply the hard push against the pagan practices of their dependents, tenants, and slaves. Bishop

Maximus of Turin (died between 408 and 423) preached a sermon to owners of estates, urging them to prohibit the offering of sacrifices on their property. "Brother, you sin when you see your peasant sacrificing and do not forbid the offering, because even if you did not assist the sacrifice yourself you gave permission for it.... For if you remain silent, what your peasant does is acceptable to you.... The worship of idols is a great evil. It pollutes those who practice it. It pollutes the inhabitants of the region. It pollutes those who look on. It seeps into those who carry it out, those who are aware of it, and those who are silent about it ... The lord of the land is polluted when his peasant sacrifices to the gods .... Where the devil dwells, whether in houses, in fields or in peasants, all things are defiled, all are abominable" (Maximus of Turin, *Sermon CVII*). Superficial conversion remained a problem. But slowly orthodox Christianity rooted itself in every part of the empire.

Conversion in Hard Times

Even as the hard push and the soft push were adding converts *inside* the Roman Empire, that empire's economic and military problems were

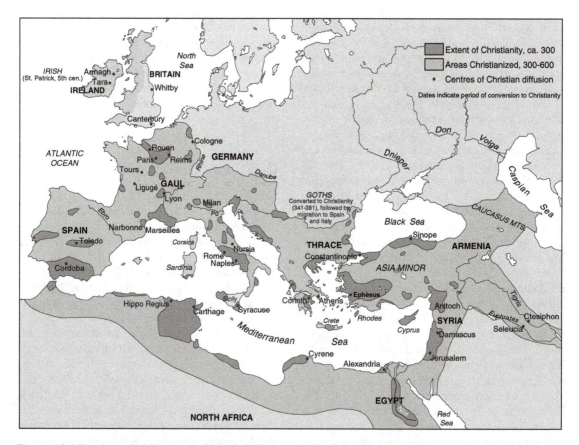

Figure 18.1 The Spread of Christianity between 300 and 600 CE. When Constantine legalized Christianity, it was strongest in scattered "islands" of churches across the empire. Even those areas were not exclusively Christian. By 600, the entire empire was legally Christian. In addition, Christianity had crossed the imperial borders into Armenia, Ireland, Axum/Ethiopia, and the Persian Empire. The conversion phase was coming to an end, but the Christianization of those vast territories was uneven and incomplete. (*After Noble et al., Western Civilization*)

creating challenges for Christianity. Although no contemporaries seem to have realized it, orthodox Christians had linked their religion to a society that was in serious trouble. To contemporaries, the empire seemed indestructible and eternal, part of God's plan for humanity. But with the benefit of hindsight, we know that from the third century onward, the Greco-Roman world suffered from interlocking economic, demographic, political, and military problems, even though there were a few periods when the problems subsided. The imperial government became more autocratic and bureaucratic even as its resources were declining. In *The Decline and Fall of the Roman Empire*, the eighteenth-century historian Edward Gibbon created an image that has been influential in modern popular and scholarly culture: The Roman Empire "declined and fell." The historical reality is more complicated. The Roman Empire surely declined between 200 and 600, but it did not simply "fall." Modern scholars increasingly write of a "transformation" of Greco-Roman society. That society evolved in so many ways that it was remarkably different in 600 from what it had been in 200. Nevertheless, Christianity adapted to changing circumstances.

The Eastern Empire

Differences between regions had always existed within the empire, but they became sharper as the empire was transformed by forces beyond its control. The eastern and western parts of the empire, roughly the Greek- and Latin-speaking areas, drifted apart. Although the eastern part of the empire, which modern historians call the "Byzantine Empire," was hard-pressed by invaders, it survived. In spite of serious losses of territory to Islamic armies in the seventh century, the emperors at Constantinople remained powerful, dictatorial rulers of a sophisticated state, which had a significant income from reliable taxation that supported a bureaucracy, a small but effective professional army, and a fleet. The emperors at Constantinople continued to have a loyal clergy, who taught in good times and in bad times that God chose the emperors and gave them a duty to defend orthodox belief and the church. The

essential features of the church-state arrangements that had begun under Constantine and had been worked out during the fourth and fifth centuries survived for more than a thousand years in the Byzantine Empire.

Some eastern emperors promoted missionary work. The Emperor Justinian (527–565) stands out. He was a vigorous ruler who legislated on a grand scale in his *Corpus iuris civilis* ("Body of the Civil Law"). He built forts, defensive walls, aqueducts, and magnificent churches, especially the Church of Hagia Sophia ("The Holy Wisdom"), which still stands in Istanbul. As steps in an ambitious plan to recover the western part of the empire from Arian Germanic conquerors, his armies subdued both Ostrogoths in Italy and Vandals in North Africa. He also sponsored missionary work beyond the northern and eastern borders of the Byzantine Empire. His military victories in those regions were often followed by conversions of rulers and their elite followers. Some barbarian rulers came to Constantinople, where Justinian himself sponsored them at baptism and became their "spiritual" father as well as their political superior. Byzantine missionaries were then welcome to work within the new Christian ruler's territory. Justinian often chose the missionaries, subsidized them financially, and wrapped them in the protection and splendor of the Byzantine state. Because such conversions depended on political arrangements, some did not last. If the alliance with the Byzantine Empire was repudiated, the missionaries were expelled and their converts persecuted. But across the centuries, the Byzantine missionary policy had great successes, the most enduring of which was the conversion and subsequent Christianization of most of the Slavic peoples between the ninth and eleventh centuries.

The Western Empire

Between about 400 and 600, the empire and churches in the west developed in directions quite different from those in the east. Over about a century (378–476), the western Roman Empire collapsed as Germanic peoples settled in its territory. Europe is called a continent, but that is flattery or perhaps a reflection of Europe's historical rather than geographical importance. You can see on a map that Europe is a large peninsula on the western edge of a huge landmass, called "Eurasia," which runs north to the Arctic Sea, east to the Pacific Ocean, and south to the Mediterranean Sea and the Indian Ocean. In a pattern that began before recorded history, peoples living in the vast grasslands that stretched from France to China migrated peacefully or violently toward the edges of the Eurasian landmass. China and India were repeatedly invaded, as was the European peninsula. Almost all the ethnic groups that inhabit Europe now, such as Greeks, Italians, Celts, and Germans, had migrated from somewhere to the north or east.

The Romans put a long pause to those migrations when they created defensible borders that ran along the Rhine and Danube Rivers. From about 100 BCE to about 400 CE, the Romans and the northern peoples faced each other across a loosely controlled border. The groups north of the border were distinct from one another, but the Romans often lumped them together as "barbarians." Modern scholars classify them as "Germans" because linguists recognize that they shared a family of languages called "Germanic." Do not let the word "Germans" mislead you. The speakers of the Germanic languages had been separated from one another for long periods of time and by long distances. Many groups could not understand one another easily or at all. Also do not be misled by modern ideas of race or nationalism. The Germanic peoples north of the imperial border were not united, although they made temporary alliances with one another in order to wage war. They fought each other constantly. The Germanic victors killed some defeated Germanic enemies and enslaved others. The Roman imperial government fought the northerners when it had to but preferred a policy of "divide and conquer," often bribing Germanic chiefs to attack one another so as to take pressure off the imperial borders. That worked as long as the empire had the money to pay the bribes. In the western empire, the money dwindled in the later fourth and fifth centuries.

Germanic war chiefs had traditionally raided the empire's territory for loot and captives, which they took back to their settlements north of the border.

Until the later fourth century, the Romans were militarily strong enough to prevent the Germanic raiders from settling permanently within the empire's borders. But as the western empire's economic and military resources declined, the ancient patterns of migration into the European peninsula reemerged. Between the later fourth and eleventh centuries, waves of Germanic peoples pushed south to settle in what had been the western Roman Empire.

A Roman military defeat in 378 changed permanently the relationship between the empire and the northern peoples. The Huns, a federation of nomadic tribes (who were not Germanic but Mongolian), migrated westward out of the central Asian grasslands. They were skilled horsemen and fierce warriors who terrified their enemies. Some Germanic tribes submitted to the Huns, but others fled from them, pushing into the area north of the Danube River. In 376, the eastern Roman emperor permitted the Germanic Visigoths to cross the Danube into Roman territory to escape the Huns. For the first time in Roman history, an entire Germanic people—men, women, children, livestock, and earthly goods—entered the empire peacefully with no intention of leaving. They brought with them their own kings and their native ways. Most important for the history of Christianity, many were Arian Christians. When the corrupt and inept Roman bureaucracy treated the Visigoths badly, they rebelled. Instead of waiting for reinforcements, the Roman Emperor Valens (364–378) met the Visigoths in battle at Adrianople, west of Constantinople, on 9 August 378. The Romans suffered a massive defeat. Valens was killed, and his body was not found. For about forty years, the Visigoths migrated inside the empire, moving westward to find a suitable place to settle. In 410, the Visigothic King Alaric shocked the Roman world when he looted the city of Rome itself, which was no longer the residence of an emperor but still had immense symbolic significance for all Romans, including Christians because it was the burial place of numerous martyrs, including Peter and Paul. Alaric, who was an Arian Christian, forbade the looting of some churches and shrines in the city, but great economic and physical damage was done. About 418, the Visigoths settled in southern Gaul and then Spain, where they created a kingdom that lasted until the Muslim invasions after 711. The Visigothic military success revealed the weakness of the western Roman Empire. In the following century, other Germanic peoples created kingdoms on what had been the territory of the western Roman Empire. In 476, a Germanic warlord in Italy deposed the last western emperor, a boy named "Romulus Augustulus." (There was still a Roman emperor in the east at Constantinople.)

Sometimes invaders intentionally destroy the culture they conquer. But those Germans living close to the empire's borders were somewhat "romanized" because of centuries of contact through warfare, trade, diplomacy, military service, controlled migration, and cultural interchange. That did not mean they read the poet Virgil or dressed in togas, but they valued such Roman practices as coined money, agriculture, military service, trade, luxury goods, and the Arian form of Christianity that had originated in the empire. Most Germanic migrants did not want to destroy Roman civilization but rather to enjoy its benefits. Even though they were Arian Christians or pagans, they did not set out to destroy the Catholic churches in their realms. There were other Germanic peoples who lived far from the Roman borders and as a result were quite unromanized, especially the Angles, Saxons, and Jutes who invaded Roman Britain. After the Anglo-Saxon invasions (about 450–600), Roman institutions, including Christianity, all but vanished from lowland Britain.

Because the imperial government collapsed in the west, the pattern of an emperor supporting the church could no longer work. For decades, no Germanic ruler shared his Roman subjects' religion, which was the Nicene form of orthodox Christianity. The kings of the Franks in northern Gaul and the multiple kings of the Angles and Saxons in Britain were pagans. The Vandal kings in North Africa, the Visigothic kings in Spain, and the Burgundian kings in eastern Gaul were Arian Christians. Even the bishop of Rome lived for a time under Arian rulers. In spite of unfavorable conditions, orthodox Christianity had its own

strengths and advantages, including numbers of adherents and resourceful leaders. The invaders killed, looted, raped, and enslaved, but the disruptions were generally temporary. The Germanic invaders came in relatively small numbers. The people they ruled, who vastly outnumbered them, were Catholic Christians. Most of the invaders wanted to live peacefully with their subjects so that they could exploit what they had conquered. The Arian Vandals in North Africa were the exception who actively persecuted Catholic Christians until the Byzantine Emperor Justinian conquered them in 534/535.

When Roman officials fled or were driven out, bishops emerged as the leaders of the conquered Catholic Christian majority. They organized resistance to the invaders and, when that failed, as it usually did, negotiated for their people to get a tolerable agreement with the conquerors. Without anyone planning it, the bishops emerged as leading figures in the west. They added to their extensive religious role an intensification of their existing prominence in the social and political leadership of local communities. They took up tasks formerly belonging to the Roman state, including military defense, the supply of food for cities, care for the poor, ransoming of captives, and negotiations with the Germanic overlords. In an age that took religion seriously, the division between Arian or pagan rulers and their Catholic Christian subjects led to instability. The Germanic rulers suspected, perhaps correctly, that many Catholic Christians favored the restoration of Byzantine rule because the eastern emperors were orthodox Christians.

Each Germanic kingdom had its own historical development. For more than a century (476–600), some Arian Germans held on to their form of Christianity, which had become their native religion and which preserved their ethnic identity in a sea of Catholic Roman subjects. A century is a long time, and contemporaries probably thought that rule by an Arian German minority might be permanent. But in one human lifetime, between 534 and 589, the Arian Germanic kingdoms in the west were either conquered by Catholic Christians or converted to Catholic Christianity. The Byzantine Emperor Justinian conquered two Arian German kingdoms, that of the Vandals in North Africa and that of the Ostrogoths in Italy. The Arian kings of Burgundy converted to Catholic Christianity in hopes of preventing conquest by the Franks, but they were nonetheless absorbed into the Frankish Kingdom. At a council in Toledo in 589, the Visigoths in Spain officially abandoned Arianism and adopted Catholicism under the leadership of King Recared. The Lombards, who entered Italy in 568, were the last significant Germanic invaders during late antiquity. Some were Germanic pagans and others Arian Christians. They undid Justinian's reconquest of Italy, although the Byzantine Empire controlled a few small enclaves in Italy centered on Ravenna, Naples, and especially Rome. But even the Lombards converted to Catholic Christianity by the early 600s. Four brief case studies will clarify the historical processes that led to conversion and Christianization among people who were not Greco-Romans.

The Conversion of the Franks

Demography can often be decisive in history. Some Germanic invaders migrated deep into Roman territory. Some were assimilated into the native Roman population, much as immigrants to the United States have usually been assimilated within a few generations. For instance, the Vandals settled in modern Libya and Tunisia. No significant reinforcements of Germanic peoples came that far south again. Settlement far from the Germanic heartland led inevitably to the Vandals' disappearance, although they did not realize that would happen. Over several generations, Vandals intermarried with the native population, forgot their ancestral language, and after Justinian's conquest in the 530s, disappeared as a separate ethnic group.

The conversion and subsequent Christianization of the Franks were important in the history of Christianity. The Franks had a different future than groups such as the Vandals. They migrated a relatively short distance into northern Gaul from their main settlements in the middle and lower parts of the Rhine River valley. They came in relatively large numbers and settled most heavily between the River Rhine and the River Loire, although there

were many Christian Romans there, too. Because of a short migration and relatively large numbers, the Franks retained their ethnic identity longer than most other Germanic invaders. When they arrived in the fifth century they were pagans, but Frankish paganism had no missionary impulse. They tried to get along with their Catholic Christian subjects, especially the bishops who led local cities. Traditionally, the Franks had multiple kings, who might better be called "chiefs." One of them, Clovis (ruled 481–511), a ruthless and ambitious man, killed his royal rivals and became sole king of the Franks. His family, called "Merovingian" from an ancestor named "Merovech," provided kings to the Franks until 751. Clovis was a pagan, but he married Chlotild, a Catholic Christian princess from the kingdom of the Burgundians. The choice of foreign royal wives for diplomatic purposes often led to conversion to Christianity. Even as a pagan, Clovis was on good terms with the bishops in his kingdom, who gave him moral and political advice, some of which survives in their letters. Gregory, bishop of Tours (573–595), a Gallo-Roman aristocrat who wrote an informative history of the Franks, recorded what were perhaps traditions within Clovis' family about how he was converted to Catholic Christianity. According to Gregory, Queen Chlotild encouraged her husband to convert, but he would not. As Clovis calculated what was in his best interests, he might have thought that Arian Christianity was the wave of the future. His kingdom was bordered on the southwest by Arian Visigoths, on the east by Arian Burgundians, and on the southeast by the greatest contemporary king in the west, the Arian Ostrogoth Theodoric. Even his sister Lanthechild was an Arian Christian. Clovis was probably under pressure to convert to the Arian form of Christianity, although Bishop Gregory wrote nothing about that. Gregory gave an account of the events around the years 496–506 that led to Clovis' decision to convert to Catholic Christianity. "The queen did not cease to urge that he confess the true God and forsake the idols. But she was not able to move him to believe these things until he made war against the Alamanni, in which he was compelled by necessity to confess what he had earlier chosen to deny." It appeared that the Alamanni would defeat the Franks. "When the king saw this he lifted his eyes to heaven, repentant in his heart and moved to tears, he said: 'Jesus Christ, whom Chlotild proclaims to be the son of the living God, you are said to give aid to those in struggle, and to grant victory to those who hope in you. Full of devotion I beg the glory of your help. If you grant me victory over these enemies, and if I experience that power which the people dedicated to your name claim that they have experienced, then I shall believe in you and shall be baptized in your name. I have called upon my gods, but as I am finding out, they have withdrawn themselves from helping me; wherefore I believe that they are endowed with no power, since they do not come to help those who obey them. I now call on you, I want to believe in you, but only if I am rescued from my adversaries.' When he said these things, the Alamanni turned their backs, and began to flee" (Gregory, *Historiae*, II.30, author's translation).

Gregory supplied the words for Clovis' speech that had occurred seventy years earlier, but his account reveals one of the attractions that Christianity had for Germanic peoples (as it had for Romans): the promise of military success. Between the first and the twenty-first centuries, Christ has been conceived in many ways, including the suffering redeemer, the stern judge, the teacher of ethics, and almighty God hidden in flesh. Clovis and other Germanic converts to Christianity saw Christ as the one who brings victory, as the Lord God of Armies, more powerful than the pagan gods and for that reason worthy of worship. Two hundred years earlier, the Emperor Constantine had thought something similar. The military successes of Christian rulers undermined paganism in ways that no theological argument could. After his victory over the Alamanni, Clovis kept the bargain he had made with Christ. Bishop Remigius of Reims instructed him privately in Christian beliefs during a sort of catechumenate. Because Clovis depended on his warriors, he would have taken a serious risk if he converted alone. Gregory of Tours reported that Clovis said to Bishop Remigius, "Most holy father, I hear gladly what you are saying. But one thing remains. The people who follow me will not permit the abandonment of their gods. I am going to talk with them according to your word." Gregory thought a sort of miracle occurred when

Clovis appeared before his people, who cried out, "O pious king, we drive out our mortal gods, and are ready to follow that immortal God whom Remigius preaches" (Gregory, *Historiae*, II.30, author's translation).

With the agreement of his warriors, Clovis' next step was baptism itself. Gregory's account of Clovis' baptism points to a second strength of the Catholic Christians—their identification with the still-strong prestige of Roman culture. The Roman imperial government had developed magnificent rituals, buildings, and costumes to impress observers and to stress the central importance of the emperor. After the empire accepted orthodox Christianity, the Christian church adopted elements of Roman public performance but refocused them on Christ, the saints, and the clergy. Even though the Roman Empire in the west was gone, the splendor of Christian liturgy impressed the Germanic peoples. Gregory's description of Clovis' baptism is rich in its stress on impressive sights and smells: "The streets were overshadowed with decorated hangings, the churches were adorned with white hangings, the baptistery was set in order, smoke of incense spread, perfumed candles gleamed, the whole church of the baptistery was filled with a divine fragrance. God granted such favor to those standing there that they might think they were located among the fine fragrances of paradise. First the king asked to be baptized by the bishop. Like a new Constantine, he moved forward to the water....After the king confessed Almighty God in the Trinity, he was baptized in the name of the Father, the Son, and the Holy Spirit, and anointed with holy chrism (that is, confirmed),with the sign of the Cross of Christ. More than three thousand members of his army were baptized; and his sister Albofled, who not long after was taken to the Lord, was likewise baptized....And another of his sisters was converted, by name Lanthechild, who had fallen into the heresy of the Arians..." (Gregory, *Historiae*, II.31, author's translation).

Gregory's account also illustrates a third important feature of conversion in the new world of Germanic kingdoms. The Frankish people were converted from the top down. The king, his family, and his warriors were baptized first. In the short run, such elite conversions probably had superficial results. Among the Frankish farmer/warriors scattered in small settlements, the immediate effects of the king's conversion were minor. But in the long run it was significant that the Franks as a people had abandoned paganism and rejected Arian Christianity to become officially Catholic Christians. When the barrier of religious difference was removed, the Catholic Christian majority supported their Catholic Frankish rulers. In the following centuries, Frankish kings and nobles supported the bishops, priests, hermits, nuns, and monks who carried out the Christianization of the Frankish people. The Franks also turned out to be the toughest barbarians. They conquered their neighbors and created the longest-lasting Germanic kingdom on the continent, the distant ancestor of such modern states as France, Germany, Italy, Holland, and Belgium. By persuasion (the soft push) and by force (the hard push), the Franks promoted conversion and Christianization in Gaul, Saxony, northern Spain, and Italy.

Conversion outside the Empire's Borders

So far, we have looked at conversion and Christianization within the boundaries of the Roman Empire, where Christianity was already rooted in the population and where bishops already presided over organized churches. Could Christianity spread into regions that had never been inside the Roman Empire? Christians asserted that their religion was universal and would eventually convert all human beings. Even before Constantine, Christianity began to spread sporadically beyond the imperial borders. The first Christians to cross the borders were often Christian merchants, prisoners of war, and slaves. They made some "retail" conversions of individuals and families, but the impact outside the empire was minimal. Beginning in the fourth century, Christianity had several notable missionary successes outside the borders of the Roman Empire, only three of which can be treated here.

Armenia

The first "national" conversion, that of the Kingdom of Armenia, was roughly contemporary with the conversion of Constantine in the first decade of the fourth century. The Kingdom of Armenia, located south of the Caucasus Mountains where modern Turkey, Syria, Iran, and modern Armenia meet, was wedged between the Roman Empire and the Persian Empire, each of which sought to control it. In Armenian history, a man named "Gregory" (about 240–332) is called "the Illuminator" because he was thought to have brought the light of Christianity to his people. In the middle of the third century, Gregory, the child of an Armenian noble family, was taken by his nurse into the Roman Empire, to Caesarea in Cappadocia (modern Turkey), to escape the slaughter of his relatives. Gregory converted to Christianity, returned to Armenia when the danger subsided, married, had two sons, and was a zealous preacher of Christianity. At first, King Tiridates III, whom the Romans had put in power, was hostile to the new religion—so were the contemporary Roman rulers. He persecuted Gregory and his converts but became favorable when he was convinced that Gregory had healed him. In about 314, Tiridates made Christianity the national religion of his people, the first time that any kingdom officially adopted Christianity. Gregory was chosen the first *catholicos* ("chief bishop") of the Armenian Church and obtained his consecration from the bishop of Caesarea in Cappadocia. In the complex interaction of war and diplomacy, Armenia remained a pawn, shifting back and forth between Roman and Persian alliances. In 387, the two great powers divided Armenia between them. Christianity survived the political fluctuations to become the strong focus of Armenian identity. Gregory the Illuminator's son represented the Armenian church at the Council of Nicaea (325). His family provided the *catholicos* for several generations. But when the Armenian church did not accept the decision of the Council of Chalcedon (451) about the two natures in Christ, it became alienated from the pro-Chalcedonian church of the Byzantine Empire and developed in its own way.

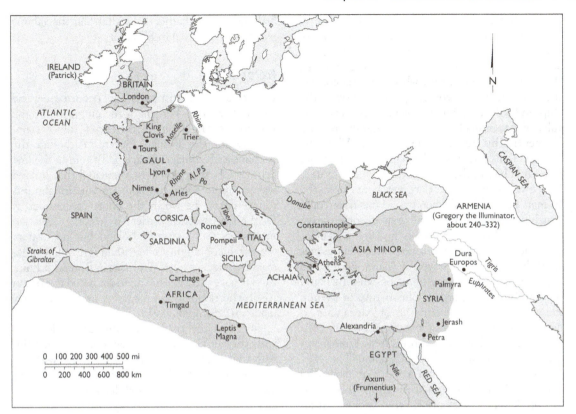

Figure 18.2 The Spread of Christianity outside the Empire from about 300 to about 450. Christianity, which was permeated with Greco-Roman elements, crossed political, linguistic, and cultural boundaries to plant roots in areas outside the borders of the empire. Conversions were not carried out by the "Church" in an abstract sense but rather through the initiative of individuals including Gregory the Illuminator in Armenia, Frumentius in Axum/Ethiopia, and Patrick in Ireland.

The conversion and subsequent Christianization of Armenia demonstrate the important cultural consequences of the conversion of non-Greco-Roman peoples. Christianity was a religion of books, above all the scriptures, but also sermons, biblical commentaries, theological treatises, saints' lives, conciliar canons, and much more. When a converted people were wholly illiterate, as the Armenians were, the arrival of Christianity stimulated literacy and sometimes the translation of religious documents into the native language. Within a century of the official conversion, Armenian Christian scholars had invented an alphabet for

their language, in which they composed original works and into which they translated mostly ecclesiastical documents that had been written inside the Roman Empire. Gregory's successor, the *catholicos* of Armenia, still presides over the Armenian church in the Armenian city of Etchmiadzin.

Axum/Ethiopia

The church historian Rufinus (about 345–410) recorded an account of the conversion of the Kingdom of Axum, which was located in the northern highlands of Ethiopia. Rufinus wrote that he had heard the details from Aedesius, one of the participants. According to Rufinus, Meropius, a philosopher from Tyre, went on a voyage to see India and took with him two young brothers, Aedesius and Frumentius, whom he was educating. On the return voyage, pirates captured the ship and killed all but the young brothers. The ruler of Axum made Aedesius his cup-bearer and Frumentius his treasurer and secretary. When the king died, his widow asked Frumentius to help her rule on behalf of the infant heir. Frumentius used his power to help Christian merchants from the Roman Empire build churches where they could worship. "Retail conversion" drew in some native people with his encouragement and financial aid.

Aedesius went home to Tyre (where Rufinus met him), but Frumentius stayed in Axum. Because he was a layman, there were limits on what he could accomplish in supporting Christianity in Axum. He went to Bishop Athanasius of Alexandria to ask for a bishop to minister to the Christian congregations. Athanasius consecrated Frumentius himself as the first bishop of Axum. The only firm early date comes from a letter of about 356 from the Roman Emperor Constantius to the rulers of Axum. Constantius, who favored Arian Christianity, wanted them to replace Bishop Frumentius with an Arian bishop. They did not do so. During the fourth century, the royal family accepted Christianity, and the conversion and Christianization of the nobles and the ordinary people followed slowly. The Ethiopian church, like its Egyptian mother church, later rejected the Council of Chalcedon (451). Anti-Chalcedonian monks from Syria had success spreading monasticism and Monophysite Christianity in Ethiopia. When Muslim armies conquered the eastern and southern shores of the Mediterranean in the seventh century, Ethiopian Christianity survived, but its isolation deepened as it was cut off from the Christian Roman Empire. In its relative isolation, far to the southeast of the Roman Empire, Ethiopian Christianity developed its own distinctive architecture, religious practices, and a religious literature written with its own alphabet in its native languages. Until the 1950s, the Coptic patriarch of Alexandria chose and consecrated an Egyptian Copt as Ethiopia's chief bishop, called the "Abuna" ("Our Father"). Until 1929, the Abuna was the only bishop in Ethiopia.

Ireland

Conversion to Christianity also occurred beyond the northwestern borders of the empire. Like the Ethiopians, the Irish were neither subjects nor invaders of the Roman Empire. Although the Romans had conquered lowland Britain in the first century CE, they probably calculated that Ireland was too remote and too poor (and its inhabitants too fierce) to be worth the effort to conquer it. By the fourth century, there were some Christian merchants and slaves in Ireland but no bishop. Christian communities flourished only a few miles from Ireland, across the Irish Sea in Roman Britain. But because the British Christians hated the pagan Irish, who raided them for booty and slaves, they made no organized effort to convert them.

Just as Gregory the Illuminator is identified with the conversion of Armenia, and Frumentius with that of Ethiopia, Patrick is identified with the conversion of the Irish. Because Patrick (about 390–about 460) wrote a brief defense of his career, called his *Confession*, we know more about him than is usual for such early figures. He was born into a Christian family in the west of Roman Britain; his grandfather had been a priest and his father a deacon. When he was a teenager, Irish pirates kidnapped him and sold him as a slave in Ireland, where he spent six years as a shepherd. He escaped captivity but later wrote that he had a vision in which he heard the voices of the Irish crying out, "Holy boy, we ask you to come and walk among us again" (Patrick, *Confession*, c. 23). He had a tumultuous and dangerous career as a bishop in Ireland, but when he died about 460, a functioning church existed in some parts of the island.

Patrick had introduced the bishop-centered Christianity that was normal in his native Britain and on the continent. But because Ireland had no Roman institutions, including no cities, no coinage, no written language, and no knowledge of the Latin in which western Christianity communicated, the bishop-centered organizational model failed to survive in the long run. Within a century of Patrick's death, a distinctively Irish

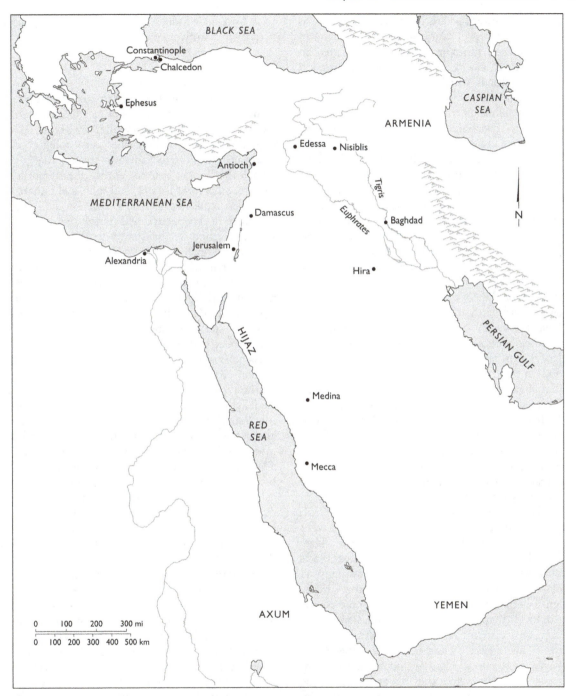

Figure 18.3 **The Kingdom of Axum/Ethiopia.** Axum was distant from the centers of Christianity in the eastern Mediterranean. Frumentius (fourth century) began the conversion. Because he was consecrated as a bishop by Athanasius of Alexandria, the church of Axum was heavily influenced by the Alexandrian patriarchs, who became anti-Chalcedonian in the later fifth century. (*After Brown, The Rise of Western Christendom* [*2003*])

way of organizing Christianity emerged, just as distinctive forms of Christianity had emerged in Armenia and Ethiopia. Christianity adapted to Irish secular society that was organized around large kin groups, which held territory under petty rulers with the exalted title "king." Monasteries that were affiliated with the competing kin groups became the backbone of Irish Christianity. Abbots, often related to the ruling family of the kin group, were the leading figures in the Irish church. To be sure, orthodox Christianity could not function without bishops, who alone could do such indispensable things as ordain clergy and consecrate things and places. But the bishops in Ireland were often monks subject to their abbot, quite different from the powerful, independent, aristocratic bishops of Gaul, Spain, Italy, Syria, or Egypt. Irish Christianity was orthodox in its beliefs: A bishop in Gaul or the pope himself would not have disagreed with an Irish Christian on a serious theological point. But important differences in liturgy, customs, and organization created tensions when Irish Christians encountered Christians in Britain and on the continent. One special feature of Irish Christianity deserves a mention because of its future significance for the conversion of the west. In Irish society, where solidarity with one's relatives was a central value, an especially meritorious form of ascetic self-denial was the voluntary abandonment of home and family. In imitation of Abraham, to whom God said, "Go from your country and your kindred and your father's house to the land I will show you" (Gen 12:1), zealous Irish monks between the sixth and tenth centuries went on what they called a "pilgrimage for Christ." They often had no plan, going where they thought God's providence took them. Irish pilgrim-monks visited or settled in what is now Scotland, the Orkney and Shetland Islands, and Iceland—some people think that they even landed in Rhode Island. They also went east to the Kingdom of the Franks, to the wilds of pagan Germany beyond the Rhine River, to Rome, to Constantinople, and even to far-off Jerusalem. Often they did not intend to be missionaries, but they were pious busybodies who criticized Christians, whom they saw as lax, and preached to the pagans whom they encountered. The yearning of Irish monks to go on pilgrimage for Christ fueled much early medieval missionary activity in northwestern Europe.

Summary

When Constantine converted in the early fourth century, Christianity was still a minority religion within the Roman Empire. By about 600, Christianity had become the chief religion of many people living within and beyond the borders of the Roman Empire. Within the Byzantine Empire, emperors, bishops, and monks eliminated or at least reduced paganism and heresy. The eastern emperors cooperated with bishops and monks to carry orthodox Christianity to the north and east into the Balkans, Russia, and parts of Eastern Europe, creating the family of Orthodox churches that is still prominent in those regions. But gains were more than balanced by losses. Resistance in Syria and Egypt to the Council of Chalcedon permanently split the eastern Christians into pro- and anti-Chalcedonian churches. The military successes of Islam between 632 and about 730 amputated the Roman provinces that lay along the eastern and southern shores of the Mediterranean Sea. In the west, Christianity turned out to be tougher than the Roman Empire. After Germanic kings and their elites accepted orthodox Christianity, they stepped into the role of protectors of Catholic Christianity. They were, however, weaker, less organized, and less effective in their religious support (and religious control) than the Roman emperors had been. After the western empire vanished, hundreds of bishops and thousands of clergy and monks found ways to cope and then to convert the unconverted. Battered, divided, and barbarized in some ways, the western church preserved important values of civilized Roman life, including a respect for order and the use of writing to record law, liturgy, theology, and group memories embodied in saints' lives and histories. The missionary strategy of demonstrating Christ's power to do such things as heal illness, expel demons, and give military victory worked over time to convert the invading peoples and the remaining pagans inside the empire. In addition, Christianity crossed significant barriers of culture, language, and politics to become the religion of such diverse peoples as Franks, Armenians,

Ethiopians, and Irish. The strategy of converting first the rulers and their chief followers, who in turn used their power to Christianize their people, was often successful.

FURTHER READING

Ancient Sources

Bertram Colgrave and R. A. B. Mynors, ed., Bede, *Bede's Ecclesiastical History of the English People*, (Oxford, 1969; reprinted 1998). A fascinating account of the conversion of the Anglo-Saxons during the seventh century.

R. P. C. Hanson, *The Life and Writings of the Historical Patrick* (New York, 1983). Read especially Patrick's *Confession*, in which he defended his missionary career.

J. N. Hillgarth, *Christianity and Paganism, 350–750: The Conversion of Western Europe* (Philadelphia, 1986). Translated sources, accompanied by good explanations of how the western empire and its Germanic successors were converted.

Thomas F. X. Noble and Thomas Head, ed., Sulpicius Severus, *The Life of Saint Martin in Soldiers of Christ: Saints and Saints' Lives from Late Antiquity and the Early Middle Ages*, (University Park, PA, 1995), pp. 1–29. An influential account of a monk/bishop/missionary.

Modern Works

Richard Fletcher, *The Barbarian Conversion* (New York, 1997). See especially chapters 1–4.

Adolf von Harnack, *The Mission and Expansion of Christianity in the First Three Centuries*, translated by James Moffatt, two volumes, second edition, (New York, 1908). Old but still worth reading for its rich details.

Ramsay MacMullen, *Christianizing the Roman Empire A.D. 100–400* (New Haven, 1984). A brief, stimulating inquiry into how the Greco-Roman masses were converted.

Arthur Darby Nock, *Conversion* (Oxford, 1933). A good treatment of the ways in which some prominent intellectuals converted to Christianity.

Rodney Stark, *The Rise of Christianity: A Sociologist Reconsiders History* (Princeton, NJ, 1996). A sociologist of religion tries to account for the increase in the number of Christians between the first and fifth centuries. His use of modern sociological insights is stimulating but not always convincing.

Ian Wood, *The Missionary Life: Saints and the Evangelisation of Europe 400–1050* (Harlow, England, and New York, 2001). A comprehensive account of the conversion and Christianization of Western Europe between the late Roman Empire and the end of the Viking invasions in the eleventh century.

CHAPTER 19

The Eastern and Western Churches Go Their Separate Ways

Ancient Christianity did not "end" abruptly. But between 300 and 600, trends in politics, economics, and religion that had been at work for centuries produced significant changes in society. The underlying development that influenced much in the late Roman world was the sometimes slow, sometimes rapid but unstoppable separation into regions at the expense of unity. Greek-speaking Christianity, Latin-speaking Christianity, and Christians across the eastern border in the Persian Empire were drifting apart. For many centuries, the churches in the west and the churches in the east believed and often acted as if they constituted a united church. But the growing regionalism contributed to their separation. When many Greek-speakers could no longer understand Latin, and when many Latin-speakers could no longer understand Greek, the eastern and western churches found it difficult to talk about such important and complex subjects as theology. Quite literally, they often talked past one another and did not understand one another. Their differing political experiences also put barriers between them. The eastern Christians lived within the framework of imperial control and support that had emerged in the fourth century. The western Christians lived mostly in Germanic kingdoms, which, even when they became Catholic, differed substantially from the empire. The east and west developed different religious customs (for example, clerical celibacy in the west and a married lower clergy in the east or unleavened bread for the Eucharist in the west and leavened bread in the east) that were tolerated when the western and eastern churches were on good terms but attacked when they were at odds. There were differences about where authority lay in the church. In particular, the extent of the authority of the bishop of Rome, which the western church accepted in a strong way and the eastern church accepted in a limited way, pushed the churches apart. Unity within the broad Christian movement remained elusive, as it always had. By 600, dissent had become a permanent fact of Christian religious life. Many Christians in Egypt, Palestine, Syria, and farther east, who could not accept the Council of Chalcedon's teaching on Christ's human and divine natures, were alienated from the orthodox church and from the empire that supported it. And yet the opponents of Chalcedon shared with their pro-Chalcedonian opponents many things, including their organization around a bishop, a scriptural canon, and a creed; their use of councils; liturgical, architectural, and artistic practices; and admiration for martyrs, ascetics, and saints.

In 600, the church was quite different than it had been when Constantine had converted about three hundred years earlier. Christianity had gained a place in society that went far beyond politics or even formal theology. Some changes were visible to the eye. The old gods, whose dominance predated written history, were going or gone. Christian teaching had transformed them into frightening beings—demons—that a person might encounter on a lonely road or in a creepy ruined temple. The pagan oracles were silent. The countless local pagan festivals during which worshippers had danced, sung, feasted, and made offerings to the gods were dead, dying, or had been reshaped by Christians for their purposes. A Christian landscape had replaced the pagan landscape. Hundreds of pagan temples were abandoned, mined for stone to build other structures, and rather rarely converted directly into churches. A huge expenditure of wealth was making the physical world look Christian. Churches, monasteries, cemeteries, charitable institutions, and martyrs' shrines transformed the landscapes visible to Greco-Roman people.

Christianity not only destroyed paganism as a functioning worldview but also replaced it in the lives of Christians. Social life increasingly revolved around the Sunday liturgy and Christian festivals such as Easter, Christmas, and saints' anniversary days. The Christian festival days combined church services with dancing, drinking, eating, and marching through the streets in processions. The outstanding events in personal and family life (births, marriages, deaths) were marked by religious services and feasting. The personal lives of millions were saturated with Christian beliefs, signs, and symbols. Many wore Christian symbols as jewelry. The rich had in their homes art showing Christian themes, and the poor had at least simple oil lamps with Christian symbols stamped on them. Christian symbols stood out on coins. Christians worshiped in buildings decorated with Christian images. Bishops, priests, deacons, monks, nuns, and ascetics were familiar figures in the cities and towns of the Roman world, integrated into religious, economic, political, and intellectual life.

Profound change is often slow and incomplete. Even by 600 Christianity had not entirely replaced the older beliefs and practices that are lumped together as "paganism." The pagan priesthoods were gone, and the intellectuals who could have explained and defended paganism were now Christians or at least silent. But in many places, especially in peasant communities, the age-old rituals with their underlying beliefs continued. For instance, about 574, Bishop Martin of Braga in what is now northwestern Spain composed a model sermon that less-educated clergy could adapt for delivery to peasants. He said that he wrote in "rustic speech," that is, simple Latin, so that his audience could understand. He assumed that his hearers were baptized and attended Christian Eucharists on Sunday. But they also held on to many of the old religious ways. Martin criticized the peasants for singing magical chants to the gods,

who, Martin said, were demons. He was angry that they lit candles at sacred stones, springs, and trees. They observed certain days as sacred to the gods. For instance, he said that on the first day of each month, some people adorned tables, hung up laurel wreaths, poured wine, put fruit on a log in the fireplace, and placed an offering of bread in a spring. The peasants chose Friday, the day of Venus, goddess of love, for weddings and were careful to travel on religiously favorable days. Martin's sermon is a reminder that the churches often lacked resources to replace entirely the survivals of pagan practice. But they had eliminated many, co-opted others, and tolerated still others. Although Jews, dissident Christians, and pagans still existed in 600, no one was unaware that the Roman world was Christianized or at least Christianizing. The continuities and the regional differences in Christianity about 600 can be glimpsed in the careers of three important bishops: Gregory of Tours, Gregory I of Rome, and John V of Alexandria.

BISHOP GREGORY OF TOURS (573–593/594)

The city of Tours, on the Loire River in Gaul, is about seven hundred miles from Rome and about nineteen hundred miles from Alexandria. Martin, the bishop of Tours, who had died in 397, remained the city's dominant inhabitant, its special saint, and protector. He was buried in a fine church, to which Frankish kings, pilgrims, and seekers of favors came from all over Gaul. In 573, Gregory, a thirty-five-year-old man of high birth and good education, became Martin of Tours' successor as bishop of Tours. Since his youth, Gregory had been in frail health. When he was about thirteen, he was struck with a life-threatening stomach ailment. He promised that if he survived, he would enter the service of the church, as many of his relatives had done. In 563, at about age twenty-five, he thought he was dying, went to St. Martin's tomb, and received what he was sure was a miraculous cure. A decade later, he was chosen as bishop of Tours. Gregory was a well-educated man, although he claimed to be self-conscious about the deficiencies of his literary style. He wrote a great deal nonetheless.

He wrote on the *Glory of the Martyrs*, on the *Glory of the Confessors*, on the *Miracles of Saint Julian of Brioude*, on the *Miracles of Saint Martin*, and on the *Lives of the Fathers*. His masterpiece was his *Ten Books of History* (sometimes called *The History of the Franks*), which began with the creation of the world and ended with the Frankish kingdom of his day in the 590s. His writings are important sources for modern knowledge of the political, cultural, and religious life of sixth-century Gaul.

Bishop Gregory was also a man of action. He virtually governed Tours, whose leading secular figure, the count, took an oath to him. Like many bishops, he protected the inhabitants of Tours, protested to the Frankish kings about new taxes, and intervened to spare the lives of condemned criminals. He acted as a mediator in bloody feuds that disrupted local life. He attended councils of fellow bishops; he went frequently to the courts of contemporary kings, whom he served occasionally as an emissary. He knew certain kings well, but he had his own opinions based on his moral assessment of them. He admired King Guntram (reigned 561–592), whom he regarded as a just ruler, and disliked King Chilperic (reigned 561–584), whom he regarded as an unjust ruler.

The context in which Gregory lived is important for understanding the situation of the Christian church in the Gaul of his day. When Gregory became bishop of Tours in 573, the Franks had been consolidating their control of Gaul for almost a century. The church in Gaul, which survived the invasions with some damage, had found ways to live with the new Germanic rulers. When he became bishop, Gregory stepped into a well-established pattern. The Frankish kings needed the help of the approximately one hundred bishops whom they directly appointed or at least approved. New bishops took an oath of loyalty to their king. The bishops also needed the kings, whom they advised, supported, and encouraged to promote Christianization. There were political advantages for kings and bishops, but the system was also built on the traditional religious conviction that the welfare of the king, his family, and his subjects depended on the church, for which the bishops spoke. Gregory functioned in a Frankish national church, in which bishops and kings were inextri-cably bound together. Not all was rosy. There were frictions over power and property. There was serious political intrigue—his *History* is full of accounts of coups, torture, battles and assassinations. But the pattern of royal and episcopal cooperation, which had taken shape in the Roman Empire, endured for centuries in the Kingdom of the Franks.

In his writings, all in Latin, Gregory mentioned the pope or St. Peter occasionally. Tours, like many Gallo-Roman bishoprics, was thought to have been founded by a (probably) mythical missionary from Rome. Rome was thus the mother church of the west and a great treasure house of relics, and above all it had the tomb of St. Peter. Frankish pilgrims went to Rome to venerate relics, bits of which might be doled out or sold to them. By chance, Gregory's deacon was in Rome to obtain relics when Pope Gregory I (590–604) was elected and consecrated. From the report of his deacon, Gregory of Tours recorded (*History*, 10) the events and the sermon Gregory I gave on the occasion of his election. From the vantage point of Tours, the popes were venerated but rather distant figures. The bishops of Rome had no effective authority in the Frankish national church. Pope Gregory I wrote letters to Frankish kings, queens, and bishops, but he was rarely in a position to demand anything: He asked for their cooperation, which they sometimes gave and sometimes withheld. Pope Gregory criticized some practices of the Frankish church, such as the buying of church offices (simony), the consecration of laymen directly to bishoprics, and the tolerance of rural paganism, but he could not interest any king or any bishop in actively remedying those faults.

The conversion of King Clovis between 496 and 506, which was treated in chapter 18, was an element in the creation of the Frankish national church. Another element was that many of the senatorial elite, which dominated Gaul before the Franks, had survived the invasions with their wealth and their social standing intact. The senatorial class had to yield militarily and politically to the Frankish kings and counts. But the Gallo-Roman senatorial aristocracy found new roles in the kingdom of the Franks. They possessed the literacy and organizational skills to enable the Frankish kings to profit from the remains of Roman administration. They also monopolized almost all the higher positions in the church, especially the position of bishop. Gregory of Tours is an illuminating example. Among his living and deceased relatives, he had many high clergy, including seven or eight bishops. Wealthy senatorial families were expected to be generous to their special saints, to churches and monasteries, and to the poor. The Frankish rulers imitated the senators in generosity as well. Gregory recorded many gifts to churches and distributions of coins and food to the poor. The spread of Christianity in the Frankish kingdom was still incomplete in Gregory's day. The kings, the senatorial and Frankish elites, and most people in the small cities were formally Christian. The inhabitants of the countryside followed a range of pre-Christian and Christian practices that is difficult for us to interpret. But the alliance of rulers and bishops slowly succeeded in spreading Christianity in the countryside.

Gregory was always conscious of his role as a bishop. He described in rich detail a Christianity that was alert to signs of the active interventions of God, who expressed his pleasure or displeasure in such things as storms, droughts, plagues, sudden deaths, or even Gregory's personal illnesses. Gregory thought that the world was moving to its last days but was not quite there yet. Gregory's pages are full of living holy men and some holy women who healed the sick, expelled demons, made prophecies, and worked miracles. But above all, he valued the dead saints in their richly adorned tombs, to which countless people came to ask for intercession with God. Gregory emphasized especially the power of St. Martin, his patron and the patron of his bishopric. In Gaul, Christianity had survived major social, political, and economic changes. Bishops, assisted by thousands of presbyters and deacons, presided over their respective churches; wealthy men and women continued to endow monasteries and nunneries; councils of bishops met when circumstances permitted; thousands of men and women lived the ascetic life in its varied forms; scribes continued to copy Christian scriptures, scriptural commentaries, sermons, letters, poetry, histories, liturgical manuscripts, and saints' lives; and Christian intellectuals continued to compose new examples of traditional literature. Many aspects of Roman culture were still visible, including writing in Latin, a vast body of traditional literature, the canon law, and the church itself.

POPE GREGORY I THE GREAT (590–604)

I apologize that I am writing about two "Gregories", one the bishop of Tours and the other the bishop of Rome. In 590, the monk and deacon Gregory became bishop of Rome at about age fifty. Gregory's career had aspects that looked back to the later Roman Empire and forward to the transformed world of the early Middle Ages. He was born to a rich, socially prominent Christian family—he had an ancestor who had been pope and had three wealthy aunts who were ascetics, although the youngest had caused a scandal by marrying the steward of her estate. He was one of those well-educated aristocrats who would have been governors and generals in former times but chose to be clerics or to retire from public life as ascetics. Before his decision to abandon worldly life, Gregory was the prefect, that is, the civil governor, of the city of Rome. At about age thirty-four, Gregory became a monk. He founded six monasteries on his family property in Sicily and founded a seventh, the monastery of St. Andrew, in his family's magnificent home in Rome, where he lived as a simple monk. What was left of his considerable fortune, he gave to the poor. Even though he was a monk, he could not entirely abandon the status he had held in the world. He was a man of high birth, personal piety, good social connections, good education, and considerable talents at organization. Such people are rare in any period. Because the Byzantine emperor and his bureaucracy were still so central to the well-being of the Roman church, in 579 Pope Pelagius II drafted Gregory from the monastery to be his representative (*apocrisarius*) at the imperial court in Constantinople, where he lived for about seven years in the company of Latin-speaking monks. At Constantinople, he made friends with important lay and ecclesiastical officials. He was godfather to one of the Emperor Maurice's sons. After he became pope, he corresponded with the Empress Constantina. But it was a symptom of the growing separation between the west and the east that in spite of seven years in Constantinople he apparently did not master the Greek language. When Pope Pelagius died during an epidemic, the clergy and people of Rome chose Gregory to be bishop. Although elsewhere many monks had been chosen as bishops, Gregory was the first monk to be pope, a choice that emphasized the importance of monks in his time and that foreshadowed the prominence of monks in the early medieval church.

Gregory is unusual in the amount we know about him. The later Roman Empire remained a world of writing. Aristocrats were proud of their literary education and compositions; writers of sermons distributed copies of their work; and hagiographers recorded the wonders of saints in lives, liturgy, hymns, and inscriptions. Like Gregory of Tours, Pope Gregory stands out because many of his writings, all in Latin, have survived. He wrote forty sermons on the gospels, twenty sermons on the prophet Ezekiel, commentaries on the Song of Songs and on the First Book of Kings, an exposition of the Book of Job, four books of *Dialogues*, and *The Book of Pastoral Care*, an important handbook of advice for bishops and priests. But other unusual documents reveal Gregory at work in political, economic, and administrative matters. The popes, like emperors and other important people, maintained archives where they kept copies of their correspondence and important documents. Wars, fires, and other calamities have dealt harshly with most documents written before the twelfth century. The church at Tours probably had an archive, but it does not survive. By good luck, about 850 letters survive from Gregory's fourteen years as pope, dealing with theology and religion but also with economic, political, legal, and military matters. As a consequence, Gregory is well known as bishop, theologian, and spiritual adviser and as the administrator of a large corporation, which is more or less what the Apostolic See had become by 600.

Gregory was a complex man. He regretted that he had given up the monastic life of withdrawal for the heavy responsibilities of the papacy. He suffered from a stomach ailment—it was attributed to his severe fasting—that never went away and sometimes incapacitated him for days or weeks at a time. Like some pious Christians in almost every period, he was convinced that Christ's return was close. He had strong reasons to believe that. The Roman Empire had lost the west in the fifth century and was under attack on all sides. The city of Rome, although still controlled by the empire, was a shadow of its great days. No emperor had lived there for centuries. The city's population had declined; once-bustling urban districts were sparsely populated or abandoned; ancient buildings were collapsing or being used as quarries for their stone and metalwork. The economic and urban decline, which had been going on for generations, was worsened by military threats. The Arian Christian Lombards, who invaded in 568, controlled territory to the north, east, and south of Rome, which they sought to capture as the ultimate prize. At some points, they were only a few hours' march away from the city. To escape the Lombard advances, thousands of refugees—nuns, monks, clergy, and laypeople—had fled into Rome, where they had to be fed and housed. The imperial government in faraway Constantinople was threatened by its own enemies, notably the Persian Empire. As a consequence, the imperial government had little practical help to send to the remnants of the empire in Italy, but it discouraged efforts to make peace with the Lombard invaders, whom it hoped in the future to defeat or drive out.

The ascetic and contemplative Gregory, convinced that the world's end was near, turned out to be a man of practical skill and action. He resembled those earlier Romans who had created an empire, devised a complex legal system, and built bridges, temples, and aqueducts that still stand. When Pope Gregory was threatened by invaders and had no effective support from the emperor, he took matters into his own hands, as did so many western bishops. The financial burdens of defense and caring for the poor and refugees were immense, but he had a great asset, the far-flung estates of the Roman church, called the "patrimony of St. Peter," much of it located beyond the threat of the Lombard invaders. He reorganized the patrimony to provide him with a substantial income. Out of those resources, he fed and housed refugees, ransomed captives, raised troops to defend Rome, negotiated with Lombard kings and dukes, and kept up diplomatic pressure on the Byzantine emperor to do something. In short, Gregory became the de facto ruler of the city of Rome and laid one of the foundations for the medieval papacy.

Gregory was a loyal subject of the God-created empire. He agreed with the traditional view that the emperor had a right and a duty to protect the church. He desperately wanted the emperor to fulfill that duty in Italy! He accepted the partnership between the emperor and the bishops, which was a central feature of the imperial church system. For instance, even though the Roman clergy and people had elected him to be bishop of Rome, he postponed the laying on of other bishops' hands until the Emperor Maurice (582–602) gave his permission. Gregory honored the emperor in language and actions and obeyed his laws, including those that regulated the church. But Gregory resisted any effort, including efforts by emperors, to diminish the rights and dignity that he thought were owed to St. Peter.

Gregory continued to think of the church as an empirewide—in fact, worldwide—institution. By 600, the five patriarchs presided over five regions in which religious customs, liturgy, canon law, and even theology had distinctive features but not so distinctive as to provoke permanent separation. The desire for a united church was still strong. Gregory reaffirmed the unity of the universal church in the traditional ways. For instance, in February 591 he sent a long letter to his fellow patriarchs at Constantinople, Alexandria, Antioch, and Jerusalem announcing to them his election, professing his unworthiness to be bishop of Rome, and expressing his loyalty to orthodox belief. In a letter of July 598, Gregory congratulated Patriarch Eulogius of Alexandria on the news that he had converted some heretics. He then informed him that the monk-missionary, Augustine of Canterbury, whom Gregory had sent to far-off Kent in Britain, had baptized more than ten thousand pagan Angles during the preceding Christmas festival.

With hindsight, we can see that Gregory's career pointed to the future in the west. Gregory's pontificate was turbulent, and his real-world position was weak. He drew on ideas of governance and religious behavior that had originated as early as the second and third centuries. He repeated the Petrine Doctrine and defended St. Peter's rights. He helped to preserve the papacy's position of honor at least in the western churches until circumstances centuries later led to greater real authority.

JOHN THE ALMSGIVER, PATRIARCH OF ALEXANDRIA (610–ABOUT 619)

There was another important bishop whose followers also greeted him with the title "pope" (papa): the patriarch of Alexandria. Pope Gregory of Rome had been dead about seven years when John, nicknamed "the Almsgiver," became patriarch or pope of Alexandria. Unlike the two western Gregorys, John left almost no personal writings. He is known primarily through lives written by contemporary admirers. The writers of saints' lives traditionally stressed the religious purity and miraculous acts of their heroes and heroines. But they usually ignored or treated superficially the practical, political, and economic aspects of the saint's career, just the sorts of things that modern historians want to know. But John's admirers included in their accounts of his life some of his practical actions as well as his pious ones.

John was born to an important family in Cyprus, where his father was governor. He had a long secular career in the service of the empire and had a wife and children, although they had died. While he was still a layman in his fifties, the Emperor Heraclius (610–641) appointed him to be the pro-Chalcedonian patriarch of Alexandria. That city was more populous and more prosperous than contemporary Tours or Rome: It was still a great commercial and administrative center. Like the bishoprics of Rome and Tours, that of Alexandria had accumulated wealth over at least three centuries from the donations of the pious, the gifts of the rulers, and business dealings. For instance, the Alexandrian patriarchate owned a fleet of ships that carried the abundant grain harvests from the Nile River valley to hungry customers around the Mediterranean. It also owned houses and commercial buildings that it rented out. His biographer wrote that when John became patriarch, his predecessor had left him a treasury of eight thousand pounds of gold. Like many great dignitaries of the later Roman Empire, John had a large household of clergy and laymen to manage the spiritual and temporal business of the patriarchate. Unlike Tours, where the Roman government had vanished, and Rome, where the imperial government was almost powerless, the Roman imperial civil service still functioned in Alexandria. Whereas Bishop Gregory and Pope Gregory did many "secular" things that the empire could not do in Tours or Rome, John faced a still somewhat effective, although corrupt and occasionally violent imperial administration.

The bloody feuding of the Frankish kings disrupted Gaul, and the Lombards were the threatening presence in Pope Gregory's Italy. At Alexandria, the schism between anti- and pro-Chalcedonian Christians was a central disruptive force. The bitter disagreements about the relation of the divine and human natures in Christ still disturbed political and religious life more than 150 years after the Council of Chalcedon (451). The anti-Chalcedonian party represented the views of the majority of Coptic-speaking Egyptians in the Nile River valley. But the anti-Chalcedonians were prone to split. Since the 450s, there had been rival anti-Chalcedonian claimants to be the bishop of Alexandria, at one point four of them. In the city of Alexandria, which was still heavily Greek-speaking, there were supporters of the Council of Chalcedon, but even there those opposed to Chalcedon predominated. Bishop John, as the pro-Chalcedonian patriarch of Alexandria, had a powerful rival, Bishop Anastasius, the anti-Chalcedonian patriarch. John depended on the financial and military support of the Byzantine government. When he became patriarch in 610 only seven churches in Alexandria were in the hands of the Chalcedonian party. John warned his flock passionately never to participate in the worship or sacraments of the "heretics," that is, the anti-Chalcedonians. When John fled from Alexandria when the Persians attacked in 619, his biographers said that there were seventy church buildings in the possession of the pro-Chalcedonian church.

The pervasive asceticism of Christianity was evident in John's life. He had not been a married man, not a monk, but as patriarch he lived as an ascetic. Like both Gregorys, he was also a patron of monks. Like both Gregorys, he had a strong sense of the end of the world and the judgment to come. Pope Gregory faced life-and-death crises in Rome. John faced religious division and the entrenched injustices of the late Roman world. Alexandrian society was deeply divided between rich and poor, the powerful and the powerless. Like many premodern societies, Alexandria was a place from which modern, western people would recoil in horror. The city had its rich and its middle class, but it also had numerous abjectly poor workers, beggars, ill, and deformed people for whom there was no effective economic relief or medical treatment. The city was periodically swept by outbreaks of infectious diseases, urban violence, and hunger. Masters and mistresses were free to inflict horrible but legal cruelty on their slaves. The rich could usually protect themselves, but middling and humble people feared the police, the judges, and the hated tax-collectors, who resorted to intimidation and torture to get what they thought was due the hard-pressed empire. The officials of the Roman state administered beatings and quick, dirty "justice" to the humbler people in society. We should probably resist being too hard on the late Roman Empire, which was in some ways comparable with a modern Third World country: The poverty, the diseases, the injustices were built into a system that even a man of goodwill like John (or either Gregory) could not change in fundamental ways.

Both eastern and western bishops had taken on a central religious role in society. Many people turned to living Christian ascetics or dead saints for healing and intercession with God. But they also turned to bishops, who often acted as the defenders of the poor and the powerless. Bishops could not change the system but sometimes intervened successfully to soften its cruelty. Unprivileged people expected that a bishop such as John (and both Gregorys) would intercede for them to shield them from the tax-collectors, torturers, and invaders. John's hagiographers stressed that he frequently advised imperial officeholders to demand evidence of a crime before they condemned an accused person to severe punishment or death. They wrote that he tried to lighten the harshness of daily life for the many, to prevent or correct official injustice, and to discourage private violence and acts of revenge. He was nicknamed "the Almsgiver" or the "Merciful," who alleviated the misery of the poor and ill. He intervened with cruel slave masters when such cases were brought to his attention. He founded seven hospitals to care for the ill, aged, blind, and other unfortunates. Even his opponents among the anti-Chalcedonians admired his charity. After his death, he was regarded, quite unusually, as a saint both by the pro- and anti-Chalcedonians.

John, like Gregory of Rome, also lived through war and invasion, but, unlike Gregory, he did not need to raise troops or organize the defense of Alexandria. Imperial officials did those things although not always well. The enemy in the east was the Persian Empire, with which the Roman Empire had periodically fought for more than four centuries. Between 611 and 622, the Persians swept across the eastern provinces of the empire, looting, burning, killing, and taking prisoners to sell as slaves or to sell back to anyone who would pay a ransom. In 613, they captured Damascus and in 614 Jerusalem (from which they carried off the relic of the True Cross). By 615, Persian armies were deep into Asia Minor. The Persian military successes set in motion waves of refugees for whom John the Almsgiver cared. He also ransomed nuns and others from Persian captivity. He sent gifts to Jerusalem to help it recover after the Persian destruction. But when the Persians threatened to take Alexandria, which they did temporarily in 619, John fled to his native Cyprus, where he died.

In summary, in about 600 leading bishops across the former empire remained united in their self-understanding and in many traditional institutions. But from east to west, from Tours to Rome to Alexandria, the effectiveness of the imperial church system grew weaker and more tattered. With hindsight, we can see that the eastern and western parts of the church were going their own ways. But the separation was hastened and made more severe when something quite unexpected, unanticipated, and even astounding happened in the middle of the seventh century: the rise and rapid expansion of Islam.

FURTHER READING
Ancient Sources

Sophronius' life of Patriarch John of Alexandria is translated in "Saint John the Almsgiver," in Elizabeth Dawes and Norman H. Baynes, *Three Byzantine Saints* (Oxford, 1948), pp. 195–270.

John R. C. Martyn, trans., *The Letters of Gregory the Great,* translated with an introduction and notes by the translator three volumes (Toronto, 2004), contains the rich letter collection of Gregory. Martyn's introduction, pp. 1–116, is worth reading.

Lewis Thorpe trans., Gregory of Tours, *The History of the Franks,* (London and New York, 1986). For Gregory's treatment of more strictly religious practices and ideas, see his *Glory of the Martyrs,* translated with an introduction by Raymond Van Dam (Liverpool, 1988), and *The Lives of the Fathers,* translated with an introduction by Edward James (Liverpool, 1991).

Modern Works

Peter Brown, *The Rise of Western Christendom,* second edition (Oxford, 2003), paints on a broad canvas the transformation of Greco-Roman Christianity into the many regional Christianities of the early Middle Ages.

Stephen J. Davis, *The Early Coptic Papacy: The Egyptian Church and Its Leadership in Late Antiquity* (Cairo and New York, 2004). The history of the patriarchs or popes of Alexandria until the city was conquered by Muslims in 642.

Frederick Homes Dudden, *Gregory the Great: His Place in History and Thought,* two volumes (London, 1905), is still worth reading in part for its extensive quotations in English from Gregory's works and letters.

Judith Herrin, *The Formation of Christendom* (Princeton, NJ, 1987), especially pp. 90–219, is stimulating.

Jeffrey Richards, *The Consul of God: The Life and Times of Gregory the Great* (London and Boston, 1980).

CHAPTER 20

Epilogue: Muhammad and Islam

Histories of early Christianity usually end at the Council of Chalcedon (451) and the subsequent emergence of permanent divisions between pro- and anti-Chalcedonian forms of Christianity. But I think it is appropriate to offer a brief treatment of the effect of Islam on the "end" of early Christianity. Developments that began in the Arabian Peninsula during the seventh century radically changed the future of Christianity. The vast Arabian desert had been on the southern fringe of successive civilizations to the north. In the sixth century CE, the Arabs in the peninsula were divided among themselves by economics, politics, culture, and religion. Bedouin Arabs wandered in the desert with their flocks of sheep and camels; oasis-dwelling Arabs were traders and farmers; some Arabs were Christians, some had adopted Judaism, but most worshipped many gods. They fought frequently among themselves and with the Byzantine and Persian Empires to the north. But they also allied with the Roman Empire or the Persian Empire when that seemed profitable. The marginal status of Arabia was changed by the emergence of a major monotheistic religion, Islam. The Near East has been remarkable for its religious creativity. Several important mystery religions of the ancient world originated within that relatively small portion of the earth, although all are now extinct. Major prophetic religions that had or still have a world impact—including Zoroastrianism, Manichaeism, Judaism, and Christianity—originated there over a period of about twelve hundred years. Islam emerged out of that religious womb as well.

The prophet of Islam was Muhammad (570–632), a younger contemporary of Bishop Gregory of Tours, Pope Gregory I, and John the Almsgiver. It is almost certain that none of them ever heard of him and that he never heard of them. He was an Arab trader from the town of Mecca who traveled in a religiously mixed world, inhabited by Arab polytheists, by various kinds of Jews, by various kinds of Christians—pro-Chalcedonians and anti-Chalcedonians, and perhaps by Jewish Christians. In 610, when Muhammad was about forty, he believed that the Angel Gabriel began to bring him revelations from Allah, a word that means simply "God" in Arabic. During the last twenty years of his life, he continued to receive revelations, which contain religious, ethical, social, and political teaching. The core of the message revealed to him was a strict monotheism that stressed emphatically that there is no God except for God, who was identified with the God of the Jews and of the Christians. In Muslim eyes, God had revealed truths to Jews and Christians, but they had misunderstood or falsified them. Muhammad's followers accepted him as the final and greatest prophet sent by God, following in the footsteps of earlier prophets such as Abraham, Moses, and Jesus. The revelations given to Muhammad were free from error. His revelations, which were originally recited orally, were apparently copied down and then gathered into a book in the 650s. The *Qur'an* (the "Recitation") was the scripture of the new religion. The word "Islam" means "submission to God's will," and "Muslims" are those who have submitted.

Muhammad's message summoned all humans to accept God's final revelation. Over time, Muhammad converted his family and other Arabs to his monotheistic religion. In a complex process of war and alliance-making, Muhammad united many Arab tribes and clans both politically and

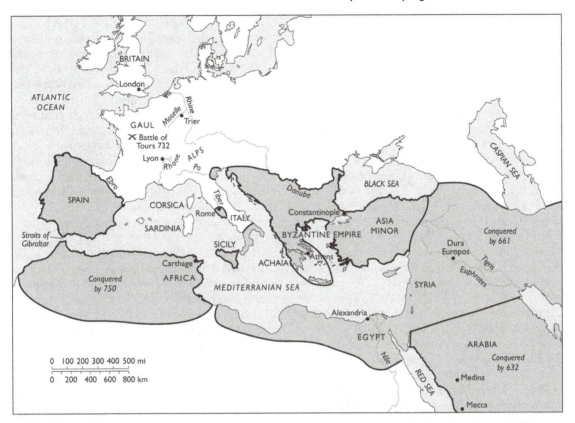

Figure 20.1 The Expansion of Islam (632–750). Arab armies, united by adherence to Islam, conquered the Arabian Peninsula by 632, then the Near East and Persia by 661, and then the coast of North Africa and the Christian Visigothic kingdom in Spain by 750.

religiously. The pattern was simple: To ally with Muhammad and his followers was to accept him as the messenger of God and the truth of the revelation that "there is no God but God and Muhammad is his prophet." A contemporary Byzantine emperor or Germanic king would have recognized the advantage of combining a political alliance with a religious conversion. When the Prophet Muhammad died on 8 June 632, the new religion united a substantial number of Arab tribesmen. They saw themselves as the "community of the faithful" and everyone else as outsiders.

The Arabs were skilled warriors who had a long tradition of attacking caravans or settled peoples for loot and slaves. United by Muhammad's revelations and political skills, they turned their military energies toward the Byzantine and Persian Empires.

Because those empires were financially and militarily depleted from years of war with one another, they were vulnerable to attack. Drought, famine, and a major epidemic in 542 (probably bubonic plague) had depopulated many Byzantine cities in Syria, Palestine, and Egypt. The Byzantines had an added weakness because their numerous Monophysite Christian subjects were alienated by efforts to force them to accept the theology of the Council of Chalcedon. Some sixth-century Christians interpreted the success of Islamic armies as deserved punishment for their sins and for the incorrect beliefs of other kinds of Christians. When Arab Muslim armies attacked Byzantine and Persian targets, they were successful, which encouraged further raiding. In a way of thinking that Byzantine emperors and Germanic kings shared, Muslims interpreted military success as a sign of God's favor. In a remarkably short time, the Muslim raids turned into conquests that changed permanently the religious face in the Near East and the southern shores of the Mediterranean Sea.

The Muslim Arabs quickly conquered large parts of the heartland of early Christianity, including Palestine, Syria, and Egypt. They also conquered Persia, where there were many Christians. Damascus was captured in 635; Jerusalem and Antioch in 637. As Muslim armies moved west across North Africa, Alexandria fell in 642 and Carthage in 698. After crossing the Straits of Gibraltar in 711, Muslim armies destroyed the kingdom of the Catholic Visigoths. In 672–678 and 717–718, Muslim forces besieged Constantinople, the largest Christian city in the world and the core of the Byzantine Empire. The city survived—just barely. In 732, near Tours in Gaul, a Frankish Christian army turned back a Muslim raiding party. Although the significance of the victory at Tours may have been exaggerated, that raid was the high watermark of Islamic advance in the far west. Within a century after Muhammad's death (632–732), Arab Muslims had gained control of a vast territory from Spain to Persia (and the era of Muslim expansion was not over). It is remarkable to realize that in 732 huge numbers of Christians, perhaps the majority of them, lived under Muslim rule. Until the eleventh century, when Italian city-states and crusaders counterattacked, Islamic pressure on the Christian coastal lands and islands from Gaul to Turkey was normal.

The history of Islamic beliefs and practices is well worth studying, but this is a book about early Christianity in which Islam's impact on that religion must be the central topic. The consequences of Muslim conquests for the development of Christianity were profound. At the most basic level, Christian societies faced a competing religion that claimed to be the final, perfect revelation of God. Islam had its own holy book (the Qu'ran) and its own language of theology and culture (Arabic). Contrary to stereotypes about "conversion or the sword," the Muslims did not force "people of the book" (Jews and Christians) to convert, even though they thought them seriously misguided. (They did force pagans to convert.)

But they placed legal, financial, and social disadvantages on their non-Muslim subjects, similar to the legislation that Byzantine emperors had issued against heretics, pagans, and Jews. Over time, the conquerors Islamicized the physical landscape just as the Christians had Christianized the Roman landscape during the fourth and fifth centuries. When compared with their Muslim overlords, Christians and Jews had a second-class status. They were eventually classified as *dhimmi*, "protected" and controlled. They were forbidden to make converts from Islam, to build new places of worship, and to carry weapons. They were required to wear clothing that set them apart from Muslims, to defer to Muslims in everyday life, and to pay a special tax to their conquerors. Over the centuries, the Christian populations under Muslim rule shrank in Egypt, Palestine, Syria, and Iraq and melted away almost entirely in North Africa west of Egypt. Some Christians were convinced that Muhammad's revelations had replaced those of Jesus; others wanted to escape the burden of extra taxes and restricted rights; and still others responded to periodic outbreaks of violence against Christians. There are still Christian minorities in such Muslim countries as Egypt, Syria, Iraq, and Iran.

Muslim conquests disrupted the system of five patriarchates that had organized and balanced the Christian church of the later Roman Empire. Antioch, Jerusalem, and Alexandria fell under Muslim control. The Christian patriarchs in those cities continued to function (they still exist), but the number of their followers, their freedom of action, and their wealth were sharply curtailed. The patriarch of Rome and the patriarch of Constantinople remained outside the Muslim orbit. But when a system with five poles of authority was reduced to a system with two poles, friction, which already existed between Rome and Constantinople, grew more severe. The end of the balanced patriarchal system and the subsequent direct rivalry of Rome and Constantinople contributed to the eventual split between the Roman Church and the Greek Orthodox Church.

The Muslim conquests also changed the religious composition of the Byzantine Empire itself. After the Council of Chalcedon, Byzantine emperors and orthodox bishops had tried either to compromise with the numerous Monophysite Christians or to force them into conformity. In a single generation, the Muslim conquests "solved" the Monophysite problems for the Byzantine emperors because most of the Monophysite Christians passed under Muslim rule. Their conquerors tolerated them because they were people of the book and there was little danger that they would want to restore Byzantine rule. The shrunken Byzantine Empire still had religious dissent but less of it because so many opponents of Chalcedon were now Muslim subjects. If the Monophysites under Muslim rule accepted their second-class status, they (and others such as Nestorian Christians) were allowed to organize their own churches and obey their own religious leaders. In Frankish Gaul, the Muslim control of the Mediterranean Sea did not end religious and economic connections with the outside but did curtail them significantly.

Muhammad died almost exactly six hundred years after Jesus died. Although sudden breaks occasionally happen, history is often marked by slow change. That was true of the history of early Christianity, which did not turn into "medieval" or "Byzantine" Christianity in a single moment or through a single event. But if one had to choose a tipping point when existing regional, political, and religious differences were solidified, it would be in the middle decades of the seventh century, when the military successes of Islam capped off about three centuries of profound change. Christianity in the east and Christianity in the west, although they continued to share a common heritage, took or were pushed onto distinct paths that influence them even today. When the Muslim expansion slowed in the eighth century, the Christian world was profoundly different than it had been. The eastern church, still closely intertwined with the Byzantine Empire, had survived. But the empire's only secure bases were in Greece and Asia Minor, from which it periodically expanded and contracted until the last remnant of the Byzantine Empire, Constantinople itself, was captured by the Muslim Ottoman Turks in 1453. In the west, churches were organized for several centuries around Christian Germanic kings and their bishops. A new, transformed world had emerged.

FURTHER READING

For an account of the millions of Christians of varying views who passed under Muslim rule, see Sidney Griffith, *The Church in the Shadow of the Mosque* (Princeton, 2008).

Michael Cook, *Muhammad* (Oxford, 1983); F. E. Peters, *Muhammad and the Origins of Islam* (Albany, NY, 1994); Carole Hillenbrand, "Muhammad and the Rise of Islam," in *The New Cambridge Medieval History*, vol. 1 (Cambridge, 2005), pp. 317–345. An up-to-date, cautious interpretation of the first century of Islamic history.

Credits

Ch 4, p. 47
First Letter of Clement, c. 5 in *The Apostolic Fathers*, vol 1, pp. 43–45.

Ch 6, pp. 66
The Didache, c. 11 in *The Apostolic Fathers*, vol 1, pp. 435–437.

Ch 6, p. 67
The *Didache*, c. 15, in *The Apostolic Fathers*, vol 1, p. 441.

Ch 6, p. 68
Ignatius, *Letter to the Smyrnaeans*, c. 8, in *The Apostolic Fathers*, vol 1, pp. 303–305.

Ch 6, pp. 68
The *Didache*, c. 9 in *The Apostolic Fathers*, vol 1, p. 431.

Ch 6, p. 72
Ignatius, *Letter to the Ephesians*, c. 6 in *The Apostolic Fathers*, vol 1, p. 227.

Ch 6, p. 72–73
Ignatius, *Letter to the Smyrnaeans*, c. 1, in *The Apostolic Fathers*, vol 1, p. 297.

Ch 7, p. 83
Epistle to Diognetus, c. 5 in *The Apostolic Fathers*, vol 2, pp. 139–141.

Ch 9, p. 117
Didache, c. 7 in *The Apostolic Fathers*, vol 1, p. 429.

Ch 9, p. 118
Didache, c. 9, in *The Apostolic Fathers*, vol 1, p. 431.

Ch 9, p. 121
Didache, c. 8 in *The Apostolic Fathers*, vol 1, p. 429.

Ch 9, p. 122
Didache, c. 8, in *The Apostolic Fathers*, vol 1, pp. 429–431.

Index